INDIANA
HISTORICAL SOCIETY
PUBLICATIONS

VOLUME 22

JOHN BADOLLET

*by Charles Alexandre Lesueur, c. 1833*

# THE CORRESPONDENCE OF

# John Badollet
## and
# Albert Gallatin

## 1804-1836

*edited by* Gayle Thornbrough

INDIANA HISTORICAL SOCIETY

INDIANAPOLIS 1963

# FOREWORD

The letters comprising this volume have been taken from the splendid collection of Gallatin Papers deposited with the New-York Historical Society by Gallatin's heirs. Permission to publish them is gratefully acknowledged by the Indiana Historical Society, and the editor wishes to thank in particular James J. Heslin, director of the New-York Historical Society, and Wilbur Leech and Arthur Breton of that Society's staff for their assistance. Dorothy Riker, editor of the Indiana Historical Bureau, was very helpful in checking the manuscript and made many valuable suggestions. I should also like to add a word of appreciation for J. G. Bowman, an attorney of Lawrenceville, Illinois, who, in 1846, acting in behalf of the widow of Albert Badollet, son of John, returned to Albert Gallatin all the letters he had written to John Badollet and which the latter had so carefully preserved. Thus the letters became part of the Gallatin Papers.

The two drawings of Vincennes by Charles Alexandre Lesueur included herein are from photographs in the American Antiquarian Society of the originals in the Museum of Natural History in Havre, France. The sketch of Badollet by Lesueur is from a lithograph in the Indiana Historical Society Library, and the William H. Powell portrait of Gallatin is reproduced through the courtesy of the New-York Historical Society.

The correspondence between John Badollet and Albert Gallatin reproduced here is of multi-dimensional interest. There are the correspondents themselves, educated, scholarly Genevans who became ardent Jeffersonian Republicans, and who in such different ways participated in the development of their adopted country. Then there are Badollet's long, detailed letters from Vincennes which constitute a remarkable source for Indiana history in the territorial period. There is also the picture that emerges from Badollet's letters of a frontier

American town and of the people who came there, some eager for adventure, some seeking to make their fortunes fast, some hoping for political success, others for military fame, and among them those who strove to develop a stable community in which to live and raise their families—a picture that has been repeated again and again as Americans moved westward. Finally, there are Gallatin's letters to "his dearest friend," written in his later years, which are probably the best source for his reflections on his life, his family, and the nation, for then he seemed to write more freely and openly to Badollet than to any one else.

The editor hopes that the reader, as he makes his way through this volume, will keep these various points in mind.

G. T.

# ILLUSTRATIONS

# INTRODUCTION

John (Jean) Louis Badollet was born in the city republic of Geneva, Switzerland, in 1758, and Albert Gallatin was born there in 1761.[1] Both came of old, respected families; the Badollets traced their line back to Jacques Badollet of St. Raval, Savoy, who was received as a citizen of Geneva in 1555, while the Gallatin family went back to 1510 when a younger son of the Gallatins, minor noblemen of Savoy, became a citizen of the city. The boys attended the College and Academy of Geneva, following the course of study known as "belle-lettres," which meant instruction in the classical languages, algebra, geometry, and natural sciences. Along with another of their fellow students, Henri Serre, they found the future offered them in the dour city of Calvin little to their liking. Their imaginations were caught by the American struggle for independence from Great Britain and the opportunity offered by the emerging nation.

Gallatin and Serre slipped off from their families in April, 1780, traveled across France, and took passage at Nantes on an American vessel bound for Boston. Family problems prevented John Badollet from joining them, and he became a theological student at Clairac, a center of Protestantism in southwestern France. The travelers arrived in Boston in July,

[1] Biographical sources on Gallatin, besides the Gallatin Papers in the New-York Historical Society, include the two excellent biographies, *The Life of Albert Gallatin,* by Henry Adams (Philadelphia, 1879) and *Albert Gallatin, Jeffersonian Financier and Diplomat,* by Raymond Walters, Jr. (New York, 1957). Biographical material on Badollet has been extracted from the Gallatin Papers and from the Badollet Papers deposited in the Indiana Historical Society Library by Vincennes University. The latter include genealogical notes, a journal kept by Badollet in 1792 and 1794 when he was surveying for roads in southwestern Pennsylvania, letters to him from fellow Genevans, various commissions issued to him including his land office commissions, a half dozen letters written to his son Albert, and miscellaneous documents and papers.

where they stayed for two months, then moved north to Machias in the District of Maine, where they spent a long, cold winter among the Indians. Here began Gallatin's interest in the American Indian that lasted throughout his life. Their enthusiasm for the country grew. They dreamed grandiose dreams of possible fortunes and wrote long letters to Badollet urging him to join them. Back to Boston and Cambridge they went, where Gallatin began offering courses in French at Harvard. In 1783, in company with Jean Savary de Valcoulon, a dreamy and impractical Frenchman, they traveled from Boston to Philadelphia. Serre then sailed for Jamaica, and Gallatin and Savary extended their explorations into Virginia. Gallatin continued his long letters to his friend, outlining his scheme for a settlement of Genevans on the American frontier.

In the fall of 1785 Gallatin and Savary leased five acres of land on the Monongahela River at the mouth of Georges Creek in Fayette County, Pennsylvania, and opened a store. The next spring Gallatin purchased a four hundred-acre farm on the river south of the creek. Here he established his home, naming the property "Friendship Hill," and here it was that Badollet joined him.

Just when Badollet reached America has not been determined, but by the fall of 1786 he was at Georges Creek, helping Gallatin with his farm and looking around for land for himself. But the dream of a Geneva settlement and a plantation life for the two Swiss friends was not to come true. Almost as soon as they were reunited their paths began to diverge. In August, 1788, Gallatin attended his first political meeting at Uniontown, seat of Fayette County. At this meeting he was elected one of two delegates to attend a statewide meeting to consider amending the new United States Constitution to include a "bill of rights." Thus began his long, almost uninterrupted career of over forty years of public service. As spokesman for frontier democracy and advocate of Jeffersonian principles he served as a member of the Pennsylvania Assembly, briefly as United States senator, and as representative in Congress, as Secretary of the Treasury from 1801 to 1813, as peace commissioner following the War of 1812, and as minister to France and to Great Britain.

Not so his friend John Badollet. His destiny was to keep him for eighteen years on the Monongahela, and thereafter, for the rest of his life, in and about the little town of Vincennes on the Wabash in Indiana.

Shortly after his arrival in Pennsylvania Badollet married a neighbor girl, Margaret (Peggy) Hannah, and five children were born to them in Pennsylvania—Albert, Frances, Sally, James, and Algernon Sidney. Gallatin's first wife, Sophia Allegre, of Richmond, Virginia, whom he married in 1789, died after a few months of marriage, and in 1793 he married Hannah Nicholson, daughter of Commodore James Nicholson, of New York City. This marriage into a family of comfortable means and excellent social and political connections was to have great influence on Gallatin's career, an influence that Badollet realized when he journeyed to Philadelphia to meet his friend's bride. Upon his return to his farm he wrote to Gallatin: "Peggy wishes eagerly to become acquainted with your wife. . . . And here I cannot help mentioning how far your Situation is in some measure Superior to mine, your wife in point of education & information will offer you enjoyments, which I must ever remain deprived of, but on the other hand, when I consider that Peggy is one of the best natured and most affectionate women, that she is superior to the rest of her sex, who had not met with more opportunity of improvement, by her contempt for slander & gossiping, & that in my circumstances & in this country I could not have obtained a better companion I remain perfectly satisfied, & confident that I have the wife that suites me best."

The two families did not mingle socially. Badollet stayed on his farm striving to make a living, and Gallatin spent most of his time in cities—in New York with his wife's family, in Philadelphia, and then in Washington. However, in 1795, the two friends, Gallatin's brother-in-law James Witter Nicholson, and two Genevans, Louis Bourdillon and Charles Anthony Cazenove, signed an agreement which they hoped would lead to the oft-dreamed-of settlement that would attract others of their countrymen. They purchased 650 acres, organized Albert Gallatin & Company, and laid out the town of New Geneva near "Friendship Hill." Gallatin had to leave the enterprise in the hands of his partners while he attended Congress, and as in most such utopian schemes the partners fell out and complained of each other to Gallatin. Only two ventures of the company, a glass factory and gun manufactory, had any lasting success. The partnership was broken up in 1799; Gallatin continued the businesses as an absentee owner, and Badollet returned to his land.

In a modest way Badollet established himself in his community. In 1792 he was appointed by Governor Thomas Mifflin a member of a commission to study the improvement of the navigation of the Monongahela and Youghiogheny rivers. In 1792 and 1794 he spent considerable time surveying for the location of roads in the Laurel Hill section of southwestern Pennsylvania. In 1795 he was appointed a member of a commission to select the county seat of the newly created Somerset County, and the following year he became an associate judge of the court of common pleas of the newly created Greene County in which his farm lay. These commissions may have come to him through Gallatin, but Badollet from the beginning was extremely sensitive about being in any way a burden to his friend. In 1792 he wrote to him, "Since we have [been] speaking together about the possibility of my getting some employment in this County as any where else, I reflected that on account of the natural envy borne against strangers & the reflexions that might be thrown upon you on my account, it will be prudent & I require it of you never to mention me as a candidate to any office in case any vacancy or new appointment would take place. If I am thought of in the County without interference, it is well, if not, which is by far the most probable, I will drudge along on my farm, taking the time as it comes & making up by resignation what is deficient in my circumstances. I will continue though to study [surveying], it can never hurt me."

In 1792 Badollet was commissioned a first lieutenant of a troop of light horse in the second brigade of Washington County militia. At this he wrote Gallatin, "You will not be able perhaps to refrain from laughing when you hear of my being elected first lieutenant of the light horse, it is really so, but I asked no body, & as it pleases generally in the company, I may as well be there as any where else. . . ." In 1796 he became a captain in the combined militia of Washington and Greene counties.

Upon his election to the Presidency Thomas Jefferson named Gallatin to his cabinet as Secretary of the Treasury. In this position he was able to do something for Badollet. The surveying and sale of the public lands lay in the Treasury Department, and here Gallatin felt Badollet could be truly useful. On July 27, 1803, he wrote to him that he had been appointed to survey, lay out, and mark certain roads northwest of the Ohio River "as will best serve to promote sale of public lands." Then in 1804 came the announcement that he had been appointed register of the newly created land office at Vincennes, capital of Indiana Territory.

On March 28, when he was considering appointments for the three new land offices in Indiana Territory—Vincennes, Kaskaskia, and Detroit—Gallatin had written to President Jefferson, "For the register at Vincennes permit me to recommend to you John Badollet, of Greene County, in Pennsylvania. I know no man of more strict integrity or better qualified for the office, and he has long been desirous to remove to that place, where his tried Republicanism would I think, be useful.

"There is but one objection to him, which is that of being my intimate friend, having been brought up at College with me and removed to the United States a short time after me. As to language, he speaks English better than I do, and has been for twelve years the only efficient associate judge of his county."

This is the only instance of favoritism discovered during Gallatin's long service in the Treasury Department, where opportunities for nepotism and favoritism were constantly presented.[2] Badollet's long and faithful service was to justify his friend's confidence in him.

The letters comprising this volume begin with Badollet's appointment.

While there is something poignant, even rather tragic, in the contrasting lives of these two intellectual young men, who had known each other so intimately from youth—the one rising to such heights as a public figure, the other forced to play a much more obscure role—this very divergence has proved of great value to us today. After 1804 they were to see each other only once, in 1825, when Badollet returned for a visit with Gallatin at "Friendship Hill." Despite their separation, their attachment for each other continued unbroken, and as proof of this we have the collection of their letters beginning with Gallatin's letter to Badollet written on May 16, 1780, at Pimbeuf, the port below Nantes, while he and Serre were waiting to sail away to America, and continuing to October 26, 1836, when Badollet, in Vincennes, Indiana, painfully penned his last letter to Gallatin. The earliest letters are in French but after 1790, with a few exceptions, they wrote to each other in English.

The flow of letters over these years is, of course, uneven and broken. Gallatin's letters from America to his friend still in Europe are longer and more numerous than Badollet's written from his school in France. While Badollet was on his Pennsylvania farm and Gallatin in New York and Philadelphia, their correspondence seemed to flow more evenly. They exchanged news about the progress of the French Revolution and their reflections on it, about local Pennsylvania affairs, about farming, their reading, and books. "I find," wrote Gallatin on January 7, 1792, "that my last winter clothes

<hr>

[2] Jay C. Heinlein, "Albert Gallatin: A Pioneer in Public Administration," in *The William and Mary Quarterly,* 3d Series, VII (1950), 72.

could do for this season, & the money which I expected to apply to new ones I have laid on books which has enabled me to get Hume's, Gibbon's, and Robertson's historical works, which will make a valuable addition to my library & our reading. I have also purchased another set of Blackstone's Comments so that you may appropriate the other set altogether to yourself."

St. Clair's defeat in November, 1791, caused uneasiness in western Pennsylvania. Gallatin wrote from Philadelphia in his letter of January 7, and again on January 20, to assure Badollet that the Governor was not unmindful of the exposed frontiers and of the plans and preparations being considered both by the State and by the United States for action against the Indians. Badollet replied on January 30, "The defeat of St. Clair is truly an event of the most dreadful consequence in our Country, it is easy to foresee what will befall on us next Spring, it would have been ten times better to let the indians capture a few boats now & then, than to convince them at the expence of so much money & blood of our imbecillity & inability to punish them. Though it would not be justifiable in me at such a distance to Say any thing about chief of that boasted army, yet considering that we must be the losers, who can blame if in the bottom of my heart I wish that our President was as lucky in appointing officers as he was once Skilfull in training them. However, perhaps would it be a more eligible plan to let alone the remote indian Country for a while & to be Satisfied with encouraging & protecting the inhabitants in their actual Settlements without carrying against the indians an offensive war, which time will Sufficiently do without us."

Later on in the same letter he rejoiced, "I look upon the acceptance of the French Constitution as the grand cause of liberty gained in Europe. She will reign in spite of the horrid Grins of the *Mightinesses, Highnesses, Serenities, & Majesties* of the earth, like Virtue she wants only to be know[n] to gain the hearts. . . ."

Unfortunately there are no letters at the time of the Whiskey Rebellion, so we do not know what reaction the impetuous and outspoken Badollet might have had to the moderate role that Gallatin assumed in that affair. There is also a break in the correspondence between 1798 and 1803.

But after Badollet established himself in Vincennes, feeling a little like a lonely exile, he poured out to his friend all his fears and misgivings about his job and his ability to cope with it, his dissatisfaction with the town, his impression of the people, his disenchantment with the government officials, his own prospects, and his discouragement. Gallatin was far too occupied with affairs of state to answer in like manner, but he wrote, now and then, letters of encouragement, advising his friend, sometimes chiding him, always assuring him of his confidence and affection. In 1809, after Badollet had written that Vincennes exhibited "a profligacy of morals not to be met with" elsewhere in the United States,[3] Gallatin responded, "It was with regret that I saw you go to Vincennes. . . . it was your expressed opinion that you could not subsist in Greene County. . . . I see no prospect of your being transferred to a nearer district . . . Still I not only feel your situation: but I *think* that your happiness in the eve of life will in part depend on our spending it in the same vicinity. I *know* that it will be the case with me."[4] This was not to be. However, Gallatin continued to feel responsible for Badollet, and in 1816, just before returning to Europe, he asked President Madison that "if the attempt should be made, he [Badollet] may not be removed [from his position as register] without sufficient cause and inquiry. This, I know," he added, "is the same thing as a request that he should not be removed at all."[5]

There are unfortunate gaps in the correspondence while Gallatin was in Europe, particularly between 1813 and 1823. Badollet was a member of the Indiana Constitutional Convention of 1816, and a report by him to Gallatin on its proceedings would have been invaluable, as well as his observations

---

[3] See below, p. 103.
[4] See below, pp. 105-6.
[5] Quoted in Walters, *Albert Gallatin*, p. 296.

on the first years of Indiana's statehood. Interestingly it was to Badollet that Gallatin felt compelled to explain why he let himself become a candidate for the vice-presidency in 1824, in one of the most interesting and valuable letters of the lot.[6] (Badollet did not agree with his decision and told him so frankly in his reply.) After Gallatin had finally retired from his active public life, his letters increased somewhat. To Badollet more than to anyone else, it seems, this statesman and scholar poured out his reflections on his life, his hopes and disappointments, and his family. In 1833 Gallatin wrote with feeling: "It has indeed, my dearest friend, been a source of constant regret and the embittering circumstances of my life, that . . . we should have been separated during the greater part of our existence. . . . And although I should have been contented to live and die amongst the Monongahela hills, it must be acknowledged that, beyond the invaluable advantages of health, they afforded either to you or me but few intellectual or physical resources"; and in the same letter, "I tell you the truth, Badollet, when I assure you that, in the course of a life which has brought me in contact with men of all ranks and of all nations, I have not known a more virtuous & pure man than yourself."[7] And, as will be seen, it was Gallatin who arranged for Badollet to receive recognition in Geneva for his service in Indiana as a public official and enemy of the introduction of slavery.

Badollet's disposition was such that he needed Gallatin's words of praise and reassurance. He was of an intellectual bent, sensitive, inclined to underestimate and degrade himself, timid, fiercely honest, unbending, excitable, loyal to his friends, and unmercifully critical of those who did not adhere to the strict high standards of conduct he set for himself. He was not an easy person to get along with; he was, in fact, a person who had to be known very well to be appreciated, perhaps liked, but one whose honesty and integrity was acknowledged even by

[6] See below, pp. 264-69.
[7] See below, pp. 309, 310.

those whom he opposed. To him people were either good or bad, and probably his judgment was not always sound. William Henry Harrison, governor of Indiana Territory, who became Badollet's chief target of criticism, wrote, "he is . . . extremely irritable & Pevish & altho possessed of a sound understanding he is so extremely diffident of himself & so little acquainted with the world that there is not a man on earth more easily duped. . . ."[8]

Badollet was a passionate believer in individual freedom and became, like Gallatin, an ardent Jeffersonian. But his high hopes for American democracy suffered early disillusionment in Pennsylvania. In a letter to Gallatin January 30, 1792, after rejoicing over the revolutionary developments in Europe, he wrote, ". . . I can hardly help deploring that in our adopted Country, true virtue, disinterestedness & genuine public Spirit are so seldom to be met with. Fair Columbia, which I have so many reasons to love, for having enlightened my mind, for having offered me an asylum when forlorn & having blessed me with many domestic endearments, Columbia fosters a good many unworthy sons. Offices sought for on account of their emoluments without regard for the qualifications they require, public bodies filled with interested men, public measures taken to answer private views & which proves that the evil is great, nobody surprised at it. I declare that I never went to an election without a painful depression of Spirits & my pride as a freeman considerably humbled." This disillusionment was to be deepened in Indiana.

Badollet had been a theological student in France, but after reaching America he was a freethinker and strongly anti-clerical. In the letter quoted above he continued, "When we consider that however good in theory a government may be, its stability and happiness of its beings it is destined to conduct, depend almost entirely upon the Sense and virtue of the people, is it not to be deplored that public instruction is intrusted to persons whose prejudices are axioms & false reasoning the

[8] See below, p. 111.

trade, who confound virtue with bigotry & morals with religion? I mean clergymen of all denominations. Would it be
so prodigiously extravagant to imagine another kind of
preachers whose discourses should instruct the people of their
duties as men and citizens & spread this idea, that the Almighty
looked down with complacency on & grant future rewards to
the man that sacrifices his interest to his country, that Serves
it with fidelity not only in a public but in a private Station by
the exertion of every virtue, in a word that forwards its welfare to his utmost. I dare say such men properly instructed
would prove far more usefull than all the hypocritical groans
of a modern Druid. Why should not a general system of
education become an object worthy of the attention of the
legislature, why should not a catechism where the natural union
of politics & morals would be established & consecrated by
plain and well conected maxims, prove more beneficial to our
youth than all unintelligible jargon of grace and election
mongers? You need not be angry with me, Gallatin. I respect
religion . . . but when disfigured by nonsensical sales, when
converted to criminal purposes, when put in lieu of virtue,
when a cloak for the wicked, then I hear her name with
horror."

This paragraph makes it clear why Badollet would be so
impressed with Frances Wright whom he knew when she was
at New Harmony, Indiana, in 1828. It was Badollet, rather
than the more cosmopolitan Gallatin, who could accept such a
woman in that day, and their exchanges relative to her and her
ideas constitute some of the most interesting paragraphs of the
later correspondence. The interest Badollet felt in education in
1792 was to find expression in his concern for the Vincennes
University and in his authorship of the article on education
in Indiana's first constitution.

Such then was the man who in 1804 came to the frontier
village of Vincennes. He at first seemed well disposed toward
Governor Harrison and other leading citizens. However, not
much time passed before he met up with the intrigue and petty

politics that inevitably had developed in the territory, and his reaction was at first shock and then bitter disillusionment and harsh criticism. The deterioration of his relationship with Harrison was complete when he realized that the Governor and his colleagues were not only countenancing but working toward a form of involuntary servitude in the territory contrary to the Northwest Ordinance. Thereafter, the picture he draws for Gallatin of the ambitious young Governor who sought fortune and military glory is, of course, prejudiced, but certainly worthy of consideration in weighing Harrison's role in Indiana's territorial history. In the editorial notes to these attacks on Harrison the editor has quoted at length from the Governor's own dispatches to Washington, letting the reader decide how wrong or how right Badollet was in his judgment of him. Likewise the depiction of the Prophet as a peaceful, almost pastoral leader by both Badollet and Nathaniel Ewing, receiver of the Vincennes Land Office, is contrary to the accepted view and is deserving of some attention.

In Vincennes there were all the elements that make up the usual concept of an American frontier. Here came young men ambitious and anxious to win fame and make their fortunes fast. Speculation in land was one attraction, and this came close to Badollet in his connection with the land office. Spirits were high, and tempers flared easily. Men were quick to call their enemies and defend their honor. Dueling was illegal, but challenges were frequent though not often carried to the final test. Men went about armed with pistols and dirks, and knifings were not unusual. The columns of the local press were a means of attack, and exchanges therein were frank and bitter.

Society was varied. On the top rungs were the Governor and other public officials and professional men, traders, and merchants of some means, all generally young, educated, and on-the-make. At the bottom were the French, remnants of the first white settlers, poor and uneducated and an element of poor, ignorant, indolent ruffian Americans. In between were American farmers and shopkeepers. And finally there were the Indians, the few who frequented the town to trade, and the tribes who lived up the Wabash and in Illinois who offered opportunities for trade, but at the same time constituted obstacles to settlement and a threat to peace.

Badollet was in his middle forties when he came to Vincennes, older than the Governor and most of the community leaders, but his education and position in the land office placed him automatically in the higher echelon in the town. He was named to the Board of Trustees of Vincennes University upon its incorporation in 1806, and served until 1811. He was a member of the Vincennes Library Company from its founding on July 20, 1806, until his death, and served as its first president, and upon his death left his personal library to the company. At the time of his death he was president of the Vincennes Historical and Antiquarian Society. As noted before he served as a member of the Constitutional Convention in 1816. He was described as a "polished gentleman," rather short, somewhat stout, and of fair complexion. In his old age he was regarded as something of an eccentric.

The letters that he wrote from Vincennes tell their story so well that it is not necessary to discuss them here. They continue up to the year before his death. He held the office of register of the land office until January, 1836, and was succeeded by his son Albert. He died July 29, 1837. His wife had died on January 6, 1834, and the next year his daughter Fanny, to whom he seemed particularly attached, also died. His family, however, had flourished, and he left beside his other four children, Albert, James, Algernon Sidney, and Sally Caldwell, no less than twenty-eight grandchildren.

In his will he laid down the following instructions which were in keeping with his modest simplicity and economy: "Whereas, an extravagant custom sanctions expenses in funerals not seldom distressing to the survivors, which it be desirable to discontinue, I hereby direct that my coffin shall be made of poplar planks, stained black, without any ornament whatever, and my shroud of common factory cotton. I also peremptorily prohibit the issuing of printed tickets of invitation to my funeral, a senseless custom of no manner of use except to put dollars in the pockets of the printer." Only the words "John Badollet" were to be inscribed on his tombstone. From time to time he had purchased land in Knox County and across the Wabash River in Lawrence County, Illinois. He had given most of his property to his children before his death, and by his will he divided the remainder of his modest estate, except for his library, among them. He was buried in Greenlawn Cemetery, Vincennes.

Gallatin died in New York City on August 13, 1849. His wife had died the preceding May. The years following his retirement from public service had been busy, as his letters show. He lived on Bleeker Street in New York, and served as president of the National Bank of New York. He continued his scholarly researches on the American Indian and helped to found the American Ethnological Society, and served as president of the New-York Historical Society. He wrote economic treatises and kept up his interest in politics and education. "During the eighteen years of his 'retirement'," wrote his biographer, "he made contributions to the civic life of New York, to scholarly and scientific research, to business development and economic thought, and to political activity which would have been notable for a young man. For a man in the seventies and eighties, these contributions were close to heroic."[9] His two sons, Albert and James, and daughter Frances Stevens, and eleven grandchildren survived him. His estate valued at $100,000 was divided among his children.

[9] Walters, *Albert Gallatin*, p. 346.

# BADOLLET-GALLATIN CORRESPONDENCE

[Gallatin to Badollet]

You are appointed Register of the land office at Vincennes. For the first year the emolument will be 500 d'rs salary as Register—500 d'rs as Comm'r to settle claims, and some recording fees—[1]After the first year 500 dollars salary and one per cent on the monies paid in the district for land, beside some trifling fees; in all about one thousand dollars a year; at least I think so. You are to give security for ten thousand dollars; but that is merely nominal and any of your friends will do; as not one cent of public monies goes through the register's hands.

If the office shall not consume the whole of your time, some surveying business may also be added to it. The salary will commence from your arrival at Vincennes & will be paid quarterly: but I will advance part of the compensation as comm'r which may enable you to proceed.

You will receive by next mail the commission and instructions.[2] Messrs. Smilie & Findley joined chearfully in your

[1] U. S. *Statutes at Large,* II, 278-79, 282 (act approved March 26, 1804). The act provided that the registers and receivers of the land offices at Vincennes, Detroit, and Kaskaskia, established by this act, should serve as commissioners for persons having claims to land lying within their respective districts. For stipulations regarding the claims see below, pp. 28-29n.

[2] Gallatin wrote to Badollet again on April 13, enclosing his recess commission from President Jefferson as register. His first duties were to receive, file, and record evidence of land claims in his district. After January 1, he and the receiver would act as commissioners of the land sales. Badollet was to be in Vincennes by September 1. Gallatin added: "As soon as I shall have been informed of the time you mean to go, I will cause to be advanced to you 250 dollars, being one half of your compensation as Commissioner. The other half shall be paid whenever the business of the Board shall have been completed." Badollet Papers, Indiana Historical Society Library.

Badollet was nominated to the Senate for register on November 12, 1804, and confirmed on November 20. His official commission signed by President Jefferson and Secretary of State James Madison was issued on

nomination.[3] I could have wished to place you nearer; but that was impossible—Give my affectionate compliments to your wife. My health is rather better.

Ever your's

ALBERT GALLATIN

[Addressed:] John Badollet Esq're one of the Associate Judges of Green C'y near New Geneva        care of Lieut. Chamberlin

[Badollet to Gallatin]

GREENSBURGH APRIL 25TH 1804

Since the receipt of yours & the commission inclosed therein, I received your favour of the Seventh per Lieut. Chamberlin, who did not come to Geneva, but forwarded your horse & letters by express to Mr. Clare.[1]

At the receipt of your official communication I felt a warm gratitude, but at the perusal of your letter, my feelings have been of a quite different nature, & have recalled forcibly to my recollection the fleeting moments of past happiness. I feel now an inward content to which I have been this long time a Stranger, & cannot but cherish the belief (if I am mistaken, do not undeceive me) that the lines I allude to, proceed from the same source, out of which formerly flowed So many endearing expressions of a warm friendship.—But forgive those

November 22. Clarence E. Carter (ed.), *The Territorial Papers of the United States* (volume II-  , Washington, D. C., 1934-  ), VII, 238. The original commission is in the Badollet Papers, as are his later commissions issued upon his reappointment to the office under act of May 15, 1820, limiting the appointment of certain public officers to four years (U. S. *Statutes at Large*, III, 582) : January 4, 1821, signed by President Monroe; January 27, 1825, signed by President Monroe; January 26, 1829, signed by President John Quincy Adams; and January 29, 1833, signed by President Jackson. His reappointments and Senate confirmations are recorded in the Senate *Executive Journal*, IV, 228, 229, 408, 412, 627, 634; V, 297, 299, 300, 304.

[3] John Smilie and William Findley, representatives in Congress from Pennsylvania. Their letter to the President, March 28, 1804, recommending Badollet, is in Carter (ed.), *Territorial Papers*, VII, 188.

[1] Thomas Clare, who had a farm on Georges Creek, near Gallatin's home, "Friendship Hill," on the Monongahela. Walters, *Albert Gallatin*, index.

involuntary effusions, they shall not recur again, & I will know how to check them, under the conviction that your time is not yours, & that whatever may be your present sentiments I have under your present circumstances, hardly a right to intrude on you the disclosure of my thoughts, the picture of my feelings.

The recovery of your health I hear with pleasure & gladly congratulate you on the subject.

Your horse is arrived very much abused, but Clare will nurse him up a while, then dispose of him conformably to your wishes. He sends you his compliments. He has lost Hagar after a severe illness & four of the rest are seriously sick of the same disorder.

At the receipt of the commission I flew to N. Ewings under the conviction that he was appointed receiver, not doubting, but his acquaintance with the Country, his knowledge of the french language, but especially his talents, his principles of honour would powerfully plead for him. But he had received no intelligence. If he has been appointed that will compleat my satisfaction. Please to let me know the name of the person that has been made choice of.[2]

.    .    .    .    .    .    .

The only return I can make to those that have been kind enough as to think of me, is to render myself worthy of their good opinion, by discharging the trust with proper diligence & faithfullness: to that end all my exertions shall be directed.

---

[2] Ewing was appointed receiver but not until October. Gallatin forwarded his recess commission from the President to him on October 15. Carter (ed.), *Territorial Papers,* VII, 226. He was nominated for the office to the Senate on November 12 and confirmed on the 20th. His commission signed by the President and Secretary of State was dated November 22. *Ibid.,* VII, 237; U. S. Senate *Executive Journal,* III, 186, 188.

Ewing was born April 10, 1772, in Pennsylvania. According to a biographical sketch he first went out to Vincennes on a trading journey in 1788. He was to serve as receiver of the land office until his removal in 1820. He died at his farm "Mont Clair" near Vincennes, August 6, 1846. Hubbard M. Smith, *Historical Sketches of Old Vincennes* . . . (Vincennes, 1903), pp. 183-85.

Present my best compliments to Mrs. Gallatin & believe me—Yours

JOHN BADOLLET

[Addressed:] Albert Gallatin
[Endorsed:] Greensburgh April 25, 1804 Badollet

[Gallatin to Badollet]

WASHINGTON 6TH JUNE 1804

(Private)

On my return from New York I found your two letters, private & public; and would have answered them sooner had it not been for the accumulation of business during my absence. As to the public business I really cannot give instructions in what relates to the business of claims, being ignorant myself of their nature. I can only warn you against all grants made by the Court[1] subsequent to the cession of Virginia to the United States,[2] and even to the Treaty of peace with Great Britain. Whether such grants for settlement rights only & when followed by actual settlements continued to this day are included within the terms of the act of last year[3] or should not

[1] The Vincennes Court, organized under the authority of the State of Virginia, in June, 1779, to preserve peace and administer justice in the community. The court generally adopted the customs and usages of the court which had existed during the French period, including the practice of granting land to French and American inhabitants.

[2] Virginia ceded her claims to the area northwest of the Ohio to the Federal government in 1784.

[3] The act approved March 26, 1804. The third section read: "That every person claiming lands . . . by virtue of any legal grant made by the French government, prior to the treaty of Paris, of the tenth of February, one thousand seven hundred and sixty-three, or of any legal grant made by the British government subsequent to the said treaty, and prior to the treaty of peace between the United States and Great Britain of the third of September, one thousand seven hundred and eighty-three, or of any resolution, or act of Congress, subsequent to the said treaty of peace, shall, on or before the first day of January, one thousand eight hundred and five, deliver to the register of the land-office, within whose district the land may lie, a notice in writing, stating the nature and extent of his claims, together with a plat of the tract or tracts claimed, and may also, on or before that day, deliver to the said register, for the purpose of being recorded, every grant, order of survey, deed, conveyance, or other written evidence of his claim. . . ." U. S.

be confirmed will be matter for consideration: but all the large speculative grants & all those of any size not followed by settlement are entitled to no regard. As soon as you have mastered the general outline of the business viz't the several species of claims which will be presented, you may write to me both officially and privately for instructions & advice. As there is no paper printed in Vincennes,[4] I presume that advertisements set up is all that is necessary to give notice that your office is opened. If you shall find it expedient to return to Green County for your family &c you may employ some person to receive the notice of claims during your absence. Perhaps you may for about 8 cents per 100 or less employ a clerk to transcribe; the law allows 12 1/2 to you; but the more you will do yourself, the better.[5] Take notice, however, that you are not obliged to receive deeds & other evidence of claims intended to

*Statutes at Large,* II, 278-79. For a study of these claims and their settlement see Leonard Lux, *The Vincennes Donation Lands* (Indiana Historical Society *Publications,* XV, No. 4, Indianapolis, 1949).

[4] This was soon to be remedied. The weekly Vincennes *Indiana Gazette* began publication in 1804 (the second number was issued August 7; no copy of the first number has survived). It continued until April, 1806. The Vincennes *Western Sun* commenced publication on July 4, 1807. On September 18, 1804, the *Indiana Gazette* carried the following announcement: "We are . . . happy in informing our readers of the arrival of Mr. Badollet, the register of the land office, in good health." The same issue carried the following notice: "The public are hereby informed, that the office for receiving and recording evidences of claims to lands within the district of Vincennes, pursuant to act of Congress passed on the 26th of March 1804, making provision for the disposal of public lands in the Indiana Territory and for other purposes, will be opened on Thursday, the 20th inst at the office of the secretary [of the territory, John Gibson]. Where the governor has issued patents or confirmed claims, it is unnecessary to record any other paper than such patents or evidences of confirmation, and except it is expressly requested by the grantees, no previous or subsequent transfer need to be recorded. In cases of claims on which the governor has not yet decided, the original evidence of claim if any, will have to be recorded in the office. And where the claim rests upon oral testimony, hereafter to be brought before the board of commissioners, a notice of said claim must also be entered within the limits prescribed by the said act. JOHN BADOLLET, r.l.o."

[5] The fee allowed the register was 12 1/2 cents per hundred words contained in the written evidence of the claims presented to the register. U. S. *Statutes at Large,* II, 278.

be recorded without the s'd fee of 12 1/2 cents per 100 words being previously paid or secured to be paid in a satisfactory manner : many would be inclined to leave the papers, have them recorded & never take them out or pay for the recording. From the date of your arrival at Vincennes which you must notify to me, your annual salary of 500 dollars as register commences, and you must let me know how you wish it paid, whether by drafts from here or Cincinnati or by drafts from you on me. As soon as the sales shall commence it will be paid as well as the commission by the Receiver. I would like extremely to see N. Ewing appointed receiver but, however fit he may be, I cannot ask for too much in favour of Pennsylvania. I wish he could get a recommendation, not from Pennsylvania, but from Gov'r Harrison & others near Vincennes & have it directed to me.

You have not mistaken my feelings—circumstances not under my controul have greatly altered the relation in which we formerly stood; but, whatever other duties and affections may have arisen, & however my conduct may have been influenced by them, you have never ceased to be, out of my own family, my first & almost only friend. Nor will I conceal that it has been with reluctance, and only from a sense of its utility to you and to your family that I have promoted by your late appointment a plan tending probably to part us forever. I had still dreams of the evening of life in which you always made one—but I will say no more on that subject. You owe yourself to your family. I have no doubt of your fulfilling your official duties with fidelity & ability, I can only advise particular prudence & frugality in your private affairs : try to save something & to secure some land on which your children may live independantly. Remember me affectionately to your worthy wife & believe me sincerely Your's

ALBERT GALLATIN

[P. S.] I enclose the letters of introduction to be sealed before they are delivered.

[Addressed:] John Badollet Esq'r

[Badollet to Gallatin]

GREENSBURGH June 1804

I have received your precious letter of the 8th [6th] instant; precious I call it, for it has produced on me an effect that no space of time can destroy & which effectually obliterates the recollections of past anguish. The unexpected benefit conferred on me by my appointment had relieved my mind from a load of anxiety & fears & awakened an adequate degree of gratitude for those who generously stepped forward in my behalf. But your last letter has effected a renovation of my whole being, has made me taste the cup of happiness.

When I began to think, (& I began late, my life having exhibited a continual scene of wild fancy, childish thoughtlessness & numberless errors,) I soon discovered that the strength of your mind & your intellectual faculties led you into a road that must for ever diverge from the humble path, which was to be my lot & upon a proper view of myself I concluded, that the part I had to act must be of a negative kind, that it must consist less in doing good than in doing no harm, less in active virtues than in an exemption of vices. I thought that prudent reflexion must stop the aberrations of my head & correct the unsteadiness of my habbits. That I have made a considerable progress in the last of those pursuits, I sincerely believe, & in this confession you will discover a proof of it. With respect to the other I need say but little. Thus far have I by slow & insensible progress advanced towards manhood, & though I passed the meridian of life, it can with truth be said that it is but lately I attained it & have learnt to know myself. In such a state of mind, from the level on which I was placed, I viewed your elevation with patriotic gladness, & did as a citizen pay you the tribute of Sincere gratitude that your labours so justly deserve.

But my heart was in pain, under the lamentable impression that the destroying hand of time or some fault of mine had given the fatal blow to an attachment so pure & so sincere, I led a life destitute of one of its most precious comforts. . . .

Your letter has removed the unwelcome delusion & I can enjoy without any mixture of alloy the prospect now opening before my eyes. My heart is satisfied, my mind happy & calm & all that is your own work.

The distance to which I have to go, is certainly great, & it will not be without a pang that I shall leave this spot: But it can be lessened once by a more frequent intercourse, when you'll wish to unbend your mind, to seek in the bosom of friendship a momentary relaxation from the weight of your arduous duties. And when retired from the busy scene on which you now act, to the peaceful shades of Fayette, when the pinching hand of want has ceased to press me, will some short but delightfull visits be out of the course of probabilities, will not then a recurrence & a renovation of our early affections spread over the periods of our separation a degree of comfort, that will be felt as long as they will last? I trust they will.

I recognize with corresponding Sentiments the hand of warm friendship, in the letters of introduction you sent me. I see however one inconveniency in them. The expectations thus raised, it will be no slight task in me to fulfill, but this much I know, that every exertion of my mind, every principle that I have cherished shall be marshalled out in the honourable attempt.

One more word I have to say, if when nearer to one another, I have in my rude bluntness involuntarily ever given offense to Mrs. Gallatin, please to acknowledge in my name my real sorrow & to sollicit her forgiveness. I am sure, her good sense will not permit her to think the less of this act of repentence, for its being unconstrained & involuntary. Present her with the offering of my respect & my sincere wishes for her happiness.

Proper measures have been taken respecting Mr. N. E— try in the mean while to have the appointment delayed till an answer from Vincennes can have time to reach you, which will be in six or seven weeks. In the wishes I presumed to express to you, I was less influenced by personal affection, than by the conviction of his fitness, not only as a man of understanding & rectitude, but as already in possession of a thorough knowledge of the country, its local circumstances & the business which must become the object of our deliberations.

Grants have been either made or confirmed by the Governor in consequence of power vested in him by law (which law I have not now before my eyes).[1] The apprehensions of the Commissioners carrying their investigations too far, & of shaking those tittles that have hitherto been considered as settled has excited considerable allarm at Vincennes.[2] But more on that subject, when I am on the Spot. I will then make a discreet use of the permission you give me to consult you.

Your advices respecting my domestic economy I gratefully receive & will faithfully observe, the more so as they perfectly accord with the plan I had formed, & which I intended to pursue.

As the outlots that you sold me enhance the value of my town lots & will facilitate a Sale, I wish you to understand that I will keep them, & when out the proceeds of their sale or any other way I shall have satisfyed you as to the balance I owe you, then my share of the military land will be relieved from the

[1] Act of March 3, 1791, "for granting lands to the Inhabitants and settlers at Vincennes and the Illinois country, in the territory northwest of the Ohio, and for confirming them in their possession." U. S. *Statutes at Large,* I, 221-22.

[2] Apparently Governor Harrison expressed some concern in a letter to Gallatin on June 4, which has not been found. The Secretary of the Treasury replied reassuringly on July 10— "On the power of the commissioners (the register and receiver) to revise any decision of the Governor in the case of complete grants, I have great doubts. At all events, it can only amount to a chancery jurisdiction, which may set aside a patent surreptitiously and fraudulently obtained, through the false representations of the party, and can never affect a *bona fide* purchaser; nor be extended to defeat a title on account of what might, by the commissioners, be considered as an error of judgment in making the grant." Logan Esarey (ed.), *Governors Messages and Letters. Messages and Letters of William Henry Harrison* (2 volumes. *Indiana Historical Collections,* VII, IX, Indianapolis, 1922), I, 102.

A summary of this letter was published in the Vincennes *Indiana Gazette,* August 21, 1804.

charge of that balance & you can make me a deed.

I will set off in July & wait till Spring to take my family down. I could not do any other way.

. . . . . .

I have long enough hindered you by this lengthy letter from attending to more important affair, I must put an end to it, but not without once more making to you an homage of my present happiness & repeating from a feeling heart that I am ever Yours &c

JOHN BADOLLET

N. B. I received your draft.

[Addressed:] Albert Gallatin Esqr  Washington City District of Columbia

[Endorsed:] Greensburg June 1804 Badollet

[Gallatin to Badollet]

TREARURY DEPARTMENT
18th July 1804

SIR . . . .

The Register of the Treasury, Mr. Nourse, will purchase and cause to be transmitted to you at Vincennes the necessary books & stationery; but, as you may, in the mean while, want a secondary book and some other articles, you may purchase them and transmit the account to him in Washington with the receipts from the persons from whom you shall have purchased.

I have the honour to be respectfully Sir your obed't serv't

ALBERT GALLATIN

P. S. A letter containing instructions and information respecting the nature of the land-claims at Vincennes has been sent to you to that place recommended to the care of Gov'r Harrison.[1]

[Addressed:] John Badollet Esq're Register of the Land Office of Vincennes now at New Geneva Pennsylvania

[1] Gallatin to John Badollet and Michael Jones, July 9, 1804. Printed in Carter (ed.), *Territorial Papers*, VII, 205-8. Jones was register of the land office at Kaskaskia.

[Badollet to Gallatin]

VINCENNES October 19th 1804

From the annexed letter you will readily perceive that I experienced a considerable degree of embarassement in the first steps I had to take, desirous of beginning right & fearfull of doing wrong.[1] I attentively studied the act of last session and your instructions, & after mature deliberation I prescribed to myself the rule of conduct, a Sketch of which you'ill see in the other letter.[2] My way of thinking is corroborated by the opinion of the Surveyor General[3] (now here) which perfectly coincides with mine. However, as I may still mistake, permit me to request your opinion & further advice. I have no doubt, but considering the novelty & importance of the business together with my natural diffidence of myself, you'll reanimate my courage by your approbation when right & by your friendly counsels when I happen to mistake.

I thought it would be improper to record in the same book, indiscriminately all descriptions of claims & considering those allowed by the Governor as forming a distinct class, I record in a Separate book all what is here termed Patents issued by him as well as orders of Surveys, the only evidences of tittle since he declined ([a]) issuing any more patents. It is to be lamented that since the passing of this act, he did not consider himself authorized to perfect the tittles he had recognized by granting orders of Survey & was fearfull of interfering with the business of the Commissioners. Had he done so, & it is my opinion he had the right, the public would have been more satisfied.

I record (or rather intend to, for the persons concerned do not appear to be much in haste) all claims which the

---

(a) number of patents are made but not signed.

[1] Badollet took his oath of office as commissioner to settle land claims before Judge Henry Vanderburgh, September 19, 1804. The document is in the Badollet Papers in the Indiana Historical Society Library.

[2] Neither the letter nor the enclosed sketch has been found.

[3] Jared Mansfield.

Governor has not taken cognizance of on another book not only because distinguished by their natures from the former, but also because if you should think that conveyances should also be recorded in the cases of hitherto unpresented claims I might upon being made acquainted with your opinion, transcribe the evidences of these claims on another book each accompanyed with the instruments of writing by which they have been transferred.

W[h]en the Governor determined to issue no more patents, considering himself no more authorized so to do, he likewise directed the Surveyor not to Survey any more till the Commissioners arrived; it therefore follows that many claimants are not able to file any platts or returns of Surveys, and as he is absent in Louisiana there is no remedy.

This town or village being situated in a prairie surrounding it on three sides, & [MS illeg.] it is extremely dear, & house rent truly enourmous. An house, similar to your house in Geneva would rent for 100 or 150 dollars a year, & any better (& there are but few Such) could not be obtained for less than between 2 & 300.(b) Those circumstances coupled with the dearness of many Subordinate objects of house keeping, which you can have in the Country, & run away with your cash in towns, make it for me a matter of necessity as it is of choice, to live in the Country. How to accomplish it I know not. I am such a poor hand at selling any thing, that the lands on the Miami which I own with you are likely to remain unsold for a good while. I wish it could suit you to take my share. I would thereby discharge a debt that you ought to have received & a balance would be left me which would assist my other small resources towards purchasing a farm.

Perhaps would it be practicable to exchange one of the Surveys for land here provided you would consent to make a

---

(b) A room a little above 15 feet square where Gen'l Gibson[4] keeps his office costs him I believe 36 dollars a year.

[4] John Gibson, secretary of the territory.

deed, on obtaining from me a lien on the land received in exchange, to secure the debt I owe you. I wish you would advise me what to do. The time will soon come, when I must bring my family here, & poor will I remain in deed, if the rent of an house, unavoidable or *useless* necessaries run away with what I can make. Add to that, that Albert who loves farming and is skillfull at it, would be a dead weight upon me instead of help, for he is not fond (though a good boy) of *head work*.

At my arrival here, owing I believe to the incessant fatigues of a journey by water when very low, exposed to a burning sun in day time & to the damps of an unhealthy country at night, I was taken sick but soon recovered. My son Albert whom I took with me, was very nigh falling a prey to an acute or continual inflammatory fever, which 4 repeated bleedings could hardly check, he is well now but a mere skeleton. Those unlucky events must account for my not paying to the business that was falling to my share, that early attention which on discovery of difficulties, would have induced me to consult you sooner.

I found a room, boarding and a most kind treatment at Col. Francis Vigo's an Italian, ancient settler in this Country a man of the most benevolent heart and unsuspected integrity. He is well known or ought to be known to government for the eminent services he has rendered to the United States during the revolution, he having been one of the efficient means of the Success of Genl Clarke's expedition, in which I believe he has sacrificed a good deal of his own.[5]

I look for the arrival of N. Ewing with the greatest anxiety, not doubting of his appointment. He possesses a thorough knowledge of this Country, and the nature of the different Species of claims that will be brought forward. There is hardly an individual here but who wishes to see him arrive invested with the office of Receiver, & no appointment could be more generally satisfactory.

[5] A biographical sketch of Vigo by Dorothy Riker is in the *Indiana Magazine of History*, XXVI (1930), 12-24.

Perhaps you do not know that Savary[6] is elected to the Assembly of the State of Kentucky by a majority of the most thinking. They place a great reliance upon him to introduce order in their finances, which are in the most allarming confusion, their warrants on the treasury losing 15 & 20 p/c. How far he is calculated to answer their expectations I know not. I hope he will not make long speeches upon the flour, for his pronunciation and phraseology having not improved, some of the members will think he speaks Hottentot. He writes however much better & I have read some political lucubrations of his, well written & full of Sound reasoning.

I hope your health continues to improve & that your family are all well. Pay my best compliments to Mrs. Gallatin & believe me

For ever yours,

JOHN BADOLLET.

[Endorsed:] Vincennes 19 October 1804  Badollet

[Badollet to Gallatin]

VINCENNES Dec'r 16th 1804

From a principle of public spirit I am now led to address you these few words, believing as I do that witholding any information the knowledge of which concerns the interest of the public, is in itself wrong & deserves censure.

It appears probable that Congress will extend their System of public Stores for the use of Indians & that perhaps one will be ordered to be kept at this place, in which case nothing would be more agreable to the natives & better conciliate their attachment, & insure an upright disposal of the goods destined for them than the appointment of Mr. Vigo. I will not expatiate upon his acquaintance with the indian tribes, his knowledge of their habbits & manners, his unsuspected integrity & known

---

[6] Jean Savary de Valcoulon. See Introduction, above, p. 10. He had gone to Kentucky by 1797, settling in Bourbon County. Badollet to Gallatin, May 10, 1797, in Gallatin Papers; *Sketch of Bourbon, Scott, Harrison and Nicholas Counties, Kentucky* . . ., edited by William H. Perrin (Chicago, 1882), p. 520.

benevolence, & the Services he has often rendered to the United States, my object being to point him out as a man worthy of trust, that you may be induced to make inquiries respecting him. By a search in the war office you will find there documents respecting that man from which you will derive further information. Mr. Ewing is also able to tell you more on this subject.

Permit me to repeat here what I have heretofore suggested respecting the propriety of granting a further allowance of time to claimants in this territory, it appearing indubitable but a comparatively small number of claims will be brought forward in time to avoid forfeiture & this consequence of misapprehension ignorance, or inability to comply with the requisitions of the act, would be uncommonly severe. Governor Harrison told me he would write to you on the same subject.[1]

When I wrote you last, I had not fully understood your instructions & my letter must have excited some surprise. I have formed I believe more correct ideas on the Subject & am acting accordingly.

I entertain serious thoughts of resigning this office    life

[1] By act of March 3, 1805, the time for presenting claims was extended until November 1, 1805. U. S. *Statutes at Large,* II, 343-45. The act also allowed additional compensation—$500 to each of the commissioners for settling the claims and an additional $500 to the registers at Vincennes, Detroit, and Kaskaskia for translating and recording or having translated and recorded the grants, deeds, and other evidences of claims in the French language. This allowed an additional $1,000 to Badollet, Michael Jones at Kaskaskia, and George Hoffman at Detroit. See Gallatin to the registers, March 13, 1805, in Carter (ed.), *Territorial Papers,* VII, 270-71. "You may," wrote Gallatin, "whenever you shall think proper draw on me for seven hundred and fifty dollars, viz't two hundred and fifty for the balance of the allowance made by the former act to the Commissioners, as such, and five hundred dollars for the extra-compensation made to you by this act for translating and recording . . . in the French language. The five hundred dollars additional compensation made by this act to the Commissioners as such will be paid, one half on the first day of November next & the other half when the business of the Board shall have been completed. For your annual salary as Register, you may draw quarterly as formerly instructed."

is so dear here that my appointments will prove in fact small & barely sufficient to make me live, for except along the Ohio, in the last purchase, no sale of land to any amount will take place. Negroe Slavery is also going to be introduced, & that circumstance alone would prove sufficient to drive me from hence.[2] I have also another reason, a very urgent one, of which I have right to be proud, but which I will explain at another time. I am sensible of the distress, which will be the consequence of such an unaccountable step, & am ready to meet it with resignation, I wish to continue to deserve your friendship & your esteem, & I trust that in mentioning these my late thoughts, I jeopardize neither. However I will tell you more on the Subject after the arrival of Ewing & if I am really impelled to return to my humble station, *never to leave it again,* I fondly hope, nay I am sure, when I think of the affecting letter you blessed me with last spring & all you have done for me, that you will not withdraw from your ill fated friend the assistance of your advices towards his future conduct.

Endeavour to steal a few minutes from your accumulated duties, to answer me a few words.

Pay my best compliments to Mrs. Gallatin & may you all enjoy health & Content. Yours forever

JNO. BADOLLET

[Addressed:]   Albert   Gallatin   Esq'r   Washington   City

---

[2] Slavery was, of course, excluded from the area comprising the Northwest Territory by the sixth article of the Ordinance of 1787. However, there was an element within Indiana Territory that sought to circumvent this and introduce some form of involuntary servitude of Negroes.

A convention of delegates from the four counties of the territory, called by Governor Harrison and presided over by him on December 28, 1802, among other things petitioned Congress for the suspension of the sixth article on the grounds that it had "prevented the Country from populating and been the reason of driving many valuable Citizens possessing Slaves to the Spanish side of the Mississippi, most of whom but for the prohibition contained in the ordinance would have settled in this Territory. . . ." This was not the first move by the citizens of the territory toward this end, nor the last. See Carter (ed.), *Territorial Papers,* VII, 89-90n; Jacob P. Dunn, *Slavery Petitions and Papers* (Indiana Historical Society *Publications,* II, No. 12, Indianapolis, 1894).

District of Columbia
  [Postmarked:] Louisville K. Dec'r 30th
  [Endorsed:] Vincennes 16th Decemb 1804   Badollet

[Badollet to Gallatin]

GREENSBURGH May 3d 1805

We have lately arrived from Vincennes Mr. Ewing & I, intending both after a few days rest to pay you a visit, in case you did not come yourself to Geneva as was expected, having some strong reasons to wish for a personal interview with you. Mr. Ewing will certainly go, if you do not come; with respect to myself, the necessary preparations for the transporting of my family down the Ohio make my absence a matter of much difficulty & render my intended journey very problematical.

I have received here from Vincennes a pacquet forwarded thither by you containing the Supplementary act of Congress passed last Session.[1] I am going this minuet to communicate it to Mr. Ewing.

I have drawn, as directed, on you for 250 Dollars, the two first quarters of my salary as Register, in favour of Charles A. Mestrezat, & will also draw for the seven hundred Dollars, as you permit me to do by your last letter, in behalf of the same person.[2]

I am happy to hear that you and family are continuing to enjoy health, my respects to Mrs. Gallatin & believe me forever Yours &c

JNO BADOLLET

PS. If you think you will come out here please to let us or Nicholson[3] know it by the next post.

---

[1] See above, letter of December 16, 1804, note 1.

[2] Mestrezat (1766-1815) was one of the Swiss emigrants who was induced to come to the United States by Albert Gallatin. He settled in Greene County, Pennsylvania, and carried on a general merchandising business. John W. Jordan and James Hadden (eds.), *Genealogical and Personal History of Fayette County Pennsylvania* (3 volumes. Lewis Publishing Company, New York, 1912), I, 124-25.

[3] James Witter Nicholson, Gallatin's brother-in-law. See above, p. 11.

[Addressed:] Albert Gallatin
[Endorsed:] Greensburg 3 May 1805  Badollet


[Gallatin to Badollet]

WASHINGTON 15th May 1805

It would have given me a heartfelt pleasure to meet you before you go to Vincennes; but unfortunately, and for the first time out of Congress session since I have been here, I find myself nailed in this city or at least within a distance where a letter may reach me in a day or two. And I take so little exercise whilst here that my health requires that I should take some short riding exercise in the neighborhood; so that if you come, you may run the risk of not finding me here or at least of being obliged to wait 3 or 4 days for my return. If you will write, however, by mail fixing the precise week when either N. Ewing or you will be here, I will take care not to be absent at the time. But I do not wish you to sacrifice money to pleasure; and if you can avoid the journey it may be a wise determination. As it relates to official business I cannot conceive why either of you wishes to see me; but of that you are the best judges; only for more than one reason, I wish not that it may be represented that you have both been absent from Vincennes at once for too long a period. Can you tell me when you intend going down the river, in order that I may judge whether there be any probability of my being with you before you go? But above all, communicate what are your views & prospects on the Wabash. Your letter in which you expressed your intention to leave the place afflicted me; & some parts were altogether unintelligible to me—Be somewhat more communicative on this subject; you must not forget that on account of the extra allowance for translating as well as on acct. of the salary as commissioner, this first years compensation is probably greater, as well as more certain, than any of the succeeding ones. I am exhausted and cannot include all I meant to say on this subject. Give my best compliments to your wife & believe me ever yours

ALBERT GALLATIN

Never write any thing of a private nature in your official communications. Try to be perfectly correct even in the most trifling ones of the last species and let your private letters be directed under two covers & endorsed [addressed] as this is

[Addressed:] *Private* John Badollet Esqre

[Badollet to Gallatin]

GREENSBURGH May 18th 1805

However desirous I was of paying you a visit before I took my final leave of this country, many reasons forbid my thinking any more of such a gratification. The Season far advanced renders a journey by water a matter of some difficulty & danger which it would be rash to increase by unnecessary delays, & the propriety of economy under the present circumstances suggests itself forcibly to my mind—Many things I had to communicate to you, many questions to ask, but I must refer you to my worthy colleague Nat'l Ewing (who is setting off for the federal City next week,) from whom you will obtain every information relative to that Country which it was our object to communicate & to whom you will be so kind as to impart every additional advice relative to my duty which it is my earnest wish to obtain. And here let me beseech you (as you may view me in the light of a prentice in the business) to furnish him, as a friend, for me, with every thing that may elucidate & render easy the manner of keeping my books, descending even to minutia. Send me a pattern for entering the lands on the days of public sale, before they are registered on the journal &c &c— Thus when I have gone through the duties of the office for a year or two & it is ascertained that I am competent to the task & do not disgrace your choice, I may pay you a visit & enjoy the pleasure of it unalloyed by fear.

Ewing will inform you both of my opinion with respect to the business of the Commissioners & of my perplexities.

From the Governour I received every mark of attention that you had a right to expect for me from him. He is a man of a fine & correct understanding, upright in his principles & conduct, a faithfull servant of the United States & highly entitled to confidence. His having been a Soldier for a long time, & his eyes having a side glance that fathom you to the soul, render his company less agreable to me, seem to repel familiarity & confidence, but it is perhaps my own fault.

It will be perhaps not uninteresting to you to learn, that from my family I derive solid comfort, every day I have new reasons to love & respect the woman whom it was my happy lot to obtain, her artless native good sense has ripened into a considerable soundness of understanding, which added to her original purity & the constant propriety of her conduct & her amiable discretion have secured her the affection & esteem of those whom it is honourable to please— My children betray no disposition, but such as must be gratifying to my feelings. My first daughter reaching the age of puberty has a remarkable good sense, is fond of study & industrious. Albert has home spun brains, which never will lead him into abstruse Speculations, but his head will be like his body solid & sound. He entertains high notions & is proud of the independance which a man owes to his industry, & begins to act from that principle. You will not laugh I am sure at those effusions of my heart, no person can listen to them, & I wanted to let some body hear my tale. Surely you were the person.

Herein enclosed a certificate of the appointment of John Rice Jones to the Clerkship to the Commissioners.[1]

Do not forget to Speak with Ewing of the propriety of

---

[1] Jones's oath of office as clerk to the board of commissioners, taken before Judge Henry Vanderburgh, is in the Badollet Papers in the Indiana Historical Society Library. A biographical sketch of Jones is given in Francis S. Philbrick (ed.), *The Laws of Indiana Territory, 1801-1809* (*Illinois Historical Collections*, XXI, Springfield, 1930, reprinted with supplementary Indiana material by the Indiana Historical Bureau, 1931), ccxxxviii-ccxlii.

having a public Store in Vincennes, & of the person fit to be trusted with it.

My respects to Mrs. Gallatin. Send me a few words about your family concerns. I hope you are all well. Ever yours

JNO BADOLLET

[Addressed:] Albert Gallatin Esq'r Washington City District of Columbia

[Postmarked:] New Geneva 17 May Free

[Note on address:] As I was folding my epistle the ink-stand over set over it & had not time to copy it.

[Endorsed:] Greensburgh May 18, 1805 Badollet

[Badollet to Gallatin]

GREENSBURGH May 23d 1805

I have received your letter of the 15th inst. & am happy in having taken the resolution you recommend, before you suggested it, the propriety of which at the present time struck me— I am much in haste, and intending to write you a few lines more before I set off. I'll mention only a few things— Mr. Ewing will be with us on Monday night on his way to the federal City, he will probably stay here a day or two—I will set off in the beginning of June, my boat is in forwardness & I will be at Vincennes in the beginnng of July, if I can be so fortunate as to have water high enough; If not I must sett off alone however great the inconveniency. I shall not dally here. I shall adhere strictly to your directions with respect to my future correspondence, rest easy on that ground.—a due attention to economy will ever hereafter be paid by me, & no money as you very properly advise shall be by me sacrificed to pleasure. My family my farm a few friends & solitude will be the only ones I'll pursue. An exalted one is perhaps in reserve, that of having proved myself worthy of your confidence—The mail sets off. I must break off abrubtly. I shall write you more at leisure & explain to you why some of my letters from Vincennes were unintelligible being the offspring of a perturbed mind. I wonder you understood them at all. Consternation to which I was a prey, will beget neither method nor perspicuity—But more in my next.

Ever yours                                JOHN BADOLLET

You mention the necessity of exercise for your health. I hope it is a *remedy of precaution* & surely a wise one

[Addressed:] Albert Gallatin Esq'r  Private

[Endorsed:] Greensburgh  May 3[23], 1805

[Badollet and Ewing to Gallatin]

[NEW] GENEVA May 30th 1805

DEAR SIR

Governor Harrison has written to us, wishing us to Second a recommendation he has forwarded to you in favour of Mr. Benjamin Parke of Vincennes for the purpose of getting him the appointment of Agent to defend the Interest of the United States before the Commissioners for adjusting the claims to land in upper Louisiana—[1] Being well acquainted with Mr. Parke we do not hesitate to say that we think him both in point of talents & integrity well qualified to discharge the duties of that office.

We are Sir with respect Your obed. Ser'ts

JOHN BADOLLET
NAT'L EWING

[Addressed:] Albert Gallatin Esq'r  City of Washington Private

[Endorsed:] N. Geneva May 30 1805  J'n Badollet

[1] This recommendation followed passage of an act for ascertaining and adjusting the titles and claims to land within the territory of Orleans, and the district of Louisiana. U. S. *Statutes at Large,* II, 324-29. Parke did not receive the appointment. He had sought appointment in the land office at Vincennes either as register or receiver. Carter (ed.), *Territorial Papers,* VII, 193, 198-99. On August 4, 1804, Governor Harrison appointed him attorney general for the territory. William W. Woollen, *et al.* (eds.), *Executive Journal of Indiana Territory, 1800-1816* (Indiana Historical Society *Publications,* III, No. 3, Indianapolis, 1900), p. 124. He was elected territorial delegate to Congress at the first session of the first territorial assembly which convened on July 29, 1805. Gayle Thornbrough and Dorothy Riker (eds.), *Journals of the General Assembly of Indiana Territory, 1805-1815 (Indiana Historical Collections,* XXXII, Indianapolis, 1950), p. 100. See biographical sketch of Parke in *ibid.,* pp. 999-1002.

[Badollet to Gallatin]

VINCENNES Aug't 31, 1805

I herein send you a few queries to which I will be much obliged to you to grant an answer.

By instructions received by the District surveyor of this place from the surveyor general, it appears that the Commissioners may direct the Survey of such lands as have not as yet been surveyed, though granted the Governor when the Act of March 1804 came to his knowledge stopped all further surveying, hence numbers of orders of surveys of tracts granted to claimants remain to this day unexecuted.

The orders of survey issued by the Governor were either special describing the place as well as quantity, or general without specification of place; these last to be located under certain regulations by him established, wherever the Grantee found a Spot to his liking. May the warrants of this last description be laid any where within the Wabash purchase, or must the Commissioners subject the owners of such warrants to some restrictions?—if so, of what nature must those restrictions be? —ought they to join surveys heretofore made or only be contiguous & parallel with the sectional lines of the general survey made under the direction of the surveyor general?[1]

Can the Commissioners issue Commissions to take depositions, when the distance or situation of the witness renders his appearance before them impracticable?— Are the depositions taken before Magistrates in this County & filed in this office to be taken as conclusive evidence or must the subscribing witness to such depositions be summoned before them?[2]— The United Illinois and Ouabache land Companies have entered their claims—their immense extent and weighty importance renders their investigation a work of too much difficulty for the Commissioners, high legal authorities will be adduced and

---

[1] Gallatin's reply to these questions, dated October 23, 1805, is in Carter (ed.), *Territorial Papers*, VII, 311-12.

[2] Gallatin wrote that the commissioners were to be the sole judges of what should be considered by them as proper evidence. *Ibid.*

they are no lawyers. What is your opinion on this subject?[3]

The Legislature has just ended its session,[4] local and interested views have manifested themselves. How few men can soar above those groveling ideas & pursue the public good with a noble independence? Our political institutions are all grounded upon the supposition that we are virtuous and enlightened, what egregious mistake! Look at our poor Pennsylvania convulsed by a french mania. How dreadfull the prospect!

Amongst the members the following deserve to be taken notice of for their enlightened views & usefullness. Col. Chambers,[5] son of General Chambers of our State, John Rice Jones & Benjamin Parke, this last is elected to represent us in Congress and is a worthy man of an excellent head and heart and of an independant mind. The member of Council for St. Clair County has resigned, a new nomination will take place, a Mr. Bond[6] will be named I believe—a conceited mule.

They have incorporated a company for opening a canal along the falls of Ohio. That undertaking which appears at a distance only, to be of any magnitude, was in my humble opinion the basis on which a plan of gigantic Speculation was

---

[3] "The Illinois & Wabash Companies," wrote Gallatin, "have not the shadow of a title to support their claim, which has been repeatedly before Congress. . . ." *Ibid.* Memorials to Congress from the Illinois and Wabash Land Companies and reports from Senate and House committees thereon are in *American State Papers, Public Lands* (8 volumes. Washington, D. C., 1834-61), I, 21, 22, 63-65, 189. The memorialists claimed certain tracts described in two deeds from the Illinois and Piankashaw Indians, one to William Murray (the Illinois Company), dated July 5, 1773, and the other to Lord Dunmore (the Wabash Company), dated October 18, 1775. The memorialists proposed to surrender to the United States all the lands described in the two deeds provided the United States reconvey to the companies one-fourth part of the land.

[4] This was the first session of the first Indiana Territorial General Assembly, which sat from July 29 to August 26.

[5] Benjamin Chambers. See sketch in Thornbrough and Riker (eds.), *Journals of the General Assembly of Indiana Territory,* pp. 962-64.

[6] Shadrach Bond, Sr. Philbrick (ed.), *Laws of Indiana Territory, 1801-9,* pp. ccxlvi-ccxlvii.

intended to rest, those views have been discovered and partly counteracted.[7]

The introduction of Slavery into this territory continues to be the Hobby horse of the influential men here. The members of the legislature have signed a petition to Congress praying for some reasonable modifications to the ordinance, but this favourite topic of Slavery, will I trust meet with a general disapprobation in Congress. Shallow politicians, who to obtain a transitory good are willing to entail on their Country a permanent evil.[8]

A Court of Chancery has been created, & who do you believe is to be the Chancell'r?—I leave it to your guessing powers—The man ho[w]ever thus selected for a post of such high importance, has I am told a sufficient degree of unfashion-

[7] The act is in *ibid.*, pp. 154-63. Thomas T. Davis, one of the judges of Indiana Territory, in a letter to President Jefferson on March 17, 1805, had urged him to hasten the appointment of members of the territorial Legislative Council so that the Assembly might convene and pass an act incorporating the canal. "The selection of some Landed property through which this Cannal must pass makes it essential for the company to be incorporated," he wrote. Carter (ed.), *Territorial Papers*, VII, 272. The company's avowed object was to build a canal around the falls of the Ohio at Louisville, but the real purpose was revealed in the provision of the act which allowed the directors after accumulating $100,000 to issue notes and set up a bank. Among the directors named in the act was Aaron Burr. The charge was made that this was part of his scheme to secure funds for his "Conspiracy." Questions about the company's intention were raised in the Kentucky papers. See particularly the Lexington *Kentucky Gazette*, September 17, December 5 and 26, 1805; January 2 and 9, 1806. For a detailed discussion see Isaac J. Cox, "The Burr Conspiracy in Indiana," in *Indiana Magazine of History*, XXV (December, 1929), 258-69.

[8] The petition is printed in Thornbrough and Riker (eds.), *Journals of the General Assembly of Indiana Territory*, pp. 101-8. It was not adopted as an official part of the proceedings of the Assembly. The Assembly passed an act "concerning the Introduction of Negroes and Mulattoes into this Territory," under which any person owning or purchasing slaves outside the territory might bring them into Indiana and bind them to service. Philbrick (ed.), *Laws of Indiana Territory, 1801-9*, pp. 136-39. The act was repealed in 1810 following the division of Indiana Territory and the creation of Illinois Territory. Louis B. Ewbank and Dorothy Riker (eds.), *The Laws of Indiana Territory, 1809-1816 (Indiana Historical Collections*, XX, Indianapolis, 1934), pp. 138-39.

able honesty as to decline an office for which he is conscious to be totally unqualified.[9]

I hope you continue to enjoy a good state of health & that your family is also well—I was taken Sick at Chilicothe during a whole week but happily recovered. Ever yours

JNO BADOLLET

[Addressed:] Albert Gallatin Esq'r   Washington City District of Columbia  Private

[Gallatin to Badollet]

WASHINGTON 25th Oct'er 1805

It is only a few days since I received your letter of 31st August. To that part which related to some points of your official duties I make an official answer, principally for the purpose of enclosing a copy of the Proclamation of 1763.[1] I forgot to mention that in 1774 Parliament passed what is called the Quebec act, which amongst other things extended the

---

[9] For the act organizing a court of chancery see Philbrick (ed.), *Laws of Indiana Territory, 1801-9,* pp. 108-12. The court was to consist of one judge appointed and commissioned by the Governor, who should hold two annual sessions commencing in March and August and who was empowered and authorized to exercise all the powers and authority usually exercised by courts of equity. Badollet's appointment as judge of the Court of Chancery by Governor Harrison was recorded in the executive journal on September 2, 1805. Woollen, *et al.* (eds.), *Executive Journal of Indiana Territory,* p. 129. Thomas T. Davis was appointed to the office on March 1, 1806. *Ibid.,* p. 132.

No session of the court was held until August, 1807. In his message to the Assembly on August 18, 1807, the Governor noted this, adding, ". . . whether the blame is attributable to the chancellor, or to the legislature, in not providing him a compensation, I shall not attempt to determine. . . ." The court met considerable opposition, and in 1813 its cases were transferred to the General Court. Thornbrough and Riker (eds.), *Journals of the General Assembly of Indiana Territory,* pp. 115n, 128, 166; Minutes of the Court of Chancery, 1807-1811, in Knox County Courthouse, Vincennes, a microfilm of which is in the Archives Division, Indiana State Library.

[1] The significant part of this proclamation by the British Crown was that it forbade granting of lands by the governors of the colonies "beyond the Heads or Sources of any of the Rivers which fall into the Atlantic Ocean from the West and North West," thus reserving the western lands to the Indians. White settlement on Indian land was forbidden as well as private land purchase from the Indians.

limits of that Province to the Ohio from the western boundary of Pennsylvania to the Mississippi. The pretended purchase of 1775 of the Vincennes tract[2] should have been made, therefore, under the authority of the Gov'r of Canada: a circumstance which I mention merely because the claimants may draw as argument (in favor of their repeated assertion that their purchase was made under the authority of Gov't) from the circumstance of Lord Dunmore Governor of Virginia being one of the Grantees. This, however, would not in any view of the subject prove any thing in their favour; and their whole claim is perfectly ridiculous.

You do not inform me whether you have taken your family, nor what are your views and prospects. Is the country sufficiently healthy to encourage a place of permanent residence and the purchase of a plantation. Considering the late purchase by Gov'r Harrison,[3] it is not improbable that before long another district & land office will be established. In that case, what should be the division; from North to South, or from East to West? and in which of the portions should you prefer to hold the office?[4]

Whilst the Republicans opposed the federalists, the necessity of union induced a general sacrifice of private views & personal objects: and the opposition was generally grounded on the purest motives and conducted in the most honorable manner. Complete success has awakened all those passions

[2] A reference to the claim of the Illinois and Wabash Land Companies. See above, pp. 47-48n.

[3] The treaty concluded by Harrison with the Delawares, Potawatomi, Miami, Eel Rivers, and Weas on August 21, 1805. This ceded to the United States all the land lying south of a line running northerly from the northeast corner of the Vincennes Tract to intersect the boundary line designated in the Greenville Treaty, running north from a point on the Ohio opposite the mouth of the Kentucky River. Charles J. Kappler (ed.), *Indian Affairs. Laws and Treaties* (2 volumes. Washington, D. C., 1904), II, 80-81.

[4] See Badollet's reply below, p. 63. By act of March 3, 1807, a land office was established at Jeffersonville for the disposal of lands lying between the Cincinnati and Vincennes districts. U. S. *Statutes at Large*, II, 448. By act of April 30, 1810, the Second Principal Meridian was established as the boundary between the two districts. *Ibid.*, II, 590-91.

which only slumbered. In Pennsylvania particularly the thirst for offices, too much encouraged by Gov. McKean's first measures, created a schism in Philad'a as early as 1802. Leib, ambitious, avaricious, envious & disappointed blew up the flame, and watched the first opportunity to make *his* cause a general one. The vanity, the nepotism and the indiscretion of Gov'r McKean afforded the opportunity. Want of mutual forbearance amongst the best intentioned and most respectable republicans has completed the schism. Duane, intoxicated by the persuasion that he alone had overthrown federalism, thought himself neither sufficiently rewarded nor respected, and, possessed of an engine which gives him an irresistible controul over public opinion, he easily gained the victory for his friends. I call it a victory; for the number of republicans who have opposed him rather than supported McKean does not exceed one fourth or at most one third of the whole; and Mc-Kean owes his re-election to the federalists. What will be the consequence I cannot even conjecture: my ardent wishes are for mutual forgiveness and a re-union of the republican interest; but I hardly think it probable. McKean & Duane will be both implacable & immovable; and the acts of the first, & the continued proscriptions of the last will most probably & unfortunately defeat every attempt to reconcile. Yet I do not foresee any permanent evil beyond what arises from perpetual agitation & from that party spirit which encourages personal hatred: but the intolerance & persecution which we abhorred in federalism will be pursued by the prevailing party, till the people who do not love injustice once more put it down.[5]

I expect Nicholson in a few days & will probably pay a visit home next spring. Ever yours    ALBERT GALLATIN

[Badollet to Gallatin]

VINCENNES Nov'r 30th 1805

Your kind enquiries respecting my present views and

[5] For a discussion of the Pennsylvania political situation alluded to by Gallatin in this paragraph and Gallatin's role therein, see Walters, *Albert Gallatin*, pp. 157-63.

prospects, I have read with gratitude, they shew me that the affection of which you have given me so many proofs, is in no danger of being extinguished. To render myself more and more worthy of it, will be my constant endeavour and if by a rational conduct, which it is my intention to pursue, I can make you forget years of error and childish thoughtlessness, I will call myself, & really be, in the possession of happiness.

I will ere long inform you of many particulars relating to myself and this Country, and consider your other questions. My mind is not as yet at sufficient liberty.

My family could not succeed at their endeavours to come down this year, Monongahela never was or kept so low, their absence is a serious source of uneasiness to me, but I must try to bear it with fortitude.

If you can pay a visit to Fayette, it is my ardent wish to be able to meet you there. Could not such a wish be gratified?

I wrote to Mr. Smiley requesting his interference in procuring a Commission in the army for one Mr. James Hurst brother of the Clerk of the General Court of this place. The Governor & other persons of respectability in & out of the army will take the first steps. I wish only Mr. Smiley to second them. The young man is deserving. Remember me to that worthy man.

Nothing contributes more to my present happiness, & inspires me with more confidence in myself, than a few private lines now and then from you. However short, they produce on me a remarkable effect.

Remember me to Mrs. Gallatin & let me know how your family is.

I remain Ever yours

JNO BADOLLET

[Addressed:] Albert Gallatin  Washington City  Private

[Endorsed:]  Vincennes  November 30, 1805  Badollet friendship

[Badollet to Gallatin]

VINCENNES Jan'y 1st 1806

You appear desirous in your last letter to know something relative to the country, myself and my prospects in this *new* world; I will endeavour now to satisfy you.

The aspect of the Country is highly pleasing, the surface being undulating exhibiting a variety of low eminences & small prairies, which furnish to persons fond of rural scenes and of a romantic disposition an easy means of uniting their views of innocent pleasure with those of greater solidity. The soil is generally rich, the first rate being generally covered with the same kind of timber, which denote our prime lands, ash, poplar, sugar-trees black & white, walnuts, honey locusts, beeches, sycamores, buck eyes &c, furnishing a comparatively small quantity of good rail timber. The oak is to be seen every where, but in very small number, and where it predominates, it denotes as with us an inferior kind of soil. In places the beech seems the king of the forest and with its confederate the poplar grow to a very large size.

There is another kind of land lying to the South East of Vincennes & extending a great way in that direction, called the barrens, not from an absolute want of fertility, of which when they lye very flatt they exhibit no small proof, but from their remarkable inferiority when uneven to the rest of the country, and their being covered either with no timber at all, or with thinly scattered small oaks, which do not prevent the wild grass from growing luxuriantly under them.

On the west of the Wabash and almost immediately on its banks begin that immense body of prairies or plains extending to the Illinois Country & reaching the lake Michigan to which the veins of timbered land which now and then cross them bear a very small proportion. Nothing can be more romantic than the view of these barrens & plains, appearing like unbounded meadows, especially in the Spring of the year, when they are decked in all the variety of an unchecked vegetation.

The cause that gave rise to these plains appear to me to be no secret, the most general production of the soil in this country is grass, growing to a very great height, in autumn it dries up & falling on the ground it matts it, in a manner similar to cured hay. The natives have been in the habit from time immemorial of Setting yearly that kind of Stuble a fire, and its violence is such that, especially when assisted by a smart breeze, it destroys every thing before it. Thus every year the constant efforts that nature is known to make for reproducing timber, are as constantly bafled and the tracts of wood land, now existing owe their preservation to some peculiarity of situation or vegetable production other than the grass before mentioned, by which that destructive element is in those particular cases effectually checked. This account is corroborated by this fact well known here, that wherever that description of land is protected by settlements from the so frequent inroads of fire, the trees visibly increase in number. And I have very little doubt, but that, if peavines, rich weeds, & similar plants were the production of this kind of land, instead of grass, the timber would have never ceased to exist in that part of the country which I have been describing.

White River, a stream of the size of Mononguehela about New Geneva, runs in a south west direction in the Wabash into which it empties 30 miles below this place, is muddy & lyable to very high freshets. Its banks alternately on one side or the other & sometimes on both, are sometimes over flowed to the depth of six feet and distance of four or five miles, which precludes the possibility of forming settlements on those rich bottoms for ages to come. To what distance it is navigable I am not able to say.

The Wabash much wider is a clear, placid stream, gliding along between banks generally low & through a country, though not generally level, yet so destitute of high hills, that the wind has a full play on its surface and sailing is not unusual here. It is the most beautiful channel of navigation I have seen on the west of the mountains, it is navigable for about four hundred miles above this place. Its rises and falls are slow and gradual, usually inch by inch. From the upper point of navigation there is an easy portage of eight miles to Fort Wayne on the navigable waters of the lake Erie, over which they frequently go without unloading their barges or perogues & you daily see at this place boats which have set off from Detroit.

The Country included between these two water courses, as you proceed Northeastwards, every information derived from respectable sources states to be handsome, fertile, irrigated by numberless excellent streams and to hold out the most alluring encouragement to new settlers. How far the same description applys to the Country westward of the Wabash and Eastward of White river I am not able at present to tell. Several banks of stone coal have been discovered, and also a copper mine but of this last fact further evidence is necessary, to entitle it to full credit.

The imperfect account I have here given you is however sufficient to prove the importance of this Country, both in a agricultural and commercial point of view. To the list of articles the produce of the western parts of Pennsylvania, cotton which grows here to perfection may be added, an object no less interesting in domestic economy than with a view to exportation. The edges of those large prairies, afford the most eligible situations for graising farms upon a large scale, & the food is so inexhaustible that those that would venture upon such scheme, would soon be able to export large cargoes of beef and to secure annually handsome profits. And on another hand, what prospect for commerce does not exhibit to the view, a River which exclusive of its branches, is navigable for five hundred and fifty miles reaches on one hand the waters of the Lake, and on the other the Ohio below all the obstructions, which except in very high waters impedes its navigation?

Those prospects flattering as they are, I have little doubt will be realised, the attention of Government now directed towards a country hitherto insulated in the middle of foes, by whose curtesy alone it was permitted to exist will invigorate the exertions of the presents inhabitants and cause a sudden increase of population, of which last circumstances we can perceive now no equivocal symptoms.

The population of this town is composed of ancient french inhabitants and of Americans. The first is an ignorant, harmless & indolant race exhibiting to the eyes of an observer an uncouth combination of french and indian manners. Their attachment to their old habits is such that the idea of living in the woods that is to say on a farm excites in them as much abhorrence as if they were dropped here from the middle of Paris. Their former opulence having disappeared with the Indian trade by which they subsisted, they live cooped up in this village (the only place in America to which that name applies with the meaning it has in Europe) with a few exceptions, in a great state of poverty, hauling their firewood from a distance of three or four miles, raising a little corn in the neighbourhood of Vincennes & following boating for employment. Nothing illustrates better their want of forethought, than the precipitancy with which they have parted with their lands for a few trifles, hardly one in a hundred being found at this day in possession of the lands granted them by the United States.[1]

You find amongst the Americans more understanding & more enlarged views, but a want of activity, an *ennui* is discoverable in every face amongst them, which has begot a spirit of gambling, but too prevalent here. To the same cause may be attributed, an unceasing attention to domestic anecdotes, a turn for gossiping & detraction, which for a well disposed mind, renders conversation uninteresting or disgusting & by imposing a necessary restraint, effectually destroys the pleasures of sociability. You find yourself solitary in the largest

[1] This observation is confirmed by Badollet and Ewing's report as commissioners to settle land claims. According to it 415 claims based on British and French grants and court grants were confirmed. By far the majority of the original grantees were French. But by 1806, the date of their report, 313 of the 415 tracts had already been sold. Lux, *Vincennes Donation Lands,* p. 470.

company. To these general observations honourable exceptions can be mentioned.

The farmers being all american, are the same kind of people, whom we find in other new settled parts of the United [States], with this difference that the majority of them coming from the souther[n] States, do not exhibit such habits of activity, such enterprising dispositions as their more northern neighbours.

I'll conclude these observations by the following fact, namely, that the french though poor and ignorant beyond conception, still exhibit something mild in their manners, whereas the Americans when placed under the same circumstances of ignorance and poverty, shew more sense or perhaps cunning attended with a savageness of manners truly repelling. But those distinguishing features begin to wear apace, the french loosing by their intercourse with the Americans, whereas these gain little by their communications with them.

As to myself the prospect is flattering: In a country where land is cheap, where the soil is fertile, and the produce of the earth is high, there is no room for dispondency, & I cannot be uneasy with respect to my family's future support if even I did not enjoy this office, & had I not by my removal here broken assunder many interresting connections, happiness might yet be my lot.

From what I have said respecting this place, you will readily conclude I am very little tempted to reside in it, but if even I could be so destitute of taste, other considerations peremptorily forbid it. My sollicitude for the morals & wellfare of my children impose on me the duty of keeping them remote from scenes of dissipation and irregularity, from the slander common aliment of conversation here, indicative of want of thought and malignity of heart, and of raising them amidst the scenes of rural life, wherein solidity of understanding can be better attained, industry better taught, vanity or false pride better checked and innocence better preserved.

Views of economy render also my choice of a country life

a measure of the greatest propriety. The first necessaries are here dearer than with us & would run away with the best part of my salaries, by raising them myself in a greater quantity than my wants will require I shall soon be able out of my savings to secure land for my boys, object whitch I shall constantly keep in view. Moreover, in this town house rent is exhorbitant, in the country I'll pay none, here I must receive visits, necessitating additional expenses, I must even on my table pay homage to fashion, on a farm, I may live as simply as I please.

But unhappily, that plan rational as it is, meets in its execution difficulties peculiar to this place & my situation, and which notwithstanding all my endeavours have hitherto baffled all my views of a settlement in the country. This town is situated in the western edge of a large prairie, and the incredible devastations of the french amongst the timber have so far removed the edge of the woods from Vincennes, that there is no plantation in its immediate neighbourhood. On the North East side: at the South West corner of the Donation tract, wherefrom the distance to Vincennes is the smallest, begin the improvements. The first farms are at least three miles off from the town and not to be purchased. The next, still more remote, either are not for sale, or cannot be obtained but at an exhorbitant price. I have offered 6 dollars an acre for two hundred acres, whereon there are thirty four acres cleared and a cabbin & I cannot get it. The ease with which they can hawl to & sell wood at Vincennes from that place only fo[u]r miles distant account for that extraordinary price. On the other sides you meet either the continuation of the prairie, or the barrens mentioned above, or the Wabash, or that zone of country whereon the *vandalic industry* of the french have annihilated every stick of timber. Was I not obliged to come every day to town, by going a little farther off, I would experience no difficulty in finding an eligible spot to settle on.— There is a tract of 85 acres on the bank of the Wabash four miles above Vincennes, a most elegant situation, with some log houses on it, whereon 20 soldiers and a lieutenant are now meditating with full leisure on tactics, as usefull here as the fifth wheel to a waggon which I would delight to own.[2] Will not the United States sell it, and if so could any means be devised, by which I might come in possession of it? There is some dormant claim against that tract, which if revived would take it from the United States or the purchaser under them, but as such revival appears improbable, the real owner having never been heard of since the purchase and having in all probability left no heirs, I would freely run the chance, not doubting but that the United States would compensate me with a piece of land if dispossessed. In the meanwhile I would have a home and time to look about me.

This country is perhaps the healthiest of those which lyes on the waters of Ohio, & though not so unexceptionably so, as the western parts of Pennsylvania, yet it excites in me no uneasiness, some particular spots generate intermittents easily checked, when the rest is free from them. The Americans living upon their farms are generally healthy, the French owe perhaps to some peculiarity in their diet generally less wholesome & more scanty, or to the nature of their occupations, or to their living all in town their greater lyability to them. I have not been a moment sick since my last arrival, last year the fatigues of a journey by water rendered me sick for a few days, and gave to my poor boy Albert a continual inflammatory fever which was very nigh carrying him to an untimely grave.

---

[2] A reference to Fort Knox, located on the Wabash three miles above the town. Carter (ed.), *Territorial Papers*, VIII, 198. The lieutenant in command was Ambrose Whitlock. In 1809 Governor Harrison described the garrison as made up of fourteen or fifteen men, the greater part of whom were frequently absent with the commander who was also paymaster for the district. The fortress consisted of open barracks and blockhouses not connected by pickets or any other defences. Esarey (ed.), *Messages and Letters*, I, 341. The land on which the fort was built had been sold by T. Dubois to Jeremiah Buckley about 1776, and then on June 11, 1803, sold to the United States Government. In 1832 the land was returned to Buckley's heirs. U. S. *Statutes at Large*, VI, 520-21 (Private Laws); Knox County Deed Records, R: 48, transcript in files of Indiana Historical Bureau.

You will ask me wether I am happy. It would argue a want of gratitude in me, not to own that I have sufficient reason to be so, but candour obliges me to say that I am not yet arrived at that enviable state from causes peculiar to myself. When I arrived first at this place, which I knew to be a nest of federalists and suspected to contain some applicant for the office I was going to occupy,[3] I expected to be scrupulously examined, and with no benevolent dispositions, that reflexion, joined to difficulties which I had not dreamed of threw me in a state of real terror which disordered my understanding. I thought myself for a while down right stupid, & that judgement of me appeared to me written in legible characters on every countenance, it is needless to tell you, the prospect of exposing you to obloquy on my account intruded itself upon my mind with additional bitterness, and was I able to draw a true picture of the state of my mind, at that time it would be a picture of the most consummate distress, so truly exquisite, that I would with tears of gratitude have kissed the hand, which would have led me away from this spot. But I was fastened & had no means of escape left me, I would not let you perceive any simptoms of my feelings, but the few letters I wrote you at that time sufficiently evince by their incoherence and obscurity the mental distress to which I was a prey. At the arrival of Ewing on whose friends[h]ip & advices I could rely I felt suddenly relieved, & my courage & confidence in myself have been ever since gradually returning. Still a certain uneasiness hangs over my mind, which never can totally disappear till experience has fully proved that I am calculated for the office. That it suits, I cannot pretend to deny.— But enough of myself.

A poisonous reptile, called Darneille of St. Louis, has been this long time traducing the character of Governor Harrison before the public in anonymous publications, for reasons best known to himself.[4] Lately appeared sundry specific

[3] A reference to Benjamin Parke. See above, p. 46n.

[4] Here Badollet refers to a series of five letters written by Isaac Darneille attacking Governor Harrison and his political associates. They ap-

charges against him, the lucubrations of the same pen with an insidious list of respectable men as witnesses to corroborate the alledged facts. I have conversed with the greatest part of them, they are indignant at the audacity of the wretch, and every thing they can prove, will turn out to be clear of criminality, or truly laudable. Making every allowance for the sallies of a man who is still young, & the foibles inticident to human nature, I consider the Governor as a man of true honour, of an unimpeachable honesty, and an excellent officer.

I have been several times tempted to entertain you on the subject of a certain judicial character here, but on reflexion, it savouring too much of delation, I seal up my lips. I'll observe however, that the interest and dignity of the United States, and the happiness of the people of this territory, seem to demand that the attention of Government should be turned toward our judiciary organisation.

I must not forget to mention that a waggon road from Louisville to this place, is a measure of primary importance, with a view to the settlement of this Country, the sale of public lands & the intercourse with Louisiana. A mere bridle path, originally opened by General Clarke, leads from the falls to the seat of Government & deters numbers of people from moving into this territory.[5]

There are but few houses here fit to secure public records,

peared first in the press and were then printed in pamphlet form for the author in Louisville, dated December 10, 1805. The title page of the pamphlet reads: "Letters of Decius, To the Members of the Legislature of the Indiana Territory to B. Parke, Delegate to Congress for Indiana, and to William Henry Harrison, Governor; Together With Charges Against the Governor Addressed to the Honorable James Madison, Secretary of State, for the United States." The letters with additional documents and an introduction by John D. Barnhart are reprinted in *Indiana Magazine of History*, XLIII (1947), 263-96. The use of the name "Decius" harked back to the letters so signed which appeared in 1788-89 in the Richmond, Virginia, *Independent Chronicle*, attacking Patrick Henry for his opposition to the Constitution.

[5] This is the old "Buffalo Trace," also called the Vincennes Trace and Clark's Trace. George R. Wilson and Gayle Thornbrough, *The Buffalo Trace* (Indiana Historical Society *Publications*, XV, No. 2, Indianapolis, 1946).

and those that would answer the purpose, could not be rented for less than one hundred dollars a year. Will not the United States allow something for office hire?

The business of the Commissioners consumes the best part of our papers & sometimes there is not a sheet to be found here. Our allowance of stationary might I think be a little more liberal. Join to it, if you please some good pen knives, erasors, folders, pounce boxes &c.

My family is still in Greene, a circumstance which poisons the little share of happiness I am permitted to enjoy, they will be here however in the spring, by my last accounts of them they were well and in good spirits. I hope yours is well also.

From Mr. Parke, our member in Congress I have received many testimonies of kindness, any peculiar mark of attention you will be pleased to shew him, will be highly gratifying to me. Please to remember me to him.

As often as you can lay aside the officer with me, please to do it. I want of more encouragement than reproof & the style of friendship will ever infuse happiness into my breast.

Fareyou well, ever yours

JOHN BADOLLET

Mr. Ewing sends you his best compliments

Be so kind as to hand the enclosed to Gen'l Smith of the Senate.

P. S. I was going to forget to answer your query, relative to the division of this district. Two reasons forbid the line of demarcation from running in any other direction than from North to South, namely, its greater extent from the line of Ohio state to its western boundary, than from the Ohio river to its northern limits, and the certainty of the lands bordering upon that river selling & settling sooner than the back parts— The line I think ought to start from the neighbourhood of Jeffersonville & run thence Northward. Our district is now ascertained to be smaller than it was at first thought, the purchase from the Delaware Indians containing much less land than at first imagined.—[6] The locating of the College township is an object of immediate importance to this country, it is generally understood here, that such location ought to take in the salt lick on the east of White river.—[7] I would like very well to live on the river Ohio, but Ewing wants to settle here & I cannot bear the idea of leaving him— I will I suppose end my days here, provided the inhabitants, when arrived at the third grade of government do not admitt the odious system of slavery, on account of which they betray the greatest uneasiness, they have all brought from the Souther States their prejudices & fondness for that nefarious system, that measure would perhaps be attended with a few transitory & present advantages, but would entail on this country serious & permanent evils. The northern & middle states can only spare popu-

[6] See above, notes 3 and 4, letter of October 25, 1805.

[7] The act of March 26, 1804, for the disposal of the public lands in Indiana Territory, provided for the reservation of an entire township to be selected by the Secretary of the Treasury for the use of a seminary of learning. U. S. *Statutes at Large*, II, 279.

On May 2, Gallatin wrote Badollet that it would be necessary to locate the college township before the land sales commenced. Carter (ed.), *Territorial Papers*, VII, 354. He instructed Badollet to confer with Governor Harrison and Ewing and report to him. On October 10, Gallatin wrote Badollet designating township No. 2 south, range 11 west (in Gibson County) as the reserve college township in the Vincennes land district. *Ibid.*, VII, 394-95.

"An act to incorporate an University in the Indiana Territory" was passed by the territorial Assembly and approved November 29, 1806. Philbrick (ed.), *Laws of Indiana Territory, 1801-9* pp. 178-84. The trustees named in the act were William Henry Harrison, John Gibson, Thomas T. Davis, Henry Vanderburgh, Waller Taylor, Benjamin Parke, Peter Jones, James Johnson, John Badollet, John Rice Jones, George Wallace, William Bullitt, Elias McNamee, Henry Hurst, General Washington Johnston, Francis Vigo, Jacob Kuykendall, Samuel McKee, Nathaniel Ewing, George Leach, Luke Decker, Samuel Gwathmey, and John Johnson. Badollet served on the board of trustees until August 2, 1811, when he submitted his resignation. Harrison resigned on the same day. Little progress was made during these years. A grammar school was opened in 1811. A seminary building was started in 1808, but was not completed until 1820. Howard Burnett, "Early History of Vincennes University," in *Indiana Magazine of History,* XXIX (1933), 114-21; "Minutes and Proceedings of the Board of Trustees for Vincennes University," microfilm in Genealogy Division, Indiana State Library, from original manuscript in Vincennes University.

lation for settling new countries. Their influx in this country & their productive industry, would be effectually [checked?] by the adoption of that measure, & the rapid population and prosperity of the State of Ohio State, sufficiently evinces which of the two slavery or no slavery most effectually invite new settlers.

[Badollet to Gallatin]

VINCENNES Jan'y 15th 1806

You must have received a letter, wherein I communicated to you my ideas relative to the line of division between this district & the one which will probably be formed to the eastward of it, embracing the last purchase of Governor Harrison from the Miami Indians. I did not venture to mention my thoughts on that subject, without consulting Mr. Ewing who readily approved of them, & with his consent I wrote.

But we forgot to say any thing on the line which is to divide this same district, from that of Kaskaskias, and is not as yet accurately described. We both concurr in the opinion, that considering the great extent of that district up and down the Mississipi, it would be proper for the present time to have the two districts separated by a line running northward from an Island in the river ohio, called Hurricane Island.[1]

I am about concluding a bargain with the Governor for a piece of land unimproved, lying about five miles from this place, it will require all the money I'll make for some time to come, to make the same compleately my own.

You must know I have sold to Thomas Graham my town and outlots in Greene, for 1600 gallons of whisky which are

[1] Demarcation between the Kaskaskia and Vincennes land districts was not determined at this time. On December 21, 1807, Gallatin was writing Surveyor General Mansfield, "Before any alteration is proposed to Congress, it would be necessary to know what *should* be the line between . . . the district[s], & to designate that boundary by the number of some one range of the lands surveyed west of the Saline." Carter (ed.), *Territorial Papers,* VII, 507. See Mansfield's reply, *ibid.,* VII, 518. In 1812 the Shawneetown land district, which lay between the Vincennes and Kaskaskia districts, was established. U. S. *Statutes at Large,* II, 684.

to be paid in four annual instalments, 70 I have received & a fine breeding mare whom I have here. I sold if I recollect well sometimes in June last I entered into an agreement to make him a deed within a year & he is bound by this same to give me a mortgage on the premises on his receiving the deed of conveyance from me. Now in order to prevent any difficulties or impediments arising in the regularity of Graham's payment (upon which my family's support & the building of an house chiefly depends) I beseech you to direct Nicholson to make me a deed for the outlots ( I have already one for the town lots) & then our friend Thomas Clare who is my attorney in fact will convey the whole to Graham & receive a mortgage to secure the payment, conformably to the terms of our agreement.

I intend to discharge the debt I owe you by partial payments, as soon as I can, & to live, (the sooner to be able to do so,) with the strictest economy. I would like to keep my share of the land I own with you in Ohio State, but I had rather to part with it, on account of the interest of the $540 I owe you. Have you any chance to sell it?—The settlement is thickening in its immediate neighborhood, the land is good but flatt. I do not think A. Cross who had purchased a part of it from you, ever saw it, the description he made of it, does not apply.

The political horizon, I am concerned to see, is very threatening & may destroy for a time, the fairness of our present prospects, but we must meet our fate with a becoming fortitude, I hope we will not be wanting to ourselves.— The general Government ought to direct its attention amongst the various objects of vast importance, which must occupy its cares, to the red river. If a storms threatens New Orleans, it will gather on the head of that stream. The garrison at Nachitoches is too weak, a Fort ought to be built at the rapids of that river, but especially Gun boats be stationed opposite its mouth, every boat coming down it to the Mississipi being obliged to cross over to its eastern bank, to avoid being sucked into the Chafalaya. This circumstance renders that spot very important in a military point of view.— This territory has not a sufficiency of arms for its defence, should the Indians be aroused by the Spanish influence, we would be in a critical situation.— A body of militia cavalry would render essential services to scour a country so full of immense plains, and there is not a sword or a paire of pistol to be had.

Forgive my desultory and careless way of writing & continue to believe me Ever yours

JNO BADOLLET

My respects to Mrs. Gallatin
Remember me to Mr. Smiley & Mr. Parke
[Addressed:] Albert Gallatin Esq'r  Private

[Badollet to Gallatin]

VINCENNES July 5th 1806

I am happy in informing you that my family are at last safely landed, in full health, and very pleased with the country and my purchase. The plantation we now are settled on, is nearly paid for and the plough which is now briskly going on, will for the future supercede the necessity of purchasing the first necessaries.

By the inclosed advice, you will see that I have drawn for the 500 dollars, which you allowed me to draw. The long stay of my family at Greensburgh has been a cause of additional expense to me & a fertile source of anxiety. I find myself partly for their support, partly for purchases of implements of husbandry and other articles not to be dispensed with, including a boat of 50 dollars, in debt to Nicholson and Mestrezat to the amount of 322 dollars. The 125 dollars I lately drew upon you in favour of Nicholson, with a part of this days draught, will clear me with him, the remainder I request him to pay to Mestrezat. I shall this fall be perfectly clear, and then I shall begin to lessen my account with you.

I lost 50 dollars I had sent to my family in bank notes by the villainy of some post master not far from hence.

The 250 dollars drawn in favour of Mr. Bullit go in part

pay of my place, to defray the expenses of my costly journey and to stock my farm.

The boat costed 30 dollars, the hire of the hands & barge to take us up to this place, costs 50 more besides 12 days provisions for 12 persons, and 50 I lost will partly account for my leaving as yet no money in your hands.

I have 1200 gal. of whisky remaining yet with which I have no doubt of purchasing some land.

Rest assured that I am pursuing a plan of rational economy, that we will go into no expense, that a strict necessity will not warrant, and that on that score, and I trust on every other, you shall be satisfied with me.

Ever yours

JOHN BADOLLET

[Addressed:] Albert Gallatin Esq'r  Private

[Badollet to Gallatin]

VINCENNES July 15th 1806

The absence of Mr. Ewing is a serious inconveniency to me, to the public business, & no less detrimental to his reputation. I have written several times to him & I believe he contemplates coming here only in the falls. Be so obliging as to urge him to come, without letting him know that I have made the present request, and that I have said any thing about him.

The surveyor General urges me to have the recognized claims surveyed, it cannot be done before the reserved tract is laid out & locations made. On that score Mr. Ewing & I are not agreed. He wants to lay out only that part of the old purchase which lyes between Wabash & White rivers, the base line and Indian boundary, without considering that there is not a sufficiency of good land between those boundaries and that the donation tract itself, contiguous to which the newly granted donation are as he thinks to be laid out, crosses White river and takes in a part of the country within the forks, eastwards of the boundary he recommends.[1]

---

[1] On August 16, 1806, Gallatin wrote to Badollet and Ewing, " . . . unless your final & specific proposition for laying out the tracts intended

Does the clause of the law respecting priority of location mean as Ewing thinks, that after having ascertained all those who have right to locate I must draw lots to determine who shall locate first second third &c, which mode would involve numberless practical difficulties, or does it mean, as it is my opinion, this only, that when two or more persons present themselves together to locate the same spot, they shall draw lots to determine who shall locate first?[2]

I have another substantial reason for wishing Ewing's presence, the sale will take place this autumn,[3] we must have

to be reserved for unsatisfied claims, as well as your opinion respecting the location of a College township shall be received within a short period, it will be impracticable to give direction for the public sales this Autumn. . . .

"It appears to me that you propose to set aside for the purpose of satisfying former claims, a greater quantity of Land than is wanted for that purpose. But whatever may be the number or extent of the tracts which you may thus recommend to be reserved in addition to the vacant lands between the Wabash & White rivers, I beg . . . that those tracts should be bounded by the boundary lines of some town or township, or by the Indian boundary line." Carter (ed.), *Territorial Papers,* VII, 381.

[2] As to determining priority Gallatin wrote, ". . . the Register must give notice that on a certain day, the priority shall be ascertained by lot in his presence, inviting the Claimants to file their Claims (if not already done) prior to that day, and to be present if they chuse. The priority or right of selection or location, must on that day be fixed by lot, for all the claims filed, whether the claimants attend or not. Those whose claims shall not have been filed & the priority thus ascertained, will be entitled to select or locate in the order in which they may afterwards present themselves for that purpose at the Office." *Ibid.,* VII, 382.

[3] The sales were not held in the autumn. On October 11 Gallatin wrote to Badollet and Ewing, "I have the honor to enclose the Presidents proclamation, fixing the time of sales of the public lands at Vincennes on the last monday of April next,—No certain account of the completion & transmission of the surveys having been received 'till very lately, it was not possible to give notice of the sales for this Autumn. You will be pleased to cause this proclamation to be inserted once a month 'till May in the papers which may be published in the territory of Indiana, and also in one newspaper at each of the following places; viz't Cincinnati, Chilicothe, Louisville, Frankfort & Lexington.

"From the sales must be excepted the tracts set aside for satisfying private claims, the college township . . . the section No. 16, in each township, & all the sections including salt springs. . . ." Carter (ed.), *Territorial Papers,* VII, 395-96, 397-98.

There was no paper published in Indiana Territory during this time,

a practical knowledge of the manner of keeping our books, that will require previous exercise, and his assistance will be necessary to enable me to begin right. The idea of possible blunders terrifies me, and I have nobody here that I would wish or it would be proper to consult— A correspondence at this late period & at the distance of 550 miles cannot answer the public's or my purpose— Had he been here, the business of locations would be in a train. Therefore I repeat it for his sake, for the public's and mine he ought to be here. Pray write to him.—My family is well. I hope it is the same with yours.

Yours for ever

JOHN BADOLLET

[Addressed:] Albert Gallatin Esq'r  Private

[Badollet to Gallatin]

VINCENNES Jan'y 14th 1807

On examining the platts forwarded to me by the Surveyor General & the Laws relating to the sale of public Lands, I find myself under great embarrassments, from the want of rightly understanding how the fractional Sections are to be offered for sale. Whether formed by the Indian boundary, navigable streams within, or bounding, the District, the contents of the whole fractional sections are only inserted and not those of the quarters or portions of quarters which compose them: Some fractional Sections are so large as to fall very short of a whole section, & others so very small that the same rule cannot apply to both with equal propriety. It happens also that a smaller or greater portion of a contiguous section cut into two parts by some navigable water course, is adjacent to a fraction on the same side of such water course, its contents are set down therein & it is necessary to know how such portions may be

the *Western Sun* beginning July 4, 1807. See above, letter of June 6, 1804, note 4. The proclamation appeared in Cincinnati *Liberty Hall*, December 9, 1806.

According to the proclamation (in accord with the act of March 6, 1804) the sales were to last three weeks. Carter (ed.), *Territorial Papers*, VII, 397. By act of March 3, 1807, the time was extended to six weeks. U. S. *Statutes at Large*, II, 447.

offered for sale. I have read over and over the sections 9, 10, & 12 of the Act of March 26 1804 and I cannot from them form a correct conclusion in relation to the mode which must be adopted. The section 12 of the act alluded to, directs the sale of fractional sections to be made by quarter sections & the contents of each entire quarter & of the fractional quarter is never expressed, but only that of the whole fraction. The Receiver is not here, & the Governor who is also by law to be one of the superintendants of the sale, is as much at a loss & myself, and advised me to write immediately to you on the subject. I'll thank you therefore to send me a system of rules relative to that subject, as will embrace every case that may possibly occurr.[1]

The happiness which I anticipated in the possession of this office is not within my reach. I am beset by a thousand terrors & my mind fertile in breeding gloomy thoughts does not per-mitt me to enjoy a moment of comfort, my appetite is nearly gone, my nights are restless, and I could willingly, nay with delight reassume a private station, could I see a prospect of being able to provide for myself & family food and raiment. I almost doubt my competency to discharge the duties of an office, wherein so much correctness is required and with the details of which I am so little acquainted. I lye at your mercy, but whatever you may be pleased to do with me, do not mistake my despondence for a symptom of indifference or ingratitude. To the last hour of my life I'll breathe blessings on the friend who has done so much much to rescue me from a state of indigence & raise me to a station wherein I could obtain by my own labour a decent competence.

If you are determined to try me a little longer, do not withold from me every assistance & advice, which you may deem usefull to be imparted to me, & be persuaded that I always shall receive such marks of your kindness with a heartfelt gratitude.

---

[1] Gallatin's instructions concerning the sale of fractional sections are in his letter to Badollet of March 9, 1807, in Carter (ed.), *Territorial Papers,* VII, 436-37.

Could you not send me by the mail Rowlett's tables of interest? They being wanted in the office, must remove every kind of objection to that mode of Conveyance. I want them as a check upon my own calculations & because, are prefixed to the work, the true principles on which the interest is calculated in the banks & public offices of the United States.

Nothing new has reached this place relative to Mr. Burr. It is a bad symptom, that such desperate ambition should exist in the infancy of our national existence. Conspirators appeared at Rome, when only every spark of public virtue was extinguished. It is easy to see that we are no Romans. That disinterestedness which formed the characteristic of that wonderfull people, for so many ages, is not a fashionable qualification of our modern patriots, and our land speculators would not readily admit, that there were any *Gentlemen* amongst those Romans so proud of their ignoble poverty.

Notwithstanding the change of climate, we have enjoyed an uninterrupted state of health. I hope your family has been visited by no sicknes.

I remain as usual ever Yours

JOHN BADOLLET

[Addressed:] Albert Gallatin Esq'r  Private
[Endorsed:] Vincennes  14 Janu'y 1807  Badollet

[Badollet to Gallatin]

VINCENNES Jan. 29th 1807

How it happens that an office, so much wished for, calculated to place me in a state of independance & to put me in possession of happiness, has hitherto produced a state of uninterrupted mental pain, I know not, but it is really so.

When I first came here, I met with difficulties which I had by no means foreseen. In the middle of the confusion in which I found the land claims & the diversity of opinions entertained relative thereto, alone and unassisted, I could with difficulty form a correct idea of the nature of my duties, fear seized upon all my faculties and a permanent state of mental agony became my lot. At the arrival of Mr. Ewing, from his encouraging counsels & cheerfull conversation I received some relief. I started home in the Spring of 1805, in his company, to fetch my family down. The low state of the waters forced me away without them & at my arrival here, my former distresses recurred and again were alleviated by the arrival of Mr. Ewing in the fall. I forgot to tell you that during my absence some scurrilous publications had appeared against Ewing, but chiefly against me originating in the disappointment of some of the Candidates for the Clerkship  Those publications hurt me exceedingly and added poignancy to the pains I then suffered. We applied ourselves with unremitted zeal to the investigation and decision of the claims & we have gone through that tedious work, in a manner wherein perhaps more talents might have been displayed but our impartiality has been firm and our integrity has remained unshaken.

After having closed and forwarded our report,[1] we set off together Mr. Ewing for Fayette & I for Kentucky to meet my family at Limestone. After waiting there for them for five or six weeks, I at last had the pleasure, and a sweet pleasure it was, to meet them all safe and to convoy them here. I might have enjoyed some quiet, had not the act for the locations of unsurveyed claims,[2] made it my duty to receive those locations & the difficulty of carrying that law into execution renewed my unhappiness & my fears. I proceeded in that work however in the manner which I conceived the best, & it is yet to be known whether I have acted right or wrong. In that unhappy disposition of mind allarmed by the mere rustling of the leaves, I

[1] John Rice Jones, clerk to the commissioners, forwarded their reports in favor of the land claimants to the surveyor general on July 26, 1806. Their reports are in *American State Papers, Public Lands,* I, 288-89, 290-303, 558-81. See also Lux, *Vincennes Donation Lands,* pp. 469-70n. An act confirming land claims in the Vincennes District was approved March 3, 1807. U. S. *Statutes at Large,* II, 446-48. Gallatin enclosed a copy of the act in an official letter to Badollet of March 26, 1807, which included his instructions concerning the recording of patents to be issued on the confirmed claims. Carter (ed.), *Territorial Papers,* VII, 441.

[2] Act approved April 21, 1806. U. S. *Statutes at Large,* II, 395-96.

anticipate a thousand practical difficulties in the impending sales, the minutia of which I cannot know, the ideas of blunders embarrassment and disgrace, persecute me in my dreaming & waking hours— I need not tell you, How my soul recoils at the idea of committing the generous friend, to whose benevolence I owe my appointment.

The agency you have been pleased to give me in relation to the laying out and opening sundry roads within this Territory, has not a little contributed to encrease the disorder of my mind. Comformably to your request, I have engaged persons to lay out and survey the three roads mentioned in your letter, namely that from St. Louis to Vincennes, that from Vincennes to the Indian boundary towards Cincinnati & that from the last to the falls.[3] A Major Thomas Orme who was well recommended to

[3] By act approved April 21, 1806, six thousand dollars was appropriated for opening a road or roads "through the territory lately ceded by the Indians to the United States, from the river Mississippi to the Ohio, and to the former Indian boundary line which was established by the treaty of Greenville. . . ." *Ibid.,* II, 397. On May 14, 1806, Gallatin wrote to Badollet, describing five roads that might be opened: 1) a road from opposite or near St. Louis, passing by or near Vincennes to meet a road running from Dayton, Ohio; 2) a road to run from Kaskaskia toward Vincennes, intersecting the first road west of the Wabash; 3) a road, a fork of the first road, running from some point on it west of the Indian boundary line drawn by the Greenville Treaty toward North Bend, Ohio; 4) another fork of the first road beginning at or near Vincennes and running to the Falls of the Ohio; 5) a road from Kaskaskia to a point on the Ohio below the mouth of the Wabash so as to afford the easiest communication with Kentucky, particularly Lexington.

Badollet was to confer with Governor Harrison concerning local difficulties and obstacles that might arise, the relative utility of the routes proposed, and the exact course they should follow, as well as the best mode of opening them, and the cost per mile both of surveying and laying out. Carter (ed.), *Territorial Papers,* VII, 360.

Badollet apparently replied on July 17, but his letter has not been found. On August 14, Gallatin, with the advice of the President, wrote that the following two roads should have priority: 1) from St. Louis by Vincennes to the Indian boundary line; 2) from that road, preferably near the point where it crossed the east fork of White River, to the Ohio at Clarksville or Jeffersonville. (Badollet regarded these as three roads, dividing the one from St. Louis to Vincennes, and from Vincennes to the old Indian boundary.) Badollet was authorized to employ person or persons

me, has undertaken the last mentioned road, has finished his
survey, and I have given him a draught upon the Receiver of
Cincinnati for the amount of 315 Dol. at $3. per mile &
cancelled our agreement.— Since that, I have received two
letters from Kentucky, (one of them from Mr. Elijah Bacchus
of Kaskaskias at present in the federal City) informing me
that the road as laid out by Mr. Orme, will not answer the
expectations. Whether the information is correct I know not,
but certain it is that that piece of intelligence, has been to me
a shock, which has plunged me in a State bordering on real
distraction. I am very unhappy indeed.

In the first paroxism of my terror I had actually begun a
letter of resignation, but the dismall prospect opening before
my eyes has stopped my pen, and I justly dreaded to determine
such a momentous question in a moment of real delirium, when
it is possible that I see things through a false medium.

Yet, as you are too much concerned in the more or less
proper manner in which I may conduct myself here, I thought
it my duty to display before you, my present impressions, my
frailties, & my errors, without disguise, or attempting to paint
them in favourable colours, that you may be yourself a Judge
of the propriety of trusting me any farther. If it be your
opinion from this faithfull picture of my mind that I ought

to lay out these roads at a cost not to exceed $2.00 per mile and make
inquiries about contracting for opening them. After the surveys were made
he was to advertise for proposals for opening these roads, and if terms
could be concluded not exceeding the balance of appropriation after surveying, he was authorized to enter into contracts for the work. *Ibid.*, VII,
378-80.

President Jefferson, to whom Gallatin had referred the whole matter,
advised him on August 31, 1806, that he agreed with Badollet that the
roads should not be opened more than a rod wide. Henry Adams (ed.),
*The Writings of Albert Gallatin* (3 volumes. Philadelphia, 1879), I, 309.

On December 8, 1806, Gallatin authorized Badollet to allow $3.00 per
mile for surveying, laying out, and marking the roads. Carter (ed.),
*Territorial Papers,* VII, 403. Badollet inserted in the Vincennes *Western
Sun* of September 12, 1807, a notice that he would receive proposals for road
contracts on the roads above authorized, to be one rod wide and fit for
loaded wagons to travel.

to be superceded, take this for a resignation & let my dismission appear, as if prayed for by me, & not to be the necessary consequence of misconduct in me. A too great fear of acting wrong & too little confidence in my own opinion & abilities, have produced in me a mental misery, which ought to be the attendant of guilt only. I have seen during the course of my life persons both in private & public stations whose actions were not consonant with the strict rules of morality, enjoying an uninterrupted state of content, & with the best intentions, with, I trust, an upright heart, with a respect for the rights of others, which I never infringed. I am doomed to internal sufferings, & a stranger to that state of inward peace, the first foundation of happiness.

If from a persuasion that I fancy difficulties which do not really exist & that I have done right in the business of locations, you are induced to leave me in the possession of this office, would you consent to delegate the business of the roads to another person, more calculated than I think myself for the conducting it according to your wishes, & less embarrassed than I am, in the duties of an office, with the routine of which I am as yet unacquainted?

Whatever may be your sentiments arising from the present disclosure of my situation, do not I entreat you, assume the tone of censure with me, I want the soothing and comforting language of friendship & how great-soever may be your displeasure at what I have disclosed let sorrow & not anger be produced in your friendly breast. I need not assure you that I have endeavoured to do right & it is the conviction alone that those endeavours have been sincere, which can afford me some consolation & much of my future happiness or misery depends upon the disposition in which you'll read this communication.

I'll look with sollicitude for an answer to this letter, & whatever advice you'll give me, whatever step you'll be pleased to take, I know that you cannot but sympathize with my present distress & wish to alleviate it.— That you may live as happy as you deserve, is the sincere wish of Yours &c

JNO BADOLLET

P. S. The annexed letter[4] relative to the business of the office I wish you would be pleased to take into consideration.

A sad experience in this Country has shewed me that difficulties instead of rousing my faculties into energy, have confused my head and disordered my understanding. Hence my fears & constant allarms. Had I only gone on for a few months in the practice of the daily duties of the office with approbation, I would be restored to a proper tone, the certainty that I can do right would enable me to do still better & happiness would be my lot. But in my present disposition of mind, you must perceive the propriety in not imposing upon me too multiplied duties, & the reasonable apology I can make for wishing to be excused from any further interference in the business of roads if you find you can without inconvenience, relieve me from that burthen. If you cannot I'll submitt.

Forgive my ravings & continue to believe that I am not unworthy of your friendship. Again Fareyou well.

[Badollet to Gallatin]

VINCENNES June 27, 1807

The apprehension of practical difficulties in the discharge of my official duty, so remote as I am from every means of information, had filled my mind last winter with such allarm, that I would gladly have resigned this office. I had always flattered myself, that Ewing & I a few months before the sale, could devote our time to that business & conducting the business of our respective offices, by means of fictitious purchases, acquire the benefits of experience, & in case that during our progress we should meet with any embarassment, that we would have time to apply to you for information. But it happens otherwise, Mr. Ewing was forced to go for his family to Pennsylvania where he was detained by the inclemency of a long and hard winter & arrived here only the evening preceding

[4] Not found.

the first day of the sales.[1] Unprepared as I felt myself, my distress is not to be described, & we went to work on the following day under circumstances extremely unfavourable. The first fruit of our inexperience was to have sold on that day 19 tracts, by far more than we could manage. Under the pressure of business so little proportioned to the time I could devote to it, surrounded by a croud of purchasers, who without feelings or discretion would teaze me with their entreaties to be dispatched & by endless questions, the extreme fear of mistakes exposed me to the commission of many. That first weeck forms an epocha in my life which I shall ever remember.

The dawn of hope however begins to beam upon me, & my mind is now accessible to more agreable impressions, than it had been these two last years, & could I but be enabled to overcome some difficulties which occurr daily in practice (of which the annexed official letter mentions some), I begin to believe that I shall be able to conduct this office with approbation. A few years more will, if I am permitted to enjoy it that time, will put me in a sort of state of independance that is to say I shall be no more afraid of wanting necessaries. The only drawback on the happiness of which I begin to perceive the harbingers, is the retrospect of a life of thoughtlessness, spent to no purpose either for myself or my country.

You are entitled to an apology from me for not having sooner discharged the debt I owe you. The difficulties into which supineness & want of proper industry & not extravagance had thrown & from which my appointment to this office has nearly relieved me, & the great expenses I have been at to remove into this country & to which the first years of my residence here subject me to, & the purchase of two pieces of land I have made, have prevented me from paying that attention to the call of justice, which ought to have been expected from me. But I thought that if I knew your heart, you would not take exception to my conduct in that respect, & you would without displeasure suffer my debt to you to be the last that should

[1] The sales began April 27, and ran for six weeks.

be discharged by me, & that you would not be displeased at my having procured in first instance a home for my family & myself. Could the early discharge of witholding of that debt, have affected your circumstances in a manner ever so trifling, I would have silenced the suggestions of what any other less friendly judge might have decreed to be selfishness, & paid you before this time.

The devastation of the timber of the United States land round this place is a matter of serious consideration. This town being situated in a prairie, every inclosure in it, & the fences of vast fields in the prairie are, are made of timber growing on the public lands on the river above this place. The timber for buildings daily renewed, is procured in the same manner so that many tracts, & the number of them is daily encreasing, will not find any purchaser.

The evil is encreased from another cause. The french inhabitants of this place, having so long lived with the Indians, have contracted their manners, they did not & do not at this day conceive the importance of timber, they formerly did & now do cover their houses, stables, barns &c (for this is really an European village) with bark, which destroys more timber than can be well calculated. A few days ago about 80 trees were barked about 7 miles from this place. When they go for fire wood they cut a tree down, lop off the branches, load a cart with them, & the next trip is the death of another tree. If you stand on an eminence in the neighbourhood of this place, or in the commons, you perceive the trees strewed over & covering the ground, just as if a west indian hurricane had exerted its destructive fury on the land, & the whole appearing like a barren waste.

I had many things to talk to you about, but the mail is going to set off & I must conclude.

Ever yours

JOHN BADOLLET

P. S. I forgot to ask you in my letter of yesterday whether, two or more persons can enter lands jointly, the practice would be attended with many difficulties & would wish, it could be avoided.

[Addressed:] Albert Gallatin Esq. Private
[Endorsed:] Vincennes June 27, 1807 Badollet

[Badollet to Gallatin]

VINCENNES October 13 1807

If ever you gave any credit to my veracity, I pray you now to attend to the subject of this letter.

It is a true but melancholy fact, that a number of persons of profligate principles, or rather of no principles at all, have taken refuge in this extremity of the Union, and contribute to render their country and its institutions hateful to that class of men; whom conquest has subjected to our laws, & whose affections it was as much our interest, as our duty to conciliate. It is a subject on which a volume could be written.

In this place are also to be found persons of a similar description, men who incapable of an act of virtue or disinterestedness, ascribe all the actions of other men, however laudable, to the sordid motives of interest, can as little understand the meaning of the word integrity, as they are acquainted with the practice of it, laugh at contempt and hold character to be an empty name.

Amongst men of this description Stands conspicuous one Henry Hurst,[1] clerc of our General Court, by whom I wish to be understood every thing that is base and profligate. He with Judge Vanderburgh and Judge Sebastian of Kentucky[2] set on foot that speculation on the large grants of Vincennes Court, the mischief of which are commensurate with the Union. That our decisions upon those claims & that of the Judge, have excited their enmity appears very probable, that the sight of

[1] Hurst served as clerk of the General Court throughout the territorial period. A Virginian by birth, he came to Louisville where he studied law in the office of Benjamin Sebastian, then moved to Vincennes at the organization of the territory. He was allied politically with Governor Harrison. Sketch in Thornbrough and Riker (eds.), *Journals of the General Assembly of Indiana Territory*, p. 29n.

[2] Benjamin Sebastian.

plain honesty and of the respect which follows it, may be odious to them must also be allowed. There may exist other motives more base, I will not pretend to decide: But the fact is that we have in them & some others a set of irreconcileable enemies determined to persecute us and hunt us down. Mr. Hurst has become the mouth piece of the party in an open manner: he has ever since the sales spread the most atrocious calumnies against Ewing, who is by him more particularly marked for destruction.[3]

A Dr. McKee,[4] of whose understanding and heart something better ought to have been expected, has suffered himself to be made the tool of the same party, and in a dastardly & insidious manner has in the paper of this place given publicity to accusations involving in criminality the three superintendants of the sales.[5]

[3] Gallatin acknowledged that Ewing had discovered a forgery in one of Judge Vanderburgh's land claims which might have prompted the charge against Ewing. See Gallatin to the President in Carter (ed.), *Territorial Papers,* VII, 466. For documents pertaining to Vanderburgh's claim see *American State Papers,* I, 303, 576-81.

[4] Dr. Samuel McKee.

[5] The superintendents were Governor Harrison, the register (Badollet), and the receiver (Ewing). The first of the articles signed by "A Friend to the Commissioners" (McKee) appeared in the Vincennes *Western Sun* on August 8, 1807. Herein he says that as a friend to the commissioners or superintendents of the land sales and others high in public office in the territory he is reporting the rumors that were circulating that foul play had been practiced by them during the six weeks of public sales, that their conduct had produced serious injury to the United States, to the territory, and their own characters, and declared that in justice to all "they ought to satisfy the public mind, by a fair and candid statement of every fact within their knowledge, which may in any way bear on the subject. . . ."

The "Friend" was answered in the issue of August 15 by General Washington Johnston, who had served as crier of the sales. He suggests that the "Friend" is serving as cat's-paw to some other person and only regrets that he had not been able to get a "finger in the pie." Johnston added that the allusions and inuendoes were intended to include himself and the clerks and Governor Harrison, "than whom, no person in the territory possesses a fairer or more unsullied reputation. . . ." However, the editors of the paper stated in this issue that the "Friend" had authorized them to state that the Governor was not included among his "commissioners."

On August 22 the *Sun* carried a letter signed by Badollet and Ewing in

For some previous falsehoods spread by H. Hurst, Ewing
has brought suit against him, in consequence of which he has
had notwithstanding his efforts to avoid it, a scufle with him,
in which our friend has been stabbed in four or five places.
He owes his life to the smallness of the instrument, which
could not penetrate deep enough to reach any vital part.[6]

answer to the "Friend." Badollet sent a copy of this to Gallatin, enclosed
in his letter of November 13, 1809, and it is printed below, Appendix, pp.
347-49.

Finally, on September 12, McKee, signing his own name this time, produced his charges. They were that the superintendents had joined companies
for the purpose of speculation and had either directly or indirectly through
other persons dealt in "hush money." He then mentioned specific land in
which the speculating companies had been interested and the transactions
on them, and added, "Let the commissioners explain them and all the circumstances attending them satisfactorily, and they will be perfectly acquitted."

The charges mentioned by McKee were among those mentioned by
Hurst in his letter to Charles Brent cited below, note 7. McKee stated that
the United States had suffered loss in revenue derivable from its lands by
the maneuvering of the superintendents, and the territory and the settlers
also had suffered. "What . . . can one poor man do when opposed by
wealthy companies with commissioners at their head?" he asked.

Governor Harrison entered the scene with a letter "to the Public," in the
Sun of September 19. He began by saying that since McKee had declared
he, the Governor, was not an object of his attack, he had determined to remain a spectator. But McKee's comments continued to appear to implicate
him. He said that he had participated in formulating the law governing
land sales, that by it the register was precluded from purchasing public
lands, but that the receiver, surveyor general, and governor acting as
superintendents were not excluded. He stated he had purchased land and
had done so in partnership with others. But he denied that "poor actual
settlers" were injured by his transactions. ". . . who can deny," he asked,
"that if I possessed the right of purchasing at all, I had also the right to
take as many partners as I pleased, and those particularly who I discovered
to bid for a tract which I myself had selected . . . ?"

This letter was followed by a statement, signed by John Gibson,
Benjamin Chambers, Samuel Gwathmey, register at Jeffersonville, Shadrach
Bond, Jr., and Peter Jones, that McKee, when confronted by Harrison,
had acknowledged he had no proof of his charges.

[6] In his letter in the *Western Sun* of September 12, McKee remarked,
"Since Mr. Ewing has sued Mr. Hurst, those tales &c may be brought to
light through a different channel, and had I anticipated such an event, I
had never meddled with the subject." Ewing's slander suit against Hurst
was filed in the General Court in the November term, 1807. He demanded

It appears that the same Hurst has had the consummate effrontery to forward to Government his falsehoods & that an investigation of that business has been ordered.[7] Though

$10,000 in damages. General Washington Johnston represented Ewing. Among those summoned to appear as witnesses were the Governor, John D. Hay, John Griffin, Parmenas Beckes, John Rice Jones, John Gibson, and John Wallace. The case dragged on until 1809. On May 9, 1809, the jury, John Hatton foreman, found the defendant guilty and awarded Ewing one penny in damages. Papers in suit of Ewing v. Hurst, General Court of Indiana Territory, Archives Division, Indiana State Library; Order Book of the General Court of Indiana Territory, 1801-10, also in the Archives Division, pp. 329, 333, 334, 336, 338, 358, 359, 364-65.

For Badollet's later reference to this suit see below, pp. 139-40n, 161, and note.

[7] On June 5, 1807, Henry Hurst wrote to Charles Brent, a merchant of Winchester, Virginia, an account of his charges of "bribery corruption & fraud" against Ewing, asking him to lay his statement before Gen. John Smith, a representative of Virginia, requesting him "to take such steps as will put it out of the power of this Ewing's acting in this fraudulent way towards the United States again. . . ." The letter found its way to Gallatin, for it bears this endorsement in his hand, "Enclose a copy . . . in the letter to Harrison and Gibson." Carter (ed.), *Territorial Papers,* VII, 457-59. The reader may compare Hurst's account of Ewing's action with that given by Badollet.

Hurst's accusations involved not only Ewing but also Waller Taylor, one of the territorial judges. Hurst stated that had Ewing succeeded in his schemes involving three tracts at the mouth of the Wabash he would have cleared as much as $4,900. The charges were regarded as sufficiently serious to warrant an investigation. On July 31, Gallatin was seeking advice from President Jefferson about who in the territory he might ask to undertake it. He mentioned Governor Harrison; he described John Gibson, territorial secretary, as incompetent; he said Badollet was honest but too close to Ewing; Judge Taylor was linked in the accusations; Judge Henry Vanderburgh had been caught in forgery of a land claim and was probably one of the instigators of the charges; and finally Gallatin said that Jefferson knew the other judge, Thomas T. Davis.

On August 13, Gallatin sent a letter to Harrison and Gibson, enclosing a copy of Hurst's letter and ordering them to investigate the charges and report to his department. *Ibid.,* VII, 466, 467.

Harrison, because of his involvement in the land companies, declined serving as an investigator. The investigating committee was finally composed of John Gibson, George Wallace, and William Bullitt. They sent an account of the results of their investigation to Gallatin and signed a certificate that Ewing had not been found guilty of any improper conduct. See below, p. 87.

On April 27, 1808, Gallatin forwarded the results of the investigation to the President, observing that, according to it, both Ewing and Governor

satisfied in my own mind that Ewing was incapable of an act of willfull impropriety, I have attended the meetings of the Commissionners (The Governor as involved in the charges exhibited by Mr. McKee, has with propriety I think declined acting and named two other persons in his room) & from the testimony received the following facts have been beyond contradiction established viz That Ewing joined a company with a view to purchase a tract on Ohio deemed proper for the building of a town, that he agreed that the majority, in said purchase, should bind the rest, that the conflicting views of two other companies having made the land run above the price which it was thought to be worth, it was forfeited, that two hundred dollars were promised to the agent of one of the adverse companies provided he did not bid, reserving to him the priviledge, if any other person bade higher than four dollars, of running up the land as high as he pleased, that such an event did really take place, and the land struck to Mr. Ewings company at 8 dollars, that having been forfeited again as too high, it was set up a third time under the same agreement, that it was run to 7 dol. & 53 cents & finally struck to another member of the same company. That at the second and last time,

Harrison had been concerned in companies formed to purchase lands, that money had been offered to individuals in the name of those companies in order to induce them not to bid for certain tracts, "but that neither the Receiver or Governor were concerned in those offers, & that the Receiver who is the person specially charged expressed his disapprobation of such proceedings." He recommended that the superintendents of the sales be informed that such conduct was disapproved.

On April 30 Gallatin informed Ewing that the report had been laid before the President and added that "the charges do not appear to be supported by evidence. But the President has directed me to state, that it is deemed improper that any Officer, superintending the sales of public Lands, should be concerned in any companies or operations the tendency of which is, by lessening competition to prevent the highest prices being obtained for the lands." On the same day Gallatin wrote to the governors of the territories and to all receivers and registers, that while the formation of companies to purchase or speculate at the sales of public lands could not be prevented by law, the President found it necessary for the superintendents of the sales to discountenance such practices and that they themselves should refrain from participating in any such companies. *Ibid.*, VII, 562-64.

when Mr. Ewing was made acquainted with the compromise, he unequivocally declared his determination not to have any thing to do with it, that he would not be considered as a member of the company, if they agreed to take or receive any money, and that if they thought the land too dear at 7 dol. & 53 cents he would himself alone take it. The deposit was paid, but since forfeited on the land being found not to possess those advantages, which it had been supposed to enjoy.

Respecting another charge made against Ewing, that he received five hundred dollars not to bid for a fraction at the mouth of the Wabash from one Thomas Jones, the inclosed affidavit will remove every doubt, other testimony will also corroborate the statement therein contained. The mouth of this river forms a place of deposit for commodities destined for this place. This Thomas Jones had built there a kind of shed dignified by the name of a whare house, & kept as agents there persons in whom nobody could place any confidence. Those circumstances induced two or three respectable merchants of Vincennes together with Ewing to purchase that spot, with a view not to speculate, but by building a sound wharehouse thereon & keeping a man of integrity to manage it, to remove the evils of which every body complained. Jones allarmed at the prospect of either loosing the tract or paying too dear for it, would actually have sacrificed a handsome sum to silence that company, employed agents to make proposals and actually induced one of Ewing's partners to desist, the other ones ware absent  Mr. Ewing seeing himself left alone and teazed by the importunities of Jones, determined to abandon the project on Jones promising to build a stone whare house and to keep a good man in it, but spurned the idea of receiving any money.

Upon the whole, during the whole of my stay here with Mr. Ewing, I have ever found him the man of integrity, of steady adherence to its dictates & of unblemished honour, & I pledge my veracity that the result of the investigation now going on, will be conformable with the opinion I here express. It is a duty I owe to an honest man shamefully persecuted, by anticipating the opinion of the Gentlemen to whom that enquiry has been committed to remove from your mind, or at least to suspend any unfavourable impression respecting my much injured friend.

Was I addressing any other person than the friend of my tender years, to whom the bottom of my heart is fully known, I certainly would not traduced as I am myself, have attempted the cause of another. But I am much mistaken, if Gallatin's mind can harbour a suspicion of his old friend. Three years have lived in this place a life of wretchedness, from an apprehension of involuntary errors, could I have become suddenly bold in iniquity?

It is cruel to see the fruits of a life of integrity snatched away from us, it is more than human patience can bear— I have sued the Dr. to force him to a disclosure or to an acknowledgement of his wrong:— will a verdict heal up the wound he has inflicted on an innocent man?—[8] I am in a state of distraction— Will the President take no notice of Dr. McKees allegations, will he not order a solemn investigation: have I not a right to expect it?

Ewing and I have lived on a footing of intimacy with this Mr. Hurst in his own house, and we had full time and opportunity to become acquainted with the profligacy of his principles, & the deformity of his heart, we know him well and of what excesses of villainy he is capable.— Unable to face the light of day & to prove one single act of impropriety in Ewing during the course of the investigation, he is now busy in the dark in collecting scraps of certificates containing mutilated statements, with which he will have the impudence to insult you.

Excuse the tone and style of this letter. I feel more agitated than I expected I should be, the sight of injustice, whoever was its victim, has always excited indignation in my breast, what must be my situation, when my friend & myself are exposed to its attacks.

[8] For reference to this suit and its outcome, see below, pp. 88, 89, 141-42.

The Inclosed paper signed by the Commissionners, will shew what are their present impressions on this business.

I remain as usual ever Yours &c

JNO BADOLLET

[Endorsed:]  Vincennes  October 7  [13], 1807  J. Badollet

[Enclosures]

We the undersigned who have been appointed to investigate certain charges exhibited against Nath'l Ewing, Receiver of Publick monies for the District of Vincennes by Henry Hurst, do certify that after having called upon the said Hurst to support the said charges, and attending three days to hear and investigate the same, we do not find (from any thing that has yet come to our knowledge) that the said Nath'l Ewing has been guilty of any improper conduct.— This Certificate is given to prevent any mistatement that may be made from partial depositions of which the said Hurst has obtained a certified copy, should he attempt to use them for that purpose. Vincennes 13th October 1807—

JNO GIBSON
GEO WALLACE JR.
WM BULLITT

---

INDIANA TERRITORY ss

Before me the subscriber a justice of the peace in and over the said Territory, personally appeared Thomas Jones Merchant of Vincennes in Knox County in said Territory who being duly sworn deposeth and saith, that at the sale of the Tract of Land at the mouth of Wabash river, and which the Deponent purchased of the Superintendants of the United States at the public sales, has neither at that time or before or since ever gave or offered to Nathaniel Ewing Esqr. the Receiver of the Land office, any sum or sums of money or any other consideration whatsoever, and he further deposeth and saith, the said Nathaniel Ewing never asked him the said Jones to give him any money or any compensation whatsoever in order to prevent him from bidding for the said Tract of Land at the mouth of the Wabash river— And the Deponent further saith that the said Nathaniel Ewing never offered any sum or sums of money to him the Deponent in order to prevent his bidding for or purchasing the said Tract of Land.— Sworn before me this 26th day September 1807 in testimony whereof I have hereunto set my hand and seal.

Signed JOHN GIBSON  SS.

Signed THOS. JONES

I do hereby certify that the above is a true copy from the original.

JOHN BADOLLET

[Badollet to Gallatin]

VINCENNES Dec'r 21, 1807

You will perhaps be surprised, that I brought suit against Dr. McKee on account of his calumnies,[1] but your astonishment will cease when you come to understand my views. It was not, as in too many cases, with an intention of mending a ragged character by the decision of a jury. Mine is, even here, above any verdict. The trial was my object. I wanted to force a disclosure of my official conduct, I wanted a mass of light to be thrown upon every one of my steps & by reducing my dastardly enemy to a disgracefull silence, to obtain a satisfaction commensurate with the evil. I wanted to prevent the inferences which would be drawn *abroad* from my tamely submitting to so odious an attack; I say *abroad* for had the evil been confined here I would have remained quiet, for I will venture to say, that there does not exist a man in this county *not even the Dr. himself* who has ever entertained an idea derogatory to my character. But I think that a public officer, like a maid, ought not only to be virtuous, but ought not to be suspected.

In the only answer that Ewing & I made to the Dr. drawn in severe but decent language, we challenged him to come boldly forward with specific charges, intending to rest there, and

---

[1] See above, p. 86, and below, pp. 141-42.

observed, with respect to the tone of our answer, *that an intemperate language looked more like the writhings of a guilty conscience, than the accents of innocence.*[2] In a reply to the said piece the Dr. repeated his vague & insidious insinuations et quoting the sentence which I have underlined, observed that we had betrayed too much intemperance, whence the inference is obvious, that we felt the stings of conscience. This outrageous agravation overcame my former resolutions & I instituted a Suit  Ewing having a chance of seeing his character vindicated by the investigation ordered by the President, declined or perhaps disdained seeking the same remedy. That investigation as far as it has gone, has made known circumstances redounding greatly to his honour cleared him perfectly of the imputations alleged against him & rendered his calumniator forever an object of abhorrence. The reports of the Commissioners will soon reach you, the absence of some persons whom H. Hurst asserted to be material witnesses, having induced them to suspend the decision that Ewing might not suffer, by the complaints which Hurst would certainly utter, that he had been dealt with unfairly. You may rely upon my word, enough has come out, to place both Ewing's integrity & the baseness of his accuser in a most conspicuous light.

As to myself my dear old friend, my greatest earthly comfort has been & is still a conscience at peace with itself, could the *trash* of a few hundred dollars be a motive powerfull enough to make me forego that enviable tranquillity? Past follies, I sufficiently lament, they were the offsprings of a head strangely constituted, & which must have often appeared to you a kind of moral anomaly, but whenever honour was concerned, whenever right & wrong were presented to my choice, my heart never misguided me. I cannot call that virtue, for I never was tempted.— But why do I go on in that strain? I know you do not suspect me. If this business has given you a single instant's uneasiness, I am unfortunate indeed.

An event has taken place in this place, to which too much

[2] See below, Appendix, pp. 347-49.

importance is attached at a distance. I mean the election of David Floyd as clerk of our honourable house of representatives. It is owing entirely to private attachment (he having been heretofore a member of that body) and family connexions. It is by no means an indication of the dispositions of the people's temper in this quarter, than which no district of the Union is more loyal, but only an egregious instance of wisdom foresight & I may say decency in our representatives. I am one of those who conscienciously believe that David Floyd was deceived by that Arch-cunning traitor A. B. into the persuasion that his project met with the approbation & countenance of Government, but when I first heard of the intended election, I immediately perceived the impropriety of the step, & foresaw the wrong inferences which at a distance would, no doubt, be drawn from it & I expressed myself in company to that purpose. The animadversions of the Richmond examiner on that transaction, which I have read lately, though justified by the appearances are I do assure you intirely unmerited by this Territory, as well as by the house of representatives who can only be charged with a momentary folly.[3]

[3] The Richmond, Virginia, *Examiner* had ceased publication in 1804. A check kindly made by the Virginia State Library of the *Richmond Enquirer*, July-December, 1807, failed to locate the article referred to by Badollet.

Davis Floyd had served as representative in the first territorial assembly and held other public offices. He was involved in the Burr Conspiracy, though there is no evidence that he ever suspected Burr's intention of being anything but strictly loyal. His participation centered around the projected Washita colony. Nevertheless, a warrant was issued for his arrest, along with Burr and two of their colleagues, by the circuit court of Washington County, Mississippi Territory. Floyd escaped to Indiana Territory where he was indicted on June 2, 1807, for aiding in setting on foot a military expedition against the King of Spain with whom the United States was then at peace. He was found guilty before a federal court of Judges Waller Taylor and Thomas T. Davis, on June 12, fined $10.00 and sentenced to three hours in jail. He was convicted entirely on his own evidence. He contended that he had been convinced the expedition had the approval of the government. Three days after his conviction he was elected clerk of the House of Representatives. Thornbrough and Riker (eds.), *Journals of the General Assembly of Indiana Territory*, pp. 125, 974-75.

The severe censure of Judges Davis & Taylor are not better merited. If I am well informed the *quo animo* which only constitutes criminality, was not made out at the trial, & Floyd appeared, more like a deluded man, than a guilty one, & I have been told that the impressions of both Jury & Attorney General[4] were so strong in favour of the innocence of his views, that both interested themselves with the Court to obtain a mild sentence. The Court being under the same impressions readily granted the request.

The Legislature of the Territory have been every year pestering Congress with petitions for the admission of slavery into it. Apprehending little danger, the opponents of that scheme have hitherto remained, but will not always remain silent. They place too much reliance upon the enlightened views of the national Legislature, they firmly believe, that the spirit of justice, philanthropy & sound policy which animates them,

There is no evidence of immediate local reaction to his election in print. In the *Western Sun* of October 3 and November 17 there are letters from General Washington Johnston and Luke Decker defending his election, but in the issues of November 25 and December 16, 1807, and March 23, 1808, there are letters signed Broken Blunderbus weighing the meaning of his election, and also in the last issue a resolution from the citizens of Randolph County denouncing it.

On January 4, 1808, a meeting of the citizens of Knox County was held to take "into consideration the appointment of Davis Floyd Clerk of the House of Representatives, and to remove the Odium which has been cast upon the people of the Territory in consequence of that Appointment." Abel Westfall was chairman and Henry Hurst secretary. The resolutions adopted by the meeting declined making any criticism of the judges for the light sentence imposed on Floyd, but were strong in denouncing the Assembly for his election. Copies of the proceedings were sent to the President of the United States and various newspapers. They are in Carter (ed.), *Territorial Papers,* VII, 511-14, and the Vincennes *Western Sun,* January 6, 1808.

Late in 1807 Floyd identified himself with the antislavery faction in the territory (see note 5 below) which may have turned the Harrison faction against him. In a letter to President Jefferson on July 16, 1808, Harrison intimates that he has come to believe Floyd may not have been as innocent as first thought. Esarey (ed.), *Messages and Letters,* I, 297-98; Thornbrough and Riker (eds.), *Journals of the General Assembly of Indiana Territory,* p. 975.

[4] Benjamin Parke.

will not permitt them to introduce into this part of the union such a nefarious system, against which the faith & honour of Congress stand solemnly pledged, and they rather indulge the hope that the efforts of all good men, will be united in endeavours, to remove by every practicable means that national disgrace.

In order to enable you, fully to estimate the degree of weight which those petitions ought to have with Congress, I'll mention a few circumstances which cannot be known at the seat of Government.

The subordinate situation of this district under a Territorial Government had prevented the birth of that spirit of curiosity for public affairs, and of the interest taken therein, which distinguish the states accustomed to self Government. That circumstance, added to the remoteness & unconnectedness of some districts prevented a general attendance at the elections since we have reached the second grade of Government. The ordinance of Congress, by investing the right of suffrage in freeholders only, excludes from any share in public business, a considerable portion of industrious & by no means despicable citizens, who having moved into the Territory, with a view of permanent residence have previous to the opening of the Land office, been not in a situation to purchase land at a price suitable to their situation. From those considerations, is it rash to conclude, that the present Legislature is not as fair a representation of the population of the Territory, as will induce a reasonable belief that they are the real organs of the wishes of the people?

Since the sales, a considerable accession of inhabitants, is taking place, whose voice has not been as yet heard on a subject of so much importance.

But I can add something more pointed than mere conjectures. From my residence in this country & the opportunities, which my office of Commissioner gave me of conversing with & knowing the sentiments of the inhabitants, aided by the informations derived from respectable sources, I am warranted in asserting, that the majority of this county deprecate the measure. Besides, my office of Register has put me in possession of a fact of which few here have any knowledge, namely that almost all the emigrants from the Southern states to a man, who have purchased or do purchase land in this office are flying from the evils of slavery, to this only part of the United States, the climate of which will permitt them to cultivate the products, to the raising of which they are accustomed, without meeting the evils they so much wish to avoid. I am informed by them that a considerable population from both North & South Carolina, of whom wealthy Quakers form a great proportion, are preparing to remove here (some have already arrived), that, could the apprehensions created by the petitions above alluded to, be quieted & the belief be solidly impressed, that Congress will not yield to those clamours, but perform their solemn promise of not permitting the introduction of slavery in this Territory, then the emigration from the aforesaid States would be very great and as it were unceasing. The emigration from the neighboring State of Kentucky is chiefly composed either of men who detest slavery from principles, or of such, as being in modest circumstances, & owing their bread to their *own* labour cannot well brook the haughty manners of their opulent neighbours the slave-holders. The members of our Legislature & their co-adjutors, whatever may be the source of their actions, prejudice or interest, have argued from wrong premises, namely that crouds of slave holders would flock here, raise the price of land and rapidly increase our population. (What sort of population, of poor black slaves, stopping the ingress of free & industrious men) What I have stated above sufficiently demonstrates the fallacy of those reasonings. I'll add but one more observation the former unanimity of the Legislature exists no more, two members of the lower house,[5] in compliance

[5] These would be Jesse B. Thomas of Dearborn County and James Beggs of Clark County. The memorial to Congress passed by the Assembly on September 19, 1807, for suspension of the sixth article of the Ordinance of 1787 forbidding the admission of slaves into the Northwest Territory,

with instructions from the Counties of Dearborn & Clarke, have seceded & opposed the measure.

This epistle contrary to my custom and inclination is pretty long winded. Permitt me to add a few words respecting my little private affairs. After having bought the place whereon I live, for which a balance of about $200 dollars remain yet to be paid yet, as soon as I saw myself in possession of something I could spare, I hastened to purchase another piece of land of 400 acres at 2 dol. for which I made a first payment of 300, trusting to the future for the remainder. Perhaps I was a little precipitate, but I thought I could not too soon *fix*, by transforming it into *real* the *volatile* personal property I had then on hand. The allarms at the prospect of an english & perhaps indian war, have, as you well see by our returns, caused a Stagnation in the sales of lands & by diminishing my profits, subjected me to temporary but somewhat serious difficulties.

This town is a perfect european village, composed of unsightly wooden buildings, stables & barns are to be found on every lot. The high price of house rents, commonly a symptom of prosperity is here a sign of wretchedness. For a small uncomfortable room hired for my office I had to pay 36 doll. a year, with the prospect of either being without fire, or of being at an additional expense of 50 dol. for a stove. In September last, an acquaintance of mine, who had purchased a tavern, offered me his house and lot for 350 dol. to be paid on the first of October 1808. The lot is excellent in a central situation, has on it a tolerable good house a well and barn. The property is cheap, could be rented at at least 60 or 70 dol. & will remain an object of increasing value. Views of future profits, or present economy did not permitt me to hesitate, another person being ready to close the bargain at my refusal,

so aroused the antislavery sentiment in Clark County that a meeting was called on October 10 which adopted a memorial to Congress praying that no action be taken relative to slavery until the territory attained statehood. Davis Floyd was secretary of the meeting. Dunn, *Slavery Petitions and Papers,* pp. 518-20.

I had but a moment given me for deliberation & I concluded.

Shall I now tell you, in that moment on whose assistance I relied, in case of need. It was on yours. Those 666 acres which I have in Ohio State, subject to a lien of 540 dol. I thought you perhaps would be agreed to take & to release me of the debt, to give me on the first of October next those 350 dol. as the balance of the value of the tract, or if you think it is worth more, to give me that surplus when it suits you. (It would be applied by me to compleating one of the instalments due for my land) But the 350 dol will satisfy me. Should that proposal not suit you, permitt me to hope, that in case I should next fall stand in want of that sum I may rely upon it as a loan. It may happen that I shall not want it, but, if the sales of land proceed next year as slowly, as they now do, it is probable that I shall.

I have now earnestly to request you to drop me a word of answer on that subject. If you are agreed on either of those terms I shall draw upon you in September next, in case I should want it for that sum, if you are not, I ought to know it soon that I may sell the property again. This is an expense justified by prudence and foresight, wherein neither extravagance nor thoughtlessness are chargeable on me.

Graham having sold the Lots & Outlots he purchased of me wrote to me lately for his deed. The lots you have made me a deed of transfer for, there remain the outlots to be transferred please to direct Nicholson as your attorney in fact, to execute the same to me & Thos. Clare will then transfer in my name the whole to Graham. This I am bound to have done.

In the agitation of my mind, I am afraid I neglected to affix the word *Private* to my last letter. I shall never again be so thoughtless.

I forgot to mention to you, when on the subject of Floyd that some of his friends in Kentucky, under signature of *Broken Blunderbuss*[6] (a term pretty appropriate) has attempted to vindicate the conduct of our Legislature, to effect

[6] See note 3 above.

which, he has gone into a long winded irony of several pages, proceeding as smoothly on as a Conestoga Waggon on the rocks of the Allegahany. A serious reproach can be made to the author of that awkward piece: that he endeavours (to be sure in vain) to excite laughter at what ought to create abhorrence, the conspiracy of B. If that piece is ever read below, its tendency will be to encrease the stream of prejudices against this poor Territory.

Fare you well; we have been in my family long & dangerously sick remember me to our two worthies Wm. Finley & Jno Smiley & keep your health and spirits. Ever Yours &c

JOHN BADOLLET

[Endorsed:]  Vincennes 31[21] Decemb. 1807 Badollet

[Badollet to Gallatin]

VINCENNES  January 23. 1808

I have troubled you with the inclosed official letter on account of the diversity of opinions entertained here respecting the subject therein alluded to, & the uneasiness I have felt on that account.[1] Except Ewing I do not choose to consult any body. Very few exist here on whose Judgement or candour I would like to rely, and I am so tremblingly alive at the fear of doing wrong, that the idea of sinister views forces itself upon my mind whenever any person volunteers his opinion to me. And I ought not to be very much blamed for this suspicious prospensity, which you know was not born with me, for of all the little towns of the United States, I do not believe there is another one, which contains so much selfishness, such disregard of principles, & where judgement is more warped by interest. The observation does not apply to all, for there exist even here some noble souls, but in general to meet with plain

---

[1] Badollet's official letter of this date has not been found. Gallatin replied to it on March 4: "The Registers certificate under the Act of 3rd March, 1807, may issue in favor of those persons designated by the Commissioners as *present claimants,* unless Governors *patents* have actually issued, in which case the chain of title should be perfect." Carter (ed.), *Territorial Papers,* VII, 530.

homespun honesty, you must descend into the valeys & leave the eminences.

I have often admired the ingenuity or Stupidity, as you will choose to call it, with which our first Legislature (with many lawyers too) have trampled on the Ordinance of Congress, in that part of it which relates to Slavery. They have passed an Act[2] permitting owners of negroes emigrating into this Territory to bring them hither and to keep them for a number of days, during which time the poor slave is at *liberty* forsooth to bind himself for a term of years (the favourite term is 99 years) or to be remanded to the state he was brought from & there to be sold. True if the Slave accept of the proferred boon, by signing the indenture (a slave signing a contract!) the master gives bond with security, conditioned for the slave never becoming a charge on the County. A sardonic grin invades my face at writing this. Could humanity, the principles of wise policy which shine in that part of the ordinance, and common-sense be insulted in a more outrageous manner? The executive gave his sanction to the laudable Act! ! ! ! So much for the first exploit performed under the second grade of Government. So much for the Solons, who give us laws.

I beseech ye to bestow a moments attention on the subject of my official letter, I want to have done with every thing that interferes with the business of the Land office, which I begin to understand tolerably well. I have another reason, a few hundred dollars of fees are depending on that business, which it would suit me exceedingly to receive. For till I have paid up my two tracts of land and a balance coming to Mestrezat partly for money paid to my father, I must & do live with a parsimonious economy, & cannot think of the comforts of a warm house. I dwell still under an old clapboard roof. This place is very dear and the support of a family is no trifle.

I wish also you would let me know your determination respecting my last proposal of selling you my share of the Ohio

[2] Philbrick (ed.), *Laws of Indiana Territory, 1801-9,* pp. 523 ff.

lands. If it could be sold to somebody for two dollars I would be afloat, but as that somebody cannot be sought after, neither by you nor me, it would be a desirable thing under my present circumstances, to be sure of as much money, as you'll deem advisable to allow me, after retaining what I owe you. A propos of my Expenses you must know that when Ewing left home with his family, he engaged a clerk for me for a year, a very estimable young man, well educated, whose salary, in the present stagnation of the sales, take besides my commission of ten per cent, a portion of my stated salary. It would be practicable to do now without him, but he came to this distance trusting to my honour.[3]

I expect that, in about two years, when my mind is completely at ease, to pay you a visit. I can then explain you many misteries of this place, which I have [neither] inclination nor patience to put in a letter nor you leasure to read.

You'll render me an essential service, by directing Nicholson to make a conveyance of my out lots at Greensburgh to me, that Mr. Clare may transfer the same together with the town lots to Thomas Graham, who has himself sold, to whom I am bound to make a deed, & who upon failure on my part might be tempted to withold this spring installment & subject me to very serious inconveniences.

I have received a letter from our friend Mussard,[4] who informed me he spent a week with you. I had the pleasure to be informed by him that you entertained no uneasiness on the score of my official conduct. Was I not from habit & principle averse to every obliquity of conduct I have too much at Stake ever to be tempted to deviate from the path of rectitude, you, Mr. Finley & Smiley,[5] to whose kindness I owe my appoint-

---

[3] The young man was Jonathan Jennings. He was soon to leave Vincennes and establish his residence in Clark County. Dorothy Riker, *Unedited Letters of Jonathan Jennings* (Indiana Historical Society *Publications,* X, No. 4, Indianapolis, 1932), pp. 165-67.

[4] A. Mussard, who operated the glassworks and gun factory at New Geneva for Gallatin. Walters, *Albert Gallatin,* p. 139.

[5] See above, pp. 25-26n.

ment, impose upon me such sacred obligations, that I would consider myself as the most abandonned wretch, if I ever was tempted to violate them, and the only suitable return I can make for such unexpected favours, is to shew myself not unworthy of them. Such you will always find me, my only ambition is to be approved by my conscience & by my friend. My head can mistake, but never intentionally, and the motives of my action will always be honourable and pure. It is a matter of great comfort to me that you have not deemed those declarations of mine necessary.— You must have by this time the result of the enquiry respecting Ewing. I know not what the Gentlemen have said, but know well what they ought to have said, & I trust that by this time you have the pleasure of being confirmed in your good opinion of him.

Adieu Ever yours

JNO BADOLLET

[Addressed:] Albert Gallatin Esqr   *Private*

[Gallatin to Badollet]

WASHINGTON 4th Feb'y 1808

I have just received your letter of 21 Dec'r last.[1] In the extreme hurry of public business, I cannot answer at large at this moment, but I lose no time in letting you know that you may draw on me at any time for the three hundred and fifty dollars. As I might be absent when your bill comes, you had better draw in favour of Ewing on me. Let him pay you the money for it, & endorsing the bill to the Treasurer of the United States remit it with one of his monthly returns, charging the amount to the United States as so much money paid into the Treasury. I will then pay the bill to the Treasurer. The bill should be drawn on Albert Gallatin at Washington, omitting the words *Sec'y of the Treasury*. Write me a private letter of advice at the same time.

My wife had a daughter in September who is very weakly.[2]

[1] See above.
[2] This daughter did not survive.

With that exception we are all well. Remember me affectionately to your wife.

Yours

ALBERT GALLATIN

[Addressed:] John Badollet Esq're   Vincennes

[Badollet to Gallatin]

VINCENNES   March 31   1808

I inform you that agreably to your permission I have to
day drawn upon you in favour of Nathaniel Ewing for 350
dollars.

In the present posture of public affairs, it does not seem
probable, that you can leave the seat of Government & pay a
visit to Fayette, but should such be your intention, please to
inform me of the time at which you would be there, an interview of a few days with you, would at present be exceedingly
agreable to me and desirable on more than one account.

I have not time to write any thing more, than as usual I
remain ever yours &c

JOHN BADOLLET

I have had much sickness amongst my children; they are
all recovered except my two daughters, who linger yet.

[Addressed:] Albert Gallatin Esqr.   (Private)

[Endorsed:] Vincennes   March 31   1808   Badollet

[Badollet to Gallatin]

VINCENNES   August 8   1808

I have last fall contracted for the opening of the roads I
was directed to have opened through this Territory,[1] with
Benjamin Chambers formerly of Franklin Co. Penn'a as
you shall be more fully informed when I render you an Official
account of my proceedings in that business. I stipulated in the
contract that, before the roads could be received, they should
be examined by two persons appointed by me. Advances have
been from time to time made to him, as the work was progressing with a liberality for which his character standing & wealth

[1] See above, pp. 74-75n.

will furnish a ready apology.[2] Notwithstanding that Mr. Chambers has been more & more troublesome in his applications for money, & upon my resisting his persecutions and declaring my determination to retain conformably to your directions, a sum sufficient to secure the fullfillment of the contract, he has abandonned himself to my face to all the intemperance of anger, has insulted me, threatened me & made upon my character in the circles of Vincennes the most illiberal, the most malignant observations, he is gone now away meditating schemes of vengeance & I have no doubt will do his best to execute them. I have attempted to do my duty, I care little for the consequences. I see daily opened and masked knavery, commanding the good things of this world, and the consideration of the croud, I see self, sordid, interest, the only motive to actions—and I receive the treatment due to guilt!

If the men whom I have sent to view the roads, report them, not opened according to contract, how am I to act, I surely must continue to withold the balance of Mr. Chamber's money in my hands, but should he become surly and refuse to do over the roads and complete them, what steps is it proper for me to take? Or should he comply, how shall I obtain evidence of his having done so? viewers cannot be appointed ad infinitum. I'll thank you to give me every advice you'll think usefull in this business, for I foresee further trouble. My agency in these roads has been to me a fruitfull source of disquietude, and I must repeat here my earnest request that I may no more be employed in a business of that kind, which I indeed cannot attend to, without a too great expense of the scanty share of happiness I am permitted to enjoy. Ewing, Judge Parke, number of others would answer the purpose better than I do.[3]

The Governor who is security of Chambers, had the in-

---

[2] In November Chambers had been paid $1,500 on his road contract. Other payments probably had been made by this time but no record has been found. For total payments made to Chambers see Carter (ed.), *Territorial Papers*, VII, 490, 498; VIII, 67.

[3] Chambers gave his version of the affair in a long letter to Gallatin on November 10, 1808. *Ibid.*, VII, 614-17.

delicacy to point out to me some of his own friends, as proper persons for viewers, and is highly incensed against me, because I paid no attention to his suggestions, answered him, that nobody should know whom I would send.— Chambers is a member of Council, the Governor has for Congress a favourite candidate—[4] all is intrigue here— I abhorr being made a Cat's paw— He may perhaps venture to join his voice, to the clamours of Mr. Chambers, but if he presume to do so. . . . Ewing and I have made a stand against the deception practised upon the public in relation to Slavery, this business will wear another appearance before long. His most excellent Excellency does not thank us for our opposition and having found out that the real, though not ostensible object of the leaders in the scheme of the second grade of Government was the introduction of Slaves.[5] The vices of Courts are not unknown in this gubernatorial climate.

Times are hard, & bear severely upon me, a year more of tolerably brisk sales would have placed me in a situation free from incumbrance, but there is no sale & I cannot make the two ends meet together notwithstanding the strictest economy, so

[4] Thomas Randolph, a graduate of William and Mary College, a lawyer, and a former member of the Virginia legislature. He arrived in Indiana Territory by May, 1808, and was appointed almost immediately (June 2) attorney general. Sketches of him are in William W. Woollen, *Biographical and Historical Sketches of Early Indiana* (Indianapolis, 1883), pp. 391-99, and Philbrick (ed.), *Laws of Indiana Territory, 1801-9*, p. ccxlii. He ran with Harrison's strong backing for territorial delegate to Congress in 1809, but was defeated by Jennings. See below, pp. 121, 124-26, 129n.

[5] The reference to "second grade of government" is to the advancement of the territorial government to semi-representative as provided in the Ordinance of 1787, with a general assembly of two houses, a house of representatives elected by the male freeholders and a legislative council of five members appointed by the President and approved by the Senate from ten persons nominated by the house of representatives. Indiana Territory advanced to this form of government when a majority of the male freeholders voted in favor of it at an election called by Harrison for September 11, 1804. That the introduction of slavery was the prime cause for Harrison's interest in this advance is also supported by Jacob P. Dunn. See his *Indiana, a Redemption from Slavery* (Boston and New York, 1905), pp. 320 ff.

dear living is in this place. However Albert works nobly, and we have this year a fine crop of wheat in the barn which will save me ninety odd dollars a year I had to pay for flour. We have oats secured and fifteen acres of corn in the ground. We have hitherto been incapable of manufacturing our own wear, proper ground for flax we have none cleared yet, flax sells here 33 1/2 cents a pound, and weaving is 16 1/2 cents a yard, so that no saving can be expected from that quarter except you can raise spin & weave the flax within yourself. This year we have raised some flax on rented ground, and as soon as I can afford the expense I shall have a loom & loom house & make Sally weave. We have made an attempt at sheep & have lost all by the wolves. We planted an acre or two of cotton but the wet spring killed every seed— James Hannah[6] has just arrived with his family— I want to hear of your family concerns, I want to see you, but I despair in the present awfull state of public affairs, of your being able to make a short excursion to the westward.

Adieu, ever Yours &c

JOHN BADOLLET

[Addressed:] Albert Gallatin Esq'r   Private
[Endorsed:] Vincennes August 8, 1808  Badollet

[Badollet to Gallatin]

VINCENNES March 7, 1809

I have received your official letter of Dec'r 21, 1808, but lately owing to the delays occasioned by the inclemency of the winter & will transmitt you the account of my expenditures in relation to the roads. I availed myself of the permission you gave me & have transferred the business to Mr. Ewing. I am very thankfull for your kindness in thus complying with my wishes & the delicate manner in which you have done it.

I have often hinted to you that this place exhibits a profligacy of morals not to be met with in no other part of the United States. The business of these roads & the means full of perfidy employed to injure me, for no other reason than

[6] Brother-in-law of Badollet.

because I did my duty, will corroborate to my assertion. Oblige me to send me a copy of Mr. Chambers' letter.[1]

Nothing I wish so axiously as to have an interview with you, tell me whether it could not take place this spring. I have thousand interesting communications to make.

I have been near loosing Peggy by a nervous fever, I have myself & children been sick. I believe the place I live on is not healthy. This reason & the demoralised state of the place, induce me to wish for a change of situation, it would be agreable to me to be transferred or to retire to a private situation wherein I could support my family— I never shall be forgiven by some here for being an honest man, for having with Ewing and few others began a plan of opposition to the introduction of Slavery, which a few men in high stations would fain have persuaded the public, was the wish of the majority. All deception and intrigues! I drew the Petition against Slavery[2] & hastily the report of the Committee of the

---

[1] Upon receiving Chambers' letter of November 10, 1808 (cited above, p. 101n) Gallatin wrote to Badollet: "Mr Chambers has in language very unbecoming, as it relates to yourself, appealed from your decision respecting his contracts for opening roads. . . . In this instance it is impossible for me to examine and decide on details of this kind; and the perfect confidence placed in you, would render it difficult to submit the question to a person better able to decide than yourself. But as you have requested on a former occasion that your services in that respect might be dispensed with . . . I enclose two open letters, for Mr. Chambers and Mr Ewing, and leave it to yourself either to finish and settle the whole, in which case you will suppress the letters, or to transfer it in the manner proposed to Mr Ewing, in which case, you will be pleased to seal & transmit the letters, and to give copy of the instructions, the contract itself, and all the necessary information to Mr Ewing." This letter and the letters to Ewing and Chambers are in Carter (ed.), *Territorial Papers,* VII, 622-24.

Badollet, as he wrote to Gallatin, turned the business over to Ewing, who was instructed to "settle Mr Chambers's account, cause the roads to be completed . . . and pay to Mr. Chambers or others, the balance which may be due. . . ." *Ibid.*

Final settlement with Chambers was not reached until August, 1811. See *ibid.,* VII, 658-59, 664-65, 679; VIII, 55-56, 67-68, 128. See also Ewing to Gallatin, November 22, 1809, below.

[2] See below, pp. 333-35.

House of Rep. on the same.[3] His excellency had the imprudence to attack Ewing & me on the subject with the rage of a despot, we repelled the attack with becoming decency & firmness, and are hated therefor! &c &c &c.

This is confidential—Fare you well Yours for ever

JOHN BADOLLET

I'll send you a genuine copy of the Petition & report. Excuse my scrawl. I am writing without fire & the mail is closing.

[Addressed:] Albert Gallatin Esq'r    Private

[Endorsed:] Vincennes   March 27 [7], 1809   Badollet

[Gallatin to Badollet]

Private

WASHINGTON 12th May 1809

I have received your letter of 7th March, and am as desirous as yourself of a refreshing interview. The summer session has prevented my going to Fayette this spring; but I must go there either in August or September. I cannot yet determine the precise week or month, & will not be able to stay more than four or five days, unless I return at that time with my family for the purpose of permanently residing there: which is not impossible tho' not yet decided on. The decision, not to induce you into mistake, rests entirely with myself. Will it be prudent for you to incur the expense & trouble of so long a journey merely in order to see me? It was with regret that I saw you go to Vincennes; for I apprehended the climate and I hated the distance. But there was no option. The Ohio representation

[3] The report of the House committee is in Thornbrough and Riker (eds.), *Journals of the General Assembly of Indiana Territory,* pp. 232-38. It has always been considered the work of General Washington Johnston who was chairman of the committee to which various petitions against the admission of slavery had been referred. Badollet indicates that the real author was himself. Jacob P. Dunn, in his volume *Indiana, a Redemption from Slavery,* describes the report as "entitled to rank among the ablest, if not the ablest, of state papers ever produced in Indiana." He then analyzes it in detail (pp. 371-76).

claimed for residents their exclusive right of filling the federal offices in that State: and it was your express opinion that you could not subsist in Greene County. The same obstacles seem to oppose a change. I see no prospect of your being transferred to a nearer district: and you will find the same difficulty in supporting your family in case you should return to Pennsylvania. Still I not only feel your situation: but I *think* that your happiness in the eve of life will in part depend on our spending it in the same vicinity. I *know* that it will be the case with me. If you can perceive any means, in which I can assist, to attain that object, state it fully & in all its details; that we may attempt whatever is practicable, but nothing rashly. What would your little property in Indiana sell for? What would be the expenses of bringing your family up the river? What are the precise ages and capacities of your children? I do not know what you can do yourself without an office: but I will not prejudge; and I earnestly wish that we may discover some means of *re-union*.

As to your squables & disappointment, they are matters of course. At what time, or in what country, did you ever hear that men assumed the priviledge of being more honest than the mass of the society in which they lived, without being hated & persecuted? unless they chose to remain in perfect obscurity & to let others and the world take their own course: and in that case they can never have been heard of. All we can do here is to fulfill our duty without looking at the consequences so far as relates to ourselves. If the love and esteem of others or general popularity follow, so much the better. But it is with these as with all other temporal blessings, such as wealth, health &c., not to be despised, to be honestly attempted, but never to be considered as under our controul or as objects to which a single particle of integrity, a single feeling of conscience should be sacrificed. I need not add that I preach better than I practice. But I may add that you practice better than I do, your complaining of the results only excepted. The purity with which you shall have exercised the duties of land officer may be felt & continue to operate after you have ceased to act. And if you have had a share in preventing the establishment of slavery in Indiana, you will have done more good, to that part of the country at least, than commonly falls to the share of man. Be that feeling your reward. When you are tired of struggling with vice & selfishness, rest yourself, mind your own business, and fight them only when they come directly in your way.

Give my best & affectionate love to your worthy wife who has been your greatest comfort in this world, and on whose judgment you may rely with great safety in any plan you may form.

Ever your's

ALBERT GALLATIN

JOHN BADOLLET    Vincennes

[Harrison to Gallatin]

Private                    VINCENNES 29th August 1809

DEAR SIR When you did me the honor to recommend Your friend Mr Badollett to me in a very particular manner I felt extremely gratified at the Confidence which you seemed to have in my disposition to shew my respect for you when ever an occasion should offer. A very slight acquaintance with B. was sufficient to shew that the partiality of the friend had not exagerated the Virtues of the Man & that he was really entitled to the encomiums you bestowed upon him— An intimacy and Confidence which knew no bounds as I believe on either part was the consequence & continued uninterrupted (for I cannot deem an interruption, a trifling misunderstanding which took place at the board of Trustees of the Vincennes University)[1] Until I discovered that Mr B. was the Author of a Petition to the Territorial Legislature which was circulated through the Counties for signatures against the law for the introduction of Negroes in which there was a severe

[1] For another reference to this see below, pp. 177-80. The minutes of the board of trustees (Microfilm in Archives Division, Indiana State Library) do not shed any light on this.

stricture upon me for having Signed it.[2] I immediately went to Mr Badollett & remonstrated with him upon the impropriety of attacking me in that way. reminded him of the intimacy which subsisted between us when the law was passed & for several years after. In all which time he never had hinted to me that my conduct was improper. I knew indeed the strength of his feelings upon the subject of slavery & had always treated them with peculiar delicacy. I demanded of him only as the price upon which my confidence and friendship would be restored an avowal that it was not his intention to condemn the *Motives* under which I had acted in signing the law— This avowal was however not given & a distant & cold politeness succeeded to our former intimacy— About this Time the dispute between Colo Chambers & Mr Badollett took place[3] in the course of which Mr B. received some illiberal & unmeritted abuse— Colo Chambers determined to appeal to the Govt & employed a lawyer of this place (an intimate friend of Mr B—s) to draft a Memorial for him— As soon as it was finished, the Colo brought it to me & requested me to examine & correct it; Upon reading the paper I was astonished to find it the Most vehement & abusive satire upon Mr B—s conduct character & person that I had ever read—I told the Colo that it was impossible for me to correct the piece—but if he would suffer me I would draw up a statement such as he ought to send & the Govt receive—that I knew the Govt would pay no attention to the silly invective which had been prepared for him & that it would even injure his cause. He acquiessed & I accordingly drew up a statement which contained the substance of the disagreement but not a single word to the prejudice of Mr B— This the Colo promised me to send on but as he demanded the piece which had been drawn by his lawyer I am inclined to believe (and some other circumstances have confirmed the opinion) that the latter was the one really sent to you— I

[2] See below, pp. 333-35, for petition and above pp. 104-5n. for Badollet's account of it.

[3] For the Chambers' affair see above, pp. 100-2, 103-4n.

sometime after related these circumstances to Mr. Ewing &
requested him to communicate them to Mr B. that he might
know the difference between a real & a professed friend—
This I believe was *not* done—& the distant politeness between Mr B & myself still continued. In the course of this
spring a series of publications appeared in the paper of
this place the joint production of McIntosh a Scotch tory
& Mr Badolletts brother in law E McNamee[4] the avowed
object of which was to establish a New criterion for distinguishing Federalists from Republicans Viz their being for
or against the admission of negroes into the Territory—No
republican it was asserted could possibly wish to admit
them— These were followed by several essays by Mr Badollett
himself[5] in which were several violent anathemas against the
people of the Southern States, amongst others, very exceptionable was an idea something like the following that the
people of the Southern States might find it convenient to
follow the laws of morality towards each other but that if
it were not so the man who could keep a negroe in Slavery
would not hesitate to steal a horse. Mr. Ths Randolph a first
cousin of Mr Jeffersons & for Six years a member of the
Virginia Legislature was a candidate to Represent the Territory in Congress—He had declared himself in favor of the
admission of negroes & against him was the fury of McName
& McIntosh particularly directed—[6]It was very evident that

[4] For Badollet's reference to McIntosh and McNamee see below, pp.
pp. 119-20n.

[5] See below, pp. 335-47, the articles signed "A Farmer."

[6] Randolph announced his candidacy in the *Western Sun* of April 15.
He said that he had been uniformly Republican and favored the introduction
of slavery, though he admitted that the great majority in the territory
opposed it. He promised that he would make no attempt to introduce
Negroes into the territory unless so instructed by a majority of his constituents. In the following issue (April 22) McNamee raised objections
to Randolph as being under the particular patronage of the Governor. "We
have heretofore had a delegate to congress, Mr. Parke, precisely under the
same circumstances, for three sessions; during all that time he may have
served his patron so faithfully, but he did not procure one solitary advantage
to the territory."

the opinions of the people had undergone a great change
in respect to the admission of negroes—three fourths were
certainly against the admission—in this County only there
was a small Majority in favor of admitting them the other
three counties almost unanimously against it— There were
two candidates in this County both friendly to the admission—[7]
The third from Clark[8] opposed to them—The result of the
Election was in favor of the latter who had a plurality of the
votes & a small Majority over Mr Randolph. In this County
every exertion was made to get the French votes for Jennings
the candidate from Clark—I am told that Mr. Badollett was
present when McIntosh addressed them & advised them to
vote for no one that had any confidence in me that I was
their tyrant—He was asked for instances of tyranical conduct—He told them "that I had given them Judges of the
Common Pleas commissioned during good behaviour Had
pardoned Hiley a Murderer"[9] (whose pardon Mr Badollett
& many other Citizens had petitioned for) "& had recommended an oppressive amendment to the Militia Law" The
amendment proposed was the insertion of a clause which is
to be found in the code of every State in the Union—[10]You
will perceive the state to which Mr B—s mind had been worked

[7] Thomas Randolph and John Johnson.

[8] Jonathan Jennings.

[9] Abraham Hiley, convicted of the murder of John Coffman of Knox
County, was sentenced to hang but was pardoned by the Governor on
October 30, 1808. Woollen, et al. (eds.), *Executive Journal of Indiana
Territory*, pp. 149-50. The reasons for the arrest of judgment and pardon
are given in Philbrick (ed.), *Laws of Indiana Territory, 1801-9*, p. clxxiv,
note 2.

[10] In a communication to the Assembly on October 20, 1808, Harrison
recommended certain changes in the militia law which would have given
the Governor the power to call out the militia in times of emergency. The
law then in force authorized him to call it out only in face of actual or
threatened invasion. Thornbrough and Riker (eds.), *Journals of the
General Assembly of Indiana Territory*, p. 240. Harrison apparently drafted
a bill which was introduced into the Council and passed but which failed
in the House. McNamee to the President of the Senate, December 12, 1809,
in Carter (ed.), *Territorial Papers*, VII, 685.

up by party spirit when he suffered these gross impositions to be passed upon the ignorant French in his presense— I must own that it excited my utmost astonishment  But you who know Mr B so well need not be told that altho he possesses more virtues than are commonly the lot of one man—he is nevertheless extremely irritable & Pevish & altho possessed of a sound understanding he is so extremely diffident of himself & so little acquainted with the world that there is not a man on the earth more easily duped—it is thus that he suffers himself to be conducted in leading strings by a man of infinitely inferior mind and who he will one day find to have been his evil genius  I mean Nathl Ewing—than whom I sincerely believe there is not a more malicious & Mischevious being in existance—To this mans arts I attribute the difference between Mr. B— & myself & to him is owing the intimacy between Mr B & several characters whom I am persuaded he secretly abhors—And I do assure you Sir most Solemnly that I have prevented a petition being sent from this county signed as I am sure it would be by at least four fifths of the citizens for the removal both of the Register & Receiver—not from any ill conduct in office (for I sincerely believe that they both conduct themselves with strict propriety in their respective appointments) but from the violence of their opposition to me & their connection with men who are looked upon to be enemies both of the Government & the Country.— Ewing has circulated a report amongst the people that the Government have lost all confidence in me at the very time that I received a letter from the Secretary of War assuring me "that I possess his entire confidence as he perceived I had already that of the Executive"[11] It is now declared that it is

[11] When Harrison assured the Administration that the Indian threat to the frontiers had subsided and the Prophet's party had dispersed, the Secretary of War had written, "It was apprehended from the first accounts that more serious consequences might ensue but a reliance on your opinion & judgment encouraged a belief, in the favorable termination which has taken place. It is with great satisfaction that I now request that you will be pleased to accept an assurance of my own, as I perceived you already

from your exertions that my removal is to be expected. this report I gave as little credit to as the other. From this statement you will readily perceive that Mr Badollett is not in his proper sphere & that the influence over his mind must have been very Strong to induce him to take for his friends such men as J. R. Jones[12] & McIntosh neither of them friends to the Govt. The later had a commission under the King of G. Britain in the Revolutionary War & is at this Moment as faithful a servant of King George as any in his dominions. About 15 months ago he published an attack upon me in the Western World.[13] Mr. Badollett was so indignant at it that he unasked furnished me with documents from his office to prove his having suborned a poor ignorant French man to commit perjury—These *Gentlemen* (Jones & McIntosh) are the principal councellors of the Kaskaskias Speculators—At the late Election they set up as a candidate for the Legislative Council E. McName the brother in law of Mr B. & a Captn Bruce for the Representatives—After making every possible exertion & bringing to their aid the prejudices of the people against the admission of negroes the most successfull of their candidates got no more than ten or twelve American votes out of 350 & about 30 ignorant French—

The interest which I know you take in every thing which relates to Mr Badollett has occasioned me to be thus particular. I write this at the moment that my horse is saddling for a journey to Fort Wayne to hold a Treaty with the Indians

I have the Honor to be with great Respect & Esteem your Hum Sert

WILLM HENRY HARRISON

possess the entire confidence of the Executive in your Communications together with the approbation of the measures adopted by your Excellency which have undoubtedly had their influence in producing the result." Letter of June 5, 1809, in Esarey (ed.), *Messages and Letters*, I, 347.

[12] See below, pp. 117-19n.

[13] A newspaper published in Frankfort, Kentucky. See Woollen, *Biographical and Historical Sketches of Early Indiana*, pp. 373 ff., for reference to these articles and Harrison's relations with McIntosh and Jones.

P. S. Ewings disposition for tatling & scandal will it is probable be the cause of Mr Jno Randolphs calling upon you for an explanation—E said some time since at a tavern that you had informed him that Mr. J. Randolph[14] was known to be entirely under British influence—Mr T. Randolph was present & retorted on him severely—& may probably have communicated it to his relation—altho' he declared his disbelief of the story at the time—

HONBLE A GALLATIN ESQR

[Addressed:] The Honble Albert Gallatin Esqr Washington City   Private

[Endorsed:] Vincennes 29 August 1809  Gover Harrison

[Gallatin to Harrison]

WASHINGTON 27th Sept'er 1809

DEAR SIR I have on my return from a short excursion found your private letter of 29th ult'o. I was and still am decidedly opposed to the introduction of slavery into any part of the Union where it does not exist or can be checked. But this is a subject on which I differ in opinion with many valuable friends: and it is with great regret that I find that a difference of opinion on that point should have produced any thing like personal hostility between you & my friend Badollet. In justice to him I must say that he has never written to me disrespectfully of you or against you. He once barely stated the fact of his being opposed to you on the subject of slavery: and I am confident that no application or even hint will come from him to me, suggesting that another Governor ought to be appointed. On that subject my opinion may not perhaps even be asked; but I have no hesitation in saying that it is in favor of your re-appointment.

As to Mr. John Randolph, he certainly admires the British nation more than I do; and I think that some of his speeches respecting our foreign relations have been very wrong & have

---

[14] John Randolph of Roanoke, representative from Virginia and second cousin of Thomas Randolph. *Ibid.,* p. 391.

done some injury to America. But I never said what I am sure is false, that he was under British influence. No man is more free of extraneous influence of any kind than he is.

I am &c

[No signature]

Gov'r Harrison Vincennes

[Endorsed:] Copy of answer to Gov'r Harrison's private letter

[Badollet to Gallatin]

Vincennes October 15, 1809

This will be handed to you by Mr. Jonathan Jennings who formerly assisted me in my Office, & who is returned as our Delegate to Congress notwithstanding the unheard of lengths to which his Excellency permitted himself to go to marr his election & send a peculiar favourite. The question of slavery formed the touch stone & Mr. Jennings being decided on that point & knowing besides a number of precious secrets, has therefor drawn upon himself the (honourable) hatred of our Executive & of his hirelings by whom he has been very indecently treated.[1] His conduct towards me has attached me to him & every attention you'll think fit to Shew him shall be gratefully acknowledged by me.

Adieu Yours for ever

John Badollet

Albert Gallatin Esqr.

[Badollet to Gallatin]

Vincennes November 13, 1809

I had fed myself my Dear Friend with the hope of paying you a visit this fall, but painful circumstances wherein however my family is not concerned have forced me to abandon that project, at least for some time to come.

---

[1] Jennings was the first delegate chosen under the act approved February 27, 1809, providing for the election of the delegate to Congress and members of the legislative council by the voters of the territory. U. S. *Statutes at Large,* II, 525-26. The election was held on May 22, 1809. For further

Your last letter's effect upon me is almost undescribable, the certainty of having my conduct approved by you diffuses through my whole frame a sensation of happiness which made ample amends for the mental pain I have been this good while suffering. The mere probability also of drawing nearer to one another of indulging those early impressions which require a renewed strength as we draw nearer to the common goal of quitting this country of moral debasement, almost electrified me and made every fibre vibrate with anticipated pleasure. But as I have at length arrived at *years of discretion* I check the cheering ideas which arise in my mind and view the practicability or rather impracticability of any change in my situation with the sober eye of prudence and the correctness of cool calculation. Thus armed, it is without any kind of danger that I permit myself to ruminate upon your letter, and here allow me to observe, that you would find me a different man from what you once knew me, instinctive integrity has been rendered immovable and ennobled by reflection. My conduct here, where I was thrown in the midle of vice and without a prop to rest upon, has convinced me that there existed in me some merit, but long concealed under a disgusting heap of rubbish; and that conviction makes me take a retrospect of my thoughts and ill spent life with bitter regrets, but it also induces me to think that I could attend business with assiduity well convinced that man is condemned to work and that a family cannot be clothed and fed upon the idle fancies of a romantic brain. So far can you calculate upon my becoming usefull, should you happen to pitch upon some plan with or near you, whereby I could provide for my family, and the attention nay the pleasure with which I discharge the duties of my Office are a sure pledge of my future steadiness and industry. But I permit these ideas to occupy my mind but transiently.

You kindly question me about my family—Albert about 21 years old is a fine porsly [*sic*] young man, retired, sober

references to it see Harrison's letter immediately above and Badollet's letter of November 13, below.

and modest as a girl, his hobby horse has too long been a mule, but that stiffness has been and is mellowing into an honourable firmness of mind. His heart is pure, his understanding though not of a superior order, is correct, his body is sound and inured to labour. Had he but a few months' residence under some proper teacher, he would be soon capable of attending business or to relieve me in my office. I had a mind to send him for some time to you, hoping that you would extend to him your friendly protection and place him under some good hand.

My eldest daughter Fanny about 18 years old is a sensible reflecting and studious girl. Sally two or three years younger is not marked with the same turn of sedateness, but both are raised to industry, are clear of fashionable follies and unacquainted with the dull, insipid, and not seldom uncharitable chat of modern female gentry. Peggy has been a treasure to me, her native good sense and innocence of heart have ripened into solid but not less amiable qualities. She is here what she has ever been loved and respected, her lips having never been polluted by the language of detraction, she excites among her female acquaintances no sentiment of reserve or fear and is every where viewed as entitled to affection and respect. Her winning example aided by fatherly advices has infused in her daughters an early sense of self-respect, which effectually remove every uneasiness in relation to the propriety of their conduct. The two boys[1] are too young yet to furnish any theme for observations.

I[n] my last letter I gave you pretty roundly my opinion respecting our Gov'r and it must have surprised you. Do not believe however that it has been rashly conceived and as rashly expressed. I have been more than two years his complete dupe, believing him a very good man, but the attentive observation of his conduct and the gradual discovery of his principles have at last flashed conviction in my own mind and forced from my pen the expressions you have read.—Moral

[1] James and Algernon Sidney.

cameleon he assumes a variety of appearances to answer his purposes, vulgar with the lowest order of mankind, polite & fascinating with the more refined, he succeeds equally in imposing on them all. With a fluency of well chosen language he veils a very superficial knowledge, and with despotic self-conceit and clamorous loquacity he reduces modest & solid merit to a mortifying silence. To him must be ascribed [in] the first instance the nefarious and impolitic project of introducing slavery into this Territory, wherein he has persisted with an unwearied pertinacity & whereby he has greatly impeded its population and filled it [with] intrigue and discord. To his suggestions or rather directions (for the Legislatures except that of 1808 were nothing better than the recorders of his edicts)—must be attributed that disgrace of Legislation, the law *concerning the introduction of negroes into this Territory*,[2] which contrary to his duty he had the audacity to sanction; and such was his infatuation that relying upon the wonted servility of those who surrounded him, he with his worthy coadjutor Benjamin Parke introduced on a fourth of July a toast in favour of the admission of Slavery which I alone unsupported as I was, made him swallow in the midle of his adherents.

One of his clan a complaisant member of the Legislature challenged at Cahokia John R. Jones whom he hated and feared. Sometime afterwards the same Bragadocio challenged his son Rice Jones who impelled by a youthfull but too incautious zeal had manifested a determination of being substantially upright and independant and of discovering unasailed by clamours and threats every malversation to the world.[3]

[2] See above, p. 97.

[3] The challenger was Shadrach Bond, "Jr.," of Randolph County. He was thus referred to, to distinguish him from Shadrach Bond, Sr., his uncle. Sketches of both and of John Rice Jones and Rice Jones are in Philbrick, *Laws of Indiana Territory 1801-9*, see index. Bond served as representative from St. Clair County in 1807 and as a member of the Legislative Council in 1808. John Rice Jones had been appointed by the President to the Council in 1806, upon recommendation of Harrison, but by the summer of 1808 the Governor, along with citizens of Knox County, was seeking to

These two challenges produced no bloodshed, but soon afterwards, after a session of the Legislature wherein Rice Jones
headed an opposition hitherto unknown and therefore the more
galling, that interesting young man adorned with every talent
steeled with every virtue, was assassinated in the streets of
Kaskaskia and another favorite of his Excellency stands now
recognized in a sum of several thousand dollars as an accessory
before the fact to that ever to be lamented crime.[4] I have not

have him removed for improper conduct. Esarey (ed.), *Messages and
Letters*, I, 296-97; Carter (ed.), *Territorial Papers*, VII, 578-79, 627-30.
Jones had become a large landowner in the western counties and was seeking
division and organization of Illinois Territory. The pro-division, antislavery, anti-Harrison movement in the western counties of St. Clair and
Randolph had become very strong by this time. For petitions to Congress
attacking Harrison and seeking division, see *ibid.*, VII, 544-54.

[4] Exactly whom Badollet refers to here as the "accessory" is not very
clear unless it is Bond. Rice Jones was shot in Kaskaskia on December 7,
1808, by Dr. James Dunlap who had served as Bond's second. Just when the
challenge of John Rice Jones mentioned by Badollet occurred has not been
determined. The encounter between Rice Jones and Bond came about as an
aftermath of the heated campaign for representative in the summer of 1808
in which Rice Jones was victorious. (George Fisher, representative from
Randolph County, had been appointed to the Legislative Council, and a
special election was called for July 25, to fill the vacancy. Woollen, *et al*
[eds.], *Executive Journal of Indiana Territory*, p. 147.) Jones favored
division of the territory, which was opposed by the Harrison faction. At a
political meeting at Kaskaskia, Jones attacked Bond, who was present, as
a tool of Harrison and opposed to the interests of St. Clair and Randolph
counties. Bond challenged Jones that evening and they met on an island
in the Mississippi. A reconciliation was effected by Jones's second, William
Morrison. Dr. Dunlap, Bond's second, endeavored to show that Jones had
made concessions to Bond in a cowardly fashion and a bitter exchange
occurred in the pages of the *Western Sun,* in issues of August 27, September
3, 10, October 1, November 5, 1808.

Jones attended the session of the Assembly which ran from September
26 to October 26. A contest of his election failed. Thornbrough and Riker
(eds.), *Journals of the General Assembly of Indiana Territory*, pp. 160,
161-62, 171-72, 184-85n. At this session Jesse B. Thomas was elected
territorial delegate, committed to work for division of the territory, which
was a blow to the Harrison faction. *Ibid.*, pp. 248-49n. Jones's report to his
constituents on this session is given below, pp. 351-56.

On December 17, 1808, the *Western Sun* carried the curt announcement:
"We have the melancholy task to record the death of Rice Jones Esqr. of
Kaskaskia, he fell by the hand of Dr. James Dunlap,—he was in the vigor

related those facts with a view to insinuate that he was the immediate instigator of such proceedings, but to shew what kind of men he fosters, and what degree of audacity they think that under his shield they can permit themselves to reach.

A certain Thomas Randolph dropped here from Virginia,[5] with a great name and talents which the Governor has increasingly proclaimed great, but of which he has hitherto given no evidence, challenged Dr. McNamee, because he dared to rend the veil that covered Mr. Harrisons official conduct.[6] This Randolph has ever since his arrival been an inmate of the Governor and I have seen the spot where he practised his shooting with pistols at a mark to make sure of the Dr's existence and the bullits can there be seen to this day. And here

of youth, and just entering the busy scenes of life.—" The paper reported nothing more at the time. Dunlap fled to Louisiana Territory. It is recorded in the *Executive Journal of Indiana Territory* (p. 151) that Harrison had written to the Governor of Louisiana to have him apprehended, but he was never returned for trial.

During the campaign for election as delegate to Congress the following spring the Jones-Dunlap affair was revived in an article signed "Spectator" in the *Western Sun* of April 29, 1809. Herein it was indicated that Rice Jones had abused Dunlap as a professional man and sought to get him out of the territory and his attacks had driven him to action against Jones. This writer had it that Jones and the Doctor met on the street. He did not say who made the first move. Apparently Dunlap attempted to use a small cane and Jones drew a dirk. The Doctor then resorted to his pistol in self-defense.

[5] See above, p. 102n.

[6] Dr. Elias McNamee, a brother-in-law of Badollet. When the editor of the *Western Sun*, Elihu Stout, identified him as the author of letters which had appeared in the *Sun* signed by "A Citizen of Vincennes" and "A Detector Detected," Randolph challenged him. Jonathan Taylor, Randolph's second, reported that McNamee denied being the author "of the most objectionable parts of the pieces, but refused to give the name or names of the persons concerned, he having authorised the printer to give up himself only, as the author. . . ." McNamee, a Quaker, did not accept Randolph's challenge. Instead he went before Judge Henry Vanderburgh and swore out the following statement: "I Elias McNamee do solemnly swear that Thomas Randolph of the county of Knox Esquire hath challenged him to fight a duel, and that he hath good reason to believe and doth verily believe that the said Thomas Randolph will take his life and do him some bodily harm." Vincennes *Western Sun,* June 10, 1809; Woollen, *Biographical and Historical Sketches of Early Indiana,* pp. 396-97.

permit me pause and to ask you what kind of heart that man must possess who can unmoved contemplate the bloody end of the friend who is sacrificing himself to his cause or of an highly respected member of Society and respectable citizen on whose life depends the support of three helpless children and their mother? And lately the same Gentleman attempted to cudgel in the streets a Mr. McIntosh[7] for the same crime, but to his great discomfiture he received two or three stabs from a dirk to which McIntosh had recourse in his own defence.[8] Such is the State of Society here, such the manner in which the Governor watches over the peace and safety of the citizens!

I pass by his intrigues in the Legislature, because however certain in the eye of the beholder (who, although not perceiving

[7] William McIntosh. He had been appointed territorial treasurer in 1801 by Harrison but he soon become a political enemy of the Governor and his followers, particularly of Benjamin Parke. The Vincennes *Indiana Gazette,* of September 21, 1804, carried a letter of Parke identifying McIntosh as the author of pieces appearing in earlier issues under signatures of "Freeholder" and "Citizen," attacking Harrison and the advance of the territory to the second grade. On August 27 the *Sun* had carried an "Advertisement" signed by Parke in which he announced: "Circumstances have recently occurred, which authorise me in pronouncing and publishing William McIntosh, an arrant knave: a profilgate villain: a dastardly cheat: a perfidious radical: an impertinent puppy: an absolute liar: and a mean and cowardly poltron." Parke later challenged McIntosh. The latter according to one account declined until he could clear his name and never did accept.

In 1807 McIntosh had assumed the role of spokesman for the French inhabitants of the territory in proclaiming their loyalty to the United States and attacking Harrison for allegedly implying doubts as to their patriotism. See Harrison's letter to Gallatin, August 29, 1809, above; Esarey (ed.), *Messages and Letters,* I, 256-59, 262-63; Carter (ed.), *Territorial Papers,* VII, 503, 536-37. See also account of McIntosh in Woollen, *Biographical and Historical Sketches of Early Indiana,* pp. 378-83. In 1811 Harrison was to bring suit against McIntosh for slandering him in his administration of the Indian Department. He won the suit and recovered $4,000 damage. Esarey (ed.), *Messages and Letters,* I, 509-10.

[8] According to Woollen, McIntosh stabbed Randolph in the back with a dirk and Randolph cut McIntosh in the face with a small pocket knife, his only weapon. McIntosh was but slightly hurt, while Randolph's life hung precariously in balance for several weeks. *Historical and Biographical Sketches of Early Indiana,* p. 395.

the wires, yet discovers by the sudden inconsistent and con-
tradictory motions of the puppets, the operations of some
extraneous agents) they cannot be easily demonstrated and as
it were made tangible—without an historical and disgusting
account of characters and a previous and intimate knowledge
of our local peculiarities.

As soon as Mr. Randolph [arrived] with his great name
and relationship to Mr. Jefferson (which the Governor was at
great pains to inculcate) he was appointed Attorney general to
the exclusion of a Lawyer of respectability who had been raised
in this place. He was next nominated as a candidate for the
Assembly (to be thence sent to Congress by usual obsequiousness of that body) but having imprudently & before he had
felt the public pulse, advocated his patron's scheme of slavery
he missed his election.

I have endeavoured to preserve a regular chain of ideas, but
in vain. I already perceive that I anticipate and must take some
retrograde steps.

After we had ascertained that the opposers of Slavery
formed a great majority in this County and to our great Surprise and joy, that the eastern parts of the Territory were
decidedly against it, we thought it advisable to bring the
matter fairly before the public by a petition to the Legislature
(which I drew) and is marked A in the inclosures.[9] The Governor became enraged against Ewing & me, accustomed to a
blind devotion to his mandates, he could not conceive such
independance, such rebellious boldness. He attempted to make
us feel the weight of his ire, but in vain, we rose indignantly
against his infuriated sally & left him the impression, that fully
acquainted with our own rights, we could no more be driven
than he had found us before disposed to be led.

To lessen the effect of our petition, which was generally
signed, another one was circulated containing a long prayer to
the Legislature to oppose the division of the Territory (a
measure very obnoxious to the County) and at the end of it

[9] See below, Appendix, pp. 333-35.

as it were hidden in a corner was added a short paragraph praying that efforts might still be made in favour of slavery. By such deceptive and dishonourable means members were made to sign what they were decidedly opposed to. Notwithstanding this stratagem and the suppression of some of our petitions which had been forwarded to this place but never reached it, the number of signatures was so overwhelmingly on our side that the majority of the lower house was with us. I was requested to draw the report of the select Committee to which the Petitions were referred, which was adopted by the house. In the Council two members who had received proper orders stood firm as rocks against every thing which could displease their employer. That report enclosed herewith is marked B.[10]

Allarmed at the approaching destruction of all his hopes and at the tendency of some essays over the signature of A Citizen of Vincennes written by Dr. McNamee he formed with Judge Park & Randolph a Caucus wherein were written & whence flew in every direction the most abusive and artfull pieces. Parke whose republicanism had been neutralized in the Governor's atmosphere, did not disdain at the nod of his master to descend from his elevated station, to enlist in the ranks, nay to place himself at the head of a faction. A series of essays confessedly written by him and signed *Slim Simon,* containing a compound of Sophistry, bilingsgate and the most damnable hypocricy were vomited against the poor *Citizen* & in defence of Slavery the object of their unceasing sollicitude. Those I attempted to refute in the *Farmer* marked C.[11] No attempt has ever been made to rebut me and I have enjoyed the pleasure of learning that my reasons had made on many a deep impression. They grew more enraged than ever, and instead of meeting us on the fair ground of argument, they

---

[10] See above, pp. 104-5n. The report is printed in Thornbrough and Riker (eds.), *Journals of the General Assembly of Indiana Territory,* pp. 232-38. No copy of it was found in the Gallatin Papers.

[11] See below, Appendix, pp. 335-47.

contemptuously designated us under the name of the Vincennes Junto: mark that expression applied to men supported by the soundest principles of humanity justice and policy and backed by three fourths of the Territory.[12]

Preparations were now made for the election of Randolph to Congress for although the public opinion had been so strongly expressed in the late elections and by the Petitions before mentioned, the Governor's daring mind, bent upon

[12] The newspaper exchanges referred to here and below appeared in issues of the *Western Sun* from January 28, 1809, on through the spring and into the summer. The chief theme at first was the party division of Federalists and Republicans and the introduction of slavery. McNamee ("A Citizen of Vincennes") contended that the Federalists generally were proslavery, the Republicans antislavery. He demanded that any candidate for elective office declare himself on the slavery question. (Issue of January 28) Parke ("Slim Simon"), in reply, denied this party alignment: ". . . as to applying the terms federalist and republican to those who are in favor or against it [introduction of slavery], you might as well have used the terms Pyankashaw and Hottentot. Your object, however, is obvious. You knew that the name, federalist, had become odious to many; and you therefore broadly assert that those who are in favor of slavery are not only federalists but aristocrats—and make the opinion of a man on this subject a criterion by which his political tenets may be, unerringly tested. . . ." (Issue of February 4) In a later issue (February 11) Parke said the real question before the country was how the slaves already in the country were to be disposed of. "I have thought it a dictate of sound policy, that their owners should be permitted to remove with them wheresoever they pleased; and that in the course of the present century, considering the vast emigration to the Western territories, they would be so dispersed, that they could be emancipated with the same ease and safety, that they have been in N. England."

On February 25 Randolph entered the picture, replying to McNamee. He condemned him for raising the slavery issue, a subject "from which no real alarm can rationally be apprehended." He announced himself in favor of the introduction of slavery into the territory.

McNamee's reply on March 4 included the observation "that slavery is acknowledged by every statesman, to be a moral and political evil, so enormous, that I must solemnly protest against the patriotism of the man who wishes to extend it."

Thereafter the slavery issue was thrust aside in exchanges on speculations in lands at the expense of the public, in which the old charges against Harrison were raised, and Jennings who was running against Randolph was accused of bidding up tracts and forfeiting them while he was employed as clerk in the land office. (Issues of April 29, May 6)

sending him there to promote his reappointment and to attend to his darling object of slavery, conceived the bold and to all appearances desperate project of getting him elected by the people themselves, to whom Congress by a very wise and just law had transferred that power from the Legislature.[13]

A miserable wretch, an insignificant insect named Edward Westfall was cajoled to father the lucubrations of His Excellency and his *honorable* associate and under the signature of Jeremiah Jingle, he has continued to retail the decent productions of his high patrons.[14] He was seen writing or rather copying in the Governor's house and what is truly ludicrous some of his numbers contain the most emphatic enumeration of Wm. H. Harrison's virtues, of his military talents, of his warlike exploits and an history of his father whose merit and patriotism it was broadly hinted he had inherited by descent. The press then more than ever was the vehicle of the most virulent, unmerited, and unrestrained abuse.

A few days before the election of our Delegate which was to take place before the succeeding number of our despicable paper could appear, an extra sheet was printed containing the piece marked D[15] which bears internal evidence of its being penned by the Governor himself. That performance wherein truth candor taste and decency are equally insulted, is a living monument of the extremities to which powerfull but unprincipled men can abandon themselves to oppress the innocent & those who dare to assume an erect attitude in defense of reason, of justice and their invaded rights. That edifying piece, witheld till the last moment, till it was too late to rebut it, was intended as a last and irrepellable blow against Jennings

---

[13] The act of February 27, 1809, which provided for the election of the territorial delegate to Congress and members of the Legislative Council by vote of those persons entitled to elect the members of the territorial House. U. S. *Statutes at Large,* II, 525-26.

[14] The articles signed Jeremiah Jingle are in the Vincennes *Western Sun of* February 25 and March 11, 1809.

[15] Not in Gallatin Papers, and no copy has been found. Apparently it carried a piece signed "Detector." See following note.

& his friends and to complete the turpitude of such a conduct, the Printer an humble slave sold to the Governor, made the Doctor understand that thence forward no writing should be admitted without the price of printing being paid; the Dr made out to write in haste the piece marked E and to pay for it. The writing signed *Detector detected* is of another hand, the manner in which it is written does not entirely meet my approbation. The author though known to me did not consult me.[16]

[16]No copy of "E" is in the Gallatin Papers, but a copy is in the collection of broadsides in the Indiana Division of the Indiana State Library. It is a single sheet, printed on both sides and contains a letter signed "A Citizen of Vincennes" and another signed "A Detector Detected." Both are answers to "Detector." In the piece by "A Citizen" it is alleged that Parke and the Governor were authors "of all the scurrilous pieces over the signatures of Slim Simon, the Voter, the piece signed A, and lastly the Detector." That Parke had written under the name "Slim Simon" is noted above (Note 11). The piece signed "A Voter" is in the *Sun* of April 29 and that signed "A" is in the issue of May 6. Apparently the piece signed "Detector" concerned the old issues of slavery and land scandals. It also defended Harrison as a Jeffersonian. "A Citizen" answered by saying that under Adams he was "a warm federalist" while under Jefferson he made great professions of republicanism.

The language of "A Detector Detected" was much stronger. "The governor," it ran, "not contented with the unbounded power given him by the ordinance for the government of the territory, by which he can make, and unmake officers with as much facility as Bonaparte can kings—add to this his veto, by which it is his pleasure whether you shall have any laws other than those he pleases; I say, not content with such unbounded power, under his influence and direction, a writer over the signature of 'Detector,' abuses one of our best citizens, for pointing out to the free and independent voters of Knox a few obvious reasons why a person under the influence of the governor ought not to be elected delegate to Congress; and for having dared to make some opposition to the Collosses of Indiana. Fellow citizens beware of your judgments, that they are not captivated with the base insinuations, and foul poisons contained under the flimsy covering of his falsehoods, and barefaced assertions, for the piece contains more falsehoods, & bare faced assertions, than any person who is not callous to feeling, or lost to truth could possibly imagine. He begins by asserting that he will strip the Citizen of his flimsy covering, and discovered him to you in his pristine deformity. Fellow citizens, had the Detector honesty enough to draw the picture truly, the Citizen would no doubt stand high in your estimation; but as for the writer of the Detector, was *Pandora's Box* and *Hell* too open, a more hideous and depraved monster could not be seen. The Detector

You cannot form a correct idea of the fertility of that man's brains in inventions to deceive and decoy. The piece marked F supercedes the necessity of a volume of comments & exhibits in a glaring point of view the depravity of the inventor, the exalted opinion he entertains of the readers understanding and their contemptible stupidity. The circular marked G entrusted only to a few choice spirits on the eve of the election, is also a precious *morceau* where Randolph's heart and head equally shine.[17]

The Salt springs to be found in the new purchase have been made an engine of corruption, he having before the election *promised* the lease or management of them to sundry different persons who are now wrangling about and in order to destroy that source of undue influence I am of opinion that some other person and not the Governor ought to have the transacting of that business.

A man warm on our side is made sheriff of Harrison County & is become since mute,[18] another also enemy to Slavery receives a Commission of a justice of the peace,[19] changes sides, becomes clamourous for it & proclaims Randolph a phoenix. Blandishments and frowns are by him successfully employed and when you reflect that every office both civil and

then tells you, that pickpockets, whores and conjurers, endeavour to keep your attention attracted, while they are picking your pockets, corrupting your chastity, &c.—Fellow citizens the Detector is a striking instance of those abominable characters he speaks so wittily of—for in his piece he gives you the friendly caution of, guard your liberty, at the very time he is endeavouring to palm upon you a man for delegate, who, he knows will represent the governor, instead of you, as the Detector well knows a man who has played more tricks within eight or nine years, than any Egyptian fortune teller. . . ."

After the election, in a series of letters published in the *Sun* on June 24, July 1 and 29, 1809, Randolph carried on the campaign issues.

[17] The items marked "F" and "G" are not in the Gallatin Papers and have not been found elsewhere.

[18] Spier Spencer. He was appointed sheriff December 8, 1808, upon the organization of Harrison County. Woollen, *et al.* (eds.), *Executive Journal of Indiana Territory*, p. 151.

[19] Not identified.

military is in his gift, you can easily guess without being an
Oedippus, the effects such a conduct must necessarily produce
in a limited community such as Indiana.

It is an irksome and difficult task to pursue that man
through the endless variety of strategems he employed to
force as it were the election of his favourite. What will you
say of his writing letters on the subject in every direction?
of his dispatching emissaries to every corner some mounted on
his own horses to electioneer, publish the praises of his dear
Randolph deride and calumniate his opponents? What will you
say of his trusting on the eve of an election to a tavern bully
an adept at catching votes, a blank commission for a Justice of
the peace (at the distance of about twenty miles) of which
that respectable agent was to fill the blanks on conditions not
difficult to divine? What will you say of his leaving a parcel
of Braves in Vincennes, all his intimates, who overawed the
election, and by their violence so terrified the voters, that numbers of them retired without voting at all, when himself was
posting to the eastern counties to intrigue amongst the people
and even harangue them on the election ground? What will you
think of these words terminating his speech "In short Gentlemen, if you want me to be your Governor again vote for Mr.
Randolph, but if you wish me not to be reappointed vote for
Mr. Jennings." By which he enlisted on his side the voters'
hopes and fears and audaciously invaded the sacred freedom
of election, for when people vote *viva voce* and each man's vote
is written down how many will be found willing to expose
themselves to his enmity or to forego the hopes of his favours?

Even the idle rumour of an indian war has been made
subservient to the same purpose with a dexterity truly admir-
able. Instead on the first allarm of distributing a well chosen
set of spies forty or fifty miles from the frontiers, to traverse
the country and cover the settlements, to train and arm the
volunteers and establish allarm posts, he posted two companies
drafted from amongst them, four miles from Vincennes, where
they spent the working season in sloth and idle mockery of

military manoeuvres.  In the mean time the line of frontiers might have been a scene of desolation and ruin before those patriotic trained bands had even suspected the catastrophe. Such are the military talents of this hero.[20]  But the election business was going on, the member of the Assembly who had reported against slavery was made adjutant,[21] although he knows as much about military affairs as I do about Pope's bulls & made to draw a handsome pay.  The consequence was that he shifted side and from the reviler became the panegyrist of his Excellency.  The Major,[22] for those two companies had a major, a man conscienciously opposed to slavery was rendered mute & made to vote against Jennings.  A decent young man[23]

[20] Harrison had received reports from Meriwether Lewis, governor of Missouri Territory, and William Wells, who was at Fort Wayne, of the hostile disposition being shown by Indian tribes on the Mississippi and Illinois rivers and those on the Wabash who were followers of the Prophet. On April 18, 1809, he wrote to the Secretary of War of his concern and said that "under these circumstances and considering the unprotected situation of this town and the neighboring settlements I have determined to organize arm and equip and call into actual service two companies of volunteer militia. . . .  Considerable progress has already been made in drawing out those men. . . .  They will be placed upon the Wabash a few hundred yards below the Garrison called Fort Knox. . . .  Standing immediately upon the frontier both it and the town of Vincennes could be surprised plundered and burned by an hundred Indians at any time without risk to themselves, as there is not a single family settled to the north and northwest to give notice of their approach.  A detachment of 12 or 15 men of the two companies called out will be placed in the settlement of Bosseron 20 miles northeast of this place. . . ."  Esarey (ed.), *Messages and Letters,* I, 340-41.

On April 29 the *Sun* carried a notice that according to the Governor the Wabash tribes appeared to be pacific and he did not apprehend danger from the distant tribes and added, "but that under all circumstances, as a party of militia had been ordered out, he had thought it best to keep them in service until he heard something decisive from governor Lewis."

On May 2, from "Camp near Vincennes," Benjamin Parke wrote to John W. Eppes, a representative of Virginia, of the hostile disposition of the Prophet, and expressed a wish that permission would be granted for two or three hundred men to march against him and surprise him in his camp. This he felt would be the most effectual way to disconcert his plans. Carter (ed.), *Territorial Papers,* VII, 650.

[21] Probably General Washington Johnston.

[22] Not identified.

[23] Not identified.

zealous in our cause was made Quarter Master and lost his speech. Parke the hypocritical Parke volunteering in this holy crusade was seen in the ranks with a knapsack on his back in the real though not avowed character of a missionary de propaganda. Several days was another confident of the Governor seen swaggering in the camp, cursing the Vincennes rascals (by which elegant expression we were designated) without whom the Country would enjoy peace and happiness. When they were dismissed they were addressed by the Commander in chief in terms of the most hyperbolic praises *You have well deserved of your Country, happy the man who will have to lead you on* &c &c &c. Libations of [MS illeg.] closed the scandalous scene & the consequence was that Jennings was stuped & Randolph, the incomparable Randolph, the only person fit to represent the Territory in Congress. Albert who was a conscript ycleped a volunteer, disdained going to the house and stood amazed at its disgusting prostitution. By such and thousand other arts eluding the powers of description the citizens of this county & a few of the others who had always been on our side became lukewarm or apostates and voted as they were bid. Still Jennings was elected by the strength of the eastern Counties who themselves had set him up.[24]

From the imperfect sketch you have read, you'll be induced to believe with me that self respect, independence of mind have all fled. Nothing is left but servility and moral degradation. I never could have conceived that it was in the power of a single man *clothed with a brief authority* to exercise such a deleterious and demoralizing influence over men born free.

The plans of the Governor being thus destroyed by the

[24] The results of the election were given in the *Western Sun* of July 8, 1809. The vote was 428 for Jennings, 402 for Randolph, and 81 for John Johnson. Jennings' large vote in the eastern counties of Clark and Dearborn gave him the election. In conjunction with Badollet's observations on Harrison's actions in relation to this election one should read Jennings' letter to William Duane, editor of the Philadelphia *Aurora and General Advertiser,* which touches on many of the points in Badollet's letter. Riker, *Unedited Letters of Jonathan Jennings,* pp. 170-72.

election of Jennings his rage equalled his disappointment. (It is then the challenge took place).[25] But his genius fertile in resources conceived the project of sending still Randolph to Congress and of making the people pay the expense. In the fumes of a fourth of July in the midle of a very mixed company, after some indecent toasts,[26] he as some of his understrappers set a subscription going to defray the expenses of a person to the Federal City (the person was not named but well understood) on the scandalous pretence that the subscribers could not consider themselves represented by the member elect. That subscription was signed that day there & since hawked through the County by the same sycophantic fool Edward Westfall. To tax thus the stupid credulity of men (and for his own self's sake) puzzled enough to make a living in a country as yet devoid of resources outherods Herod himself. Randolph is now there, mark him.[27]

I'll say little about the public sales of Lands, wherein he was as usefull as a fifth w[h]eel to a waggon, and with a parcel of speculating partners, he hung like a cormorant on the simple purchasers to fleece or deprive them of their lands, at the very time that his too generous country paid him six dollars a day for doing nothing, because Dr. McNamee is writing to the President on the subject and will state a number of facts descriptive of his exalted disinterestedness.[28] This Doctor son

[25] Randolph's challenge of McNamee. See above.

[26] One of the toasts at the Vincennes observance of the 4th, with Harrison presiding, was: "Jonathan Jennings—the semblance of a delegate—his want of abilities, the only safety of the people.—3 groans." Vincennes *Western Sun,* July 8, 1809.

[27] Randolph contested Jennings' election and went to Washington to plead his own case. The House finally seated Jennings. The proceedings are well covered with documents and notes in Carter (ed.), *Territorial Papers,* VII, 661-63n, 694-95, 697-703.

[28] McNamee addressed two letters to the President, but they have not been found. A letter to the President of the Senate, December 12, 1809, opens thus, "Having written two letters to the President of the United States, in which I have stated some of the misconduct of William H. Harrison Governor of Indiana Territory.—I deem it right to lay the same facts before the Senate of the United States. . . ." *Ibid.,* VII, 682-86.

of the good old Quaker who burnt the bricks of your house, is a good sensible and principled man, any thing that His Excellency or Randolph may have said to the contrary notwithstanding, he is possessed of a considerable share of political virtue and of course marked for destruction, at which because he is a new comer, more helpless than any one of us, whom our stations in some measure protect, they work with a demoniacal perseverance.— Permit me to observe that, that pyratical war which Mr. Harrison, being Governor, waged against the emigrants coming to increase the prosperity of the Country entrusted to his guardianship & that abandonment of decorum and duty of which in the capacity of superintendant of the sales he was guilty, are circumstances of such a serious nature that the Administration cannot in my opinion pass them over and to countenance such proceedings by a reappointment would be a stigma on the justice and honour of the United States and a fatal blow on the scattered & desponding remnants of virtue that may still be found amongst us.

Without too confidently relying upon the expected services of Mr. Randolph he had three remaining resources to prop his sinking credit at the Federal City namely a purchase of indian lands and recommendations from the people and Legislature. These two last evince the boldness of his conceptions and his success the dexterity with which he can reduce them to practice.

He had sent word to the Wabash Indians to meet him in Council at Vincennes but they did not chuse to do it, but as he was determined to effect a purchase, he setts off with his suite for Fort Wayne, but instead of going there by the direct road, he leisurely travels through Clarke & Harrison to Dearborne

The letter covered the matters of Harrison's alleged speculation in lands and use of "hush money" to further his ends; his efforts toward the introduction of slavery; his engaging in an enterprise for trade with the Indians contrary to the law prohibiting him as superintendent of Indian affairs to do so; his dissolution of the Assembly in 1808; and finally his proclamation in April, 1809, apportioning the territorial representatives following division of the territory.

County visiting every nook, cajoling the people, tampering with the members of the Legislature, inviting them to accept free quarters at his house during the approaching session, painting Ewing & me in a variety of odious or ridiculous colours. He at last reaches Fort Wayne & with much difficulty obtains from some of the tribes a strip of country along our north eastern boundary and another adjoining Dearborne.[29] You may well believe that there is no man here who would not rejoice at an addition being made to the Lands of the United States above us, yet such is the wickedness and profundity of his schemes, that he has spread the impression and even hinted to the Legislature that [he] had met with difficulties in his negociation from the macchinations of certain enemies of their country residing at Vincennes by which black suggestions he endeavoured to direct the torrent of public odium on Ewing on me and others of our friends.[30] I know not what means he

[29] On route to Fort Wayne Harrison stopped at Cleves, near Cincinnati, from September 7 to 10, home of his father-in-law, John Cleves Symmes. He was accompanied by Peter Jones, John Harding, James Dill, two Frenchmen, and two Indians. Beverley W. Bond, Jr., *The Correspondence of John Cleves Symmes* (New York, 1926), p. 297.

The treaty was concluded on September 30. For the text see Kappler (ed.), *Indian Affairs. Laws and Treaties,* II, 101-2. By it a tract almost seventy miles square containing approximately 3,000,000 acres was ceded to the United States. Compensations were annuities of $500 to the Delawares, to the Miami, and to the Potawatomi, and a $200 annuity to the Eel Rivers.

[30] Harrison in his message to the General Assembly, October 17, 1809, in stressing the need for the reorganization and strengthening of the militia, said that his earlier attempts in this direction had failed, and then continued, "I cannot suppose that those unfounded Jealousies of the accumulation of power in the hands of the Executive which have been propegated amongst the People with so much industry, and so little success have ever found admittance within these walls, although not well informed as to their source, it is not impossible to beleave that they have a common origin with those unremitted exertions to excite our Indian neighbors to hostilities against us, that infamus policy which would kindle the fury of blood thirsty savages and direct it against our unoffending People, would not be too delicate to attempt by any means to paralise the force which would defeat their machinations. . . . ." Thornbrough and Riker (eds.), *Journals of the General Assembly of Indiana Territory,* pp. 321-22.

used to induce the Indians to consent, but it is really a fact that rumours have been heard here of discontent amongst the Tribes and of their having been under the influence of fear.*

During his absence recommendations drawn in a style of fullsome exaggerated and unmerited praise were industriously circulated every where for his reappointment. His humble tools were seen at work with the teazing importunity of beggars, letting none escape however young, however unknown, however despicable. The streets were watched, the abodes of intemperance were penetrated for that purpose and I have myself seen on an evening of horse races that petition handed about through the confused ranks of an intoxicated croud by boys and persons incapable of seeing the indecorum of their conduct. Examine the signatures and you'll find there wanting the names of those who could alone have given it respectability and weight, and I have reason to believe that he would yet willing resign some scores of those names for those of a few of us. And such is the way that an upright Administration can be imposed upon.[31]

But his masterpiece of tactics is to be seen in his manage-

---

*Gen'l Gibson and Col. Vigo could purchase from the Indians more land in two hours than the Gov'r in ten years & such the influence they have amongst them and the esteem entertained toward them, that the Gov'r applied to them to extricate him out of the difficulties in which he had some years ago involved himself and the U. S. by his purchase from the Delawares, in which they perfectly succeeded.[32]

[31] Petitions to the President and the Senate for and against the reappointment of Harrison are in Carter (ed.), *Territorial Papers,* VII, 703-4, 705-7, 710-11.

[32] The treaty with the Delawares, concluded August 18, 1804. Kappler (ed.), *Laws and Treaties,* I, 70-72. The Miami claimed the lands ceded in this treaty by the Delawares, saying they had not conveyed them to the Delawares, but only allowed them to live thereon. There was considerable discontent among the tribes, and Vigo and Gibson were dispatched to Fort Wayne where they held council with the Delawares, Miami, and Potawatomi, and invited them to come to Vincennes. Esarey (ed.), *Messages and Letters,* I, 133, 137-40, 147. The Miami in the treaty of 1805 acknowledged the right of the Delawares to sell the tract. Kappler (ed.), *op. cit.,* I, 81.

ment of the Legislature in order to obtain their recommendation. In consequence of the division of the Territory he under
the old law made a new apportionment of the members between
the Counties of Indiana, he gave eight to the lower house.[33]
When the Act of Congress[34] taking that power from him and
transferring to the Legislature the apportionment of not less
than *nine* members, was known here, he did not recall his
proclamation but chose rather to exercise a power no more
belonging to him, than to forego the advantages he had
promised himself from the apportionment already made whereby the County of Knox which is not the largest, but the most
obsequious had five members out of thirteen which were to
compose the whole Legislature. Thus he laid the foundation of
his hopes of a recommendation, and a Legislature was formed
illegal in every point of view, which if ever brought into operation must throw the Territory into embarrassments and difficulties. But these were in his eyes subordinate considerations.
You must know also that surprised at the symptoms of independance displayed in the last session he in a fit of anger
& mortification petulantly dissolved them, circumstance of
which Congress appear to have been ignorant, when they
framed the Act giving to the Legislature the apportionment
of their members between the Counties.[35]

He had summoned this anomalous body to meet on the
15th of October last; Although the eastern members came with
unfavourable impressions and surely aware of his designs, he

[33] The proclamation announcing this reapportionment is in Woollen,
*et al.* (eds.), *Executive Journal of Indiana Territory,* pp. 154-55.

[34] Act of February 27, 1809. U. S. *Statutes at Large,* II, 525-26. This
provided that the House should have not less than nine nor more than
thirteen members.

[35] The Governor had dissolved the 1808 session of the Assembly;
according to the Ordinance of 1787 he had this authority. Thornbrough and
Riker (eds.), *Journals of the General Assembly of Indiana Territory,* pp.
268, 314. McNamee, in his letter to the President of the Senate, December
12, 1809, said that he had acted when he found that body not as subservient
to his will as the previous session. Carter (ed.), *Territorial Papers,*
VII, 685.

had the dexterity of bringing four of them (bag and baggage) to his house, while he consigned two others to the *hospitality and guardianship* of Peter Jones one of his Arguses and a zealous and devoted member of the cabinet. Two only would not leave their tavern.

He made them a speech when they met, wherein he had the Tartuffian hypocrisy of ascribing the difficulties he had to encounter in his administration to the same cause which put the Tomahawk and scalping knife in the hands of the Indians, to british influence, to british emissaries! God of Justice! Is it at those marks you'll recognize Mr. Ewing and your old friend? He gave it as his opinion that they might proceed to business and enact laws, provisional if they pleased and not to take effect till Congress had legalized their political existence.— They now declare themselves a constitutional body, presently entertain douts, draft a memorial to Congress to mend the matter, and exhibit every symptom of embarrassment and irresolution. After a few days spent in that ridiculous manner, in doing nothing, the grand object of their convention is at last ushered in. The member from this town who last session stood conspicuous in the ranks of opposition to Slavery, who penned himself so many violent resolutions, who upon being made adjutant and promised more, had nimbly faced about; that very same member moved a resolution for recommending the Governor to the President for a reappointment,[36] those who were in the secret and properly attuned hail the proposal, the members from the East, of whom their constituents expected another conduct, having been plyed at the Governor's & his friend's board with good advice, good drink and good cheer, could not in gratitude give a dissenting vote, said nothing, stupidly believing that their silence could not be construed into acquiescence; One from this County, a very good

---

[36] According to the Assembly journal it was John Johnson who introduced this resolution. Thornbrough and Riker (eds.), *Journals of the General Assembly of Indiana Territory,* p. 338. However, Badollet probably means General Washington Johnston. See above, p. 128n.

man, heroically evaded the difficulty by withdrawing. one alone in the Council had the *boldness* to say *No*.[37] No sooner was this all important affair terminated, than another creature of his Excellency rises, moves a resolution praying the Governor to dissolve them, the resolution passes, the prayer is most graciously granted and thus the indecent farce terminates, and the representatives discovering at last the disgracefull part they had been made to act, steal away home overwhelmed with shame.[38]

> Baissant la queue & portant l'oreille
> Comme un renard qu'une poule auroit pris

Not a whisper, not a cry of indignation was heard. The prostituted penn of Parke drew the recommendation.

I forgot to tell you by what stratagem he obtained the respectable name of Col. Vigo. That worthy man had denied signing the Governor's recommendation, but on a day of general muster a parcel of officers (all appointed by him) invite the good old man to a tavern: form themselves into a committee and place him in the chair before he could divine their business. Then a recommendation in behalf of themselves and the regiment is moved and adopted and the poor Col. seized with the endemical disease, is made to sign it as chairman and is doomed to the unavailing regret of having sanctioned with his

[37] The joint resolution praying Harrison's reappointment is printed in Ewbank and Riker (eds.), *Laws of Indiana Territory, 1809-16*, pp. 770-71. It was signed by General Washington Johnston, speaker of the House of Representatives, and Thomas Downs, president pro tem. of the Legislative Council. Jennings' letter to William Duane (cited above, p. 129n.) was prompted by the appearance in Duane's paper, the Philadelphia *Aurora*, of this resolution. Jennings said that he wrote "as a friend to the honour and interest of the United States, and as a foe to all speculating and intriguing men in office. . . ."

Harrison was nominated by President Madison for reappointment on December 19, and confirmed by the Senate the following day. Carter (ed.), *Territorial Papers*, VIII, 3.

[38] The proceedings of this session of the House, including Harrison's message, may be followed in Thornbrough and Riker (eds.), *Journals of the General Assembly of Indiana Territory*, pp. 315-44. No copy of the journal of the Legislative Council has survived.

hitherto revered name a paper which ought to have raised a blush in the writer's cheek, if he could blush at all.[39]

The same virtuous and patriotic Governor of Indiana, was in partnership with a merchant of this place, who during the firm had the contract for indian supplies and numbers suspect him of being so still, but the connection being more carefully concealed, it is very difficult, if not impossible to ascertain it.[40] And since I am about partnership, I cannot omit that I have no doubt of his being in partnership with Chambers; that conclusion I form from several circumstances remarkably striking, from his notorious thirst for money, evinced in his conduct at the public sales & the fact just above mentioned in his having charged in his accounts of superintendant six sundays, & in his having constantly opposed the termination of the sale before the six weeks were elapsed, from his having made the contract and received the advance of 1500 dollars himself during the absence of Chambers who having appointed an attorney in fact to sign the said contract had directed him to *sign* only and to leave the arrangement to Governor Harrison, from his having pumped out of one of Mr. Toussaint Dubois the proposals which he would make for one of the roads, from two persons having

[39] This resolution signed by Vigo, colonel of the Knox County militia, and David Robb, captain and secretary of the board, appeared in the Vincennes *Western Sun* of November 4, 1809, and is printed in Esarey (ed.), *Messages and Letters,* I, 385-87. According to its contents it was passed by a meeting of the officers of the Knox County militia on October 28, 1809. The resolution expressed confidence in the Governor, in his military talents, his ability to govern the territory, his integrity, patriotism, and attachment to the general government, and prayed his reappointment.

[40] Elias McNamee had been specific in the matter to the President on December 12, 1809, writing, "There is a law of congress which prohibits agents & superintendants of Indian affairs to be concerned in trade with the Indians.—Nothwithstanding which Governor Harrison has been engaged in a merchantile partnership with the contractors for furnishing Indian provisions Indian goods &c.—This fact can be proved by the other partners (viz) Genl John Wilkens Junr of Pittsburgh & George Wallace Junr of this place & by the clerks of said company, (viz) John D. Hay of this place & Saml McConnel of Kentucky." Carter (ed.), *Territorial Papers,* VII, 685. See deposition of George Wallace, Jr., denying Harrison had engaged in supplying the Indians, below, p. 169n.

offered themselves to me for viewers, one of whom *however*
*honest* was & perhaps is still his partner, the other the same
turn coat adjutant mentioned before, from his having himself
dared to recommend to me as viewer one of his most obsequious
valets, from the uncommon zeal manifested by him in behalf
of Chambers, from his having penned for him a letter to you
very *friendly* to myself, from his and his friends displeasure
at my refusing to let Chambers have more money in fine from
the curious proceedings before Parke [in] relation to those
roads.[41] And now that I have mentioned that Parke once more,
permit me to tell you, that, if you want to form an exact idea of
the degree of abject subserviency to his master's views a man
may condescend to stoop to, your eyes must alight upon that
very same judge. Just now a new effusion from his chaste
pen or that of the Governor has appeared before the public,
wherein the devoted Doctor is assaulted in the most disgusting
language of ribaldry, is made out the inventor of the rumours
on the late treaty, which he only related, is called *a lyar* upon
the pretended authority of Mr. Wallace; a man of character &
who could do justice to the Doctor, but wisely declines, because
forsooth he must by doing so break out with the Governor.[42]

[41] See above, pp. 100-2, 103-4n, 108-9.

[42] In the Vincennes *Western Sun,* November 18, 1809. In relation to the
treaty of Fort Wayne (see above p. 132) the piece said, "There is little doubt
but that some abandoned profligate, in the garb of an American, attempted
to frustrate, entirely, the treaty. The Indians had been told, that the President did not want the land; that he had given no instruction for the purpose,
and that the governor was desirous to make the treaty, to retrieve his
declining popularity. . . . News of the treaty no sooner reached this
place than attempts were made to deprecate it, and to induce a belief that
unfair means had been used to obtain it. It was said the purchase would
ruin this place! A story was circulated that there was a number of mal-
contents amongst the Indians; that the Potawatamies and Delawares, and
some of the Miamies, were about to send, or had sent a deputation to the
President of the United States to enter a protest against the treaty. The
tale was thought to be so malicious and unfounded, and of so mischievous
a tendency, as to authorise tracing out its author. Application was therefore
made to colonel John Small, who it was said had related it, for his author.
The colonel, with promptness and candor, wrote to Governor Harrison
that doctor E. McNamee related it to him. Mr. George Wallace then called

I mention this to shew you to what degree of servile apathy they have sunk here, since a man above the vulgar, confessedly full of honour, is willing to abandon an injured man to unmerited obloquy, to avoid the frowns of a petty despot.

Upon what follows you may make your own comments.

Mr. Ewing having brought a suit against Henry Hurst, the intimate of Mr. Harrison for having most outrageously calumniated him, after a number of unnecessary delays the cause was at last brought to trial. Hurst did not even attempt a justification, he pleaded Drunkenness, the Governor only witness summoned by him was allowed by the Court to address a long speech to the jury before he gave his testimony calculated to make wrong impressions on them. That jury composed of the dregs of this place, as incapable truly to appreciate the importance of character as blind men to judge of colours, for men must have attained a certain degree of refinement, to comprehend in its full extent the real value of a good name; that Jury, chosen by a sheriff appointed during pleasure by the Governor found a verdict in favour of the Plaintiff of one cent! It must be observed in this place that by a late statute of this Territory known only to lawyers, in a suit for slander, the plaintiff to recover costs must obtained a verdict of [blank] dollars and some few cents,[43] the Court did not inform the Jury of that Circumstance, made not one single observation recorded the verdict and remained deaf to a motion for a new trial.— I do not believe another instance can be produced of such mockery of justice. But Ewing must receive his reward for

on the Doctor, who, with faltering accents, and with confusion in his face, said, that he had never told colonel Small any such thing ! ! !"

The piece then continued, "It may be thought an humble task to record a circumstance of this kind; But when it is recollected that this *creature* (called M'Namee) holds a distinguished rank in a certain *corps of worthies;* that he has been their drudge, and performed their dirty work for some time past, it will not be considered altogether useless to brand him, in public, with the name he deserves . . . the Doctor cannot escape; and he may hereafter be content to live under the opprobrium of having propagated a wilful, malicious falsehood. . . ."

[43] Philbrick (ed.), *Laws of Indiana Territory, 1801-9,* p. 454.

having presumed to oppose the patriotic plans of his Excellency.[44]

After Doctor McKee had charged publickly the superintendants of the sales with malpractises, a paragraph appeared in the next paper to this purpose. The Editor is authorised to state *that in the charges made against the superintendants of the Sales by a Friend to the Commissioners Governor Harrison is not alluded to.*[45] Mr. Ewing and I who had determined to take no notice of the publication, because no body could mistake the drift of the Doctor, became indignant at the wretch who could thus in contempt of justice and truth turn upon us the torrent of public odium which ought to have over whelmed the guilty Governor alone and I drew in our joint names the piece marked H the only one we have published on the subject.[46] The Doctor in another piece reiterated his accusations, by which the Governor who had thought himself secured from suspicions, was so incensed that in the plenitude of his might he

[44] For earlier reference to this matter see above, pp. 82-83n, and notes. Immediately upon the decision of the court Ewing asked for a new trial because several of the jurors were not freeholders and because the verdict was against the evidence. The court ruled the first cause was entered too late, and in regard to the second said that the court could not grant a new trial because of the smallness of the damages allowed. The court stated, "The Jury's *pennyworth* of damages has vindicated the character of the Plaintiff from the charge brought against him by the Defendant, as fully as tho' he had recovered ten thousand dollars; and I cannot conceive that either in fact or law this explicit declaration of his innocence can be disparaged from the circumstance of his having to pay the costs of suit." Nor could a retrial be granted because one of the jury thought the penny damages would carry cost of suit. "I trust," said the court, "we are not yet quite so degenerate as to graduate character by the paltry scale of pence and farthing. In actions of personal *torts* the damages are imaginery; it is the province of the Jury to estimate the quantum; and I will never contest their verdict unless it should be *outrageously* excessive. . . ." Order book of the General Court of Indiana Territory, 1801-10, pp. 364-65. The court gave reasons why a special jury should not be called and ruled the plaintiff should receive the penny damages and recover no costs.

[45] In Vincennes *Western Sun,* August 15, 1807. See above, pp. 81n, 82n, for previous mention of this.

[46] See below, Appendix, pp. 347-49. This letter was published in *ibid.,* August 22, 1807.

summoned McKee in his office, where he had previously convened a number out of his *faithfull commons* and made an
attack upon him so violent and unexpected, that the poor
Doctor fairly stunned, stammered out some unmeaning
sentences which were by the bye slanders certified and signed.
That certification by the Governor ostentatiously published in
a piece written by him to establish his *own innocence* and in it
were read the following remarkable words. *After the declaration made by the Editor that I was not alluded to I had determined to remain an unconcerned spectator of the contest that
was to ensue.*[47] Cold hearted must the miscreant be who could
see unconcerned the sufferings of injured innocence, when he
at once enjoyed the applause due to integrity & pocketted the
sweeter fruits of guilt! I then brought suit against the Doctor,
that suit never could be tried. Judge Vanderburgh was excepted to by my Attorney, Judge Taylor who had been a
partner of his Excellency at the sales, did not relish that his
name should be so often mentioned in the testimony and of
course would not attend Judge Parke, the delicate Parke could
not sit because forsooth he had once when only a lawyer, said
incidentally in conversation that the offense of the Doctor was
actionable, but he had no objection against sitting in the cause
of Ewing, although he had himself conducted the beginning of
that suit. Thus was mine hung upon tenter hooks to accumu-
late costs, till the Doctor put an end to it by—dying.[48]

Now, in order fully to comprehend this business, you must

[47] In Vincennes *Western Sun,* September 19, 1807. See above, p. 82n.
[48] Henry Vanderburgh, Waller Taylor, and Benjamin Parke were the
judges of the General Court of Indiana Territory, holding their positions
through recommendation by the President and confirmation by the Senate.
Badollet's attorneys were John Johnson and John Rice Jones. The suit of
Badollet *v.* McKee may be followed in the Order Book of the General
Court of Indiana Territory, 1801-10 (pp. 329, 356, 375, 379, 399, 400), from
the September term, 1808, to the April term, 1810. In the April, 1810, term
there is the following entry: "This suit abates by the death of the Defendant." According to a letter of November 29, 1809, from Ambrose
Whitlock to the Paymaster General, McKee died on November 15. Pay-
master General, Register of Letters Received, in National Archives,
Washington, D. C.

know, that the Doctor intended in his defence to prove not mine, that he could not do, but the Governors malversations, flattering himself that, by proving one of the superintendants guilty, he would have made out his case and avoided costs. That is the reason that my cause could never be tried. The paper marked I[49] the original of which is in my hand will throw some additional light on the subject. Such was the fear the Governor had, of having his own conduct exposed in the trial of my suit, that not withstanding his rage against the Doctor who he had called in my presence a perfidious wretch, that subduing resentment & pride, he one day stretched out his hand to him with these words, *come Doctor let us think no more of what is past and come to my house to take a grog with me.* Auri Sacra fames &c.

If what I have attempted to relate, is not sufficient to convince you of the debasement of this unfortunate Territory, you'll be perhaps induced to believe it when I assure that all the circumstances I have mentioned and a thousand others I could add thereto, create no surprise, excite no indignation, the most unexceptionable characters are sunk in a criminal neutrality or rather indifference and in a degrading torpor. A palsying influence is spread over the land. In a word, it is impossible to repell the idea that the nearly total annihilation of that noble sense of independance which ought to animate every american breast, the disappearance of every manly feeling, the extinction of all moral virtue are the fatal fruits of the administration.

There are however some noble exceptions, I would name in this place a number of independant minds who disdain to grace the train of a man whom they cannot esteem and have every reason to detest.

You would feel both pity and indignation could you but see to what company, from the defection of good men he is reduced, who are his intimates & his privy councellors. If there is any political virtue left it is to be found amongst the opponents of this enthroned Machiavel.

[49] See below, Appendix, pp. 349-50.

It may be with truth be said that we live under a system of terror, violence and diffamation are the orders of the day, all social intercourse is destroyed, every mouth is closed, the effusions of the heart are drained in their source, a mutual distrust, too well justified by multiplied instances of perfidy reigns every where, those attractive and amiable dispositions of the heart which unite & draw men together are supplied by a repelling selfishness. Like in the dreary wastes of Asia man is afraid here of meeting his fellow men.*

I must not omitt here to tell you that Chambers made a last attempt upon me through the means of a lawyer, who was then upon friendly terms with me (this fact is another specimen of Vincennes morals) and who for some twenty dollars promised or paid him, attempted to circumvent me and with infernal artifice to induce me to make with Chambers a new arrangement which would have effectually cancelled the contract by which I held him. Seeing me firm, he communicated to me that Chambers would complain at the Treasury of my Official conduct. To such a speech I made the following answer.— *To cut the matter short Mr. Johnston,*[50] *if the sacrifice of my Office must be consequence of my adherence to the plan of conduct which I have prescribed to myself, well, let it go. I have been poor, I can be poor again.*

It appears to me that two reasons militate against that man's reappointment if no other existed. One is the principle of rotation in office which every day more is becoming a vital part of our institutions and which ought to be more so in territorial Governments where so unlimited powers are improperly lodged in & rapidly corrupt the Executive who has no reason to dread public opinion and who can by friends and intrigue secure a reappointment, which in the different States of the

---

*To complete the picture you must know, that here as at Naples or Lisbon stilettos or dirks with a blade about three inches long are in general use among the Gentry who wear them night and day concealed in their bosoms.

[50] General Washington Johnston.

Union is the honourable reward of talents and virtue. And even there the Constitutions wisely guard against too long continuance in Office. The second no less cogent is that as long as our Governor is really or is thought friendly to the admission of Slavery, this Territory will know no peace and its increase will be impeded. Our next Executive ought surely to come from either the State of New York or Pennsylvania, no more Virginians.

Under the circumstances of which I have endeavored to give you a faint idea you will easily conjecture that my life is far, very far from being enviable. Reasons of policy and the difficulty of the undertaking have hitherto protected me against his inveterate malice, how long those causes will continue to operate, is not in my power to tell, in the mean time erect, supported by an approving conscience, convinced that my principles are correct, that my motives are pure, I view undismayed the gathering storm (impavidum farient ruina). But at intervals the idea that an unworthy Officer may receive from Government new marks of confidence, that the wrongs of this Territory may be overlooked, the expiring sparks of virtue it contains may be totally extinguished, that myself & friends may ultimately fall devoted victims, that my fair name, my almost only earthly blessing may at last be blasted, that idea almost unmans me and leaves me a prey to fits of unspeakable anguish. But my mind soon resumes its energy.

When I began to write I little suspected that my letter would swell to such a size, but the subject is inexhaustible & yet I have not said the tenth part of what might be said. There are thousands minute details which perhaps would lead more immediately to the perfect knowledge of this man's heart and principles, which it is almost impossible and which I despair being able to unfold in a letter.

Thus far my much valued friend I have poured my sorrows in your bosom & would be happy in an answer. I entreat to you to bestow some leisure moments if any such you enjoy on the means of getting me away from home. I'll face every difficulty, even poverty itself rather than to live any longer (if no change takes place) in this earthly hell.  Permit me also to entreat you to let me know whether there be any danger of his reappointment, which communication shall remain sacredly buried in my bosom, that I may myself prepare my mind to the event & ruminate in time upon some practicable mode of removing myself to another spot.  Never again should I be found under these accursed territorial governments.  Fare you well and accept the sincere wishes I form for you and yours.

Ever yours

JOHN BADOLLET

P. S.  The report is now running through the County that Ewing is aiming at being Governor himself.  Where that pretty piece of invention to destroy his influence has taken rise is not difficult to guess.

I cannot close my letter without a word more about the Doctor McNamee.  That intelligent man of considerable professional abilities, whom I have known these ten years respectable and respected for his candour veracity & honour having taken a bold Stand is doomed to be a first victim.  In answer to the scandalous piece issued against him from head quarters, he offered a vindication to the printer who refuses peremptorily to publish it.

Pray get the Certificate marked I[51] published in the intelligencer.

I accidentally laid my hands upon the paper marked K[52] containing a striking instance of the base artifices employed to delude the public  The number of *the Citizen of Vincennes* attached to it, is also transmitted that you may form an opinion of his manner of writing & the motives which actuate him. You must know that no other writer, that we know of on the Governor's side than the Governor himself, Parke or Randolph, that they form a kind of partnership to retail sophistry and abuse.  Edifying occupation for an Executive and a Judge!

[51] See below, Appendix, pp. 349-50.
[52] Not in the Gallatin Papers.

The papers marked A B & C are the only ones which I have written. They have been written too much in haste to be passable, but I trust that the reasons are solid and arguments correct. Do not destroy them. I have preserved no copies.

The paper marked L[53] is the production of either the Hero of the tale himself, or of his amanuensis E. Westfall under his direction or of the noble Judge. The piece is worth reading. T[h]e documents I have thus enclosed you are all worth your perusal; they will explain better the situation we are in than ten pages of mine, and give you a better idea of the man who is the prime mover & soul of the party.

[Ewing to Gallatin]

VINCENNES Nov'r 22d 1809

SIR I was in hopes to have been able to have sent you my accounts respecting the roads for settlement by this mail,[1] but have been disappointed by the surveyor who laid out the part of the road on the direction to Louisville which Coll. B. Chambers had contracted for laying off, but which has been rejected by the Vewers as altogether impasable. This part is laid out and opened but not yet measured. as soon as I receive the plat of it I will forward it with my accounts to you.

I have compleated the road from Vincennes to the Boundry line on the direction to Cincinata also the road to Louisville. they have cost upwards of one thousand dollars. the road from Vincennes to St. Louis remains in the same situation it was left by B. Chambers & is altogether impasable for Waggons. it will cost between 3 & 400 dollars to compleat it—

On receiving your letter requesting me to lay the business of the roads before Judge Park, I desisted from compleating the western Road untill his report should be made to you. I however cannot help suggesting that this report ought to be received with caution. I know not what It contains, but I know that Coll. Cambers procured the depositions of some of the

---

[53] Not found in the Gallatin Papers and not identified. It is probably a clipping from the *Western Sun.*

[1] For earlier references to these roads see above, pp. 100-1, 101-2, 104n.

most unprincipled & worthless men in the Territory to contradict the report of the Vewers. I have also good reason to blieve that governor Harrison is in partnership with Chambers in this Contract he has however taken a Verry active part for Chambers, & Park has always been his Creatur.[2]

It is almost impossible to have any public business done here with good faith intrigue & speculation runs so high— I hope to be able to send all my accounts relative to the roads with my next monthly returns.

I am Dr Sir with sincere esteem your obt Servt

NATH'L EWING

THE HON'BLE A. GALLATIN ESQ'R

SECRETARY OF THE TREASURY

[Addressed:] The Hon'ble Albert Gallatin Secretary of the Treasury

[Endorsed:] Vincennes 22 Novemb 1809 Nath'l Ewing

[Badollet to Gallatin]

VINCENNES December 10, 1809

I herein enclosed send you an address of young R. Jones to his constituents after the session of the Legislature wherein Jesse B. Thomas was elected to Congress notwithstanding the most scandalous tricks of intrigue had been played off to carry Michael Jones of Kaskaskias, a favourite at Headquarters.[1] A few days after the appearance of this piece, that unfortunate and interesting youth was assassinated in broad day! ! !

[2] On June 29, 1809, Chambers complained to President Madison that money justly due him was being withheld by Badollet and Ewing, and begged a hearing before one of the judges of the territory. Carter (ed.), *Territorial Papers*, VII, 658-59. The President referred the matter to Gallatin who requested Judge Benjamin Parke to investigate and report to him. *Ibid.*, VII, 664-65. On November 2, Judge Parke reported to Gallatin that he was still engaged in the investigation, that both parties had produced a number of witnesses, and that Ewing still had evidence to submit. *Ibid.*, VII, 679. Adjustment was made according to the Judge's report, but Chambers was still not satisfied. The matter was finally settled in August, 1811. *Ibid.*, VIII, 55-56, 67-68, 128.

[1] The address is printed in the Appendix, below, pp. 351-56. For earlier reference to this election see above, p. 118n.

Fare-you well, remember your devoted friend

JNO BADOLLET

P. S. The rage was such at the disappointment, that J. B. Thomas was hung in effigy on the Gallows. We did not see the perpetrators of the indignity at that noble work but are morally sure of the quarter whence it proceeded.

[Badollet to Gallatin]

VINCENNES January 1, 1810

This will be handed to you by the Reverend Urbain Guillet Superior of the Community denominated la Trappe now settling in the Illinois Territory. Their institution besides religion embraces objects of no small importance in a country where ignorance & a too deplorable want of active industry have excited in every philantropic mind the most painfull emotions. The Diffusion of the rays of scientific knowledge, the teaching of a variety of usefull arts, the blessings of education where it is lamentably neglected or out of the reach of the greatest number, are objects which in a patriotic point of view, cannot but be considered as of the first importance, and the men who devote their lives to their attainment must become interesting to an enlightened Government and have strong claim to its protection, to its fostering care. That religious community possesses men of Science, artists of merit and mechanics of unusual skill. They have obtained four hundred acres of land, which, considering the magnitude of their intended establishment, fall short of the quantity requisite for rendering it complete. They wish to purchase more from the United States, provided they could be allowed a longer credit, than is usually granted. Such is the object of the respectable person whom I have taken the liberty of introducing to your notice, & he is gone to the Federal city to present a petition to Congress for that purpose. Should the view, which the developpement he will present you, of their plan and of their means, lead your mind to such conclusions as I have formed, I feel no hesitation in believing that you'll consider the ad-

vantages likely to flow from their undertaking, as greatly out-
weighing the trifling loss which the United States may suffer
by granting their request.[1]

I remain as usual Ever Yours

JNO. BADOLLET

[Addressed:] Albert Gallatin Esqr  Secretary of the
Treasury  Washington City

Fav'd by Rev'd Urbain Guillet

[Endorsed:]  Vincennes 1 January 1810  Badollet introduces Rev'd Urbain Guillet

[Badollet to Gallatin]

VINCENNES May 29, 1810

A business is preparing here of which I thought it proper
to give you timely information.  The Wabash company is going
to bring their claim before our General Court.[1]  Harper in
behalf of the Company has written to Gov'r Har'n to appoint
him the Company's agent.  The *exalted virtue* of his Excellency
prevented him from accepting the trust, but he took care to
committ the business to two lawyers of this place the most
venal wretches in existence.  I have been told that he wrote to
you to have the defense of the suit entrusted to Tho's Randolph
who not yielding in point of *virtue* to his Ex'y would not act
against the U. S. & of whose independance of mind & talents
you may, by this time, be able to form a pretty correct judgement.  The plan is to bring an ejectment against a purchaser
within the claimed limits, and when we consider the materials
of which our court is composed and that there is no appeal
from its decisions, this business bids fair to become as prolific
a source of trouble to Congress as the Yazous claim.

It is likely that some lawyer from abroad will be appointed

---

[1] A petition to Congress by Urbain Guillet, dated November 29, 1810,
for additional land for the Trappist association located about nine miles
north of Cahokia, is in Carter (ed.), *Territorial Papers,* XVI, 140-41.
See also pp. 89-90. This group of refugee Trappists from France resided
in Illinois only from 1809 to 1813. *Dictionary of American History* (5
volumes plus index. New York, 1940), V, 312.

[1] For earlier reference to the Wabash Land Company see above, pp.
47-48n, 51.

to defend the suit, but should it be thought proper to appoint one from this Territory either as principal or assistant I deem it my duty to mention John Johnson[2] as a man of fair character, of no despicable ingenuity and possessed of *no less* professional knowledge than Mr. Randolph.

I'll say no more on this subject, it is very probable you'll see as far into it as myself.— In our days splendid villainies pass for virtue, they indicate grand and daring souls! Woe to the wretch who steals a pony he goes here to the gallows.

If you recollect the mention I made of a Tavern bully going into the country at the eve of the election with blanc commissions of justices of the peace[3] you'll think it not preposterous in me to mention, that Mr. Joseph Dunlap son of the Principal of Canonsburgh college, is the man who was called upon to fill the blancs with the name of the person then selected or rather bought.

Sometime ago I presented to General Gibson an assignment accompanied with an acknowledgment received by an *acting* Magistrate to have a certificate and the Territorial Seal affixed to it. He told that he knew of no such Magistrate no such name was on his record, that the Governor was in the habit of sending frequently blanc commissions and of making him test them. Those Commissions are as convenient as bank bills, the bearer whoever he may be, is intitle[d] to the benefits conferred by them and number of Magistrates exercise their judicial powers in this Territory whose very names are, at least for a time, unknown to the Executive. This is discharging one's duty with a vengeance, but it is such an excellent stratagem before an election.

You'll come to Fayette this year, pray let me know in time. Fare you well. I remain Ever yours

JOHN BADOLLET

[Addressed:] Albert Gallatin Esq  Private

[2] See sketch of Johnson in Thornbrough and Riker (eds.), *Journals of the General Assembly of Indiana Territory,* pp. 985-87. No evidence of such a suit being filed has been found.

[3] See above, p. 127.

[Badollet to Gallatin]

VINCENNES June 24 1810

Averse to writing, unable to do it without much labour, it is with reluctance I take up the pen even to commune with the friend of my youth, and that reluctance is increased by the considera[tion] that in the midle of his multifarious and important occupations, there can hardly be an interval left for the enjoyment of private correspondence. But our situation here is so singular and in the mean time so awfull, that I claim a few moments of attention to what follows.

I think that I informed you once, that rumours were afloat concerning the late treaties with the indians, as having been concluded under circumstances not very short of compulsion.[1] These rumours have kept increasing and the Governor himself added weight to them by boasting in presence of witnesses that one Winemack (or some such name), a young Potowatamie lately made chief by him, had declared to the Miamis, that if they did not sign the treaty he would drive them into the lake.[2] The Potowatamies being a powerfull tribe, that threat had the desired effect. No other tribe I am informed, has any claim to the land adjoining Vincennes district if you except the Weahs Kickapoos and Piankishaws. You may remember my having informed you, that the greatest part of the tribes which had been invited to Vincennes last fall declined coming and that on their not appearing the Governor went himself to Fort Wayne.

Some time ago the salt sent by the Governor to the Prophet,

---

[1] See above, pp. 132-33.

[2] Winamac appears in the journal of the proceedings of the council and treaty as one of the leading figures. Esarey (ed.), *Messages and Letters*, I, 362-78. Harrison wrote to the Secretary of War on May 15, 1810, "I have confidence in Winamac, a Potawatomi chief who is now with the Prophet, and I am certain that his utmost exertions will be used in the first place, to prevent hostilities or if he should be unsuccessful in this to give me information of their designs." *Ibid.*, I, 420. See also pp. 427, 433-34.

was refused by him and sent back,[3] and a young man named John Gamlin entrusted with the salt told me that the Prophet had declared to him, that, if any attempts were made to Survey the lands lately purchased, the Surveyors should survey no more. That Prophet, a Mahomet in miniature appears to have taken advantage of the indians' discontent to augment his influence by espousing their cause. In the mean time Indians were daily seen passing up the Wabash even from the Missoury and numbers occasionally tarried in the town.

Last monday I received a message from the Governor, by which my presence was requested at the Secretary's office; I was very busy in mine & not conceiving myself under the obligation of neglecting my business to attend his Summons, I answered that I was not at leisure, but being soon obliged to go to the Receivers office, I reflected that since I was out, it would be more becoming to go. On drawing near, I perceived the room was full of people & made every little doubt but that he had there convened that croud to witness some inquisitorial lecture he was going to give me, a thing not seldom practiced by him, as you'll see in the sequel and I prepared myself to resist and resent it. On my entrance he was speaking and interrupted himself to address me with a recapitulation of what he had been saying. He mentioned that he had received numerous informations of an intended attack on the part of the Prophet and his followers whose numbers he represented as truly formidable. He added that the Prophet was to come with a few to his house, dispatch him first, and then give the signal to the rest dispersed unsuspected through the town to begin a general slaughter. He painted his fears in lively colours and said that if it was not for fear of spreading too great an allarm, he would immediately send his family to Kentucky and convert his house unto a fort. He expressed doubts and embarrassments about the mode of conduct proper to pursue, and a great

[3] Harrison reported this incident to the Secretary of War on June 15. Esarey (ed.), *Messages and Letters*, I, 426-27. The Prophet is Tenskwatawa or Elskwatawa, a Shawnee, twin brother of Tecumseh.

unwillingness to take any measure without the advice of the most *respectable* part of the Gentlemen of the Town and of the different officers of Government. By this time I had surveyed the group & found that excepting three or four, it was composed of men on whose obsequiousness he could rely. That modesty and diffidence being things very unusual with him, I suspected some hidden views. I suspected a trap. I saw at least plainly enough that he intended to shift the responsibility of a serious step from his own shoulders upon ours, and determined to be silent. Somebody suggested the organizing the militia (which by the bye ought to always [be] organised) on which, suddenly catching the idea, he said, Well since it is your advice Gent'n I'll immediately order out two companies of militia. At these words the idea of the farcical and unmilitary means of defense adopted last year,[4] so little calculated for effectual protection rushed into my mind and uncommonly allarmed I said in an audible voice that spies ought to be employed upon which a short conversation ensued relative to the subject. You must know that before those honest unpremeditated expressions dropped from my lips, my fears had been considerably encreased by the opinion of a Mr. Dubois[5] a respectable Indian Trader of this place, that the danger was real and very great.[6]

The information flew like wild fire, some laugh at it, but

[4] For Badollet's reference to this see above, pp. 127-29.
[5] Toussaint Dubois.
[6] On June 19 Harrison sent an account of this meeting to the Secretary of War: ". . . I was extremely averse to create any alarm until the necessity for it should appear unequivocal, but since the return of the salt boat the report of the crew of the number of Indians collected around the Prophet and the insolence of their conduct has created so much apprehension upon the part of the citizens that I deemed it advisable to assemble the public officers the merchants and other respectable citizens to take their advice upon the subject of putting the country in a state of defence. To these gentlemen the danger appeared so imminent that they unanimously urged and advised me to call two companies into actual service and to put all the rest of the Militia upon the alert—this has accordingly been done and alarm posts established and such other measures adopted as the

with the greatest number the terror is great and distress inexpressible. Removals out of the Territory have begun and are likely to multiply. Under the impression that our danger arose out of the discontents created by circumstances of the late treaties, discontents artfully improved by the Prophet, with the repetition of the scenes at Wyoming before our eyes, with our woods and streets filled with indians who upon a signal might be converted into sanguinary enemies, with a militia in a most lamentable state, it may be well conjectured that our distress was no common one. Some of us were considering whether there existed not some practicable means of averting the impending danger and met at my office to converse more at our ease. We had learnt that the above mentioned Mr. Dubois who is well known by and has many friends amongst the indians, had offered the Governor to go himself to the Prophet and learn the cause of their discontents to which proposal the Governor had made an evasive answer.[7] On the supposition that such cause would be found in the late treaties, we all feared that that information might not be readily communicated to Government. Some proposed that we should openly send a man to the Prophet with instructions to ascertain the cause of the indians' dissatisfaction and to assure them of the friendly dispositions of the inhabitants towards them and that we should lay the information received before the President. Mr. Ewing and I could not be brought to approve of

occasion called for and my means would allow." Esarey (ed.), *Messages and Letters,* I, 428.

The Vincennes *Western Sun* of June 23, carried an interview with Harrison on the status of Indian affairs in which the same picture as that sent to the Secretary of War is given. Here it also states that it was the unanimous opinion of those present in the Secretary's office, which included the secretary of the territory, a judge of the supreme court, the representatives of Knox County, the register of the land office, and county officers, that two companies of militia should be called immediately into service.

[7] On June 15, Harrison had written to the Secretary of War, "As soon as I hear that the Indians have generally collected at the Prophets I shall send them a speech such as I think calculated to reassure our friends and intimidate those that are hostile." Esarey (ed.), *Messages and Letters,* I, 428.

that plan. I urged that such a step would have the appearance, and undoubtedly would be represented as a preposterous interference with the province of the legal organ of Government, and perhaps as intended to impede its operations. On the suggestion that I was affraid, I observed that I felt when conscious of my innocence, that I possessed the fortitude to dispise even calumny, but yet when I meant to do right, I was not disposed rashly to seek for the rewards of guilt. I insisted that the only practicable and safe plan was to encourage Mr. Dubois to go for the Governor, that honest and blunt he would conceal no truth. It was proposed, if Dubois did not go, to request one Benako who had to go up the Wabash in hunt of horses, to go to the Prophet's residence and to learn the real cause of the threatening attitude said to be assumed by him and his numerous adherents, but before we came to a final determination I was desired to go to Mr. Dubois, to ask whether he was still disposed to go for the Governor, & if not, whether he would go in a private capacity. Thus we parted.

On my way to Mr. Dubois' house, my dislike to any interference of private persons grew every minute stronger & the impropriety of such step presented itself to my mind in a more forcible manner. I considered that not only the intentions must be pure, which was certainly the case with us, but that the means must also be lyable to no objection, & I finally determined to put a stop to the project.

Mr. Dubois answered me that if the Governor would send him he was still willing to go for him but for him alone. I commended his determination and entreated him to persist therein. I must confess that I had but faint hopes of the Governor consenting to employ him.[8] I hastened to Ewings, whose objections to the plans proposed at first had all along been even greater than mine, & communicated to him my settled determination. He then informed me that the Governor had

[8] On June 26 Harrison reported to the Secretary of War, "I have dispatch'd Col. Vigo to the Miamis and a Mr. Dubois another french gentleman to the Prophet." Esarey (ed.), *Messages and Letters*, I, 434.

caused Judge Johnson to be brought before him in the Secretary's office, where he had summoned a number of witnesses, and then and there in an angry magisterial and insulting manner had called him to account for his having been with us & imperiously made him declare what he had seen & heard.[9] You may see by this, what better check we have in this Territory upon the Judiciary under such an all vigilant Executive, than you can boast of with your impeachments &c— This indignity has been highly resented by his Son an attorney of character who was also with us, & some letters have past between the Governor and him which may eventually lead to disagreable consequences.[10]

Thus this unrelenting Tyrant believes that he has at length got hold of the so much wished for opportunity of injuring us and he no doubt will improve it. He exults in the idea that he will make us smart severely for our daring perseverance in

[9] In the *Western Sun* of July 7 there is a statement by James Johnson regarding this meeting. It is practically the same as his affidavit given for Ewing (p. 165, below). He opened it by saying that he had been charged with holding a private seditious meeting in Badollet's office on the evening of June 19, 1810. He declared that the gentlemen present had no intention of interfering with the proceedings of the Governor and that the door to the office was not locked. Johnson had served as judge of the Knox County court of common pleas since 1801 and as territorial treasurer since 1805. Woollen, *et al* (eds.), *Executive Journal of Indiana Territory*, pp. 92, 96, 129, 131.

[10] The son was John Johnson. It is of interest to note that the *Western Sun* of June 30 reported a meeting of Knox County citizens called by John Johnson to consider the Indian situation. Apparently a pro-Harrison faction seized control. John Gibson was elected chairman and William Prince secretary. Johnson moved that a committee of correspondence be appointed of persons living throughout the territory to give alarm of impending danger and also a committee to procure ammunition. This motion was not seconded and thus fell. General Washington Johnston then moved that the Governor be invited to attend and address the meeting on the Indian situation and the steps that had been taken for the security of the territory. The Governor complied and thereafter resolutions were unanimously adopted warmly approving the action of the Governor. It was also resolved, "That it appears to this meeting that the proceedings of certain individuals in calling public and private meetings for the purpose of adopting measures relating to the present crisis, have been dictated rather by personal enmity to the Governor, than motives of public benefit, and that they deserve public execration."

opposing his darling and never abandoned plan of Slavery. Convinced that we know him well, that he has no bait for us, he hates because he is forced to respect us, & he contemplates in our dismissal a gratifying revenge for the contempt we hold him in. He has been a long time bent upon our destruction, & Mrs. Harrison has been heard to say that Dr. McNamee being now reduced to beggary (which is not true by the bye) the Gov'r would soon bring us to the same condition if he could. We may be dismissed for ought I know, from the same causes which so unaccountably procured his Ex'y's reappointment, and we will rejoice that in our Country two men can be found of a more irreproachable conduct than ours. But let not those two men be sought for in Vincennes, where many are panting for our places & where the Governor [has] so many flexible sycophants to reward.

Since those circumstances have taken place, my conjectures have been fully confirmed, in the very first paper printed, the Governor has had a piece inserted, wherein I and few others are singled out and affectedly mentioned by name—as the advisors of the measures now in operation and such an incorrect information will no doubt be officially communicated to the President.[11] He will represent himself as forced into a measure for which he panted. Should the danger be not real (which may God grant) the object of the present warlike attitude can be no other than that of awing the discontented tribes into silence about the purchase of their lands, as the military farce of last year was so evidently intended to persuade the Wabash indians that the only mode of preserving peace with the United States was to sell them more land.

Acquainted with the unblemished virtues of the President, accustomed to view him as the legal and zealous guardian of our happiness, we always thought that a direct manly application to him never could be improper, still less be treated with a marked contempt and great have been both our Sorrow and astonishment, that the important communications of Dr. Mc-

[11] See note 6, above.

Namee made little or no impression. We hoped at least that the President would pause—[12] Having everything to fear from the resentment of the Governor and nothing to reap from that step, but the noble pleasure of contributing to a general good, the Dr manly stepped forward unappalled by the Colossus he dared to prorogue. We are yet to learn that humble merit, unattended by the pageantry of wealth, a sounding name or the glitter of office is not a sufficient passport to obtain a prudent degree of attention, we have yet to learn that in a government as we have the happiness to live under splendid connexions are the indispensable requisite for permission to approach our common father— Mr. Ewing and myself knowing that a faithfull discharge of our official duties was *all* that could be required of us, have endeavoured to fullfill them with rectitude; we are yet to learn that by becoming officers of the United States we forego the priviledges of Citizens and are excused from the duties which that title imposes. We are yet to learn, that in order to preserve our stations we must bow in humble subserviency to the will of a breveted despot and assist or at least not oppose measures of short sighted and criminal policy,— measures which in return for some transient and very questionable advantages will entail upon us and our posterity cruel and endless regrets, we are yet to learn that we must see our sacred right of election trampled upon, a shamefull traffick of offices in open operation & number of other transgressions and remain silent. Virtue is strength, it is by exerting that strength that we attempt to resist the tide of corruption which in this place threatens to overwhelm morals independance of mind and political virtue in our common ruin. In such disposition of mind, we look down upon the preservation of our offices as an object of minor & subordinate consideration, which we would not obtain at the price of a single *pang* of conscience. We know we are not wedded to them, from Mr. Jefferson we received them, Mr. Madisson may resume them without excit-

---

[12] A reference to McNamee's letters to the President and the President of the Senate. See above, pp. 130-31n.

ing in our breasts a single murmur. But in such a case, we claim from his justice, and we implore your assistance therein, that he will condescend to assign his reasons for withdrawing his confidence and not leave us by an unceremonious dismissal exposed to the inference of prevarication in office. We can disdain the loss of our stations, but a stain upon our reputations would *make us poor indeed*.

Farewell my dear Friend et do not forget Your poor exiled

JOHN BADOLLET

[Ewing to Gallatin]

VINCENNES June the 26th 1810

DEAR SIR

I hope you will pardon me when necessity compells me to apply to you for protection against the persecutions of Governor Harrison. I have borne with patience all his malice & injustice from the consolation that I had incurred it by adhearing to my duty as an officer of the United States and am truly sorry for the necessaty which oblidges me to make this communication.

The speculations of this man had involved him in debts greater than what he could spair from his salery would satisfy. he became importunate with me for to assist him. this was out of my power in any great degree without injury to myself and betraying the trust reposed in me. but no excuse I could make was satisfactory and nothing would do but a positive & flat denial. he immediately withdrew his friendship and presently became my persecutor which he continues with unremitted violence.

It was my misfortune to apply to him to sign the recommendation for my appointment. the letter which contain'd this application he had safely kept and to shew my ingratitude he had this letter hawked about the whole country.

You can have no idea of the tyrannical disposition of that man his whole system of government is by terror and corruption.

At the public sales in 1807 this mans speculation ware scandelous he wish'd to draw me in for a partner but did no succeed he associated with four or five others their plan was to discover the numbers of fractions or sections intended to be purchased by the people attending the sales. (for none of them knew any thing of the country themselves) when this done the[y] ware sure to mak a speculation by getting money to prevent them bidding.

I will relate one of many cases of the Dexterrity of this man & his associates an Old Dutchman of the name of Funk had selected a fraction to purchase. the Governor & his company found by some means the number and on the morning of the day on which this tract was offered for sale one of the company went to Mr. Funk & informed him that he understood that he intended to bid for such a fraction. Mr. Funk said he did the speculator told him that he intended to bid for it also, but added that if he Mr. Funk would not bid but let them get the land at the lowest price he should have it for a trifling compensation. to this the old man agreed & they got the land at two dollars, but you may judge of the surprise of Funk when he was told that the trifling compensation was between six & seven hundred dollars. Mr. Funk remonstrated against it as unjust & hard but the Gov'r told him that if Mr. Rector had not mad that promise, he should not have the land for $1000, as he that day saw a letter from a Gentleman in Kentucky to his friend here authoriz'g him to bid as high as fifteen dollars per acre for that fraction the old man was oblidged to comply and give them their demand.

The Governor & his company herd that I had intended to purchase a fraction at the mouth of Wabash him & Judge Taylor came to me in the name of Tho's Jones & told me they would bid against me. I replied verry well let him bid, they asked how much I would give if he would not bid. I replied nothing. some time after Governor Harrison came to me again & offered that if I would not bid for that fraction he would give me $350, certain & all that the land could be got for less than $3.50 pr acre. I told him I wanted none of his money and was surprised at his offer, but since he appeared so anxious I would have nothing to do with it. Taylor & Rector went immediately to Jones & made him give $200 or they would bid against him. I relate those facts both to give you some Idea of this mans principles and because I have had to suffer for *his* crimes. On investigating my official conduct on the charges made against me by H. Hurst, it was discovered that it was the Governor who had been guilty of misconduct but he had the address to keep the evidenc which would have criminated him from the record, and he immediately made friends with Hurst to prevent his making charges against him this will account to you for his pretended friendship to me in the letters he wrote to you on that subject he wished to have an end put to the business.[1]

Another great crime I have committed against him I dared to express my opinion in respect to the admission of slavery and have also dared to join in opposition to it. this has been a darling plan of his ever since he has been governor of the territory.[2]

This man has carried his vindictive wrath against me to such a lenth as to address a Jury before whome I had a cause depending to prevent my obtaining justice and was suffered by the court to do so, & that jury summoned from the verry dreggs of the people by a sheriff holding his office from him and during his pleasure. jurors are not selected here by ballot but by the sherif for to answer any purpose.[3]

He has lately raised a dreadful alarm of Indians has drafted two companies of militia put them in the service of the United States and stationed them at the upper end of the Town of Vincennes near his own house. this shews that he does not believe there is danger or that it is only his own safety he seeks & not the protection of the country, in general as the men

[1] For earlier reference to this see above, pp. 82-83n, 139-40n.
[2] See above, pp. 102, 121, 156-57.
[3] A reference to Ewing's suit against Hurst.

are drawn from the frontier which is left to be protected by the women and children. in this situation a few Citizens who had not confidence in the governor proposed a meeting at Mr. Badollets office.[4] I was requested to attend I told them I would have nothing to do with it that however good their intentions might be they would be misrepresented but having some business at the office I went up with Judge Johnson whome I wished to take the acknowledgment of a conveyance. there ware perhaps six or seven still there who was conversing on the subject of Indian hostilities & I found that they all ware of oppinion that the alarm was unfounded as it was last year—propositions ware mad by some of them to ascertain whether there ware any grounds for the alarm but what the[y] ware I do not positively recollect. nothing however was concluded on  Mr Badollet said that Mr Dubois has offered his services to the governor to go to the Town of the Prophet and that he would ascertain it if the governor would send him. The people then went out in less than fifteen minutes after I went in during the whole time I was there I did not open my mouth on the subject. I avoided having any thing to do with this business knowing the malignant enmity of the governor against me. immediately when the people went out Governor Harrison had Judge Johnson taken up to the Secretarys office & there interogated him in an imperious manner as to the purport of the meeting[5] the judge related all he had herd  he enquired whether there ware any officers of the United States there, and exclaimed he would level them he would have them dismissed from office. accordingly as we are informed he made charges against us to the President, but I hope the President will not condemn us unherd.

We had but just got over the alarm he raised last year and the people had began to come into the Territory when this new one took place. The inhabitand are flying from the country and governor Harrison said in a public meeting if it was

---

[4] For Badollet's reference to this meeting see his letter of June 24 above.
[5] See above, p. 156.

not for creating *too* great an alarm he would take his family to Kentucky & give his house for a Block-house to defend the upper part of the Town. this had the effect to increase the fears of the people and you cannot conceive the suffrings of those families on the frontiers whose men ware drafted to be stationed in Town.

The Shawnea Prophet of whome he protends so much fear has his Town on the Wabash between this & fort Wayne, People are passing every week they say that him and his people are peaceble and treat them well. They are buisely employed cultivating their corn of which they have between 100 & 200 acres under good fence they are getting a tolerable stock of cattle, and prohibits spiritous liquors from being brought to this town. It is as he says one of the commandment of the Great Spirit not to taste it, as it is the poison of the White People. he protends to have personal communication with the deity and it appears to be his object to unite all the Indians N W of Ohio & Missippi in one goverment of which he wishes to be the great chief. For this purpose he has laid hold on superstition & protends to have personal communications with the deity, & and when he becomes strong enough those who will not believe in him he will compell by force. This is in my oppinion what occations the disturbance amongst the indians, but without any intention to meddle with the whites.

This business may end unpleasantly the indians are and have always been constantly in our settlements the white people are truly alarmed and cannot know whether they are friends or enemies some may perhaps be killed we will then have war in earnest, as many of the Indians now believe it to be the intention of the governor to make war on them.

I hope you will excuse the trouble I put you to by reading those statements as I have been compelled to make them. I Enclose you one of the Gov'rs letters to me and also the certificate of Judge Johnson to corroborate my assertions. I am Dr.

Sr. with the greatest esteem your Obedient Serv't

NATH'L EWING

ALBERT GALLATIN Esquire

[Addressed:]    Albert Gallatin Esqr Secretary of the Treasury *Private*

[Endorsed:] Vincennes June 26 1810 Nat Ewing Wants to be protected against G'r Harrison

[Enclosures]

GROUSELAND 1st Decr 1808

DEAR SIR

When Capt'n Johnston commanded here I borrowed of him $1000 which he has transferred to a gentleman who is now here—determining not to disappoint him I sent out to Mr. Elliott & offered him my lot No. 47 which he has long wanted—but unfortunately he had disposed of all his money for other land. Esq'r McClure & his brother in law Scott both want it, but neither have the money in hand—the former has a considerable sum at New Lancaster, in Ohio & he has offered me a Draft for any part of it that I wish, but this will not answer as the Gentleman who holds my note lives in Tennessee. If you can by any means find me a few Hundred Dollars to assist in making up the Am't I want it will confer a great obligation & I will deposit McClures draft with you & will also bind myself to send for it any time you require it. If I cannot command it by other Means when you wish it paid I shall certainly have it in my power to retire it in the course of a very few weeks & will satisfy you on that Head—Give me an order on Wallace for any sum you may choose to spare.

Yours with Regards

WILL'M H HARRISON

N. EWING Esq'r                              turn over

In order effectually to guard against disappointment when you want the money I will give both Wallace & Bullitt as securities.

W H H

On the evening of the nineteenth June Eighten hundred & teen Being in the Burrow of Vincennes I met with Mr. Ewen Receiver of publick monys at the store of T. Jones. He asked me to walk with him. I accordinly did on the way he told me he wanted that I should call at Mr. Vigos and take the acknowledgment of a conveyance for a piece of land he had bought of him and that he was going to Mr. Badolets office and as soon as he got his horse he would ride out with me When we arived at the office I found there Mr. Mcintosh[1] A. Marshal[2] P. Rieue [?] J Caldwell[3] E. Minimee[4] & Jno. Johnson perhaps one or two more. The Conversation turned on the common report of the Indians being hostile it appeared to be the general opinion of those present that there was no truth in the report which coincided with my own. An observation was made by Mr. Mcintosh on the propriety of a Varble message to the Indians by the people to ascertain whether or no the[y] ware displeased with or intended to make war on the setlars at or nare Vincennes & that Dubois should cary the message as he was suposed to go on business for the Governor and that J. Badolet and one other should wait on Dubois to ascertain wither he would deliver the message or not I observed that it would be well in doing this not to infring on the prorogative of the Governer as he had the exclusive superintendance of Indian afairs. Mcintosh and some others present said the[y] did not intend to interfer with the proceedings of the Governor in any respect whatever. This is all I recolect that pased at Badolets office which on my interrogation I related to the Governer.

JAS. JOHNSON

P. S. not more than fifteen minutes after Mr. Ewen and I arived at the office the people went away and I do not recollect of Mr. Ewen making any observation dureing our stay at the office

JAS. JOHNSON

[1] William McIntosh.
[2] Antoine Marechal.

[3] John Caldwell.
[4] Elias McNamee.

[Badollet to Gallatin]

VINCENNES September 25, 1810

I am Slowly retreating from that fatal bourn from which for several weeks I contemplated eternity having been brought there by a singular kind of slow or nervous fever which has produced in me a nearly total prostration of mental & bodily powers and left me nothing but the sense of suffering. My distress was greatly increased by the circumstance of there being nobody here to whom I could or would delegate the business of my Office; at last about the sixth or seventh week of my illness Mr. Jennings providentially arrived and by easing me of that trouble contributed to my recovery. Mr. Caldwell, who does the business of Mr. Ewing, was kind enough to make the entries in my book of entries for me;[1] but could not, on acc't of his own occupations, do any thing else, so that, till the arrival of Mr. Jennings, my journal ledger &c were in arrears. I mention this circumstance to obviate any possible charitable reticence of Mr. Parke in the account he has given you of the state of my books.[2] I begin to attend the Office but remain extremely weak & my lower extremities swell, except when I am lying down. This will sufficiently account for my delays in answering some official Letters I had received from the Treas'y Department.

We are here in a singular and awfull situation, the warlike attitude of the Governor and the fears he has excited throughout this county— are such that a spark may produce an indian war, some fearless man may believe that by Shooting an indian he'll perform a deed of heroism and by exciting retaliation

[1] John Caldwell received pay as clerk to the board of commissioners. Carter (ed.), *Territorial Papers,* VIII, 123. See sketch in Thornbrough and Riker (eds.), *Journals of the General Assembly of Indiana Territory,* p. 962. He was to become son-in-law to Badollet, marrying Sally (Sarah) Badollet on February 10, 1814. Knox County Marriage Records, I, 180, Genealogy Division, Indiana State Library.

[2] Benjamin Parke served as examiner of the books of the register and receiver.

kindle a general conflagration. Those who see more deeply
in those matters, remain persuaded that all this bustle is owing
to the late treaties, which have excited a general discontent
amongst the Wabash Tribes, they aver that these military
movements, the parading of the militia, the arrival of regulars
is intended to awe them into silence and they laugh at the idea
of a coalition amongst so many nations to fall upon us at so
many points at once. It is a fact that if the Indians do not like
us they fear us and except in the event of a british war will not,
at least this side of the Mississippi, dare to provoke us. Those
terrible tales brought down in rapid succession have been
contradicted & the Account given by Gamelin the patron of
the boat which took up the salt & which I mentioned to you
before, has been unanimously denied by the whole of his boat's
crew. But the fellow knew how the land lay.

Much is said about the Shawnee Prophet & many bloody
views are ascribed to him, but the discerning are not so ready
to grant an implicit credit to them. It is a fact of public
notoriety that that singular man has collected round him two
or three hundred men, whom he himself leads daily to work
in an immense field beautifully fenced in, a village of com-
modious houses is growing, and the use of Spirituous liquors
entirely abandoned. He has thus conjured at once a most
inveterate habit among his followers, and a no less inveterate
prejudice, and had effected more towards civilizing them &
thereby seconding the benevolent and philantropic views of the
General Government than all the indian agents that have been
or may be sent amongst them. His views as far as I can see,
appear to be to Unite the Indians, to prevent their extinction
and to make a nation of them dependent on themselves. To
be sure he uses like other Superior minds have done before him,
Superstition as an irresistible engine of influence but it is of a
wild kind. Whoever is conversant with the history of man in
his different relations of hunter Shepherd or husbandman,
must know that the adoption of agricultural pursuits is no

strong indication of premeditated hostilities, no evidence of the existence of a warlike system.

The hostile preparations made in this county last spring and the ferment and allarm they created excited such uneasiness and fear amongst the clan of the Prophet, that his brother, a war chief came down to see the Governor & learn the meaning of such a threatening attitude. In several conferences he spoke to him with a freedom and sense which excited surprise, he reproached him in the face of day, with having bought the land from tribes which had no right to it, or from persons whom he himself had made chiefs, listening to the tales of every discontented blackguard who chose to come down from the indian villages with pretended news, he boldly challenged him to name a single indian of respectability, who had said or could say that he had ever heard his brother avowing any hostile intentions against the whites.[3] It is easy to consider that, the other tribes or rather some of their chiefs, and those who receive pay for land which did not belong to them, uneasy at his growing influence, will readily attempt to throw an odium upon him. It is my opinion that Government ought to look closer into this business, and rather to cherish than exasperate that man, that the indians want nothing but good treatment to become well disposed to the United States and that there is some mystery in the indian agency. I myself have observed one Pishoowah or Richarville a half blooded indian who speaks french as well as I do, is with his uncle Pacawn, a grand chief of the Miamis & besides very much of a gentleman, I have seen that man, for some hidden reason affectedly thrown in the back ground and treated with very little ceremony which usage he has deeply felt.

There is a singular circumstance in the late purchase, namely that the Tract annexed to this district & lying on the

---

[3] Tecumseh, brother of the Prophet, came to Vincennes, arriving on August 12 and departing on the 21st. Harrison's account of his meetings with him and a copy of one of Tecumseh's speeches are in Esarey (ed.), *Messages and Letters*, I, 459-69. An account was also carried in the *Western Sun* of August 25.

North of it, is precisely that part of the Wabash company's claim, beginning at the mouth of the *river du Chat* (Racoon creek) & ending at Pointe Coupée, to which the indian title had not been extinguished. Query. Was it a plan to put the United States in possession, so that the company might recover the *whole* instead of a *part* of their claim & has the Governor no interest therein? Why did not the Governor decline every interference in an affair that affects so seriously the interest of the U. S. in the first instance, without first appointing lawyers to bring on the suit? Why are hundreds of the Pamplets containing the Indian deeds, petitions to, & reports of Committees, Congress and other documents, relative to that gigantic claim, now distributed through the County, by G. Wallace the former partner of his Excellency[4] & his present friend, is it to create in the public a prejudice in favour of the claimants & to prepare thus before hand a propitious Jury?

That almost unpremeditated conversation we had at my Office under the impression of the most agonizing fears, at which attended a Juge a Lawyer and a member of the Legislature, which terminated in the abandonment of the transient idea of learning from the indians by the means of a Gentleman going there, the real cause of their Discontents, and in desiring Mr. Dubois to go, if requested for the Governor *alone;* that conversation has been transformed into a *treasonable* meeting, the object of which was to bring the indians on us, the report

[4] See above, for earlier reference to this alleged partnership. On October 20, 1809, the *Western Sun* carried a deposition of George Wallace, Jr., dated October 19, made before Judge Henry Vanderburgh stating "that he has for several years past farmed the contract for supplying the provisions which may be wanted at this place for the public service, from James Morrison, Esq. of Kentucky, and that neither Governor Harrison, nor any other person is concerned with him in the said contract, or in any mercantile business . . . and . . . that as a considerable part of the business of the Indian Department at this place has passed through his hands, he is enabled to declare, that the Governor's method of doing business is such, that it is nearly impossible for any fraud whatever to be committed, and that he possesses documents which prove unequivocally, the fairness and integrity with which the affairs of that department have been administered by the Governor."

artfully spread has increased in malignity, *vires acquiriteunda* & it is now pretty well understood, that numbers of us had a close correspondence with the Prophet and had agreed with him upon signals designating those who were to be sacrificed & those who were to be spared. Ewing & I are named as the chief conspirators! Thus our characters, as I had foresaw, are now openly attacked, but in a way that I never would have thought of.[5]

The Governor had openly boasted that he would soon reduce E & me to a private station, as Officers we defied his malice, but that awkward meeting furnished him with a luky opportunity, and this is the way he man[a]ged it. A grand jury was prepared with twelve men whom he considered as dead shots at the head of which were Wm. Prince Justice of the Peace, Auditor of the Territory and Captain in the service of Burr, & George Wallace his Partner, the nine others were respectable men but formed the minority. Two persons who had been at our meeting, being examined as witnesses deposed that nothing improper had passed there, that Ewing remained silent & myself combated the idea of coming at the knowledge of the cause of the indian's discontents by any other means than the Governor. Dubois being also examined deposed that I had urged him to go for the Governor & him alone. An indictment was first moved against us, eight of the select band voted in the affirmative, but the other four ashamed of such proceedings opposed the measure, they tried next a simple presentment, which met the same fate and were at last disappointed in their last resource, namely that of carrying a vote of unqualified censure against the dangerous and treasonable interference of certain ill disposed persons in public affairs &c. &c. &c. The plan was to forward that indictment, presentment or vote of censure to the President and to procure a Petition for our dismissal from some of the inhabitants, which he can effect whenever he pleases, by employing the same means that proved so successfull in procuring him a recommendation for a reap-

[5] See above, p. 132.

pointment. The unexpected return to honesty of four men from whom the Governor had a right to expect another conduct, rendered abortive his diabolical plan; but what will you think of a Country, where eight wretches can be found, capable of voting a bill of indictment, when no law had been violated, when in fact there was no statute to violate, in a word who could put respectable men, some officers of the U. S. upon their trial without either law or evidence?

Such is the influence of that man!

Since I began this letter, which want of strength forces me to interrupt, orders have been issued for the marching out of four or five companies of militia amongst which is a company of light horse, armed with switches, shewing three caps and four unifor[m] coats and commanded by the formidable Ben Parke, who appears to be tired of a knapsack.[6] Those companies are to escort to the New indian boundary the already strong regular force lately concentrated here [7] The Indians are in dismay. God grant that fear may not precipitate them into desperate measures— The brother of the Prophet told the Gov'r that he would himself go to the President and lay the indian's grievance at his feet, from such

[6] Benjamin Parke was appointed captain of cavalry of the first regiment of Indiana militia by the Governor on September 22, 1810. Woollen, *et al.* (eds.), *Executive Journal of Indiana Territory,* p. 164.

[7] No evidence has been found to support Badollet's suspicions that troops were actually being used in some way to support Harrison's land acquisitions. The Governor was eager for the boundaries established by the Fort Wayne treaty to be run, but the Indian situation made it unsafe for surveying parties to start working. On October 5, 1810, Harrison wrote to the Secretary of War: "My plan was if I had received authority from you by this mail for so doing, to have called out 150 or 200 militia and with these and the regular troops to have immediately proceeded up the Wabash and upon some convenient site (as near the upper line of the purchase as such a one could be found) to have erected a strong picketed work." Esarey (ed.), *Messages and Letters,* I, 474-75. The Secretary, after consultation with the President, vetoed the establishment of the post at this time because of the lateness of the season and because the situation in the area of West Florida might demand all the available U. S. forces. Letter to Harrison, October 26, 1810, in *ibid.,* I, 482. This decision may have been influenced by Badollet's letter and Gallatin's endorsement, below, pp. 174-75.

a step the Governor had every thing to fear and I venture to foretell, that means will be found to stop him.

I do not want every one of my words to be implicitly believed, but I say that something wrong and very wrong is going on here. In the name of God, let the Government direct an inquisitive eye toward this man and our situation, we are certainly on the brink of a precipice.

I have a volume to write, but my head is as yet weak, my ideas confused and my expressions obscure, it is better to stop and assure you that I do & will remain

Yours

JNO. BADOLLET
turn over
October 9, 1810

P. S. An intelligent member of the Assembly of this place whose word cannot be doubted, read himself the journal of the expedition of the Governor to Fort Wayne, by which it appears that when he arrived the Miamis did not attend, that he concluded a treaty with the Delawares & Potawatomies for the Weah's land, those two powerfull tribes could not be difficult about the terms, not a foot of it belonging to them & they now receive pay for selling the property of others! ! ! The Miamis not attending, the Governor sent an express to them who brought some of their chiefs, to all his fine speeches and expostulations, they uniformly answered, that the land he wanted belonged to the Weahs (a miami tribe) & Kickapoos that they might sell if they chose, but as to themselves they were determined not to sanction what had been done nor sell any of their own. The Potawatomies then threatened the Miamies to drive them into the lake. Still they refused. Much time was consumed, at last the Governor went at night to the Miamie camp telling them that it was unfortunate that his red children would let him go back *sorrowfull* and hanging his head &c, to which they answered that rather than to let [him] go *sorrowfull* they would do what he wished them to do. Mark that the word *sorrowfull* cannot be translated in the poor language of the indians, but by a word conveying the complex idea of sorrow anger and revenge. The next day when the deed or deeds were offered to them for signing, they made a last effort to resist but in vain.[8] The above facts and greater details were owned by the Governor himself in the presence of the same Gentleman and of Judge Vander Burgh, in an unguarded moment, when he thought none were near him but his choice Spirits and they are ready to give those depositions. Call upon Mr. Jennings he can shew you a letter from the same member of the Legislature, wherein the substance of the Governor's journal is better & more fully detailed.—

Gracious God must we picture that the Senate & President are privy to such doings & have knowingly sanctioned treaties made under circumstances which cannot be justified at the tribunal of honour and rectitude? must we believe that the Government of the United States, which professes to treat with the same impartial justice the weak & the strong, can stoop to the use of deception and unfair means, in order to compell poor defenceless natives to part with their paternal inheritance? No it cannot be, they must have been ignorant of such unwarrantable and culpable means having been employed.

Do you remember the purchase of the land between the Wabash & Louisville made from the Delawares, mere tenants at will of the Miamies, which, being resented by these last, gave so much uneasiness to President Jefferson. Do you remember that the business grew serious & that Gen'l Gibson & Col. Vigo were sent to the Miamis to accommodate matters, which they effected?[9] Well, the same conduct has been pursued in this instance, except that his Ex'y took care before he left the spot to obtain by fair or foul means the signature of the Miamies.— The Present moment is for us pregnant with

[8] The journal of the treaty proceedings is printed in Esarey (ed.), *Messages and Letters,* I, 362-78. The member of the legislature to whom Badollet refers may have been John Caldwell who was elected representative from Knox County at the general election on April 2, 1810. See also above, p. 166n.

[9] For earlier references to this see above, p. 133n.

serious events. I have very little doubt but that the very great warlike preparations now going on, will induce in the indians, the belief that the United States are bent upon their destruction, and their despair may cause the spilling of much innocent blood. This opinion is now that also of many reflecting men in this Country.

Pardon my blottings and scratchiness I cannot write now *currents calams* (nor in fact ever could) & I am to weak to undergo the fatigue of a copy.

The Partnership is now *proved* & *at last owned* by Wallace, which is one of the reasons that numbers have lost all confidence in the Governor.[10]

[Addressed:] Albert Gallatin Esqr   Private
[Endorsed:] Vincennes 25 Sept'r 1810 Badollet
[Endorsed by Gallatin:]

The enclosed letter from the Register of the Land office at Vincennes was received since the meeting of yesterday at the President's. The writer, having differed with Gov'r Harrison on the slavery question, is inimical to him & may see through a deceptive medium. But I know him intimately, & can vouch for his perfect integrity, to which he adds some share of intelligence.

I had some time ago received intelligence that the Wabash & Illinois Companies who have a purchase claim of several millions of acres derived from a private Indian purchase by a certain Murray in 1774, had instituted a suit in the Indiana terr'y to try their title, that they had applied to Gov'r Harrison, and that he had refused to interfere but had recommended some lawyers to them.[11] The hint in this letter that his last purchase from the Indians, which is for nearly the same tract is connected with that claim should not be lightly believed. But upon the whole, I feel a perfect conviction that it would be improper to continue military operations & to establish an advanced post, and that the complaints of the Indians should

[10] See above, p. 169n.
[11] See above, pp. 149-50.

be listened to & fully understood, before an attempt is made to enforce the treaty. It will be perceived by the style of this letter it is from a friend to his friend, without expectation of its being communicated.[12]

[Badollet to Jennings]

December 25, 1810

It is with a heartfelt pleasure my Dear Jennings that I am able to inform you that all the members of the Legislature from the Eastward started at the prorogation[1] more your friends than ever and that R.[2] notwithstanding his constant assiduities gained nothing & is by them thought less of than ever.

Every art now tried, & every insinuating stratagem was used to induce the members to take lodgings at Veto Hall,[3] they resisted and put up at Evan's not deeming P Jones a more becoming place than head quarters.[4] Beggs[5] went to Buntins.[6] However Roue and Overman[7] at last yielded & Decently took headquarters at his Exc'y's & became proportionably more frigid in the cause of their oppressed country. The law about slavery has at length been repealed[8] and an investigation of

[12] To whom Gallatin forwarded Badollet's letter is not known. Perhaps it was the Secretary of War. See note 7 above.

[1] The first session of the Third General Assembly of Indiana Territory ran from November 12 to December 19, 1810.

[2] Thomas Randolph.

[3] Probably Harrison's home, "Grouseland."

[4] Robert Morgan Evans opened a tavern on Market Street in Vincennes in 1809. See sketch of him in Thornbrough and Riker (eds.), *Journals of the General Assembly of Indiana Territory,* p. 972. Peter Jones's first tavern was located on Water Street, "at the sign of Thomas Jefferson." In 1807 he sold this and opened the Vincennes Hotel on the same street. *Ibid.,* pp. 991-92. He was a member of the House of Representatives.

[5] James Beggs of Clark County, a member of the Legislative Council. *Ibid.,* 959-60.

[6] Robert Buntin. He served as clerk of the county court throughout the territorial period.

[7] Richard Rue and Ephraim Overman, representatives from Dearborn County.

[8] By an act repealing the act of 1805. Ewbank and Riker (eds.), *Laws of Indiana Territory, 1809-16,* pp. 138-39.

the acc'ts of the Treasurer & Auditor which has, as was expected, redounded to the shame of Mr. Peter.[9] Calwell[10] has conducted himself most nobly & was the most usefull member. He convicted Peter of negligence and incapacity & of guilt in paying money beyond and without appropriations. He has shown that our Territory loaded with a debt of 8 or 9 thousand dollars could not obtain credit for a quire of paper, when between 1300 or 2000 dol. should be in the Treasury after all debts [were] paid if the Auditor that man of *standing* & *property* that child of his Excel. had been able and willing to do his duty, and has carried a resolution directing the G'r to put his official bond in suit.— The Gov'r having asserted in his speech to the Legislature that the Prophet's brother had said that a man of this place had held correspondence with the indians to render them dissatisfied with the treaties, Calwell in his presence asserted that to be false & made him eat his own words, as you may see by an official correction communicated at Calwell's request to the Legislature. He also carried a resolution to request the G'r to lay before the house such documents as were in his possession, proving the existence of a treasonable correspondence between persons of this place and the indians, & to name such persons; at the receipt of the resolution our honest Proconsul started, stammered, was silent, stammered again & laying after a little recollection his hands upon his heart, declared to Caldwell who presented the resolution, that upon his sacred honour he had not alluded in his address to the Legislature to any in Vincennes nor within one hundred miles of it,[11] asserted a moment afterwards in a fit of

[9] James Johnson was treasurer of the territory. On April 13 William Prince was appointed auditor, vice Peter Jones, resigned. Woollen, *et al.* (eds.), *Executive Journal of Indiana Territory,* pp. 129, 159. Unfortunately no journal for this session of the Assembly has survived. The treasurer's account book is printed in Thornbrough and Riker (eds.), *Journals of the General Assembly of Indiana Territory,* pp. 906-49.

[10] John Caldwell.

[11] In his message to the Assembly Harrison said, "It will be worthy of your consideration also, whether some penalty might not be advantageously

ALBERT GALLATIN

*from an engraving made for the American Bank Note Co.
from a portrait by Gilbert Stuart*

JOHN BADOLLET

*from a carte-de-visite lithograph, inscribed by Gallatin*

ALBERT GALLATIN

*by William H. Powell, oil on canvas, 1843*

JOHN BADOLLET'S AND GOVERNOR HARRISON'S HOUSES,
Vincennes

*by Charles Alexandre Lesueur, 1833*

VIEWS OF VINCENNES FROM BADOLLET'S HOUSE

*by Charles Alexandre Lesueur, 1834*

stammering that there was one person, but the next instant repeated the first declaration, swore that the meeting at my office[12] was owing to the best of motives, that in his opinion there was not a Gentleman there who was not actuated by views of the purest patriotism &c &c &c. Read that & remember the indictments. You remember the constant efforts made by the G'r & his sycophants in the board of trustees to employ the capital of the institution[13] in paying masters, efforts which as constantly were resisted by us & produced the quarrel which took place between him and me. Well that plan so often de-

imposed upon those who, by improper interferences, and by circulating falsehoods amongst the Indians, counteract the intentions of the government, and lay the foundation for distrust and enmities which may produce the most serious consequences. It is believed that to intrigues of this kind we are indebted for much of the uneasiness and disatisfaction which has prevailed in the Indian country for the last six months—The brother of the Prophet expressly declared in the presence of a large audience, that two secret visits had been paid to his town by different white men, who urged him to oppose the execution of the late treaty, and who assured him, that his pretensions would be supported by a considerable portion of our citizens. . . ."

And later, "Although I am persuaded that the blackest treachery and hatred towards our government and nation [a reference to Great Britain] have produced some of the intrigues of which I complain, I am also convinced that much mischief has been done by others, who, actuated by no views that were inimical to their country, have suffered their passions, prejudices, and personal animosities to lead them astray, and to do that which their cooler judgments must condemn. Whilst a penal law would perhaps deter the former, it would be the means as an expression of the public sentiment, of reclaiming the latter to their duty. Should you think proper to take the subject under your consideration, gentlemen, the original documents in my possession, in support of what is here advanced will be submitted to you." Thornbrough and Riker (eds.), *Journals of the General Assembly of Indiana Territory*, pp. 352-53, 355.

The Assembly passed an act which among other things made it a high misdemeanor for unauthorized persons to converse or correspond with an Indian or Indian tribe "in relation to any negociations or treaties, disputes or controversies with the United States or this territory," with intent to influence the conduct of any of the tribes or to defeat any measure of the Government. Ewbank and Riker (eds.), *Laws of Indiana Territory, 1809-16*, pp. 150-56.

[12] See above, pp. 154-56n.

[13] The Vincennes University. See above, p. 107.

feated by which the depositories of a sacred fund would have been consumed for the benefit of their own families and a few Gentlemen of Vincennes a property which the benevolence of Congress had reserved for the whole Territory and the future generations that plan had never been seriously abandonned as you will see.

Towards the close of session late in the afternoon on pretense of want of funds to finish the building, Gen'l Johnson (a tool fit for every dirty business) brings in a bill dissolving the present board of trustees & creating another composed of himself Prince, P. Bacchus R. M. Evans D. McClure Wallace & Wm. Jones with leave to sell ten more quarters, that work of darkness was concluded in a few minutes, every rule being dispensed with & sent up to the Council who were expected to proceed with the same precipitation. Fortunately the Treasurer of the board was present and drew out of his pocket a statement showing that there was owing to the board 1800 dollars a sum more than sufficient to pay the Carpenter. The Council paused & referred the business to the monday. In the interval the plan took vent & created a general indignation, the members of the committee collected information, reflected & reasoned & finally gave it a final negative, so far so good for the present

But the danger though avoided this moment is not removed, & the interference of Congress becomes necessary to save that precious capital. You know my dear Jennings that the Legislature considering themselves as vested with the Township located for the use of a Seminary of learning, passed an act incorporating a board of trustees & gave them leave to sell 4000 acres.[14] The first transactions of the board were rather precipitate & not tempered by reflexion. Although members had some doubt about the power of our Legislature to legislate upon a property not vested in them & to authorise the sale of a part thereof, they were at first driven with such rapacity by his Ex'y & the other knowing ones that the land was exposed for sale, the building contracted for before they fairly

[14] Philbrick (ed.), *Laws of Indiana Territory, 1801-9*, pp. 178-84, 532-39.

knew the ground they stood upon. For having gone so far they may say what in truth was the fact, that in voting for the construction of the building they did not part with but only changed the denomination of a part of the capital appropriation. But still this can be only called a palliation and not a full justification of their involuntary error, and I must confess that I was myself carried away by the rapidity of the moment. You know yourself how when we once discovered the course we were running we made a full stop, how the gang was enraged & how we have since stood firm.

Now the business which ought to engage your attention is this. Whereas doubts begin to be entertained in relation to the legality of the sales made by the board under the law of a legislature who had perhaps no right to legislate upon the business, I advise you & it is the opinion of the sound part of the board, to procure an act of Congress legalising the sales already made (for quieting the purchasers) and other steps taken by the present board, and creating another board of Trustees in which the part as yet unsold of the reserved Township that shall thereby be vested with a prohibitory clause that the new board shall never under any pretence whatever alienate any part of the capital except the price of the land would rise to [MS blank] dollars per acre, in which case it should be lawfull for the board to sell the same & to place the proceeds in bank stock. Thus every contingent dilapidation of the aforesaid capital would be effectually barred against. We had in mind to convene the board & move a resolution praying Congress to pass an act as mentioned above, but we are afraid of opposition intrigues & defection or miscarriage by the casual non-attendance of some of the members on our side & I have thought it not preposterous to mention it to you. Rely upon it, if you succeed you'll obtain the thanks of all good men. That in such a case Congress may chuse if they think proper some of the present members, I here subjoin their names *Wm. H. Harrison, Gen'l Gibson, Benj. Parke, H. Vander Burgh, Char's Smith, R. Buntin, George Leech, James Johnson, John John-*

*son, L. Decker, A'm Kuykendall, P. Jones, T. Dubois, Dr. McNamee, N. Ewing, J. Badollet, F. Vigo.* You knew yourself those whom we constantly opposed, observe only to retain the Governor, for if it be put out of his power to do mischief, he can be a very usefull member. As to myself I had rather be left out.[15]

As much as Caldwell gained credit by his conduct in the Legislature just as much shame did G. Johnston & P. Jones reap. The first drew amongst others the following bills out of his prolific brains, which met a similar fate with that dissolving the present and creating a new board. A bill making the marriage of a man or woman to a Shaker void at the end of a year with priviledges to the person having then married of retaining the property of his former consort, with a preamble containing something about the scarcity of men & the necessity of their production. A bill making a justice lyable to a fine of 150 dollars for every prophane oath which he did not punish  A bill preventing under severe penalties every body except native born Americans from medling directly or indirectly with elections. A bill empowering notories public (id est himself) to receive acknowledgements of deeds[16]  A bill empowering practising attorneys (id est himself) to be justices of the peace. In the bill for the compensation of the members, a clause allowing a sum to an assistant Clerk (id est

[15] No such act was passed. Gallatin, however, made very clear his interpretation of the act of Congress in reserving the township and his opinion in regard to the sale of a portion of it, in a letter to Badollet on April 18, 1811. "It appears evident to me," he wrote, "that all those sales are unauthorized & void ab initio. The township has never been granted or vested in trust by Congress to the Legislature of the Territory or any other persons. It has simply been excepted from the public sales and its use designated: but the title remains altogether with the United States. . . .

"Permit me also to observe, that the intention of Congress appears to be defeated by these premature sales, which for the sake of some temporary and immediate advantage, sacrifice the fund [land?] itself, the rents of which were intended to provide permanently for the education of future generations." Carter (ed.), *Territorial Papers,* VIII, 118.

[16] This bill became law. Ewbank and Riker (eds.), *Laws of Indiana Territory, 1809-16,* pp. 111-12.

himself) A bill forcing every body to swear or affirm on the holy evangels, besides the famous Trustees bill & some others not recollected  the above may be parts or clauses of bills intended for other purposes. I may be not quite correct in form but certainly so in substance. Peter did not understand the half of his time what was going on, & in order not to keep him quite useless, they sent him galoping with enrolled bills to the Governor for his signature, an office which he performed with great dignity and dispatch.

The Governor as usual attended the house with a strict punctuality, taking share in the debates and suggesting arguments to the members, which condescension Caldwell had the impudence to reprobate.

Upon the whole, considering the difficulty of their task, the baits by which they were tempted, the intrigues by which they were surrounded and the frailties incident to human nature, it can be said with truth that the members have manifested symptoms of an independance unusual at this place; which is I trust the harbinger of an approaching resolution. You'll be indebted to your worst enemies for your future success, they having behaved in a manner calculated to create disgust. Amongst other traits I'll mention but one. P. Jones the man of standing and property the worthy creature of his Ex'y at a supper given by the respectable G'l Johnston, called the members from the Eastward to their faces a d—m set of rascals who came there to ruin their Territory, which elegant speech drove from the entertainment Roux and Overman and had well nigh broke it up.

Downs[17] is nobly independant. Pennington[18] was fast shaking off his shackles. Manwaring [and] Templeton[19] have

---

[17] Thomas Downs, representative from Clark County. Sketch in Thornbrough and Riker (eds.), *Journals of the General Assembly of Indiana Territory*, pp. 970-71.

[18] Dennis Pennington, a member of the Legislative Council from Harrison County. *Ibid.*, pp. 1002-4.

[19] Solomon Manwaring, a legislative councillor, and John Templeton, a representative, both from Dearborn County. *Ibid.*, pp. 996, 1012-13.

acted right, the most of them made us promises to correspond with them.

I must not forget to mention to you that if a land office is created in Dearborne county, Mr. Templeton requests your friendly offices to procure the office of Register.[20]

Do not forget to send me a weekly Aurora,[21] that if it please me I may have time to write to you to Subscribe for me and to discontinue the one I now receive.

Fare-you well my dear Jennings, write to me as soon as possible & believe me

Your sincere Friend

JNO BADOLLET

You'll receive Johnson's petition,[22] if compulsory process could be obtained, few depositions, enough could be proved to put an end to the reign of Richard III— My best compliments to J. R. Jones.

[Badollet to Gallatin]

VINCENNES  August 6, 1811

It is a long time since I have not entertained you with news from this ill fated Country, not that the matter was wanting, but from an insuperable dislike of treating such a disgusting subject. A volume could not contain the wrongs of this Territory but I'll confine myself to what relates to indian hostilities, about which much noise is made abroad no doubt, but of which we here would remain entirely ignorant, if the infamous western sun did not exist.

You remember my having told you that the Indians of the Wabash were highly dissatisfied at the late purchase made of them under circumstances little short of compulsion. The details of all this I cannot now give you, but will refer you to the treaties themselves[1] as now given to the public in the

---

[20] No land office was ever established in Dearborn County.
[21] A Philadelphia newspaper.
[22] Not found.
[1] The four treaties of 1809 concluded at Fort Wayne and Vincennes. Kappler (ed.), *Laws and Treaties,* I, 101-5. The first was signed by the

volume containing the laws of Congress, on the perusal of which the following queries will present themselves. How are the Potawatomies a powerfull tribe made a party to the sale of lands of which not an inch belongs to them. Why are the Delaware, who are similarly situated, among the subscribers to the deed of Sales? Why are these last declared in the same instrument joint owners of the soil to which they had not the least pretension? Why were the Weahs, a Miami Tribe, the real owners of the land sold, brought to sign a sale in which they were so materially concerned after the whole business was already concluded between the Governor and other strong Tribes which they dreaded to offend? Why do the United States pay presents and annuities to two tribes who give no compensation therefor?— Who does not see in that Transaction, especially if acquainted with the character of the Negotiator, and a number of circumstances which it is not easy now to detail, an undue advantage taken of the poor nations, must be willfully blind indeed. There is no man attached to his country and alive to what can tarnish his honour, but must lament that the United States have sanctioned a negotiation conducted under such suspicious circumstances the consequence of which has been a general discontent amongst the indians, and a belief obtaining amongst them that the United States aim at dispossessing them ultimately of all their lands. I am convinced that it would be no difficult matter to secure their good will and their attachment and the pursuing measures which may eventually endanger both is under our present embarrassments a matter of serious concern to everyone who is truly attached to his Country.

This is the third year that rumours of indian war have been issued forth from head quarters here and the parades of the militia have taken place in consequence thereof. It appears plain to me that the first allarm and the mock precautions

Delaware, Potawatomi, Miami, and Eel River tribes; the second, a supplementary treaty to the first, was signed by the Miami and Eel Rivers; the third was signed by the Wea; and the fourth by the Kickapoo.

resorted to, were intended to pave the way to the treaty, the second to stifle the discontents of the Indians arising therefrom this present apparent panic has the same object and to induce a belief at Washington that the Prophet is a chief of banditti, a very designing and dangerous man, from whom the United States and especially this place have every thing to dread. The fact is he, or rather his brother *Tecumseh,* has spoken in disapprobation of the last sales in a most able and spirited manner and his extirpation or forcible removal appears to be the ardent wish of our Executive. Wether or not he is a chief of banditti, you will be able to judge yourself. He has settled on the banks of the Wabash with the consent of the adjoining tribes, numbers of whom have joined him, where he and his followers have cleared, fenced in and planted in corn a space not less than three miles in length. He has built comfortable houses, they drink no ardent spirits and go regularly to work every morning & their hands become callous are an indubitable evidence of their being in earnest. They appear to be governed by regular kind of institutions, & rise, go to their meals, and to their rest at stated hours with as much regularity as monks, they seem to taste the comforts of civilized life. Nothing can be more interesting to a reflecting and philantropic mind, than the accounts given of them by travellers, and the sundry heralds whom the Governor has been sending to their village. How that can indicate hostile intentions I with many others am at a loss to discover. The more I think of that man and the measures he pursues, the more I am convinced, that his superior mind (I mean Tecumseh) has seen the impending destruction of the indians in their present mode of life, he has seen with sorrow the fatal effects of spirituous liquor amongst them, their criminal imprudence in destroying the game to supply the avarice of traders, and cutting off their own resources to obtain European trinkets and deleterious drinks, to prevent their ultimate annihilation, the unavoidable consequence of such a thoughtless conduct, teaches them how to draw their subsistence from their own resources, to abandon the use of ardent spirits and to cultivate the soil. Nobody could have seconded the views of a philantropic and liberal Government, with more zeal and more success than this man has done. I have seen many of them at a conference which the Governor had with them & Since, and was struck with the look of sobriety thoughtfulness, and decency by which they were distinguished. I was not alone in making these observations. His purpose is to induce other tribes to adopt his principles and mode of life, and several journeys, which he has taken, and which will be represented as made with hostile intentions have I believe no other object. He said himself at a council held a few days ago and of which more anon, that when he could get the different tribes to speak with one heart and one mouth he would go then to his Father the President and explain to him his views.[2]

We were in perfect peace and in full hope that the allarms of the two last years would not be renewed, when rumors of hostile designs all of a sudden broke upon us, although travellers daily passed the Prophets station non only undis-

[2] Tecumseh came to Vincennes on July 27 and remained until August 5. In reporting to the Secretary of War his meetings with him, in a letter dated August 6, Harrison related that Tecumseh said that "after much trouble and difficulty he had at length brought all the northern Tribes to unite and place themselves under his direction. That the White people were unnecessarily alarmed at his measures—that they really meant nothing but peace—the U. States had set him the example of forming a strict union amongst all the fires that compose their confederacy. That the Indians did not complain of it—nor should his white brothers complain of him for doing the same thing with regard to the Indian tribes. As soon as the council was over he was to set out on a visit to the Southern Tribes to get them to unite with those of the North. . . . That a great number of Indians were coming to settle at his Town this fall . . . that he wished every thing to remain in its present situation until his return . . . that he would then go and see the President and settle every thing with him." Esarey (ed.), *Messages and Letters,* I, 544-45. Harrison added that Tecumseh's coming with so large a force was interpreted by many to mean that he had intended to strike a blow at the whites at this time and for some reason had had to alter his plan. He said that Tecumseh's manner throughout the council was embarrassed and that the speech he made was not the one he had planned. *Ibid.,* I, 546. Accounts of Tecumseh's visit are in the *Western Sun,* July 27 and August 3, 1811.

turbed but well treated. Some salt sent up to the Wabash indians was detained during Tecumseh's absence by his people who did not know how to act,[3] remembering the noise which had been made before on their refusing to take any portended the most sinister events, at the same time letters from Chicago from General Clark[4] and from Governors Edward and Howard[5] announced the approaching storm and the intended sacking of this place, a murder committed by the Indians on the Mississippi was the opening of the Campaign, some families on the little Wabash were cut off &c. But it would be well to ascertain whether those letters represented as proving by their concurrence the threatened general attack, were not written in consequence of the same information being sent from Chicago to Governors Edward & Howard & to General Clark & whether the Chicago information did not originate nigher the Wabash, whether the murder on the Mississippi was not an act of private resentment committed in consequence of an act of savage outrage perpetrated by some of our savage frontier men in digging out of his grave an indian warrior & taking away the trinkets and ornaments deposited with him by the piety of the Survivors? whether the families cut off on the little Wabash are not now full of life and whether the travellers have not continued to traverse the country as unmolested as before.[6]

In consequence of the portentions now the militia were called to Vincennes from the remotest part of this immense County in the midle of Harvest and after having drank plenty

[3] Reported in the *Western Sun* of June 22, 1811, and in a letter from Harrison to the Secretary of War on June 19. Esarey (ed.), *Messages and Letters,* I, 518.

[4] William Clark, general agent of Indian affairs in Louisiana-Missouri Territory.

[5] Ninian Edwards, governor of Illinois Territory, and Benjamin Howard, governor of Louisiana-Missouri Territory.

[6] For Harrison's correspondence concerning these Indian threats see Esarey (ed.), *Messages and Letters,* I, 506-25, *passim.* Accounts of murders by Indians appeared in the *Western Sun* of June 29 and July 6 and 13.

of whisky and listened to a military harrangue of the Commander in chief returned home. The Prophets brother some days afterwards in consequence of sundry messages from the Governor, sent word that he was coming to see what was the matter, and do away any misunderstanding. The militia were convened again, the Light horse put upon duty, the merchants powder sent to the Garrison, an excellent precaution, & every thing wore the appearance of real or affected allarm.[7] Tecumseh arrived with about 30 or 40 men with women and children, he stopped some time with a harmless set of enthusiasts called shakers,[8] where their hunger was charitably allayed and they behaved with the utmost civility. The woods were in the same time said to be filled with *invisible* bands all bent upon the same bloody purpose. Some Miamis came also and were as usual seen along the streets smoking, dancing, trading and chatting with the inhabitants. The militia were mustered and there the Governor clad in a hunting shirt, and addressing them by the familiar name of fellow soldiers, drew an animated picture of the meditated blood shed with such success, that it was with difficulty, that they could be refrained from running to Tecumseh's camp and there exhibiting the second volume of Williamson's expedition,[9] & seizing that

[7] Harrison wrote the Secretary of War, "To intimidate and to prevent him [Tecumseh] from attempting any enterprize against us I made as great a display of force as possible. The day of his arrival I had a review of the neighbouring militia at which there were between 700 and 800 men under arms. The Two infantry companies on duty were increased to three and these being relieved on different days by some management in marching and changing quarters it appeared to the Indians that four or five companies were on constant duty. The elegant troop of Dragoons commanded by Parke (who is also one of our supreme judges) were exhibited to the greatest advantage and nightly patrols both of horse and foot announced a vigilance which defied surprises. The Indians were in astonishment and Terror and I believe most of them went off impressed with the belief that Vincennes was not as easily to be taken as their chief would have convinced them." Esarey (ed.), *Messages and Letters,* I, 546.

[8] A settlement of Shakers was at Busseron north of Vincennes.

[9] A reference to the massacre of Christian Indians at Gnadenhütten, Ohio, by Col. David Williamson's command in 1782. Paul A. W. Wallace,

critical moment he added, what would you say fellow Soldiers, what would your indignation be, if I was to tell you that men high in office or that Officers of the United states are the friends of that bloody savage, the words may be some what different, but the substance as here stated. To be thus held up to an infuriated multitude as the friends of the enemies of the Country is a deed of atrocity worthy of a Roman proconsul!

You will not readily admit that your old friend & N. Ewing both with families, both men of principles, full of attachment to their country are capable of such odious views, nor does he believe it himself. Such fact however shews the man. He has conceived an unextinguishable hatred against us both, because we have assisted in defeating his favourite scheme of introducing slavery here, because we have discovered his views of applying the capital of the seminary to the paying of professors and thus destroying a fund belonging to posterity, and we defeated them but he hates us for a better reason, because he is conscious that we know him.

On the day that Tecumseh was admitted to a conference, the regulars of Fort Knox were drawn up, with the light horse and several companies of militia, he was introduced through a passage formed by the military drawn up with bayonets fixed and glistening in every direction. The poor naked Savages were surprised but not appalled by such formidable reception. Tecumseh amongst other things observed to the Governor that it was as little his interest as his wish to go to war, that the year before, he would receive no salt because he had no right to it, that it gave him offense, that this year his people during his absence did not know how to act, that they had taken all the salt which had been since distributed, that he was thereat also displeased, that he would thank him to let him know how he should thenceforward behave to avoid his displeasure, that he had followed his advice by applying to the cultivation of the Land, &c &c. La Poussiere a Weah chief observed that

"The Moravian Record," in *Indiana Magazine of History,* XLVIII (1952), 149-50.

contrary to the Stipulations of the Treaty of Greenville their lands had been purchased without he having ever been consulted, that the Treaty has been made with the tomahawk over their heads &c &c.— To conclude the Indians are all gone the military dismissed and every thing as quiet as if no danger had ever existed, although those formidable tribes are not perhaps fifty miles off.— The militia having drawn two days rations and dispatched their whisky, were assembled, a string of resolutions were ready made, presented to them for their approbation and passed, it would have been dangerous to object. A Committee was formed to address the President composed amongst others of Two clergymen great friends of his Excellency (who affect a great veneration for the Clergy) and professionally used to impress obedience, of a stupid elder and of Col. Vigo who although a good man has through age lost all energy of character.[10] The sentiments expressed in the address and resolutions ought to be received with great caution, as being put in the mouth of men in no condition to judge soberly and generally too ignorant to be consulted on public measures. This is one of the trics of our immaculate Governor, when he apprehends that his proceedings may not meet with the approbation of Government he shifts the responsibility

[10] By the account in the *Western Sun* of August 3, 1811, the committee was appointed by a meeting of Knox County citizens to consider the safety of the territory. Its members were the Rev. Samuel T. Scott, the Rev. Alexander Devin, Luke Decker, Ephraim Jordan, Daniel McClure, Walter Wilson, and Francis Vigo. The meeting resolved that in the opinion of those present the country would never be secure until the combination formed by the Prophet was broken up; it was also resolved that this combination was a British scheme; that the assemblage of the Indians excited the most serious alarms; "and but for the energetic measures which have been adopted by our executive, it is highly probable that the threatened destruction of this place, and the massacre of the inhabitants, would have been the consequence."

The letter which the committee prepared, addressed to President Madison, expressed great confidence in, and sincere respect and esteem for the Governor and reiterated these resolutions. "The people have become highly irritated and alarmed, and if the government will not direct their energies, we fear that the innocent will feel the effect of their resentment, and a general war be the consequence. . . ."

from his own shoulders and gets the people to praise him and extoll his talents so to suggest the steps he himself would take, he has commonly one of his valets to put the machine in motion for him, in this last farce the resolutions in the hand writing of the Governor and address were brought forward by one Sullivan[11] & Gen'l W. Johnston the same wretch of whom I spoke to you before and who can in this business be considered in no other light than of a puppet moved by wires in the hand of the Governor, addressed the people in a speech prepared for the purpose.

I think I have told you that the Governor held out the idea and asserted publickly on sundry occasions, that there were men in Vincennes in a criminal correspondence with the Indians, he had the audacity to repeat that in his communication to the Legislature. I suggested to John Caldwell whom you must have known, now a member of the Legislature, the only one who has uttered the sentiments of a freeman in that body, the propriety of moving a resolution calling upon him for the names of all such traitors & for documents to establish their guilt, he did so, was named a committee for that purpose, when he waited upon the Governor with the message, this last was confounded, stammered a great while and asserted that there was no such ill disposed persons in Vincennes, nor within one hundred and fifty miles of it. This business in a body so obsequious, though begun vigorously ended into nothing. He had also asserted in this speech to the Legislature that Tecumseh had said that there were two men in Vincennes who had intrigued with him, Caldwell on the floor of the house in his face averred that it was not true, that Tecumseh had said no such a thing, the Governor acknowledged it and upon being requested to do so by the house, he gave in writing an *errata* or correction of his message. Notwithstanding that acknowledgement he caused a law to be passed predicated upon the reality of such a traitorous correspondence, making it

[11] Daniel Sullivan.

highly penal to hold conferences with the Indians.[12] He caused also another act to be passed, which I believe he penned himself empowering him to call out the militia when he pleased.[13] It is impossible not to perceive some connexion between these two acts of the Legislature and the scenes which have just taken place.

Amongst the multifarious means employed to injure Jennings in his election, take this and *ab uno disce omnes*. Mr. Randolph carried affidavits in every part of the Territory purporting that Ewing and I had written to you with a view to prevent the Memorial of our Legislature praying for an extension of credit to the purchasers of public lands &c from Succeeding,[14] that was a very wicked stratagem which took from Mr. Jennings a great number of votes. Well, the Governor hearing a Clergyman declare that I denied having medled with such things, observed to him that if I denied it it must be true, for I spoke truth, and yet he sent his own Servant ninety or one hundred miles with pacquets of circulars calculated to injure Jennings, to be read in every district on the day of election (Mr. Jennings had copies of them) and amongst those papers was one signed by two of his intimates renewing the same accusation! He harangued the electors on the election ground and treated Jennings in a language too mean to be repeated outraging at once truth decency and our freedom of election. Was I to tell you all the tales, all the misrepresentations, which have been traced up to that source to injure that poor young man and to raise his insignificant competitor I would fill a volume. In Vincennes, the Sheriff and the same G. W. Johnston a clerk of the election had a third column opened for *Jenni* as a third candidate, by which Jennings lost 46 votes, altho the French declared that they meant the man

[12] See above, pp. 176-77n.

[13] Ewbank and Riker (eds.), *Laws of Indiana Territory, 1809-16*, p. 182.

[14] The memorial is printed in *ibid.*, pp. 776-80. The committee of the House to which this memorial was referred reported against granting the petition and the House concurred. *Annals of Congress*, 11 Congress, 3 session, pp. 672, 748.

then in Congress, and such a disgracefull trick has passed
unchecked & the two men are applauded & high in favour
for their ingenuity.[15]

To return to the Indians, it is to be wished that Government would place the indian agency in other hands, than those
of a mad man, the Indians have confidence in Quakers, why
not employ them?

This last allarm has done an injury to this Territory which
it will take many years to repair, the sale of public lands is
nearly stopped the population repelled from our shores and all
the evils of a Territorial Government entailed on us for a
longer period.

A dreadfull event has taken place here, which will help to
[MS illeg.] the state of moral degeneracy of this place.
Captain Thornton Posey killed Lieut. Jennings in Fort Knox
not in a duel by the successive discharge of two pistols. That
act of atrocity excited no other sensation than that of a slight
surprise. The sympathy felt was all for Posey. Poor Posey
were the only words heard to the right and left, one was heard
to say that Posey had done very right (right to murder!),
another, to observe that he was sorry the accident happened
not so much for Jennings whose prospect were not very bright
in this world, but for poor Posey a man *with an handsome
fortune;* the enjoyment of which would thereby be spoiled!
Posey slept that night quietly at an house half a mile off

---

[15] Jonathan Jennings was re-elected as delegate to Congress, rolling up
margins in the eastern counties sufficient to overcome Randolph's lead in
Knox and Harrison counties. Dunn, *Indiana, a Redemption from Slavery,*
p. 410.

Petitions were sent to Congress signed by citizens of the territory
complaining of the improper interference of the Governor in their elections,
of "his unexampled interference in our late Congressional election, by
harranguing the electors at the Polls by riding through the country, and
by writing and Sending into maney, if not all the Counties in the Territory
violent electioneering letters, which your Petitioners conceive to be in
direct opposition to the principles of a Republican Government, and
distructive of their rights as freemen." Carter (ed.), *Territorial Papers,*
VIII, 142-47.

belonging to one of the better sort, was furnished with horses by the same and proceeded leisurely along the big road to Lewisville, where he has remained undisturbed ever since, a magistrate warrant was issued the next day at [blank] o'clock which the sheriff has kept snug in his pocquet no proclamation issued no step taken to apprehend a criminal with *a handsome fortune!*[16]

[16] On June 23, at the garrison of Fort Knox, Capt. Thornton Posey shot Lieut. Jesse Jennings. The *Western Sun* reported this in the issue of June 29, adding ". . . of the causes or circumstances which led to this fatal catastrophe we forebear to comment, as it is probable a judicial investigation will be had. . . ." Harrison reported the shooting to the Secretary of War on June 25, "They were alone in the room of the latter [Posey]," he wrote. "The circumstances which are known are infinitely shocking and I fear that if viewed in the most favorable light for the Captain they are such as to attach an imputation upon his character which he will never be able to wipe off if indeed he should escape ignominious death. . . . Captain Posey has made his escape and took with him a sergeant of his company."

In his next letter to the Secretary, Harrison gave the following account, as reported by the commissary of the garrison, ". . . upon looking out at the window he [the commissary] saw that Lieut. Jennings had fallen out of the Door of Captain Posey's Quarters apparently dead, that upon going up to him with others he was at first told by the Capt. to stand off—but in a little time the latter asked him to come in, upon his asking for an explanation of the scene before him he said that Lieut. Jennings had come into his room, that some altercations had taken place between them, that he had insisted upon the Lieut. fighting him and had offered him the choice of pistols, that he had put one of them into the Lieut.'s hand and that the latter instantly siezed him by the neck or breast when he (the Capt.) shot him, upon being asked how he came to shoot him the second time he said that he could not account for it, but supposed that Jennings had dropped his pistol and that he had taken it up. Jennings received one ball in his right breast which passed through his body and the other behind the left shoulder which ranged along his back and came out at the right shoulder, his clothes both behind and before were burned with the powder. Jennings was certainly unarmed when he went into the Captain's room. It is equally certain that the Captain told two persons two days before the fatal affair that he expected that Jennings meant to assassinate him and that he had been twice to his room door in the night, he believed for that purpose. I am told that Mr. J . . . s. told two different persons some time before that he would kill the Captain if he could." Esarey (ed.), *Messages and Letters*, I, 525, 527-28. Posey went on to Washington, D. C., to present his case to the Secretary of War. He was apparently cleared for he continued in the army, being advanced to lieutenant colonel in the 7th infantry

If Government could once institute an investigation into the Gov'r conduct, John Caldwell Esq: would give some interesting information respecting the late treaties and the speculations at the public Sales. Now I think of it, why was an examination ordered of Ewing's conduct,[17] upon the solitary information of a most abandonned wretch, and why is the Governor receiving every day marks of confidence, although guilty of the most shamefull conduct during the sales, and the President has been repeatedly informed of the circumstance?[18] Is the balance of justice to be affected also by the *handsome fortune* of the criminal? Are we to cease placing confidence in the first Magistrate? Are we to believe that virtue is an empty sound, or a piece of furniture out of fashion; but I forbear I feel indignation swell my breast. I finish. Fare you well, Forever yours

JOHN BADOLLET

Forgive my warmth, had you lived here as long as I have done, and seen what I have seen, your mind would be convulsed with the same agony.

[Badollet to Gallatin]

VINCENNES October 15 1811

We are my dear Friend in a most undescribable situation in this Territory the din of war, a military force of 1200 or 1300 men marched up the Wabash,[1] and not a solitary act of hostility on the part of the Indians comitted, travellers in every direction, north & south, east and west passing and repassing unmolested, every thing quiet in the Illinois Terri-

on April 30, 1813. He was honorably discharged June 15, 1815. Francis B. Heitman (comp.), *Historical Register . . . of the United States Army . . .* (2 volumes. Washington, D. C., 1903), I, 800; Secretary of War, Register of Letters Recd., P-74, 75.

[17] See above, pp. 83-84n, 87, 89.

[18] See Carter (ed.), *Territorial Papers,* VIII, 72-75, 76-85, 87-102, 108-11.

[1] The expedition leading to the Battle of Tippecanoe on November 7. Harrison started up the Wabash on September 24. His command included the 4th U. S. Regiment under Col. John P. Boyd and numbered about 1,000 men including 140 dragoons and 60 mounted riflemen. Esarey (ed.), *Messages and Letters,* I, 589-90.

tory, Governor Edwards betraying no symptom of allarm and resorting to no means of defence and as I am informed Governor Hull[2] foreseeing no approaching danger. Projects ascribed to the Prophet and his brother, which I believe and every body believes, they never dreamt of, entirely absorbed as they appear to be in their favourite plan of bringing the Indians to the habits of sobriety and the arts of industry. Their town to a reflecting and philantropic mind exhibiting the comforts of civilized life and their regulations the appearances of social order. What can all this mean? The whole can be resolved into a personal enmity of the Governor against Tecumseh and the Prophet and a wish to stifle the murmurs of the Wabash Indians in relation to the late treaties and the unwarrantable means employed to effect them.

Where did the National Intelligencer[3] find the accounts he has presumed to give of Tecumsehs views of his visit to Vincennes, of his intention of sacking it, of the number of men he had with him? The whole is a mere fabrication. The Governor sent successively one Laplante[4] a french trader of this place and one Captain Wilson[5] to invite Tecumseh to Vincennes, he came with 30 or 40 men their wives and children as they are accustomed to do, and when arrived was received in the midle of bayonets. If all this be not an imposition on the Administration say that I have become a knave.— All I fear is that such a madman will goad the Indians into some act of despair to make good all what he has got published of their pretended bloody views. Oh God! Oh God!

I believe that I told you[6] that Lieu't. Jennings of the 7th Reg't has been killed in broad day light by Cap'n Posey, the same Captain repaired undisturbed to one James Scot's one of the Governor's flock, half a mile from the Fort slept there, was furnished with horses and provisions and next morning

[2] William Hull, governor of Michigan Territory.
[3] Issue of September 17, 1811.
[4] John Baptiste La Plante.
[5] Walter Wilson.
[6] See above, pp. 192-93n.

travelled leisurely to the Falls where he arrived safe. At ten O'clock of the morning after his departure a warrant was issued by a magistrate *forma causa* and evaporated into air. No proclamation was issued by the Executive to apprehend the felon, but a pretended account of a traveller fabricated here, has been published, broadly intimating that Jennings had formed the design of dispatching Cap. Posey. None more infernal story was ever invented, and to load with obloquy the memory of that unfortunate young man is an act of atrocity worthy of a *Cartouche* or rather of this place. When the melancholy tidings reached Vincennes, some were jocular on that subject, some said Posey had done right, some said Poor Posey! & the deed and the deceased were soon equally forgotten. At hearing such unfeeling expressions at witnessing such imperturbable indifference I could not contain myself and I have observed "Property is before life in this accursed place, had a poor wretch stolen a pony of four dollars, or had a poor negroe fled from the lash of a unfeeling master, all the Gentlemen of this town would have volunteered their services, they would be flying in every direction to apprehend the fugitives, but it is nothing more than a man killed! This Country is in a real state of disorganization.["]

Lieu't. Ambrose Whitlock sent a statement of facts to the Secretary at war, on the subject of which he has not received a word of answer, whence he infers that his letter has been intercepted, for it cannot be admitted that the Secretary at war and the President would suffer such a transaction to remain uninvestigated and the culprit to remain peaceably at Louisville. A propos of Mr. Whitlock I wish you would endeavour to know whether nothing has been written from this place to lessen his credibility and whether the Governor has not some hand in it? I'll pledge the little I have, nay, my very life, that the American army does not contain an Officere more true, more full of honour than Whitlock, and any attempt to injure his good name, if any such attempt has been made, must be the work of a fiend.[7]

Fare you well my dear Friend I remain ever your's J. B.

I wish you would examine wether my returns have been ever opened before they came to hand.

Since I wrote the above news have come down from the camp, that the Prophet has sent word to the Governor that if he meant to advance, he was ready for him. His force is stated at 1300 men. From that circumstance (if true) and there being no act of hostility comitted on his part or that of any other Indians, it may be fairly inferred that the Prophet means only a defensive war to protect his infant settlement, which he has made on the Wabash with the consent of all the tribes concerned. Be it as it may a new draft is ordered here and expresses have been dispatched to Kentucky for one thousand men of reinforcement. What therefore has begun by a farce may ultimately conclude by a Tragedy. That man is carving out a pretty work for the United States. What confidence can be placed in a man who had the audacity to designate Ewing and me as the coadjutors of the Prophet and his brother, the first I saw on the Governors farm in a Council, the latter I never beheld.[8] Calumny is the order of the day, woe to the wretch who dares to maintain an erect attitude to respect himself and presumes to be virtuous.

My poor son Albert is in the army, dark forebodings haunt [MS torn][9]

---

[7] For Whitlock see above, p. 60n. Whitlock had been under arrest earlier in the year, but was tried and acquitted. Register of Letters Recd by Paymaster General, May 29, 1811, and Letter Book of Adjutant General, May 14, 1811, in National Archives. Upon reporting the shooting, Harrison recommended Whitlock to succeed Posey. Esarey (ed.), *Messages and Letters,* I, 525-26. On August 11, 1811, Harrison wrote that the Secretary of War had had no objection to Whitlock being placed in command of Fort Knox except that it might interfere with his duties as district paymaster. Zachary Taylor succeeded to the command. *Ibid.,* I, 548, 551-52.

[8] Badollet should have written: "The first I never beheld, the latter I saw on the Governors farm in a Council."

[9] In the Badollet Papers in the Indiana Historical Society Library there are three letters which John Badollet sent to Albert, addressed

The communication with the army from every point of the Co[m]pas is kept up by the means of single messengers, not one hair of their heads is hurt. A shot has been fired, by which a regular has been wounded in the thigh, it is generally believed in the camp that it proceeds from an accident, it may have been done through *devilment* it may have been done by Winamack Party, who knows that the deed will be fathered on the Prophet. A wretch has been found who asserted it was done by Indians, that he hailed them & his eye sight happened to be so accute that although some hours after night he discovered they were Winebagoes, some of the Prophets clan! !¹⁰ The same man has been sent to Kentucky to excite an additional allarm and to urge the sending a reinforcement of 1000 men.

"Albert Badollet in Capt'n Parke's Company, Camp on the Wabash." They are dated October 16, 18, and 29, 1811. They show the father's affection and concern for his son. Albert apparently grew very unhappy with the army and anxious to come home, and wanted his father to procure a substitute for him. Badollet questioned whether a substitute would be acceptable and added, "There is another consideration in relation to a substitute which has its weight, as long as there is a possibility of danger, which I do not believe and sincerely deprecate, the idea of withdrawing oneself from it has some thing in it, which a man of true spirit must loath, and I leave it to you wether the pleasure of an earlier meeting with us, a pleasure which I every day pray for, can compensate you for the malignant insinuations of which you might become the object." Albert, as will be seen, stayed with the army and was in the Battle of Tippecanoe.

¹⁰ Harrison reported this incident to the Secretary of War as follows: "I had always supposed that the Prophet was a rash and presumptuous man but he has exceeded my expectations. He has not contented himself with throwing the gauntlet but has absolutely commenced the war. His parties were in our neighbourhood [site of Fort Harrison at Terre Haute] for the first time on the night of the 10th inst. our Centinels were fired on and one of the best men of the 4th U. States Regiment badly tho not mortally wounded." He added that the Prophet was demanding assurances from the friendly Delawares that they would join against the Americans and declaring that after the Indians' victory over their foe, the tribes who had refused to join would repent it. "From this statement of Facts Sir," Harrison wrote, "you will no doubt be of opinion with me that the return of the Troops under my command without affecting the desperation or humiliation of the Prophet's Party would be attended with the most fatal consequences." Esarey (ed.), *Messages and Letters*, I, 599, 600.

The Assembly who were summoned for the 28th of October is to day prorogued to 8 weeks later,[11] to give time for the expresses to reach Kentucky, the reinforcements and new supplies to reach the camp and the campaign to be ended. the Heroes of Jena and Austerlitz must hide their diminutive heads.

[Addressed:] Albert Gallatin Esqr.  Private
[Endorsed:] Vincennes october 15, 1811   J. Badollet Indian War

[Badollet to Gallatin]

VINCENNES October 26, 1811

Since my last nothing new has occurred here, peace under the garb of war still lasts, the camp, as a neighboring town is daily visited by travellers and marketting people, the woods are traversed in every direction with the greatest safety, and that bloody Tecumseh with his small band, keeps snuggly at home without injuring any body as sure proof that he meditates sanguinary deeds! How long this farce will last or how it will terminate none but the knowing ones can foresee. Be it as it may the first act of the Legislature, which if not prorogued again, will meet in two weeks, will undoubtedly be to praise the patriotism and foresight of the Governor, and to address the President with a high coloured picture of the dreadfull calamities of which he has delivered us. I have no doubt but that it is already drawn up as usual by himself, his friend Parke or some other amanuensis, and is ready for signing. Some appointments made with a proper degree of sagacity ensure him a majority in a weak and obsequious legislature, and he will palm upon the Administration what he will have dictated to them for the genuine effusions of the representatives of the People.— There is no man whose indiscretion or ill will he may have reason to dread, none whose

---

[11] On October 14 the Governor issued a proclamation postponing the meeting of the legislature until November 11. Woollen, *et al.* (eds.), *Executive Journal of Indiana Territory,* p. 178.

former services deserve reward, but who finds his accounts & makes money by this expedition. Two Colonels to command a body of militia of about 700 men, three captains to command about a few more than one hundred horsemen, a body of spies at a high salary a day, two of whom are lads whom I know to be acquainted with the streets of Vincennes only, but their connexions will duly appreciate the favour. Mr. G. Wallace his Excellency's former partner, exhibited all of a sudden out of his warehouse, an extraordinary quantity of blankets, buckets, tincups, camp ketles, and other articles requisite for soldiery far beyond the demands of his usual customs, and I heard him myself replying to the Governor who asked him whether he had any flints that he had about four thousand left. From this fact alone if no other existed I am perfectly correct in inferring that the present state of things does not grow out of recent occurrences, but is the result of a premeditated plan & was contemplated last winter, the time at which Mr. Wallace set off for Philadelphia to lay in his assortment.

A rascally Potawatomi chief called Winemack, who has all summer been bringing lies of the Prophet and his brothers and who finds his account in doing so, who is frequently in town, genteely dressed, of whom the Governor pointing at him has said, "There is the best friend of the United States, far better than some in Vincennes who call themselves citizens," well, that same fellow has lately stolen a number of horses from a neighbouring settlement, but luckily being pursued were discovered, otherwise the poor Tecumseh would have been charged with it, a result of which Mr. Winemack is perfectly aware. He is also not without some reason suspected by many (or his gang) of having fired at the sentry. A propos of that sentry I was incorrect in my last, the real or supposed Indian who fired, having been hailed by the Centinel and not by the person whom I mentioned.

Since I began this letter information has reached us from the camp that the Governor has set off with the army for the

Prophet's town, after having in vain by repeated messages endeavoured to induce him to come down to him. What he will do when there, God only knows, the Miamis or Wabash Indians, terrified half to death, have come to him with assurances that they want to live in peace with the Whites, which implies (if not positively expressed) that they will say not a word more of the late treaties and other causes of complaint.

When arrived at the Prophet's station, it is my idea that the Governor will find him still adhering to the plan he has hitherto pursued of passive tranquility, of avoiding every act that could bear the least colour of enmity, and that satisfied with having succeeded in stifling the murmurs of the Miamis, a single reiteration on the part of the Prophet of his so often repeated declaration of his determination to live at peace, will furnish the Governor with a sufficient reason to stop further proceedings, and a pretence for withdrawing his forces with *honour*. Thus will end an incomprehensible expedition by which the U. S. will be gulled into a serious expenditure of money.— If the Prophet should in defense of his *Penates,* assume a resisting attitude, or should an act of imprudence on the part of such a rable of militia kept in a state of unusual ferment by the frequency of his Excellency's inflammatory speaches, be resented, the most dreadfull consequences may well be apprehended.

It is really a matter of reflexion, that the Papers should resound with noise of an indian war, when not an authenticated fact of hostility committed by the Prophet's party or Wabash and neighbouring indians can be produced. The purchasers of public lands flock to other parts of the Territory, nay immense deposits of money have been made at Cincinnati for purchasing lands at the public sales of that part of the new purchase which is annexed to Cincinnati district, and is much nigher to the Prophet than Vincennes, and this ill fated County of Knox harassed by military parades and requisitions, allarmed by repeated pictures of threatened depredations, is kept from receiving its proportion of emigrants and even loses some of its inhabitants. Why war hoop here and security there?

One of the great Sources of the dissatisfaction of the Indians is to be found in the mode of paying them. If they are to receive any stipulated sums in hands, it is delivered to them in Such goods as the Governor's* and three other merchants' stores ill provided for indian demand can supply in remnants & such articles as can not obtain a ready sale and at prices on which there is no check. It would be a little curious to look at the prices charged by the merchants here for goods delivered to the Indians on the U. S. account, and to see whether or not they are charged higher than the common retailing price in a place where goods sell already much higher than at Louisville. The Governor well knows that by thus securing the interest of the merchants, he holds pretty fast the vast number of those indebted to them. In viva voce elections this is found to be of immense service.

In addition to what I have already told you respecting the murder of Lieu't. Jennings,[1] I will now mention that no witnesses (though all recognized to appear) presented themselves before the Grand Jury which was dismissed the second day of the Court! There is undoubtedly a mystery of iniquity in all this, I have even seen attempts made (originated here) to calumniate the unfortunate victim now in his grave. Nothing can be more shocking, and convey a more lively idea of our lamentable situation, than the commission of such an horrid crime in day light, its being laughed at by some, palliated by others and forgotten by all, and the insulted laws being palsied, the foul deed unatoned for. Not a step has been taken and to the shame of this Territory, to the shame of the U. S. the criminal is at large and unconcerned in Kentucky, within sixty or one hundred miles of this place.

---

* The Governor was undoubtedly partner of Wallace when I came here and since, what he is now God only knows.[2]

[1] See above, pp. 192-93n, 195-96.
[2] See above, p. 169n.

November 6

Today some persons have arrived from the army, no Indians to be seen, although our warlike Proconsul is drawing near the Prophet's town, some say that if the Prophet does not come to make proper submission, he will cause his town to be set a fire and will thus consign to destruction the homes, the comforts of an harmless set of human beings whose only crime is in my eyes, to have made some rational and successful advances towards civilization, a pretty work indeed! Is Government asleep?

When I told you that Tecumseh came down at the requisition of the Governor with about forty of his people besides women and children I believe I was incorrect, the number of such as are within his controul was much Smaller. A small gang of Winebagoes et some Miamis who came down at the same time not acknowledging his authority. Where did Mr. Gales find the pretty stories of seven or eight hundred men coming under the command of Tecumseh to burn Vincennes, he had better give his authority, that the Public might know who has the audacity to utter such falsehoods.[3] The women themselves laugh at such clumsy tales. The Governor keeps up the spirit of infatuation of his supporters by repeated speeches, wherein he roundly ascribes to the opposition the stopping of provisions to marr the expedition and charges them with corresponding with the Prophet to prevent him coming to meet him &c he names nobody but leaves it to his well tutored followers to make the application, if he had the spirit to mention a name, I would soon make the wretch produce the evidence on which he grounds such dark insinuations.— The opposition as he terms it, is composed of all those who have honour & principles, and who view the most flagitious administration to which a poor Territory can be entrusted, with a merited abhorrence, the only thing they can be reproached with, is their being too tamely passive and of submitting to evils, which

[3] A reference to the article in the Washington *National Intelligencer* of September 17, cited above, p. 195.

it would require only a little spirit to remove.

I forgot to tell you that in addition to three captains to command perhaps one hundred and twenty horse, his Excellency has appointed a Major, a certain self important affectedly whimsical being of Kentucky named Joseph Daveiss known by a very indecent pamphlet against Mr. Jefferson.[4] That man did not like the Governor, the appointment may stop his mouth and shut his eyes.— A Joseph Baron[5] interpreter if he could be secured against the fear of losing his bread by a dismissal from his employment, can discover some precious secrets about the late treaties, but he must be examined at the seat of Government and not here— A call from Congress for the correspondence of Gov'r Harrison would also exhibit some interesting circumstances, explain some curious mysteries.

If my son Albert come back Safe, he can do the business of the office very correctly, could you permit a short absence? I want to see Pennsylvania once more; I want to see you before I die, you'll be glad to see your old friend, you'll find that he has not given you occasion to blush for him, you'll find that he is not unworthy of your friendship, that placed in the bosom of vice and corruption, if he has incurred the hatred he also commands the respect of his enemies. Such a meeting will add ten years to my life.

My family is well, my daughters give me every satisfaction, industry and propriety of conduct mark their steps, their natural good sense is improved by solid reading; Albert has the purest morals and never was seen to mix with the dissipated of his age. My wife is still what you knew her affectionate & kind, loved by every one who is acquainted with her—

---

[4] Daviess had been appointed U. S. District Attorney for Kentucky by President John Adams, but was removed from the post by Jefferson, which occasioned the issuing of the bitter pamphlet. *Dictionary of American Biography* (20 volumes plus index. New York, 1937), V, 80.

[5] Joseph Barron served as Indian interpreter for Harrison. He was with Harrison throughout the proceedings in connection with the treaty concluded at Fort Wayne in 1809.

These details will not I am Sure be uninteresting to you.

Fare you well For ever yours

JOHN BADOLLET

turn over

P. S. The plan of the Wabash Company is to bring an ejectment against a purchaser of the public lands. George Wallace is the ostensible manager; but the Governor appears to be the real one behind the curtain, the first consulting me about certain documents necessary to support that claim, shewed me unguardedly a paper wherein he was directed to procure them and I read on the top Extract of a letter to Governor Harrison— When the suit is entered against an Individual, he'll make no defense, what will be the result, would it not be advisable in the U. S. to furnish the defendant with able council and to defray the expenses of a suit? The action is not entered yet would it not be proper in Congress to pass an act at this session & in time allowing an appeal from this poor Court to a Federal Court?[6]

[Addressed:]  Albert Gallatin Esq  Private

[Endorsed:]  Vincennes  October  26, 1811  J  Badollet He supose the Legislature will praise the conduct of the Governor

[Badollet to Gallatin]

VINCENNES November 13, 1811

At last my dear Friend what I anticipated has taken place, by advices from the camp the following particulars have come to our knowledge, not in regular official accounts by [but] by the unanimous testimony of such persons as have come down.

The army continued their march and on the 6th inst. were encamped within gun shot of the Prophet's village, and such was their perseverance in adhering to an inoffensive system that the Governor rode round it unmolested. Some parleys ensued wherein it was at last concluded to have a conclusive conference on the next day. But it appears that a Negro in

[6] See above, pp. 149-50, 174.

the camp, of notable vicious disposition went over in the night
to the Indians, with the information, that the last day's proceeding were mere stratagems to decoy them into security,
and that the plan was to attack them the following day and
burn their village.[1] The consequence of which information was
that the Indians attacked the army thrown into a state of false
security a little before day light, with the fury of lions, they
would have made a cruel slaughter of the militia undisciplined
and insubordinate, had not Col. Boyd made a spirited charge
with his regulars which decided the action. It was a bloody
and dearly purchased victory,[2] amongst the slain are Joseph
Daveiss, Wm. Mahon,[3] Isaac White, and Thomas Randolph
of the Light horse, Major Robb,[4] Capt. Spier Spencer, Thomas
Berry & Jacob Warrick of the Militia, and Capt. Bain[5] of the
Regulars, amounting in all to about 172 killed and wounded
some mortally. Albert is safe yet. The Prophet's village was
next burnt and thus the efforts of some year's industry and
perseverance & the fruits of the first rational attempts to
reach the comforts of civilized life spontaneously made by the
northern Indians have been involved in a common ruin. Thus
we are plunged in the horrors of an indian war.

The army is returning and serious apprehensions are entertained here about their safety, an attack from the enemy now

[1] Another reference to a Negro informant is in Capt. Peter Funk's
narrative of the campaign: "It appeared that the indians had been
impressed with the idea that the army had cannon, but on the 6th the negro
driver of Gen. Harrison's cart mixed among them and informed them that
no big guns accompanied the expedition. For this treachery the negro was
by a court martial forthwith convicted and condemned to be shot, provided
an attack from the indians should ensue— The sentence however was not
carried into effect— It is supposed that had the expedition been provided
with Cannon, the indians would have been deterred from assaulting our
force." Esarey (ed.), *Messages and Letters,* I, 720.

[2] Accounts of the battle may be found in Esarey (ed.), *Messages and
Letters,* I, 608 ff.; see also Alfred Pirtle, *Battle of Tippecanoe* (Filson
Club *Publications,* No. 15, Louisville, 1900).

[3] Probably Richard McMahon.

[4] Probably Badollet means Capt. David Robb. However, he was not
killed.

[5] W. C. Baen.

driven to starvation and despair is with terror looked for. The Indians left about 50 dead on the field of battle.[6]

Such is the account I could collect from the runners sent down our situation is dreadfull, our scattered and unconnected settlements will exhibit scenes of desolation if the Indians will resent their injuries in their usual way. Government cannot too soon look this way. If there is any way to heal such a gaping wound it ought to be attempted. Some men of weight and humanity could not too soon be sent.

Fare-you well my Friend if any thing occurs of moment I'll let you know. Yours for ever

JOHN BADOLLET

[Addressed:] Albert Gallatin Esq  Private

[Endorsed:] Vincennes November 13, 1811  J Badollet A battle with the Indians

[Badollet to Gallatin]

VINCENNES Novr 19, 1811

The army my Dear Friend is returned unmolested, but not without constant fear of being attacked. These brave men by their intrepidity repulsed the enemy coming upon them un-expectedly & finding them encamped on a most disadvan-tageous ground. Whatever the untutored valour of the militia could do has been done, and the Reg't of Col. Boyd has behaved with the Skill and gallantry of veterans. The military talents of the Commander in chief appears to be of a piece with his virtues.—I have seen the wounded arrive, my God, what heart rending sight! what scene of woe! From an enemy we expect no mercy, but when at the hand of our friends, country men, of those we have defended, we meet with the most culpable neglect, the most unfeeling indifference,

[6] On November 18 Harrison reported to the Secretary of War that he was convinced that the Indians had lost many more men than he had. They had left 36 to 40 dead on the field, but had carried off an unknown number of both dead and wounded. As to his own forces he reported 37 killed on the field and 25 since dead of wounds. Esarey (ed.), *Messages and Letters,* I, 630.

when our sufferings excite no sympathy*—enough, the cadaverous smell which fills the small rooms wherein so many mangled human beings are crouded, has left upon my mind an impression of horror not to be effaced. Waller Taylor aid de camp of his Ex'y set off to day with the official account of the battle,[1] his military talents will be set forth therein in due colours, his foresight will appear in his being surprised, his vigilence in having issued no orders, sunk into a neglect of the necessary precautions, given to the troop no watch words & his skill & coup d'oeil in hemming them like St. Clair between swamps. When you read all that, remember Volney's observations on History, remember also *Sic vos no vobis vettera fortis.*

Parke, Judge Parke is commissioned bull dog to bark into silence and terror those who presume to think, he has publickly accused the opposition of having stopped the supplies of the army,* had the audacity to caution Caldwell a deserving member of the Legislature against speaking, other wise it would fare bad with him, & he has threatened another member so seriously that he has fled home to Clark County.[2] Dark hints are whispered about, we do not consider our lives as safe. I wish to God I was away. Never did I dream I ever would in America witness such things! We dread assassination, if ever those black calumnies come to be credited.

The opinion which I entertain in relation to our Indian affairs is that of most every body far & wide, & to this minute it is amongst the reflecting part, a settled belief that the indians were sincere in their so often repeated assurances they wanted peace and no war, that if the Governor had built

---

* this picture is perhaps too high coloured   much has been done for alleviating their suffering, but apathy reigns here et enough of unavoidable misery is left to rend the heart.
* which were never interrupted

[1] Printed in Esarey (ed.), *Messages and Letters,* I, 618-30.
[2] Thomas Downs probably. He was granted leave of absence for the remainder of the session on November 19. Thornbrough and Riker (eds.), *Journals of the General Assembly of Indiana Territory,* p. 380.

a garrison in the tract reserved by the treaty of Greenville, not a murmur would have been heard, but that his rashness in violating their territory, his approaching the Prophet's town with such a force and in such a menacing attitude, have convinced them that their destruction was intended, et driven them to despair.

Fare you well, remember your old friend

JOHN BADOLLET

20th.   Twenty three wounded have died since—My son who has made pretty correct observations during the campaign, tells me that to the day of his death he will believe that the object of the Governor was to bring on an indian war— He has a poor idea of his military talents, but an high one of his personal courage.— (Major Robb is not killed.)  When the army arrived at the Prophet's village, the Light horse passed through their corn field, and when he was asked why he had done so and what he came for, the answer was my young men are tired now   I'll let you know tomorrow morning.

[Addressed:] Albert Gallatin Esq'r   Secretary of the Treasury   Washington City  D. C.

[Endorsed:] Vincennes   November 19, 1811   J Badollet the army is returned unmolested

[Badollet to Gallatin]

VINCENNES  December 4, 1811

We are My Dear Friend in a state of awfull suspense here in relation to the consequences of that deplorable action with the Indians, but we are not however without hopes that they will now (as before) sue for peace. Their affections to the United States must however be totaly alienated, if not regained by a conciliatory and magnanimous conduct on their part.

I reported no act of hostility has been committed by the Prophet's band previous to that fatal night, & the evening before their fears excited by the appearance of that formidable military force, were increased greatly by witnessing their corn field opened crossed and trampled by the light horse & mounted

Rifle men; a pacific measure with a vengeance. The report of the Runaway Negroe must have no doubt contributed toward precipitating the Catastrophe.

The following facts are True, a Potawatomy tribe extolled by the Governor for their attachment to the U. S. and not the Prophet's people stole some horses from Bosseron settlement.—[1] One Henry Raimbaut a boatman in the Contractors employ was killed in the boat by the accidental explosion of his own gun which burnt his coat, and not by the Prophets people, as reported, the other hands were on the bank cooking their supper.[2]

Intrigues are now at work to prevent the legislature from praising too much Col. Boyd. Saturday a great meeting is to take place of those who were in the expedition & I am egregiously mistaken, if some fullsome address is not produced to praise his valour his foresight and generalship, & to averr that the imaginary dangers which the expedition was predicated on, were real & of the most dangerous nature.[3]

For protection I enclose a letter to Mr Jennings[4] I wish you would be so obliging as to deliver it to him.

Cordially yours &c

JOHN BADOLLET

[Addressed:]  Albert Gallatin Esq

---

[1] On April 23, 1811, Harrison reported to the Secretary of War that four Potawatomi who were living with members of their tribe "between the Wabash and Lake Michigan at no great distance from the Prophet's Town," had invaded the Busseron settlement twenty miles north of Vincennes and taken twelve horses. He identified them as belonging to the same band responsible for the murder of four whites in the fall of 1810 on the Missouri. On June 6 he reported that four of the horses had been recovered at the Prophet's town but that Tecumseh and the Prophet had denied having anything to do with taking them "altho' they acknowledged that it was done by the part of the Potawatomi tribe which are under their influence." Esarey (ed.), *Messages and Letters,* I, 506-7, 512.

[2] On November 2 Harrison reported that an attack had been made on a provision boat ascending the Wabash to his camp. It had been fired on four miles above Fort Harrison and one man had been killed. *Ibid.,* I, 606.

[3] See below, pp. 214-16.

[4] Not found.

[Endorsed:]  December 4 1811  J Badollet non hostility Committed Since the fatal night

[Badollet to Gallatin]

VINCENNES December 17, 1811

An event my Dear Friend as unexpected as it is ignominious has happened as follows.

At a moment that nobody even dreamt here that the Governor would dare to hope a single word of approbation from the Legislature, all of a sudden one of his supporters in the House of representatives rose and reading an address to the President replete of praises for every talent and virtue which the Governor does not possess and praying for his reappointment, moved for the adoption of the same. Three ayes were heard, the rest thunderstruck did not collect their spirits in time to utter one single nay. It was sent up to the Council who negatived it, sent up again for reconsideration and negatived a second time. The title then was altered from the *Legislative Council & House of Representatives* to the *House of representatives* only, and during the absence of the rest of the members, the Speaker & three other members, against the rules of the House which require a majority to form a quorum, adopted the said address with much precipitation & have forwarded it by the last mail, to the great terror of all the honest citizens.[1] Thus the President will be guided,

---

[1] Harrison's commission as governor would not expire until 1813. On December 12, 1811, James Dill, representative from Dearborn County, introduced the petition to which Badollet refers. It is given in Thornbrough and Riker (eds.), *Journals of the General Assembly of Indiana Territory,* pp. 452-53. As Badollet says it was rejected by the Council, which refused to reconsider its decision (*ibid.,* p. 459). Dill then, on December 14, submitted the same petition, but as coming from the House only, which was passed by the House (*ibid.,* pp. 463-64). None of the votes are recorded in the *Journals,* so it is impossible to verify Badollet's statement about the infraction of the rules. The passage of this resolution by the House is curious in light of the anti-Harrison sentiment expressed in resolutions which it passed praising Boyd and his command and pointedly omitting reference to Harrison. See *ibid.,* pp. 393-94n.

General Washington Johnston, representative from Knox County, in a letter to his constituents which was published in the *Western Sun* of

the territory is degraded, and our allarms are increased. There never was such a prostitution of language such a debasement. What will become of us? Will the truth never reach the first Magistrate? Must we in vain hope for redress? Never [has] human nature appeared to me under such an hideous shape. In the midle of depravity perfidy and baseness, I am weary of my very existence, a cruel experience has altered my unsuspecting temper, into a settled state of gloominess and fear & I can hardly credit my own senses, when told that I stand on American ground, the boasted seat of manly independance.

A member of the Legislature, after having in conversation with me, descanted with much heat on the evils of Territorial Government, and in particular on those we Suffer, concluded by observing that our only means of salvation was to enter into a state Government, he added that he would move a resolution to that effect, requested me to draw a memorial to Congress and desired me in writing it to dip my pen *in gall*. I went to work, not with gall, but what I thought a decent degree of vigor, telling boldly some wholesome truths. It appeared to meet his and others approbation; but behold, it went through such corrections and amendments, that it appeared before the house changed into milk and water: exhibiting incongruities and inconsistencies in point of style and matter, & shewing to the least observing eye the humiliating symptoms of fear, of intermitting with occasional paroxisms of awkward boldness. Some would have adopted it in its primitive shape. If I can restore the original I'll send it to you.[2]

December 28, wrote, "Considering the talents, valor, and equanimity of Governor Harrison, the House of Representatives petitioned the President and the Senate of the United States, to continue him in office. In thus acting, I feel not the least hesitation in believing and declaring, that our conduct will meet your most hearty and entire approbation; for although he has enemy's they are few, very few in comparison to our whole population."

[2] The memorial as submitted to the House is in Thornbrough and Riker (eds.), *Journals of the General Assembly of Indiana Territory,*

The facts mentioned above in relation to the address to the President are litterally true, if he take it to be the genuine expression of the general sentiments, he will mistake egregiously. Sycophantic adulation vegetates as luxuriently here as at the Court of the first Cesars, and as there, the honest part of the community emits only impotent and unheeded murmurs.

Fare well my Dear Friend Yours for ever

JOHN BADOLLET

Did you ever know that in 1805, a joint memorial of both houses of our Legislature for slavery which had been negatived, was restored out of doors, the signature of both Speakers affixed thereto by some means or another, was transmitted to Congress and read there by Park.[8] I[s] such an act plastered over?

[Addressed:] Albert Gallatin Esq'r Private

[Endorsed:] Vincennes December 17, 1811    Badollet do not like the G'r be so much praised.

VINCENNES December 17, 1811

I have just time to enclose you the subjoined pieces, and to inform you that since the battle, as before not one act of injury has been committed by the Indians to this day, whence it appears that they fought *pro aris and focis.* The Governor

---

pp. 442-44. It was opposed in the House by James Dill of Dearborn County, Richard Rue of Wayne County, and Peter Jones of Knox County. *Ibid.,* p. 968. Jones and Dill sent a protest to Congress saying the population of the territory was too small for statehood and the expenses would be too great. Carter (ed.), *Territorial Papers,* VIII, 147-48. On the other hand, Johnston, in his letter cited in the preceding note, wrote, "The economical advantages which the general government will derive from this measure, induces me to hazard the belief that it will be acceded to." Vincennes *Western Sun,* December 28, 1811.

[8] Printed in Thornbrough and Riker (eds.), *Journals of the General Assembly of Indiana Territory,* pp. 101-8. It opened with the statement that it was "a petition of the subscribers, members of the Legislative Council and House of Representatives of the Indiana Territory, and constituting a majority of the two Houses." The committee of the U. S. House of Representatives to which it was referred spoke of it as the "petition of the Legislative Council and House of Representatives of said Territory." *Ibid.,* pp. 101n-2n.

wanted to usurp a military name, he has waded in blood to obtain it. He now must of course supercede his patron & friend G. Wilkinson[4] & I expect to hear he is appointed.

Fare you well yours for ever     JOHN BADOLLER

[Addressed:] Albert Gallatin Esq'r Private

[Endorsed:] Vincennes Decemb 17, 1811 John Badollet Indians peacefull

[Enclosures][5]

At a numerous meeting,[6] (public notice for that purpose being given) of the Officers and Non commissioned officers, or privates of the Militia corps (Hargroves company excepted) of the county of Knox, which served on the late campaign under Gov. Harrison, met at Beckes's Inn, in Vincennes, on the 7th December, 1811, Col. Luke Decker was appointed Chairman, and Major Benjamin Parke, Clerk.

A paper purporting to be an address from *"A number of the citizens of Vincennes and its vicinity,"* and signed by Henry Vanderburgh, as Chairman to *Col. John P. Boyd,*[7] being read, the following resolutions were thereupon unanimously agreed to.

1. *Resolved unanimously,* that we can not consider the said Address in any other light than as *one* amongst the *many* attempts which have flowed from the same source, to wound the feelings and injure the character of Governor Harrison.

2. *Resolved,* That the said Address in attempting to bestow the merit of the *masterly conduct* in the directions and manoevering of troops in the late action to any other than the Commander in chief asserts a notorious untruth, which will be acknowledged as such by the whole army.

3. That our indignation is justly excited at the false and contemptuous manner in which the *Militia* who served under Governor Harrison are treated, in the said address; being

---

[4] Badollet probably means Gen. James Winchester.
[5] Clipped from the Vincennes *Western Sun,* December 14, 1811.
[6] For Badollet's account of this meeting, see his following letter.
[7] For Badollet's report on this address, see his following letter.

there represented as an *untutored undisciplined* band, possessing, indeed courage, but none of the other requisites of soldiers; and owing eternal gratitude to Col. Boyd and his Regiment, for the preservation of their lives.

4. That the *Militia* which served under Governor Harrison were neither *untutored* nor *undisciplined,* but in common with the Regular troops they shared the attention of the Commander in Chief, and that by his *personal exertions,* both the Militia and Regulars were brought to a state of perfection in that kind of manoevering calculated for Indian warfare, and that they were enabled to perform all the directions of the Commander in Chief with promptness, facility, and precision.

6.[5] That it is a notorious fact, known to the whole army, that all the changes of position made by the troops during the action of the 7th ult. and by which the victory was secured, were made by the direction of the Commander in Chief, and generally executed under his immediate superintendance.

6. That we cannot but view as a most dangerous usurpation, the meeting of a few individuals, not more than from seven to ten, in a private house, without any previous or public notice being given, and to pass resolutions and addresses in the name of a neighborhood.—And we do further view the conduct of said individuals, (*almost every one of whom are the avowed enemies of the Commander in Chief—and several of whom have uniformly discountenanced and opposed every measure of the government, in respect to the Shawanoe Prophet and his party, and none of whom were on the Campaign*) in daring to speak in the name of the Militia, as highly presumptuous and unwarrantable.

7. That it was owing to the skill and valor of the Commander in Chief that the victory of *Tippecanoe* was obtained.

8. That we have the most perfect confidence in the Commander in Chief, and shall always feel a cheerfulness in serving under him whenever the exigences of the country may require it.

9. That we would prefer serving under him to any person that could be designated by the government for that purpose.

10. That when commanded by him, honor will be atchieved; and we have every confidence that victory will be obtained.

11. That in expressing the above opinions, in respect to the reprehensible conduct of the *Addressers,* we desire it to be distinctly understood, that we have no idea of wounding the feelings or injuring the character of Col. Boyd, but we are free to declare, that we believe his conduct during the actions, to have been that of a gentleman and of a soldier.

12. That we feel the highest respect, and shall always recollect with gratitude, our brothers in arms, the Officers and *Privates* of the U. S. Troops.—*We have often heard. . . . We have* now seen *what* YANKEE's *can do!*

13. That in obeying our country's call we shall feel a proud satisfaction in being associated with *Kentucky* volunteers.

14. That the above resolutions be inserted in the *Western Sun*—and that such Printers as may give publicity to the Address above mentioned, be requested to publish also the aforesaid resolutions.

LUKE DECKER, Chairman.

B. PARKE, *Clerk.*

---

[Done at Vincennes by some one of the sycophantic crew] Extract from a letter to a Gentleman in this place. [Vincennes][8]

SIR,

Your observations in your last, when speaking of certain characters, endeavoring to detract from the well earned merit of His Excellency WILLIAM HENRY HARRISON, was correct. When an individual upon earth will not even know that an enemy to him ever lived—his name and character will be

---

[8] On this clipping from the *Western Sun* of December 14, Badollet wrote the words enclosed in brackets.

revered by those yet unborn, and when spoken of it will be with admiration. No doubt, but the future page of history will do justice to his merit, and if so, his honorable fame will be lasting as a WASHINGTON or a WAYNE.

I have not to hesitate when saying he is the first military character in the United States—and as to his capacity in other respects equalling any man, is a matter not even questioned.

[Badollet to Gallatin]

VINCENNES December 30, 1811

Read and stare my Friend. At the return of the army from that ever to be lamented expedition, although the militia who had shared the dangers of that dreadfull night, were unanimous in proclaiming that the army had been *saved* by Col. Boyd and his brave Regiment yet from apathy or through some secret influence, those gallant men were received here with the most chilling coolness. A small number of us indignant at such reception met and resolved to address that meritorious Officer. I was desired to draught the address, which I did, Judge Vander Burgh & myself were appointed to wait on the Col. with it, which we accordingly did. The address is as follows :[1]

"Sir, Permit us to convey to you and through you to the Officers and men of the Regiment you command, the exalted sense we entertain of the masterly and spirited conduct which you have displayed in the late engagement with the Indians at Tippicanoe and to express the gratitude which fills our hearts for so many lives which your gallant exertions have contributed to preserve. Your near departure from this country prevents a more general and public manifestation of these sentiments, which are not peculiar to ourselves; we find them universally entertained, and *Those Brave Regulars,* expressions repeated with enthusiasm by that spirited but untutored militia, who witnessed and emulated your cool intrepid-

---

[1] This address was published in the *Western Sun* of January 4, 1812.

ity, evince at once the importance of the service you have rendered, and the warmth of their gratitude. In endeavouring thus to pourtray our feelings on the present occasion, we present you the only reward it is in our power to bestow the homage of thankfullness and truth, not the less gratifying to noble minds, for being spontaneous and artless.

"A great good Sir will flow from your example, our fellow-citizens will be convinced that valour without Science cannot, however duly exerted, lead to certain successes, and may eventually cause an useless effusion of blood, that an armed force without military knowledge is little better than an inefficient multitude and they will learn to submit with cheerfulness to that discipline and subordination which alone can render its efforts consentaneous and irresistible.[2]

"In addressing you thus Sir, we are satisfied that we are discharging a duty of sacred justice, and we will reluctantly take leave of you, with prayers to the author of all good, that he may long preserve you and your gallant companions in arms for the honour and defense of our common country

Signed HENRY VANDER BURGH Chair'n
JOHN JOHNSON Secr'y

To JOHN P. BOYD,
Col. 4th Reg't U. S. Inf'y["][3]

Well, it seems that the above well meant and honest effusion of our hearts gave much offense to the Commander

[2] A meeting of the volunteer mounted riflemen on the Tippecanoe campaign resolved among other things, "That that part of the letter of Henry Vanderburgh, which say that the militia were an untutored and undisciplined band, is considered by us as a groundless and malicious falsehood, and is calculated to take from them, (the militia) the never-fading laurels they won by their heroism, their bravery and their firmness. . . . That we view the address of Henry Vanderburgh, as an unjustifiable attempt to wound the feelings of the commander in chief of the late expedition. . . ." Vincennes *Western Sun,* January 4, 1812.

[3] Colonel Boyd's reply was printed in the *Western Sun* of January 4, 1812. It expressed his gratitude and that of his regiment for the approbation given to their conduct: "it is the soldiers boon and if we have deserved it of our country, we are gratified by your public appreciation of our exertions, which are ever ready to meet the commands of our country."

in chief, who was not unwilling that the honour of having invigorated the militia by their example and saved that little army from the danger into which his rashness and incapacity had brought it, should some way or another be filched from the real owners. A meeting of the militia who had returned from the campaign was advertised, a motley croud met on the 7th ins't and the whisky circulated lively. Judge Parke, that fit instrument of a petty Despot, headed the mob and ascending the rostrum with the malignity of a fiend, represented the above address (which if read might have testified for itself) as designed to vilify the militia, spoke of our meeting & especially of Judge Vander Burgh John Johnson and myself in terms worthy of a calumniator and a blackguard and wrought the rage of that multitude to such a pitch, that they openly threatened to tarr & feather us. He read the address then, and in such a manner that it was not understood or understood wrong. Resolutions were then entered into, which, if not ashamed of, when become sober, they will have the impudence to forward to Government.[4] The evening which followed was a scene of fights & riot. Deplorable indeed is the situation of a country where a Supreme judge relying upon the protection of his master, can and mindfull of the sacredness of his Office, be the instigator of, and sharer in, Such excesses. Be it as it may you have our guilt under your eyes, read again the above address & see whether there is an expression therein, which can warrant the diabolical interpretation & inferences of that exalted wretch. The members of our meeting were Henry Vander Burgh first Judge of the General Court, James Johnson Presiding Judge of the Court of Common Pleas, Francis Vigo former Colonel of the militia of Knox Co. John D. Hay recorder of Knox Co. James Crow now & Christopher Wyant formerly High Sheriffs of the Same, John Caldwell member of the Legislature, John Johnson clerk of the House of Representatives, Nathanial

[4] These are the resolutions enclosed by Badollet in his letter of December 17, above.

Ewing Receiver of public monies, several other respectable Gentleman & myself.(a)

I see the reason of his Ex'y's irritation, it was surely hard for a man who had taken such pains to lecture General Scot of Kentucky on the campaigns of Pelopidas & Epaminondas, on the cuneus & the phalanx &c,[5] not to be eulogised in high coloured strains but he ought to have considered our Silence as a high compliment, because the less is said of him the better.

The truth is that the army was completely surprised that the undaunted countenance of the 4th Regiment and the superiority of their discipline, invigorated the militia and inspired them with a noble emulation, that all strove gallantly to repell the enemy & and finally succeeded but at a price upon which the humane must shed tears, at the expense of more than one hundred brave men besides the great number of those who cripled & deprived of their limbs will with their families be a prey to poverty & wretchedness.

The little band of the Prophet and his brother, were not a banditti as I see them affectedly called in the public papers, they were a set of orderly sober and industrious men, who exhibited an appearance of decency and order worthy of imitation, whom we have driven to despair, in spite of their repeated cries for peace. This act does reflect no honour on the boasted of justice of the United States. The powerful oppressing the weak is a spectacle which always distresses my heart and which I fondly hoped, never would be exhibited by the United States.

---

(a) except Judge Vander Burgh & another none of us had any acquaintance with Col. Boyd or his officers.[6]

[5] A reference to two long letters which Harrison wrote to Gen. Charles Scott, governor of Kentucky, on the "Discipline of the Militia of the United States." They were printed in the Vincennes *Western Sun,* August 11 and 18, 1810, and reprinted in Esarey (ed.), *Messages and Letters,* I, 400-17.

[6] The *Western Sun* of February 15 identifies those present beside Badollet and Vanderburgh as Ewing, John Johnson, John Caldwell, and William McIntosh.

It seems to me that the only means of making up that enormous breach & of conciliating for ever the lost affection of the Indians, and the only one worthy of a magnanimous nation, would be, after the conclusion of peace, to cause their town to be rebuilt & furnished again with the conveniencies instruments of all kinds & provisions which have been too wantonly destroyed.

The Legislature are passing an act for the removal of the seat of Government[7] the bill has passed the lower house, at that stage of the business & to stop its further progress Mr. Henry Hurst, clerk of the General Court, Clerk of the Court of Chancery, aid de camp to his Excellency and his confidential Councellor wrote the inclosed in the Representatives Chamber, and delivering it to Wm. McFarland member for Jefferson County requested him to hand it to the Council. I have to apoligize to you for placing under your eyes a piece of writing of such a disgusting & filthy vulgarity, but it conveys a more lively idea of our degradation and of the nature of the yoke which presses hard upon us, than one hundred comments of mine, I wish it could be shewn with propriety to the President, that he might have a correct idea of our situation, of the degree of audacity which the friendship of our Executive can inspire, of the kinds of men he appoints to and continues in high offices and of the ignominious situation to which we are reduced.

[7] When Indiana Territory was divided with the creation of Illinois Territory, it was generally understood that the capital of the former would be moved somewhere closer to the center of the territory. The bill provided that after the 1st of May, 1812, the seat of government of the territory would be in Madison and remain there until a permanent capital was fixed upon. It carried other provisions concerning removal, including one that the governor should be in Madison during the sitting of the legislature. Harrison vetoed the bill. For its provisions and the veto message see Thornbrough and Riker (eds.), *Journals of the General Assembly of Indiana Territory,* pp. 429-30, 469-71. Harrison gave as one of his reasons for vetoing the bill that it had passed both houses by a bare majority and in the House two members of the nine were absent, who he felt would probably have opposed the measure. These two were representatives from Clark and Harrison counties, and their opposition seems like

Fare you well my Dear Friend remember me drop me but one single line, it would be to me a powerfull comforter.

Ever Yours

JOHN BADOLLET

[Addressed:] Private Albert Gallatin Esq'r

[Endorsed:] Vincennes Decemb 10 [30], 1811 J. Badollet enclosing an address to Col'l Boyd

[Enclosure]

An Act providing punishment for certain Offenses

Be it enacted by the Legislative Council and House of Representatives and it is hereby enacted by the authority of the same, That no member of the Legislative Council shall under the pains & panalties hereafter mentioned vote for or anywise give countenance to, either as member of the Council or as a private citizen, a removal of the seat of Government of this Territory from Vincennes to any such nasty dirty . . . hole or Hawksnest as Beech town alias Madison in the County of Jefferson in said Territory, and any member of the said Council or other person herein offending shall for the first offense, being thereof duly convicted before any Court of record or Honour, receive on his bareback twenty five lashes, and for the second Offence fifty lashes as aforesaid and be . . . driven out of the Territory.

[Badollet to Gallatin]

VINCENNES February 26, 1812

The period is drawing near, when it will become my duty to expose for sale all those Tracts for which the complete payment shall not have been made at the time required by law. Of the manner of conducting that business, which will be attended with some practical difficulties, I have no kind of information, & I am at too great distance from every other land office to avail myself of their experience by repairing there. I would therefore be glad of some directions from you,

wishful thinking on the part of the Governor. The three members from Knox County voted against the bill. *Ibid.,* p. 430. The capital was moved to Corydon in 1813.

on the proper entries to be made in the book of entries & journal, in case of either forfeiture or sale, on the mode adopted to close the individual accompts in short on every point which may have any relation to the subject.

The Indians have hitherto remained perfectly quiet, sending frequently messages for peace, but I am very much afraid that such a calm may eventually be followed by a storm, if by this time Government has not taken some measures to avert it, which in my opinion and that of every reflecting man, may be easily effected provided negotiators in whom the Indians can have confidence are employed, for you may rely upon it, no cordial accommodation can be accomplished through the agency of Harrison or any of his subordinates, he is too much disliked & mistrusted.

We are told that Tecumseh is coming down with a small attendance of men women and children, with pacific views no doubt, he blames his brother for not confining himself to the defensive, his wish is to go to the President, but I believe he is mistrustfull of the interpreters. That man could unfold a tale— The Democratic presses are vapouring about british intrigues, but if they have in reality excited the Indians, they have excited them to pursue the arts of peace, to seek in their own labour a less precarious means of subsistence than the chase, to abandon the use of liquors, & to tye themselves to the soil by cultivation & the erections of convenient & comfortable buildings. Such are their acts of enmity and no other can be produced, any thing in Official communications to the contrary notwithstanding.— Again if the Indians have been excited to hostilities by the British, why does the President tell us that all the Tribes, the solitary instance of the Prophet excepted, are disposed for peace. The dangerous projects of the British have then been confined to the raising against us 2 or 300 men, poor devils who had been these three years at their hoes! Plans of such a dangerous magnitude may well raise the indignation of the whole of the United S; it is not the first time that they have been gulled, & the army raised by John Adams to resist a french invasion, as well as the legislative praises bestowed upon Mr. *Would-be* prove too clearly that the nation is credulous and unthinking, if not worse. Have you seen the huge *Veni Vidi Vici* of our proconsul,[1] it takes up half a paper of little trivial details throwing but a visible obscurity on the Skirmish of that night, on the great tactics of the rival (says a grave judge & a important member of the legislature) & equal of Washington O god! oh god! at reading the despatches, such puerile egotism raises a sardonic grinn of contempt, but the indignation seizes the soll [soul] at reading the praises bestowed upon a bad man— Such a prostitution of language!

I am not an unattentive observer of passing events, & I must confess that the spectacle imparts very little enjoyment and raises very few hopes, I see too much, not to begin to believe, that our boasted institutions look better in prospect, than on a near approach, & when I see intrigues & depravity triumphing, modest & solid merit unattended to, the honors which the people or the administration can bestow lodged in hands unworthy of them, my respect for our republican system is on the wane. What do you think of the absurd doctrine that the Representatives are bound by the instructions of their constituents, it is pregnant with innumerable & momentous evils, & I am afraid that if the public opinion, in relation to that subject, does not undergo a change, it will go very nigh towards ruining us. We republicans may perhaps verify the old adage, *let him have rope enough & he will hang himself.*

If there be such a book in existence as Geography for the use of schools by the Rev. J. Goldsmith,[2] I wish I could through

---

[1] Probably a reference to Harrison's report on the Battle of Tippecanoe, cited above, p. 208. It was printed in the Vincennes *Western Sun,* February 1, 1812.

[2] "Rev. J. Goldsmith" was a pseudonym for Sir Richard Phillips, author and bookseller, who produced among a variety of writings a number of manuals and texts for school children. Badollet probably wanted his *Geography, Illustrated on a Popular Plan,* which went through several editions.

your means get one of them.

Fare well   Your   &c

Jno Badollet

[Addressed:]   Albert Gallatin Esq'r   Private

[Endorsed:]   Vincennes february 26, 1812   J. Badollet
Wants some directions in Case of forfeiture

[Badollet to Gallatin]

Vincennes April 8, 1812

An event has just taken place at the consequence of which
every man not entirely swallowed up in sordid pursuits, feels a
lively interest, namely the sudden death of H. Vander Burgh
Presiding judge of our General Court. If the President does
not chuse to appoint an Successor out of the Territory,
amongst the law characters who may be pointed at, many
consider John Johnson (and I am of that number) of this
place as not undeserving of the trust. I know him well: to his
professional or legal knowledge, he unites a correct and discerning mind and an unimpeachable moral rectitude & will I
doubt not be recommended.

If the President should wish to make a choice some where
else than this Territory, you'll acknowledge with me the
propriety of appointing a man clear of the prejudices of the
Slave states, from Penn'a for instance, many important questions in relation to a class of men every day injured and
oppressed in broad day light and in defiance of ordinance and
law, being in process of time to come before our General Court
for decision & to require vigorous and unbiassed minds. But
above all Save, my dear friend, oh save this Territory from
the misfortunes and the U. S. from the ignominy of seeing
such a wretch as H. Hurst exalted to the honourable post, to
which I doubt not he will find here characters sufficiently
profligate to recommend him.[1]

[1] James Fisk, a representative from Vermont, was appointed to succeed
Vanderburgh on July 1, but he declined to serve and James Scott was ap-
pointed on January 29, 1813. Carter (ed.), *Territorial Papers*, VIII, 214n.
Scott had moved to the Northwest Territory in 1797 and to Clark County

I wish you would be so kind as to have a few words on the subject with Messrs. Finley, Smiley and Jennings. In relation to the administration of justice this Territory deserves compassion.

With the same sincerity of attachment I remain yours &c

JOHN BADOLLET

[Addressed:]   Albert Gallatin   Private

[Endorsed:]   Vincennes Apl 8 1812   J Badollet

*Note.*[2] By the ordinance, slavery is forever forbidden in this territory. The effort of Gov'r Harrison to have an alteration in that respect, has been the source of all the territorial dissention w'h have taken place.   A. G.

[Badollet to Gallatin]

VINCENNES April 29, 1812

DEAR FRIEND

The expedition of last fall up the Wabash can be considered in no other light than that of an outrageous aggression on an unoffending & peaceable neighbour, and a wanton waste of treasure & blood. But whatever opinion may be entertained in relation to it, the consequences are at this moment as disastrous as real. The bloody tomahawk is now *in fact* raised, the work of murder has begun, a whole family has been destroyed in the new purchase, the bones of which have been found in the ashes of their house, last friday about seven miles from this place One Harriman his wife and five children were murdered[1] & it is now ascertained that large collections

in 1810. He was recommended for the judgeship by Jennings who also recommended John Johnson and Elijah Sparks. Jennings also said that either General W. Johnston or Henry Hurst would "be illy received as Judges, by the great majority of the Territory." Hurst was recommended by Parke and others. *Ibid.,* VIII, 175, 176, 178, 186. See sketch of Scott in Thornbrough and Riker (eds.), *Journals of the General Assembly of Indiana Territory,* pp. 1011-12.

[2] This note is in Gallatin's hand.

[1] This wholesale murder was reported in the *Western Sun* of April 25 and in letters from Governor Harrison to the Secretary of War on April 22 and 29. In the second letter (written on the same day as Badollet's) Harrison reported other Indian atrocities, adding, "It is impossible Sir to give

of Indians are forming on the Wabash above us, with a view it is said and believed of retaliating upon this place the inhuman burning of the Prophet's town. The terror is inexpressible, the Scattered settlements fall back a few forts are formed & the country hitherto flourishing is fast returning to a state of wilderness. The town is crouded with fugitive families & which is worse than all our *consummate* general panick struck, has laid down all his heroical airs & is in a state of *inertia,* unable to devise a single step for the common defense. He betrays his incapacity by inviting the citizens to meet and adopt plans of resistance, they meet and meet again, separate again and again, as was to be foreseen, without a plan. This wretched idea of consulting every old woman, every Peter, Jack, & Harry augments the general despondence by exhibiting in a striking point of view the wants of talents of the Commander in chief. At a last meeting they at last adopted the wise plan of dividing the town into a certain number of districts, the respective inhabitants of which are to repair to and defend certain designated houses, thus admitting the enemy in the midle of the place, permiting him to set fire to it & depriving themselves of the advantage of United exertions. The consequences must be fatal. As to myself it is useless to describe my distress, my house the last towards Vincennes is fast becoming a frontier residence. I have these several nights slept with my family at Ewings, who has a brick house & I know not what to do, either make a stand there or to go to Vincennes, in either case my House & all, if I should escape, will be burnt down.

you an adequate Idea of the alarm and distress which these murders have produced. . . . Families, abandoning their homes and flying they know not whither and many of them without any means of support, are seen in every direction. Nor is the situation of this town by any means such as offers security to the fugitives. The expected departure of the regular troops and the revival of the design by the Prophet and his Party . . . to surprise it by a water expedition cause it to be viewed as a place of greater danger than any other and the fugitives pass through it as expeditiously as possible." Esarey (ed.), *Messages and Letters,* II, 41-43.

Unfortunately at this critical moment the mock treaty[2] held at this place has reached Government with the assurances of our Gov'r that there is no more danger, that peace is restored, unfortunately also the 4th Regt. has this minute receive[d] order to march to Dayton.[3] We are thus left with a militia without discipline without subordination & without an effective Head. Let the adulations of Waller Taylor be repeated, the application of all those fullsome praises is not to be made here.

Such is the disastrous situation of a country not long ago progressing in peace, all is blasted, the Territory is ruined for years to come, and all that by the crime of One Man!

Whatever may be the event, I recommend those who may survive me to your paternal care. If things turn out better than is contemplated I'll give you early information.

Fare you well my dear Friend  Ever Yours

JOHN BADOLLET

The Governor has called for no assistance from Kentucky— Why does not the State of Ohio make a diversion in our favour from about Fort Recovery to the Wabash, which is so near to that place?

[Addressed:]  Albert Gallatin Esq'r  Secretary of the Treasury  Private

---

[2] Harrison apparently held a council at Vincennes with deputies from the tribes which opposed him at Tippecanoe sometime between February 26 and March 4, at which time the Indians indicated that they were anxious for peace. Esarey (ed.), *Messages and Letters,* II, 26, and Carter (ed.), *Territorial Papers,* VIII, 179.

[3] By orders of April 4, the 4th regiment was ordered to leave Vincennes for Dayton, destined for Detroit. On May 14, after the outbreak of Indian atrocities, this order was rescinded and the 4th regiment was ordered to remain at Vincennes until Harrison felt that the United States rangers and regular troops commanded by Col. William Russell were equal to the protection of the territory. However, by the time this order reached Vincennes the entire regiment had departed. Carter (ed.), *Territorial Papers,* VIII, 181; Esarey (ed.), *Messages and Letters,* I, 708; II, 67; Mary Crawford (ed.), "Mrs. Lydia B. Bacon's Journal, 1811-1812," in *Indiana Magazine of History,* XLI (1945), 60.

[Endorsed:] Vincennes April [2]9, 1812 J. Badollet the expedition of last fall an agression on our nebours

[Badollet to Gallatin]

VINCENNES May 6, 1812

Our situation is still the same if not more allarming, a new murder[1] on the East Fork of White river.— The consummate General is fortifying his own house & leaves the town to shift for itself. he diffuses despondence and distrust by observing that the town is in real danger & *kindly* offering an asylum within *his* strong hold to such as will accept of it, no measure for the general protection, the country which last year exhibited the preparations of military enterprise, where the banners of war were ostentatiously unfurled, where drums & trumpets were sounding, looks in the present moment when the enemy is at our door in a deadly lethargy. Every thing that is done is the work of unconnected individuals collected in groups forted in forts scattered throughout the settlements & leaving wide uninhabited intervals through which the enemy can safely penetrate. The great military ardour of the famous Hero of Tippecanow seem to have Sunk into a selfish sollicitude for his own safety & that of his family and property. The former he has sent to Cincinnati the latter he secures by a stockade. Some of the Citizens & favoured Gentlemen have seized upon the Seminary which they fortify for themselves, the land Officers are left without with the public records under the protection of—Providence. No patrole, no scouters no spyes to detect the approach of the enemy. Dreadfull is the situation of the country governed by a man who has the greatest interest in blowing up the flame of war; the Indians by their *present* murders and depredations play into his hands, & will give a colour of truth to his past assertions & the treaties, by which the Indians were *politely forced* to part with their lands, as well as the guilty negociator will be forgotten in the tumult of a bloody warfare. Such is

[1] John McGowan was the victim's name. Esarey (ed.), *Messages and Letters,* II, 44.

the awfull situation of our country. As to myself my situation
is peculiarly distressing within 3 miles of the town towards
which I am the last habitation; having on the west an uninhabited extent of barrens and marshy grounds partly covered
with thikets terminated by the Wabash, beyond which no
settlement, except a few families enclosed in one fort, can
be discovered till you reach the Illinois country, 150 miles
off. In such an exposed spot I cannot promise myself any
safety, I have hitherto gone to Ewings, but his house situated
one mile off in very thik woods, although it might afford
security for the night cannot secure me against the daily
dangers of an ambush in going to my Office. To go to town
would be preferable, if the place was under a rational system
of defense, (& the danger is great there the prevailing
opinion being that the Indians will make a bold attack on it
& burn it down) but my place must be left defenceless, my
house & all may be pillaged & consumed, my horses & cattle
lost or killed. My situation is truly distressing— Under such
awfull circumstances ought we not to be relieved from the
necessity of attending our offices? But unfortunately this
is the fifth year since the sale & the lands unpaid for, must be
exposed for Sale. I wish I could be transferred or had a way
to live somewhere else, not altogether on account of the present
distress, but also on account of the power unaccountably left
in the hands of a man who unextinguishable hate will pursue
to destruction, those who will not forsake their own esteem for
the sake of his favours, who dare to think & to speak the
language of manly truth. If ever I can see you I can shew you
that our fears are not quite visionary.

Adieu Ever yours &c

JOHN BADOLLET

[Endorsed:] Vincennes 6 may 1812 J Badollet he don't
think himself safe in his house.

[Badollet to Gallatin]

VINCENNES May 19 1812

We are my Friend in the awfull calm which precedes a

storm, attended with all its dark forebodings. The panick which has seized on the country is evinced by the abandonment of habitations and retiring into multiplied but weakly manned forts, led by the more serious emigration which still continues & becomes every day more allarming. This place, which it is the prevailing opinion, the Indians intend to destroy is left without any means of effectual defense. The Governor, whose military phrenzy last year in the midle of peace converted Vincennes into a camp, is now reduced to the standard of an "old woman" or something worse. He, without taking one *single step* for the general defense, has dwelt upon the grandeur and urgency of the danger advised wooden walls & to shew the example, has set about picketting his house & taking in as many as he could for *their sake*. This measure, which has spread in town a tenfold panick, has been imitated by some who have retired in and fortified the Seminary and by a few others who have picketted their own houses. Hence flow lamentable consequences, the strength of the place is frittered away and must become of no effect, the militia companies are dissolved and there is no head to which the people can look up for directing their efforts in the common distress. It is also attended with a moral effect no less to be deplored. Instead of keeping alive the (correct) idea that in united and consentaneous exertions, the general safety is placed, that the interest of one individual cannot be separated from that of the whole, in a word instead of kindling a generous patriotism, a spirit of dastardly selfishness is created or vastly increased, and those who have taken refuge behind their pickets, will not peek out of them in the moment of danger & the rest separated dispirited & without an officer to direct and animate their steps, would with their houses and families successively fall a prey to the flames and Tomahawk.[1] The picketted gentry themselves may learn too late the folly of their measures by not

---

[1] On May 6 Harrison wrote the Secretary of War, "Most of the citizens in this country have abandoned their farms and taken refuge in

being able to withstand the attack of an enemy flushed by success.

Thus my Friend that brillant meteor in the galaxy of military heroes, who has sung & caused so many sycophantic pens & venal presses to sing his unparalleled military talents, is at last eclipsed behind a wooden fence, and the New Washington has sunk into a pitifull and selfish Sir John Falstaf not daring to defend those he has exposed, nor to face the enemy he has ostentatiously and wantonly provoked.

Many circumstances too minute to detail have given rise to an idea that he exaggerates the danger, and not few believe that he would not be sorry that matters were utterly and irretrievably embroiled, and it is but too true that a general indian war would with the superficial and unthinking, instead of the consequence of the last fall's *unprovoked* aggression, be taken as an evidence of his foresight and vigilance & have the retrospective effect of washing off the foul stain, and he knows it well.

Some Miamis chiefs have lately come down and have assured the Governor that the Miamis Delawares, Kickapoos and Winebagoes & Shawnes wanted to remain at peace, that the last murders were committed by a few of the Potawatamies & that they would kill them. I am told that the Governor observed "I believe you the people of Tecumseh have often

such temporary forts as they have been able to construct. Nothing can exhibit more distress than those wretched people crowded together in places almost destitute of every necessary accommodation. Unless something can be done soon to enable the people to return to their farms I fear that there will be little or no corn planted this season."

On the 13th he wrote, "I am perfectly at loss as to the orders proper to be given in the present state of the country. I do not conceive myself authorized to order out any militia at the expense of the United States. . . . Altho the people of this part of the Territory are generally in Forts it is impossible to make any disposition of a company of Rangers to prevent small parties of Indians from penetrating the settlements to do mischief, and our line of frontier is so extensive that even the kind of protection which the Rangers do afford, cannot be extended to more than one fourth of it. I must beg leave to call your attention to the enclosed statement of the deficiency of arms. . . ." Esarey (ed.), *Messages and Letters,* II, 44, 48.

threatened Winemack on account of his attachment to the United States"— No said the Miamis, but because he is a villain, robbing the Red & White & carrying falsehoods between them. This Potowatamie chief Winemack is the greatest villain amongst the tribes & knows well, that whatever mischief is committed by him, will, (such is the *voluntary* prejudice of the Governor blindly adopted by the multitude) be ascribed to Tecumseh and his Shawnese.[2]

The information of those Miamis uncoroborated by the fact that the three acts of murder which I mentioned to you, and one of a man on White Water, all following one another at short intervals, have been followed these two weeks by no other, which repells the idea of (as yet) a general combination.

I live yet in my house, with blinders to my windows and doors, & my boys with a young fellow working on the place for defense, my situation is far from comfortable, inasmuch as I must & do come every day to town weakening by so much our strength. The town looks like a desert & with the measures or rather the no measures taken for its defense, is far from becoming a place of Safty. The Country people (who have not emigrated) will not leave their forts & families, all idea therefore of assistance from that quarter is done away & in fact there exists no more any organized military force. Those things ought to have been foreseen last year, they ought to have been foreseen at least after the battle & measures taken, but Government have believed as our Governor had asserted that the action at Tippiconoe had been a decisive victory! Yes, it has decided that the prospect of this Territory should be blasted for years to come. How long shall we be

[2] In his letter of May 6, cited above, Harrison referred to Winemac, and not in the vein attributed to him by Badollet. He said that the chief was desirous of coming to Vincennes but that he and his party were being retained at Fort Harrison for fear that they would be killed in Vincennes. "Those people were at Fort Harrison when the Murder was committed on McGowan and very probably by a part of the same tribe [Potawatomi]. It is thus we are served," he continued, "by these scoundrels. Whilst some of them are making warm professions of friendship and enjoying our hospitality others are murdering our citizens." *Ibid.*, II, 45.

left under the sway of a man betraying such incapacity & so much vice?

An opinion is darkly whispered about that those who do not fort are the friends of the Indians, this may be the harbinger of darker deeds, bravos are not wanting here and indian paint can easily disguise a person & be washed away.

Upon the whole from what I can hear & see I am still of opinion (& I am not the only one, some of the most thinking ancient inhabitants here are asserting the same*) that it is yet in the power of the United States, by a conduct candid just and generous, to preserve the friendship of all the Indians of Ohio State Michican & this Territory, but not a moment must be lost and above all & I cannot dwell upon this too much, Harrison must not be employed, he is detested by them all, and believed by none. Proper measures will put it out of the power of the British to seduce them.

If you read the G'rs paper the Western sun, which I hope you do not, you will observe that whatever the Indians may say or have said in deprecation of war, is always done away by a salvo, that they are not sincere or such like, it serves to deceive government & keep up here the fever of fear & rage. If this fever is not soon allayed the taste for indiscriminate indian killing will be revived, the Tribes who would fain be our friends and are averse to wars, will be goaded into revenge by the savage brutality of our own people & we may have them all on our backs. A lamentable instance of this kind has lately occurred. A Delaware Indian who had with his family been living these several years in the settlement near Ohio, who informed his neighbours of his having discovered indian tracks and cautioned them to be on their guard, was taken with his family & confined & ultimately butchered in cool

---

* amongst them, Toussaint Dubois, Francis Vigo, John Gibson, those three men have more influence with the Indians than all the Harrisons in the Universe. They are men of truth. Dubois I am afraid has lost their confidence by joining the Governor.

blood. And the Delawares are our friends. His wife and children are now in Town.[3]

Last year, when the President was addressed, as I had foretold, in a language so gloriously depicting our dangers, the addressers were not in earnest & were obeying an extraneous impulse, which is made evident by their remaining as merry as ever, thinking no more of the subject, taking no one single precaution & travelling in every direction as their business or pleasure required it, now the tone is changed, they say nothing, but have forted & both country & town appear desert. The President has been sadly imposed upon. I thought him a man of sagacity & penetration. There is something incomprehensible in this.

If any thing was wanting to place the veracity & principles of the Gov'r in a proper point of view, he has furnished it himself by recommending (which I am informed he did) H. Hurst for a Judge; a man whom he knows, and represented to me & Ewing as one of the *villains* by whom he was surrounded. Parke has also (I am told) prostituted his name by a similar step.[4] For curiosity sake ascertain the fact. Tell me, who, except marmorean apathy, can contemplate such doings, without feeling his breast convulsed by a tempest of indignation? And that man continues in favour!!— In the short span which has elapsed since the revolution, we have lived 500 years and have reached the age of the Syllas & Marius, our infancy has been healthy & promising, our manhood short lived, & our premature decrepitude exhibits the disgusting spectacle of complicated infirmities & garrulous insanity portending approaching dissolution. Such is the view I take of things, may it please God that I mistake.

We have just received a confirmation on the intelligence that Gen'l Clark[5] has set out for Washington with Kickapoos,

[3] Probably the Delaware squaw and her three children referred to in note 2, below, p. 239.

[4] For recommendations for the judgeship see above, pp. 225-26n.

[5] Col. William Clark, of Louisiana-Missouri Territory.

Potawatamies & Osages Indians, good symptom. I am also told that Tecumseh persists in declining any negociation with Harrison & in his plan of going to the Federal city to lay his projects & wrongs before the President & ask for justice. I cannot vouch for this last intelligence, although I am inclined to believe it, but the Gov'r will marr that plan. Upon the whole my spirits are not quite so depressed.

Fare you well, remember your poor exile  Ever Yours

J. BADOLLET

P. S. By this mail you'll receive John Caldwell's official bond[6] signed by Tho's. Jones, Will'm McIntosh, John Johnson Esq'r & Chris'r Wyant. Le first undoubtedly the wealthiest man of the Territory in money & land, some of the finest bottoms on Ohio below Pittsburgh being his, the second having in early times stipulated in lands here is at this day a large holder. Johnson a respectable lawyer, Wyant a former sheriff respectively owning sundry valuable tracts of land.

[Addressed:] Albert Gallatin Esq'r   Private

[Endorsed:]  Vincennes May 19 1812  J. Badollet

[Badollet to Gallatin]

VINCENNES May 27, 1812

Every thing is in status quo here, of murders no more accounts are heard, from which an impression arises that a general war on the part of the Wabash and other Indians is not decided on, and that the several attacks which I have mentioned are the works of some individuals. Yet the allarm is not abated, people remain in their forts, and the town is left defenceless against a sudden attack. The Governor's house contains a portion of the inhabitants, who with their beloved chief form a choice *patriotic* band, the Seminary contains some more, besides those hidden behind the pickets surrounding three other houses, the rest who will not or cannot ask or find admittance are left defenceless, their dwellings scattered

---

[6] As receiver at the Kaskaskia Land Office. He was appointed on March 30 and approved the following day. Carter (ed.), *Territorial Papers,* XVI, 174.

amongst deserted houses, without means, without orders to make any resistance & must in case of an attack, necessarily fall. I staid last night in town & took a walk through the streets at bed time & was struck to indignation with the spectacle it exhibited. Except the solitary houses, which in such an extensive village lye scattered at an inconvenient distance from one another and contain their owners, the rest exhibited the appearance of compleat solitude. The moon shone bright, not a solitary step save mine, disturbed the general silence, the idea then of a body of indians floating down the Wabash, & dispersing themselves through the streets in the night and unperceived and at one moment the flames & tomahawk compleating the scene of desolation, when our tarapin gentlemen and our *consummate general* wrapped up in a cloak of dastardly selfishness, would not peek from their hiding places but behold unmoved the general devastation, that distressing idea seized & convulsed my mind. Can you conceive any thing so wretched?

How does it come that every kind of information which may have a tendency to mitigate our fears makes him angry & is either denied by him or modified so as to loose its effect or to produce a contrary one? How does it happen that generally speaking, persons coming from Fort Harrison or above, give a less favourable account after having seen the Governor than at their arrival? Some days ago, two men came from the above mentioned place and being met by Ewing and General Gibson & John Johnson Esq'r, were asked what news they brought. Their answer was peace & plenty, we have about 70 acres of corn planted in the neighbourhood of the Fort. Being asked whether there were any Indians, their answer was that there were but two, one hunting for the Garrison, the other had gone to carry a letter from the Governor to Tecumseh. The news took flight and as soon as the Governor heard them, he came angry to General Gibson with whom were then Col. Vigo & Ewing. The poor General excused himself by repeating the three questions he had put to the two travellers and their answers, when he mentioned the letter to Tecumseh, the Governor coloured deeply, and appeared so confused, that the Gen'l the Col. & Ewing took notice of it, he stammered and when recovered he said I wrote only two or three words. What could he write to a man whom he loads with abuse & paints as the real and only author of every mischief? who is his correspondent near Tecumseh to translate & read his letter? What can this mean? I have repeatedly told you that an indian war was the only means that the Gov'r possessed of escaping censure & punishment for his last years (equipée) expedition and there is a degree of cruelty to leave us in the hands of a man who is & must necessarily be the enemy of our peace & who could not be sorry to raise a smoke behind which he could hide himself. I wish you would relate the preceding anecdote to the President.

After their interview with the Gov'r the information communicated by the above mentioned travellers varied (as usual) from what they had first said to the Gen'l & Ewing.

Yesterday morning a Mr. Wm. Cook of New York in the contractors employ, came down from Fort Harrison with Lieut. Weaver, with dispatches from the com'g officer, & related that the Indian Council on the Wabash had broken up, that the result was a general determination for peace, excepting a few Potowatamies with the famous Winemack who said he wanted no peace and left them, in proof of which a number of Wabash Indians had come to Fort Harrison with a number of stolen horses which they returned, with information that the late murders had been comitted by the gang of Winemak, that friend of the United states *whom it would be criminal to suspect* & by Harry a young rascal of the same nation who used to live at the Governor's, both well knowing that whatever they may do, whatever outrage they may commit, will by this friend (his Ex'y) be laid to the accompt of Tecumseh & that Government will believe him. This favourable account which was received with gladness and avidity, has been *as usual* done away by the Western sun & its editor the Gov'r.[1] What does all this mean? is it to take effectual measures of defense? No, the country looks like a desert, where now and then, you meet a wretched inclosure wherein are penned up women and children & men who cannot be brought out for the defense of either country or town, this last looks as if already surrendered. Walls Walls Walls are the only words now that the danger press which come out of the mouth of the man who last year impudently & publickly told that *we had no business to think, that he watched when we were asleep,* and the same hero who last year like Job's war horse foamed & stamped the ground eager for the onset (on a foe begging for peace) is now, where—behind a picket leaving the town of Vincennes under the protection of—Providence.

The old Story of traitors here communicating with the indians is again audaciously revived in the western sun,[2] that may lead (& perhaps it is the object) to crimes. you know the back country people & of what they are capable when indian cruelties threaten them but you know not the people here a number of us are already marked & if that insinuation could

[1] Vincennes *Western Sun,* May 26. The opening line, after reporting Weaver's arrival with dispatches was, "We are sorry to say that they do not contain any evidence of the return of the Indians to a friendly disposition towards the U. States. . . ."

[2] In the story in the *Western Sun* of May 26, there appeared the following paragraph: "But although their speeches [of Chiefs Lapousier and Stone Eater] contain no evidence of a favorable alteration in the minds of the tribes who are supposed to be hostile, they contain indisputable evidence of another kind—that there is some secret communication between some person here and the Indians, by which the latter are informed of every thing that passes amongst us—Lapusier in his speech requires of the governor to send him a Delaware squaw & three children, which he says the governor detains in this place as prisoners—the squaw and her children were brought here from the Ohio, yesterday fortnight, since which there has been no Indian here, at least none that was publickly known—nor, as ensign Weaver asserts, has any one arrived at fort Harrison from this place from whom the information could have been obtained—indeed it appears that Lapusier was the first person who mentioned the circumstances at fort Harrison, and as he came from the upper part of the Wabash, he could have received it in no other way but through some secret messenger from this place whom he met on the way."

gain a general credit, it is not difficult to foresee the consequences. Will not Government extend a protecting hand toward us.

Adieu my friend remember Your          J. BADOLLET

I will continue to inform you of what passes. In one of my next I'll speak to you of my Son James & ask your advice & assistance respecting him.

[Endorsed:]  Vincennes  May  27  1812  J  Badollet  a number of Indians returned stolen horses

[Badollet to Gallatin]

VINCENNES June 7th 1812

The probability that there will be no general Indian combination against this Territory becomes every day grater, for there has been no sign of Indians to this day and the account given by the Miamis Chiefs that the small Winemack's party were the perpetrators of the murders which spread so much terror appears more and more to be true. How it happens that allarming intelligence is spread with promptitude and commonly with exaggeration, and that every information which may have a tendency to lessen our fears, is either kept a secret or so qualified that it fails of producing its effects, I leave to you to conjecture. I know that favourable letters have come from Fort Wayne and yet we are left in the secret about the nature of the intelligence they conveyed.[1] It appears also, by the information of the same Miamis Chiefs communicated by them to one Stover on their return, that since the last murders, the Wabash Indians are in the utmost distress, apprehending another expedition, an idea which the movements in Ohio State contribute to render more probable. The utmost care ought to be taken not to offend those friendly tribes, but that is not the object of our Proconsul.

But, although the situation of the Country is so far meliorated, ours & that of some of our friends becomes every day more critical.

[1] The *Western Sun* of June 7 reported that an express from Fort Wayne to Governor Harrison had arrived but contained nothing new.

I have informed you before that dark hints were thrown out by the Governor that some persons kept up a treasonable correspondence with the Indians, it was boldly repeated to an intoxicated regiment of militia, with such designation as would apply to Ewing & me, without committing him. He has of late spread the same report in Speaches & in print and it is spreading. Last year Congress did not pass any act for the relief of the purchaser of public land, that was ascribed to us & the Governor sent his own servant in a distant county with the printed lye & a horse load of other stuff. The Act for the relief of the militia employed on the Wabash, falls short of what they had been made to expect, we are also the cause of that.[2] Waller Taylor David Floyd & William Prince are not appointed officers in the new army & we have prevented their appointment. The rage which this last miscarriage has created in the cabinet is incredible, and has produced the event I am going to mention.

Some time ago an advertisement was posted up inviting the Officers and Privates of the militia engaged in the late expedition to meet at the Court house. The impression was made and received that it was to petition Congress in their own behalf. As soon as met, without any previous notice, resolutions were introduced, reflecting to [?] Ewing & myself as the authors of all evil, were rapidley read, put to votes and adopted by four or five tools saying *ay* when the rest surprised & confounded could summon neither presence of mind nor firmness (except two) to say no. Park that organ of his Excellency ([a]), was there to direct the machinery and a Committee was appointed to prepare or rather to sign a petition already written, praying for our dismission. This business which lasted only a few minutes, was not however terminated

---

(a) who is ever at the head of every riotous meeting, to enlighten their deliberations, & direct their movements.

[2] U. S. *Statutes at Large*, II, 704-5.

before the Gov'r who was in waiting entered, and putting his right hand upon his breast, with a tone rendered tremulous with affected sorrow, & with the same look of benevolence with which an inquisitor prays on the victims which he drags to the flames, be observed that he was grieved to mention that there were persons in the County who were in correspondence with the Indians &c. Upon which he retired & the meeting was adjourned. The address to Col. Boyd[3] was again made use of as containing insults on the character of the militia to enflame & properly tune a senseless multitude.

These atrocious charges the credulous do, the profligate affect to, believe and the black hearted gang which form the Council of the Gov'r rejoice in a scheme which may perhaps lead to the perpetration of some black deed. Already it would be dangerous for us to go to some of the forts and many have been heard to say, amongst them one Hornback, "let the Gov'r only say the word and we will soon gave a good account of the rascals." If such calumnies once get a good hold, it is easy to conceive the possibility of some person made frantick by the loss of some relatives lately murdered, revenging this & his country's injuries by the dispatch of the wretches who can join and abet its enemies, or which is more probable some subservient bravo may under the appearance of an indian secretly through the bushes as we go to or from the town or at night at our own house deprive us of our lives. Our situation is truly awfull & I do not know how long I may enjoy the pleasure of conversing with you. We ought to be rescued from this situation by some means or other.

Our real crimes are these. We have always felt, often expressed an honest indignation at every act which law or morallyty could not warrant. In the institutions of our country we never were taught the lessons, in the habits of the citizens of *States* we never learnt the practice of Servility, & we never can admit the ungenerous idea that a Subordinate officer of the United States is bound by the nature of his Office to view

[3] See above, pp. 217-18.

in ignominious silence & base submission every official act
of a petty despot in hostility with the laws or violating the
rights of our country. If what is praise worthy in others, is in
us a crime, with a manly pride we plead guilty. We must
despise what is despicable, hate what is hatefull and depravity
even on a throne never will, never can obtain from us the
respect so justly due to real worth, & by no possible means
can we be made the accomplices, the approvers or even the
indifferent Spectators of proceedings which cannot be excused
or justified.

To dissipate the gloomy ideas which what precedes is apt
to generate, I enclose you the effusions of the Knox Co. Poet
laureat.[4] You'll see therein that the idol, for want of a purer
incense, can relish with pleasure the nauseous effluvia of
grovelling stupidity, it is smoke still.

Fare you well   Yours forever

JOHN BADOLLET

I do not know whether they will dare to transmit those
resolutions & petition to the President, nor do I much care, my
conscious tells me Thou doest thy duty.

[Addressed:]   Albert Gallatin Esq'r   Private

[Endorsed:]  Vincennes  June 7, 1812  J Badollet Supose
it will be a combination of Indians against the Country

[Badollet to Gallatin]

VINCENNES June 30, 1812

Affairs remain, my Friend, as in my last, not a single
instance of injury done by the Indians, has occurred, and even
the Post rider a few days ago met with three Shawnese near
the licks, who let him pass unmolested, apparently busied in
hunting. Hence the opinion that the murders which I have
mentioned to you have been perpetrated by a few Potawatamies
as asserted by the Miami Chiefs, gains every day more strength,

---

[4] The enclosed clipping, which is from the *Western Sun* of June 2, 1812,
is in the Gallatin Papers. It contains "An Eulogy On the Heroes of the 7th
Nov. 1811," by the Rev. Isaac McCoy, Baptist minister. He was later to
become a missionary to the Indians.

& from [MS. illeg.] of Governor Hull I begin to indulge the hope that, as it is wished by every good man in the Territory, the management of Indian affairs is withdrawn from our Proconsul and entrusted to the former Gentleman: from which procedure the most happy results are to be wished for.

I enclose you the resolutions[1] alluded to in my last as precious specimen of stupid insincerity, exhibiting at once the profligacy of the Governor, of his Mirmidons, and of Parke their leader: as well as these last's base subserviency. The annexed address to the people of the United States,[2] I leave to your own comments, that elaborate production of candour and truth, was brought forth several weeks before the meeting by the Governor or Parke or both, and delivered to the nominal Committee, (some of whom cannot write & all unable to write any sense) already dressed up with all its spice and seasoning. Dubois[3] was of them; a good man, who can neither read nor write, never knew any thing of the business till he heard his name read out of the Western Sun and has publickly disavowed any agency in the profligate Scheme.[4] The main object is to prevent Jennings' election[5] & carry a certain Waller Taylor (now a candidate) placed on the bench at a time I presume when men of strong & correct mind & of legal knowledge were not easy to be found.[6] But, if affecting to take sight at us they

---

[1] Clipped from the *Western Sun* of June 23, 1812. See below, pp. 249-51.

[2] There is a long letter signed by officers of the 4th Regiment of Indiana militia, Luke Decker, Waller Taylor, Noah Purcell, Thomas Scott, William Hargrove, Andrew Wilkins, James Smith, Toussaint Dubois, Daniel Sullivan, and William Prince, in the *Western Sun* of the 23d immediately following the resolutions. It was written "to rescue the fame of the Indiana militia from that weight of odium and reproach which has been so industriously heaped upon them, and which, in despite of official statements from the highest and most respectable authorities, have made their way, and gained belief in the public councils of our country." It went on then to rehearse the story of Col. Boyd, Governor Harrison, the regular troops, and the militia on the Tippecanoe campaign.

[3] Toussaint Dubois, whose name was signed to the address as captain of spies.

[4] See second enclosure below.

[5] Elections for the General Assembly and delegate to Congress were to be held on August 3.

[6] Waller Taylor had been serving as territorial judge since 1806. On

hit both Jennings & us, the joy will be the greater. Thus far about one happy Territory.

I have two sons the youngest of my children,[7] whom my daily absences from home injure in their education; there is no other resource here but a certain latin school, where a few scraps are taught, good or bad, no body here knows, & where I certainly will not send them: so that left at home they cannot improve without an overseer & guide. One being absent the other would derive more fruit from my lessons. I am not able to maintain one at a seminary of learning, nor do I relish much the kind of education they receive there. The institution at West Point presents advantages perfectly suited to my views and circumstances usefull information & small expense. James my second, whom I have now in view, is intelligent, desirous of knowledge & such a plant should not be suffered to wither for want of cultivation. He is besides of an intrepid & persevering turn, hardy as a pine knott & admitting that he would progress so well as to be placed in the corps of Engineers, he would I think make a good Officer. Not that my object is a military commission (except in the corps above mentioned) my aim is to furnish him with usefull information such as mathematics, natural philosophy & some living language, of which he would feel the advantage in any station of life & which he would contribute to the happiness of my declining years. After a few years spent there, if promotion could not be obtained or was deemed inadvisable, well he might return with such acquirements as would rather promote than impede his progress in the way of making a living. Besides possessed of a stock of military knowledge he could, under favourable circumstances be usefull, by seconding the effort that Government must make, to diffuse the military science, inspire & create a spirit of military subordination. Nothing will hinder him from resuming the labours of agricul-

June 23 the *Sun* announced his candidacy for delegate to Congress, running against Jennings.

[7] James and Algernon Sidney.

ture to which he is accustomed & he can then pursue them in a more intelligent & rational manner. I confess the idea pleases me, I wish you may not raise objections against it, in which case, if you will grant me leave of absence; I'll take him to the Federal City in the fall, whence he may be sent by water to his destination. He writes, a pretty good hand, knows arithmetick, has a general idea of Geography & seems fond of reading.[8]

But be it as it may, I beg that I may be permitted to leave this place for a short time, as you have feelingly expressed it, a *refreshing* interview would renovate my dejected mind. Before I receive my mittimus, let me see the friend of my youthfull days. I entreat you to answer me on the subject of this letter, I know you have no time to spare, but I am not unreasonable; once in two or three years is a very moderate allowance. It would be unkind to deny me.

I cannot proceed to the sale of unpaid lands without your instructions on the mode of proceeding in that business, & knowing the construction put in the Department of the Treasury on the last law of Congress on that subject &c &c I wrote to you in time to have had an answer ere now & yet I receive none.

The poor Solomon would make I think a good Officer, being possessed of more practical knowledge of military affairs than the ninety nine hundredths of the Americans. Would not a commission in the army promote his and the public interests? Is there any impediment?[9]

[8] James P. Badollet did become a cadet at the Military Academy, entering on April 26, 1813. He was commissioned 3d lieutenant in the light artillery on July 21, 1814. He transferred to the corps artillery May 17, 1815, and was advanced to a 2d lieutenant October 1, 1816. He resigned from the army on August 1, 1818. Heitman (comp.), *Historical Register of the United States Army*, I, 180. His appointment to the Academy signed by John Armstrong, Secretary of War, is in the Badollet Papers in the Indiana Historical Society Library.

[9] There are twenty-odd letters from Louis Solomon to Badollet in the Badollet Papers in the Indiana Historical Society Library and at least two letters from Badollet to Solomon in the Gallatin Papers. He was a Genevan

It will not escape your penetration, that the resolutions mentioned above, furnish a strong presumptive evidence, that our conduct as Officers has been correct, for the Governors hatred against us being so intense, the party in lieu of the ridiculous charges made against us, would, *if they* could urge something more substantial. Be it as it may if these resolutions ever formally reach the President, we hope & request that an investigation of our conduct may take place, and that the persons entrusted with it, may be instructed even to seek & invite evidence against us. But in the name of God, let them not be of this Territory. If we cannot obtain we have endeavoured to deserve a continuation in our Offices, that is all that concerns us, the rest is of little moment & is the business of the President. But ours shall be the care, that our dismissal shall not be a disgrace. The Governor by holding us to public views, gives us a consequence we never durst to dream of, we are driven to self defence & it shall be commensurate with the extent of the injury, we will tell the people of the United States, why we are the Governors enemies, we'll make an history of his Official conduct, of his corrupt practices, of his Indian Treaties & of his unwarrantable expedition of last fall in open violation of the supreme law of the land. We'll try the experiment whether in these United States a splendid name can alone without either virtue or merit overwhelm the modest men whose only arms are truth, their only shields rectitude.

Not only Dubois but Capt'n Hargrove James Smith & Waller Taylor were not at the meeting, and seems that this last has since *politely* assented to the use made of his name in his absence. What do you think of a cause supported by forgeries?

Do not I beseech you subject us to the unpleasant visits

who had settled in Pennsylvania near Gallatin. On December 26, 1805, and again on June 9, 1806, Badollet had written to Solomon, urging him to move to Vincennes and offered him a clerkship in the Land Office. He did not come. Sometime before 1814 he moved to Washington. His letters, for the most part in French, are warm, friendly, and gay, and exhibit a strong affection for Badollet.

of such a man as B. Parke, the man sold to the Governor soul & body who is the ever ready tool to execute the most unprincipled schemes. Any other friend or foe will be agreeable to us. The most capable here is a merchant named John D. Hay, he is a most respectable man.[10]

What would the President say if he knew that the address & resolutions of last year which seem to have caused the march of the 4th Reg't and all the concomitant war measures,[11] had been drawn in conclave at head quarters, was presented read & adopted without time for reflexion: that the Comittee was a farce, the work being already done & fixed; & that the same men who had sanctioned with their names the dolefull picture of dangers & sufferings which did not exist, never bestowed another thought thereon afterwards & remained as merry as the day was long, forgetting there was an Indian in existence. It is the Governor's practice when he wants to shift upon the people some exceptionable measure, to prepare with his confident resolutions, to invite a sudden meeting, Parke harangues proposes & reads the resolves ready made, puts the question, two or three persons properly placed say aye, the rest gaping with a vacant stare, not understanding a word of the business and the whole is ushered into the world through the Western sun, alias Governors private Gazette, as resolutions *unanimously* adopted a *respectable* meeting &c. The fact is, respectable people stay at home on those occasions, knowing that it is both useless & dangerous to oppose such proceedings. You'll observe always a certain Col. Decker,[12] chairman, he is an old settler, made an officer by his discerning Excellency for wont not of a better, but of one more obsequious, a dignified doll, which he dexterously uses as a fugel man, when Parke commands the facings.

[10] Parke served as examiner of the Vincennes Land Office, as noted above (p. 166n). Hay acted as his deputy upon occasion. Carter (ed.), *Territorial Papers,* VIII, 36, 207.

[11] See above, p. 189.

[12] Col. Luke Decker. Sketch in Thornbrough and Riker (eds.), *Journals of the General Assembly of Indiana Territory,* pp. 964-65.

The Gov'r Parke & Taylor have set out on a crusade against Jennings to the upper Counties, this holy league of the Executive & Judiciary against the freedom of our elections, is worth a volume of comments on the wretchedness of Territories.

Fare you well &c

JOHN BADOLLET

[Enclosures][13]

At a numerous meeting of the militia officers and soldiers who served on the late campaign under governor Harrison, public notice for that purpose having been previously given, at Vincennes, on the 30th May, 1812; col. Luke Decker being called to the chair, & Peter Jones appointed secretary, the following resolutions were moved and adopted.

WHEREAS it appears from the law which has been lately passed by congress for the relief of the officers and soldiers who served upon the Wabash campaign, that not only the bounty of an additional month's pay, which they, the said officers and soldiers had been taught to expect, has been with-held, but that payment for the horses which were unavoidably lost in the action of the 7th November last (those only excepted which were killed) is also denied: *And whereas* it appears from the declaration of a member of congress in his place (the honorable mr. Stewart) that the supposed misconduct of the militia in the said action was the cause of the rejection of those favorable clauses which the bill first contained: AND WHEREAS it is but too evident that all the unjust odium which has been cast upon the conduct of the militia in relation to said action, is to be placed to the false and calumnious statement which was published by col. Boyd and capt. Prescott, and to the misrepresentations which were made by the former of those officers in every place, and upon all occasions throughout his journey from this place to Washington, and from thence to Boston—therefore,

*Resolved,* That a committee be appointed to prepare an

[13] Clipped from the Vincennes *Western Sun* of June 23 and 30, 1812.

address to the American people, in vindication of the reputation of the militia—that they give therein a concise account of those occurrences on the campaign, which, in their opinion will tend to elucidate the subject, and explain the causes which led to the dislike which the colonel has declared existed towards him on the part of the militia, and which he has most improperly asserted to be owing to the exactness of his discipline.

As it appears that the vindication of the conduct of the militia, against the aspersions of col. Boyd and capt. Prescott, which was published in the Western Sun, was only republished in one or two other papers, when the calumnious piece of the said colonel was published perhaps in every paper on the continent— *Resolved,* That the said committee use their exertions to cause their statement, and the whole, or such parts of the commander in chiefs' vindication, and the documents attending it, as they may think proper, [to be published] in at least ten of the public papers, and if the same will be admitted on no other terms, that the publication be paid for, and the expences thereof paid by a subscription amongst those who served upon the late campaign.

*Resolved,* That a respectful petition be drawn up by the said committee to congress on behalf of the officers and soldiers praying that the horses and other property which was unavoidably lost during the campaign or action, in consequence of their being abandoned by an order which they could not disobey, at least be paid for by the government.

*Resolved,* That the secret meeting which was held in November last, at which six or eight persons undertook to represent the inhabitants of the town of Vincennes and its neighborhood was the foundation of all the misrepresentations, the calumny and injury to which the militia who served on the late campaign have been exposed.

*Resolved,* That the support and countenance which was given to that meeting by John Badolett & Nathl. Ewing, (the Register and Receiver of the Land Office) was highly criminal and improper—but is of a piece with all their conduct, which, for years past has aimed at the injury of the governor of the territory, at the expense of any injury of the people thereof.

*Resolved,* That the committee appointed upon the several resolutions be instructed to petition the president of the U. States to remove the said Badolett & Ewing from their offices.

*Resolved,* That we will never give our votes to any person that was concerned in the said secret meeting for any office in our gift, and we recommend a similar resolution to all those who served upon the late campaign.

*Resolved,* That col. Decker, majors Taylor & Purcell, captains Prince, Scott, Smith, Dubois, Hargrove & Wilkins, and adjutant Sullivan, or a majority of them, be a committee for the purpose aforesaid.

*Resolved,* That the foregoing resolutions be published in the Western Sun, and also that the committee forward a copy of the same to the president of the U. States.

---

MR. STOUT,

It is with no little surprise that I see myself in your paper of the 23d inst. made a member of a meeting which adopted certain resolutions wherein Nathl. Ewing and John Badollet, two respectable officers of the U. States are traduced and indecently treated, of that meeting I never was apprised, of its proceedings I knew nothing, and in it I ever would feel ashamed to have acted a part.—Such doings cannot pass unnoticed, and are calculated to rouse the indignation of every honest man. Please to give a place in your paper to this declaration, that the world may know of what stamp are the gentlemen who conducted that decent business.

Dubois[14]

VINCENNES, 30th June, 1812.

[14] Among the 4th of July toasts reported in the *Western Sun* of July 7 was one by William Prince, "The militia of Indiana who fought at the battle of Tippecanoe—may they never follow the example of Toussaint Dubois—let them scorn the influence of an iron chest, and stick to truth and honesty." This brought another letter from Dubois to the editor of the *Sun,* in the issue of July 14, "We have and see so many strange things

[Badollet to Gallatin]

VINCENNES August 5, 1812

I am my Friend in a great perplexity, the law granting further time to purchasers of public lands,[1] having been transmitted to me too late to advertise the sale thirty days before the Court, now I hear of a supplementary act being passed, extending to assignees the benefit of the aforesaid law & granting this privilege of reentering a forfeited tract, &c. which may reach me too late.[2]

By a copy of the bill sent to me by Mr. Jennings I see that if it has passed, those whose lands have reverted to the U. S. may reenter the same & apply to the payments thereof the monies they had paid, (which virtually does away the back interest) and that must be done, if I understand right, in september, for lands forfeited before the end of this present month. Now what must be done, may I enter in the books of this Office, reversions of lands which have not been advertised for, nor can be exposed to sale (before September,) & If I may, where is the possibilities now of placing those reversions under their respective dates in the book of entries, which under the old law were to be declared & entered in the said book, on the day only of sale, if the Tract was not bidden for? The first amendatory act passed during this last session bred confusion the second renders it more confused, it would be well when a law is making, to keep an eye on the Officers whose duty it is to execute it & not to suppose that a distance of 500 miles, when they are enjoined to act, they can then apply for instructions.

daily at Vincennes, that it is not at all surprising that I should, unaspiring as I am, be the subject of a toast on the 4th of July, the decency of the insinuation contained therein, that I should have accepted money for rescuing my name from disgrace, and that the receiver of public money should betray his trust, forms a more complete panegyrick on the principles and heart of the toaster, than volumes of elaborate writing." He concluded then with an allusion to Prince's connection with Burr.

[1] Approved April 23, 1812. U. S. Statutes at Large, II, 742.

[2] The supplementary act was approved July 6. Ibid., II, 782-83.

A law it seems to me ought to be general and comprehensive if it contain exceptions, it will soon like the scripture require comments to which comments will become necessary. it was pitifull to except from the benefit of the act those few who had purchased more than 640 acres, a supplement has been unavoidable, & now the Register here cannot keep clear of inconveniencies and error.

The last time that I saw Mr. Jennings I desired him to speak to you on, and to obtain from you instructions respecting the manner of conducting the sales of lands unpaid for, and making the proper entries in the books. he answered that I need not be uneasy, that I would receive them together with forms, that request I repeated to you in a private letter and yet I received nothing from you. Please to consider my situation, desirous of acting correctly and fearfull of doing wrong. I am in a situation very unpleasant.

It is as a friend that I now address you, and draw a picture of my embarrassment. I could not communicate with the Department of the General Land Office with the same liberty & I hope you will be so kind as to suggest to Mr. Tiffin[3] the necessity of furnishing this Office with instructions & forms. It must also occurr to that Officer that an early transmission of every law which may affect this office and directions in relation to the mode of complying with them, is indispensable. As the system must be uniform throughout the different ramifications of the Land Office, the rules for construing laws relating thereto, removing the difficulties in their execution & preserving & pursuing the same forms ought to flow from the head & not be left to individual discretion.

[4]No act of hostility since my last has been committed in

[3] Edward Tiffin, appointed Commissioner of the General Land Office on May 6, 1812. The General Land Office was created by act of April 25. The Commissioner served under the direction of the Secretary of the Treasury. Carter (ed.), *Territorial Papers,* VIII, 203n.

[4] This and the following paragraph have a line through them, probably drawn by Gallatin before he forwarded the letter to Tiffin. See his endorsement.

this Territory, but our fears are not removed, the war being declared,[5] it is to be feared that the efforts the English must undoubtedly have made to alienate the Indians from us, may be successfull & soon produce their dreadfull effects. I have at last seen the dispatches of Gov'r Harrison, they are curious & furnish an ample food for reflexion— The Post rider, who was killed between Kaskaskias and this place, appears to have been assassinated by a white man, it being known that he was carrying a considerable sum in bank notes, and a suspicious man having passed through Vincennes immediately after—[6] The boat which is said to have been attacked by the Indians on his way to the army & wherein a man is said to have been killed by them, was a contractors boat. One of the hands, one Henry Rimbault, before starting borrowed a gun from one Anthony Oneille, who on delivering it, observed to Rimbault, be cautious, this gun goes off at half cock. The man was addicted to drinking & when he was fumbling in the boat, he was killed, his clothes burnt by the powder, not the shadow of an human being perceived by those who were on the bank cooking their supper & who had it been indians, would have been the first victims.[7] Ab uno *disce omnes*— The true cause of the Indian discontents was the treaty and had it not been for that and other circumstances, the tampering of the British with them, would not have detached them from our cause (at lea[st] those of the Wabash) but now I am much afraid the British have succeeded or may succeed in making them their allies.

In this Territory, old Democrats are *Tories* & Burrites *Patriots* such is the incredible perversion of language & the more incredible perversion of the Governor & his tools who have the audacity to class us so. I am in the courtly language

[5] The United States declared war against Great Britain on June 18, 1812.

[6] The post rider on the route between Vincennes and Kaskaskia was murdered in the summer of 1810 and his body staked down in a creek bed. Vincennes *Western Sun,* July 28, 1810.

[7] See above, p. 210.

a Tory! It is asserted with such an unblushing effrontery, that my and a few others' situation is truly dangerous, should the Indians commit cruelties on this county, the rage of the sufferers fanned by these demons in a human shape, may vent itself in deeds of blackness.

Fare-you well my ever dear Friend  Yours for ever

JOHN BADOLLET

As double security I had written in time to Winn Winship Esqr. at Cn [Cincinnati?] whom I know personally, who acts as Register there, and had politely invited me to write to him, whenever I met with any practical difficulty, to obtain from him a copy of the different entries to be made in case of reversions or repurchase at the sales, and directions how to state & close the different accompts, but my letter must have been mislaid (or suppressed) for I received no answer. Could not Mr. Tiffin direct him to furnish me with the necessary information?

P. S.  I just receive the law supplementary to an act &c. but no forms.

[Addressed:]  Albert Gallatin Esq.  Private

[Endorsed: in Gallatin's hand]  Vincennes Aug. 5, 1812 J. Badollet Mr. Tiffin is requested to give the necessary instructions in the first part of this letter. by his obed't serv't Albert Gallatin  The letter (particularly the end) is private.


[Gallatin to Badollet]

NEW YORK  May 8th 1816

Ever since my return from Europe,[1] I have expected to

---

[1] On May 9, 1813, Gallatin sailed for Europe to join a delegation consisting of himself and John Quincy Adams, minister to Russia, and James A. Bayard, senator from Delaware, appointed in response to an offer from Czar Alexander I to mediate peace between the United States and Great Britain. This mission was a frustrating failure and Gallatin proceeded to London, where he received his appointment as one of the peace commissioners. Following the long-drawn-out negotiations at Ghent he went to Geneva, then back to London for the final signing of the peace "convention," and sailed for home on July 22, 1815. He returned to Europe as

hear from you; and I have every day designed and delayed writing to you. Yet I had the enclosed from Geneva for you; but I knew it brought you no pleasing intelligence. Your sister is an excellent woman; but I did not encourage her coming over, to which she did not feel disposed, and which indeed would have been at this time impossible. On one score you may be easy. As I return to Europe, have there a small annuity, and God has given me a sufficiency, j'aurai soin que ton père ne lui sont pas à charge.

To prevent any difficulty in case of the death of either of us, I sign and enclose duplicates of a settlement of accounts between us. Sign one, and enclose it to Thos. Worthington at Chilicothe Ohio, to whom I have given a power of attorney; unless you prefer & can pay the money and keep the land. In that case, give him notice as I have authorised him to sell; and I will instruct him to convey one third on payment of the balance. But if you do not give him immediate notice, it will be taken for granted that our agreement, that I keep the land in payment, is in force. I think indeed that it is better for you that it should be so.

It is not without reluctance, and for reasons too long to explain in this letter, that I return to Europe; and I hope that my stay there will be short, & that I may once more have the happiness of seeing you. If you write to me, send your letters to the Department of State at Washington, and they will be safely conveyed. I have seen James, and wish he had, before his becoming an officer, have remained longer at West Point.[2] He wanted a furlough, to which some difficulty was made; and I did not know whether it was right to press for it.

Give my most affectionate compliments to your wife. God bless and preserve you and yours, at all times & under

minister to France, sailing on July 11, 1816, where he remained until May, 1823. Walters, *Albert Gallatin,* pp. 258 ff.

In the interim when he was home he wrote to President Madison about Badollet, requesting that Badollet be continued as register. See Introduction, p. 16, above.

[2] See above, pp. 245-46n.

every clime. Ever your's

ALBERT GALLATIN

John Badollet Esqr
Vincennes Indiana
[Enclosure:]
John Badollet in acc't with Albert Gallatin

| | | | |
|---|---|---|---|
| 1803 May 20th | To his balance as pr account settled this day .......... | | 553.70 |
| 1802 to 1807— | To his third part of taxes on lands in Ohio | 12.58 | |
| 1808 May — | To his draft fav'r N. Ewing | 350.00 | |

————

916.28

1816 May — By his third of acres 2033 1/3
                  in state of Ohio, de-
                  duct lost by prior
                  claim of E. Dyal.. 200

————

                      acres 1833 1/3
                  611 1/3 acres taken in pay-
                  ment by A. Gallatin at 150 pr
                  acre Principal and interest of
                  this acc't—               916.66

May 9th 1816—Settled the above account this day, which
we declare to include all accounts & claims whatever between
us to this date; and do hereby mutually release each other
from any claim or demand whatsoever, on account of any
former advances, agreements, & transactions between us.

     Signed by Albert Gallatin       Signed [blank]
         in presence of [blank]

     [Endorsed:] May 1816 Account with John Badollet.
Sent him for signature & to be sent by him to Tho's Worthington at Chilicothe

     [Addressed:] John Badollet Esqr Register of the land
office Vincennes Indiana

     [Postmarked:] New York May 9

[Badollet to Gallatin]

VINCENNES Sept. 10, 1823

MY DEAR FRIEND

Unable to write without suffering, I have hitherto, much against my inclination, declined the attempt. Having so much to say, the herculean task under that unfortunate circumstance always terrified me & whenever I took up the pen, I dropped it in despair, referring to a personal interview, which I fondly anticipated, but which it never may be my lot to enjoy, all I had to say on myself, family, the country & past events.

My first object in attempting to write at present is to tender you Mrs. Gallatin & the rest of your family my sincere congratulations on your happy return to your country & friends, my next by a pleasing illusion to annihilate distance and enjoy a moment of converse with yourself my dear friend with whom every moment of my existence is connected by the most endearing remembrances.

The country, to which I have been exiled, labours under all the evils which afflict tropical climates. Bilious affections from the mild remittent bilious, through every gradation up to the yellow fever; are endemic in this region. Three times have I been brought to the brink of the grave; medical assistance has cost me to this day a sum amounting to 510 dollars. In September 1821 in the height of my troubles under the relief law,[1] I was seized with a highly dangerous disorder of an anomalous nature, which sunk my vital power to the limits of its extinction, for six months a shrivelled skin to the bones, a cadaverous look, a total prostration of muscular strength and of all bodily & mental powers, a loss of feelings which from the extremities was gradually approaching the trunk left no doubt in my & the physician's mind about the catastrophe. Yet I survived & my broken constitution has by slow and insensible degrees recovered part of its lost tone & I still live; though much altered for the worse but in

[1] The act approved March 2, 1821, for the relief of purchasers of public lands. U. S. *Statutes at Large,* III, 612-14.

daily fear of an attack of autumnal fevers, now raging, which I shall not be able to resist.

You would have found me in Pennsylvania at your arrival, as I had determined to pass the sickly months there, but my finances forbade it. The feeds [*sic*] which flowed in so handsomely under the relief law, have ebbed away as rapidly for the support of a great number of extra clerks, whom I employed; fearless of consequences, to carry that law into effect; now I am in debt. Congress do not seem to understand the business, having after two readings left amongst the lumber [ ?] a bill for our relief (the land officers).

From the reduction in the price of land, & in the quantity that may be purchased,[2] the paucity of purchases & from the amount remaining here being frittered away into four, six and eight installments, the commissions remaining the same, it results that the office is worth to me but little. Add to that a misfortune peculiar to myself, my unability to write my books I consume in the hire of a clerk all my stated salary.

I do not know whether the complex system adopted by Mr. Crawford[3] could have been more simple, but this I know, that the duty that became incumbent upon me to perform in relation to the relief law,[4] under the instruction of the Secre-

[2] By an act approved April 24, 1820, the minimum price per acre for public land was reduced from $2.00 to $1.25 and the smallest possible purchasable unit was fixed at 80 acres. The credit system was abolished; the entire amount of the purchase price was to be paid at time of purchase. U. S. *Statutes at Large*, III, 566-67. By act of April 20, 1818, the compensation of the registers of the land offices had been set as follows: an annual salary of $500 and a commission of 1 per cent on all money shown on receipts entered by them and transmitted to the Secretary of the Treasury, the total compensation, however, not to exceed $3,000 a year.

[3] William H. Crawford, Secretary of the Treasury.

[4] Under the relief act of 1821 it was made the duty of the registers and receivers "according to the forms and instructions which shall be given in that behalf by the Treasury Department, to assist in carrying this act in [to] execution, to keep full and faithful accounts and records of all proceedings under the same; and, within the terms of the three months after the said thirtieth day of September next to transmit to the said department a correct report of the quantity of land relinquished to the United States; the quantity on which full payment shall have been made; and the quantity

tary of the Treasury, has been completed only last June, having kept in constant employ five extra-clerks during a great part of that time, & lessening their numbers as the burthen became gradually lighter.

The moral climates of this country is not less deleterious than the physical: I have witnessed all the gradations between simple knavery & downright villainy, & which is truly deplorable, exciting neither surprise nor detestation, nor lessening the usual courtesies of life. I have seen two men equally cunning, hypocritical and depraved, the one wallowing without disgust in the slough of infamy to make a dollar, the other wants to unite the privileges attending a good name, with the more tangible advantages of a course unfettered by troublesome rules of morality, has procured a meritricious celebrity by enlisting praisers (proneurs), and there has been no lack of them. The former has no country, the latter would subject his own if he could. It is however comfortable to learn, that one is sunk never to rise again, the other is sinking apace.[5]

This is between you and me. I put no names for good reasons the riddle I shall explain, when we meet & I shall then submit to your consideration some facts which will, I think, simply justify the severity of my censure.

All my children have married. Albert who conducts the office has lost his wife & only child, is the treasurer of the County.[6] Fanny, who for her good sense and affection is

on which a further credit shall have been given, distinguishing the amount of the debt on which a further credit shall have been allowed; and the registers and receivers, respectively, shall be entitled to receive fifty cents from the party relinquishing, for each half quarter section, quarter section, half section, section, or legal subdivision of a fractional section, so relinquished." U. S. *Statutes at Large,* III, 614.

[5] One can only surmise who are the two men to whom Badollet refers. Perhaps the former is Nathaniel Ewing who had been connected with the failure of the Vincennes bank and the latter William Henry Harrison.

[6] Albert Badollet was serving as his father's deputy. He later succeeded his father as register. See below, p. 326. He had married Jane M. Agun on February 13, 1817. Knox County Marriage Records, I, 137, in Genealogy Division, Indiana State Library.

the flower of my family is married to a Gentleman[7] in moderate or perhaps humble circumstances, who is respectable and respected & who, by his attachment & affectionate proceedings, renders her truly happy. Sarah is married to John Caldwell Receiver at Shawneetown,[8] one [of] the best appointments made in the department of the Land Office in point of order correctness and integrity. He will go to Washington City next winter with other Land Officers on the subject of our common suffering. If you should see him I dare to rely upon a share of your attentions to him as a man, my son in law, but especially as an estimable officer. James after some folies, to relieve the effects of which I have in part incurred the debts alluded to above & which could not exist, if Congress had been just, has betaken himself to farming, is a pattern of industry, has been once elected Major & is now a County Commissioner. Sidney is living with me & manages my farm. My sons are all in good repute, but they have been in one respect a corroding sore to me, being all adverse to study, mental gratifications & litterature.

It is unfortunate that, when called upon to form a constitution a territory is in the most unpropitious circumstances to success for the want of men of intellect and political knowledge, attending a country in the incipient state of population. This was woefully verified in our case, for though our convention contained several thinking men, the majority was composed of empty bablers, democratic to madness, having incessantly the *people* in their mouths and their dear selves in their eyes, who resist every effort to avoid those defects which are so justly chargeable to our constitution. I was for my sins elected to that body, not through any choice or effort of my own, as you may believe, but my unconquerable timidity rendered me almost useless. I use the qualifying word *almost* because in fact some little good may in some degree be attributable to me. Convinced that to change and better the manner

---

[7] Fanny Badollet married Henry Gilham April 1, 1815. *Ibid.,* I, 98.
[8] See above, p. 166n.

of a people, moral causes operate more effectually than prohibitory enactments & the disgusting repetition of penal statutes, I introduced with that view the 2d 3d 4th & 5th Sections of Article IX the tendency of which cannot escape you.[9] The

[9] The convention to frame a state constitution met at Corydon on June 10, 1816, and adjourned on June 29. Knox County delegates besides Badollet were John Johnson, William Polke, John Bennefield, and Benjamin Parke. Jonathan Jennings, a delegate from Clark County, was elected president. Woollen, *et al.* (ed.), *Executive Journal of Indiana Territory*, pp. 87-89. Badollet served on the rules committee, education committee, the committee on the preamble and bill of rights, and the committee for general revision. Journal of the Constitutional Convention of 1816, reprinted in State Bar Association of Indiana, *Annual Report,* 1912, pp. 142, 152, 153, 190.

Article IX concerned education. The sections Badollet wrote were as follows: "Sect. 2. It shall be the duty of the General assembly, as soon as circumstances will permit, to provide, by law, for a general system of education, ascending in a regular gradation, from township schools to a state university, wherein tuition shall be gratis, and equally open to all.

"Sect. 3. And for the promotion of such salutary end, the money which shall be paid, as an equivalent, by persons exempt from militia duty except, in times of war, shall be exclusively, and in equal proportion, applied to the support of County seminaries; also all fines assessed for any breach of the penal laws, shall be applied to said seminaries, in the Counties wherein they shall be assessed.

"Sect. 4. It shall be the duty of the General assembly, as soon as circumstances will permit, to form a penal Code, founded on the principles of reformation, and not vindictive Justice: and also to provide one or more farms to be an asylum for those persons, who by reason of age, infirmity, or other misfortunes, may have a claim upon the aid and beneficence of society; on such principles, that such persons may therein, find employment, and every reasonable comfort and lose, by their usefulness, the degrading sense of dependence.

"Sect. 5. The General Assembly, at the time they lay off a new County, shall cause, at least, ten per cent to be reserved out of the proceeds of the sale of town lots in the seat of Justice of such county, for the use of a public library for such County, and at the same session, they shall incorporate a library company, under such rules and regulations as will best secure its permanence, and extend its benefits." Charles Kettleborough, *Constitution Making in Indiana . . . Volume I, 1780-1851 (Indiana Historical Collections,* I, Indianapolis, 1916), pp. 114-15.

Badollet was a member of the committee appointed by a joint resolution of the Indiana legislature in 1821 to draft a bill "providing for a general system of education. . . ." *Laws of Indiana,* 1820-21, p. 139. The report of the committee is in the *Senate Journal,* 1821-22, pp. [I]-XX. What part Badollet played in its preparation is not known.

preamble[10] was added by another member of the Committee, it does not amalg[am]ate well with the sequel, but I would move no amendment lest our democrats should meddle with *it* & substitute schools for the poor or such other wise provision.

I missed one of my objects in my visit to you; the pleasure of seeing you, Mrs. Gallatin & children was one which I enjoyed fully, the other to communicate many things on this country, its climate, inhabitants & influential men, I could not effect without inhumanely encroaching on your few hours of rest, but in your retirement on Monongahela, annoyed no more by the stateliness & glare of office I can unbosom myself as in days that are long past.

I wish you to believe that I have had good sense and honesty enough to withstand every solicitation to join the bank of Vincennes since so celebrated for its infamy.[11] My instinctive aversion to banks has increased tenfold, since I [have] been a witness of their power & their crimes.

I want also [to] see you, in order to regulate our accompt of supplies furnished to my father & sister, if Congress do us justice I will liquidate it, if not I will be much distressed but I have some property sufficient to meet that sacred debt.

Nearly a whole day of pain has been spent upon the present scrawl. I am unable to trace another line, drop me a few

[10] Kettleborough, *op. cit.*, pp. 112-13. The Preamble may have been the work of James Scott, a delegate from Clark County. This is implied in a letter from John H. Farnham to Badollet, July 12, 1827, in the Badollet Papers in the Indiana Historical Society Library. See also John H. Farnham, *Oration Delivered at Salem, Indiana, On the Fiftieth Anniversary of American Independence* . . . (New Albany, Ind., 1826), supplementary note, pp. 17-18.

[11] For the story of the Bank of Vincennes see Logan Esarey, *State Banking in Indiana* (*Indiana University Bulletin*, X, No. 2, Bloomington, 1912), pp. 222, 226-42; R. Carlyle Buley, *The Old Northwest, 1815-1840* (2 volumes. Indiana Historical Society, 1950), I, 570, 572. Nathaniel Ewing's name had headed the petition to the territorial Assembly in 1814 praying for a charter to establish a bank at Vincennes. The Assembly passed an act "to incorporate the President, Directors, & company of the bank of Vincennes." Ewing became its president. Its failure in 1822, linked with the failure of the Vincennes "Steam Mill" Company, cast a shadow of corruption on those associated with it.

words, let me be assured by your own mouth that you are become a private man, it will be glad tidings to me.

I cannot conclude without tendering my respect to Mrs. Gallatin & my kind compliments to James.

Remember me affectionately to Mr. Griffin & Nicholson. Fare you well  Yours &c

JOHN BADOLLET

[Addressed:]   Albert Gallatin Esq'r  New  Geneva Fayette Co. Pa.

[Endorsed:]   Vincennes  10 Sept.  1823

[Gallatin to Badollet]

NEW GENEVA  Penns'a 29th July 1824

My dear old friend, I have delayed much too long answering your letter of last year. I have ever since been on the wing, uncertain where I would fix myself. The habits of my wife and children, Albert excepted, render this a very ineligible place of residence to them: but the impossibility of subsisting on my scanty income in one of our cities, and the necessity of attending to a valuable but mismanaged and unproductive property have left me no choice; and we are all now here, including James's wife.[1] My health & that of my daughter[2] are delicate: the other members of the family are well. With the exception of James Nicholson, all my old friends are dead or confined by old age to their homes: there is not in this quarter the slightest improvement in the state of society or indeed of any kind: but my children are good and very affectionate; neither of my sons brought up to business, Albert, with considerable and varied talents and acquired knowledge, but as yet wanting perseverance & steadiness, James & Frances more fitted for a court than a wilderness, my wife just as she was 24 years ago.[3]

The last seven years I spent in Europe, though not the

---

[1] Josephine Mary Pascault whom James Gallatin married April 23, 1824. Walters, *Albert Gallatin*, p. 327.

[2] Frances Gallatin.

[3] For an account of Gallatin's life at this time see *ibid.*, pp. 317-18.

most useful were the most pleasant of my life, both [MS illeg.] of my reception in Geneva where I found many old & affectionate friends (Hentsch,[4] Dumont,[5] the [MS illeg.] &c) and from my standing with the first Statesmen & men of merit in France and England. Where you do not stand in the way of any body, instead of collision and envy, you meet with much indulgence if you can fill with credit the place you occupy; and this was a disposition to which I had not been accustomed towards me, and the want of which I now, on that account, feel perhaps more than formerly. These feelings would and ought naturally to have induced me, and you expressed the same wish, to withdraw altogether from public life; and my wife, irksome to her as is her residence here, was of the same opinion. I will briefly state what has brought my name before the people for the office of Vice President.

During the 12 years I was in the Treasury, I was anxiously looking for some man that could fill my place there and in the general direction of the national concerns, for one indeed that could replace Mr. Jefferson, Mr. Madison & myself. Brackenridge[6] of Kentucky only appeared and died: the excentricities & temper of J. Randolph soon destroyed his usefulness; and only one man at last appeared who filled my expectations. This was Mr. Crawford, who united to a powerful mind a most correct judgment and an inflexible integrity; which last quality, not sufficiently tempered by indulgence and civility, has prevented his acquiring general popularity: but notwithstanding this defect, (for it is one) I know so well his great superiority over the other candidates for the office of President, that I was anxious for his election and openly expressed my opinion. I would not ever compare Jackson or Calhoon to him, the first an honest man & the idol of the worshippers of military glory, but from incapacity, military habits, and habitual disregard of laws & constitutional

[4] Henry ( ?) Hentsch.
[5] Etienne Dumont. See below, p. 277n.
[6] John Breckinridge.

provisions, altogether unfit for the office, the other a smart fellow, one of the first among second rate men, but of lax political principles and of a disordinant ambition not over delicate in the means of satisfying itself. John Q. Adams is a virtuous man, whose temper which is not the best might be overlooked: he has very great & miscellaneous knowledge, and he is with his pen a powerful debater: but he wants to a deplorable degree, that most essential quality, a sound & correct judgment. Of this I have had in my official connection & intercourse with him complete and repeated proofs, and although he may be usefull when controuled & checked by others, he ought never to be trusted with a place, where unrestrained his errors might be fatal to the country. Mr. Clay has his faults, but splendid talents and a generous mind. I certainly prefer Mr. Crawford to him although he is far more popular; and yet, notwithstanding that popularity, I believe that, particularly since the West is split between him & Jackson, it is impossible that he should be elected & that the contest is in fact between Crawford & Adams. Almost all the old Republicans, (Mr. Jefferson & Mr. Madison amongst them) think as I do: but they were aware that Mr. Crawford was not very popular and that the bond of party, which had with great many produced the effect of patriotism & knowledge being nearly dissolved, neither of the other candidates would withdraw, and they were at a loss whom to unite to him as V. Pres't.— I advised to nominate no body for that office, or if any body some person from N. York or New England. The last was attached to Adams: there were contentions in N. York. The friends of Mr. Crawford thought the persons proposed there too obscure & that my name would serve as a banner & shew their nomination to be that of the old Republican party. I thought and still think that they were mistaken, that as a foreigner, as residuary legatee of the federal hatred, and as one whose old services were forgotten & more recent not the more useful were but little known, my name could be of no service to the cause. They insisted, and being nominated both by those members of Congress and by the Legislature of Virginia, I could not honorably withdraw, though my reluctance was much increased by the dead opposition of Pennsylvania which is & no where more than in this vicinity, Jackson-mad. From all I can collect I think Mr. Crawford's election (notwithstanding this mistake) nearly certain and mine improbable.[7] So much for my apology which I could not make shorter. I have now said every thing I believe respecting me which could interest you; and I have only to entreat you not to disappoint the hope you gave me and to come and spend those unhealthy summer and autumnal months with us where at least fevers have not yet penetrated, although they prevailed last year every where east of Cumberland & West of Wheeling. In summer I must necessarily to preserve health be at rest, and, if, to effect an interview, probably the last, so dear to both, it is necessary that you should have the trouble and fatigue of the journey, it is but strict justice, (if that was any object between us) that the expence should be defrayed by me. Let not that therefore stop you and come once more to see your old friend and refresh your old age by recollections of ancient times. I will add to the stock much that is pleasing from Geneva: Seventeen years of French yoke have united the parties as far as union is practicable in a free country. If there are differences of opinion they apply to details of administration: the old distinctions so odious to the people are done away. To the general Council & to that of 200, has been substituted a large elective representative council, where as far as I could judge, virtue and talents are almost the only titles for admission, where the most obscure & newest names are mixed with the oldest of the Republic, where a Dumont, Bellamy and two Pictats are in opposition to Descartes, D'Yvernois and most of the old wigs (which have been however set aside)— But what kind of opposition? I have read many of their debates; and independent of the

[7] For a detailed account of this election and Gallatin's role see Walters, *Albert Gallatin,* pp. 318-25.

interest I felt for questions to others of small & local importance, any one may admire the train of close and logical reasoning they display and must be delighted with the candour &
mutual forbearance which characterise them. They are like
discussions conducted amicably but with perfect freedom by
members of the same family respecting their common concerns.
Nor are the antient manners much altered  A few amongst
the most ignorant and vicious, the remnant of those who
disgraced Geneva in 1794, not above 3 or 4 hundred, hardly
any of the old bourgeoisie, have I am told been corrupted by
the French whilst in power & their morals have been affected;
but those of the great bulk are better than before the revolutions; and they are as pure Genevans, as little Frenchified as
you could desire. Speaking of old bourgeoisie, the distinction
does not exist—citoyens, bourgeois and ratifs are in every
respect, civil & political, on the same footing. And here let me
observe how powerful is the moral effect of virtue and
knowledge. Whilst Venice, Genoa, Belgium &c &c have been
bartered away without scruple or regard to the wishes of the
people, not only have Holland and Switzerland escaped unhurt,
because they had both a national character and were truly
nations: but even little Geneva has been respected and restored
to its independence, whilst more than 40 Imperial cities have
been left in the possession of the Princes who had usurped
them with the permission of Bonaparte. I might say much
more but must reserve it for the time when we meet. In that
hope and with my love to all the members of your family I
remain Ever Your's

ALBERT GALLATIN

My wife and Jas. Nicholson send their best compliments.
By the bye you owe me nothing. Your sister was too
proud to permit me to join in the support of your father; and
your brother's return in 1818 relieved her difficulties. I have
not heard from them since that time, and was not in Geneva
subsequent to 1817.

[Addressed:]  John Badollet Esq're  Receiver of public monies Vincennes  Indiana

[Postmarked:]  New Geneva  Pa.  31 July

[Endorsed:]  29th July 1824

[Badollet to Gallatin]

VINCENNES Sep'r 5, 1824

MY DEAR FRIEND

Your letter, so anxiously expected has been received, and read with a pleasure which I will not attempt to express. The undiminished affection which it breathes, has darted a ray of sunshine on the gloomy evenings of my days, alleviated the burthen of present distress, and mitigated the sense of past errors, which of late had destroyed the peace of my mind. This language must appear enigmatical to you; although you are fully acquainted with every circumstance, which causes me to use it. The fact is that the retrospect of my past life, is far from producing feelings of a pleasant nature, and self condemnation sits like an incubus on my spirits and weighs them down. To be relieved, in some measure; from that painful state: by pouring my sorrows into your friendly bosom and to devise with you the means of making such atonement within my power as would ease my mind, (amongst other powerful motives, of which easily guessed at, impelling me irresistibly to that step) was the object of my intended visit.

But unfortunately two obstacles will prevent the *present* gratification of that ardent wish of mine. The first you have kindly offered to remove, but I cannot consent to it, for although our proceedings towards each other are not to be judged by common rules, yet something seems to tell me, that however kind & friendly in you to make the tender, it would be unjust in me to accept. The other obstacle is of a nature not to be easily surmounted; the act of last session in relation to lands purchased under the credit system; render my absence improper if not impracticable until the 10th of April next, after which day I shall be at liberty to go, and I hope also that the fees allowed by that act[1] will, not only relieve me from my present embarrassment, but also enable me to gratify the fond wish of my heart without drawing upon the kindness of my indulgent friend. Tell me then, where you will be at that time. I hope it will be in Fayette, there alone can we be at full liberty to enjoy an unrestrained and mutal interchange of thoughts, much interesting matter you must no doubt have to communicate: both of a private & public nature; to me of the highest interest, & much have I to say on this country, where a residence of nearly twenty years has not been unproductive of observations on men and things.

I have not the physical power, if I were so inclined to lengthen this scrawl by animadverting on the part you are acting in relation to the pending election of President & Vice President of the U. S: I[n] my humble opinion, you might have done better, at least for your own happiness, not to have permitted your name to be mentioned, the venom of party rancour, of which you have received your full share, & which had remained quiescent for so many years, will be again revived & you are likely to feel the effects of its renovated malignancy, an insult which no philosophy can deprive of its bitterness, and which is the more galling for being inflicted by those whom, as a part of our great community, you have so ably & so faithfully served. Besides, admitting, which I think with you improbable, that you will succeed, you are at once replunged in the turmoils of politicks, exposed in your conspicuous situation to the shafts of slander, and deprived of that repose, which, after years devoted to the service of your country, is as desirable as it is necessary.

I have been rather unlucky in this official station. For a number of years, this part of the country being little known, purchases were slow and I had little to boast of in point of ease and comfort. The debts to pay in Pennsylvania, the

---

[1] Act of May 18, 1824, in U. S. *Statutes at Large,* IV, 24-25. The fees allowed the registers and receivers under this act were double those allowed by the act of 1821. See above, p. 260n.

purchase of a farm the erection of small house thereon for a shelter and home; and the demands of a family of five children kept me struggling against wind and tide untill the sales of 1816 and the two following years enabled me to bring up the lee-way, to purchase an hou[se] and lot in town & one half section for my daughter Fanny (a deservedly dear child). Unfortunately the Canadian warrants being nearly all located in this district,[2] I lost my commission on the great amount of land covered by them, lands which if sold would have averaged $4 or $5 per acre, and I had to perform all that troublesome and necessary duty without one cent's compensation. Had that land been sold, my commission thereon, added to the indemnication which justice could not, but Congress may probably deny me for the expenses incurred in the performance of the heavy duties under the relief laws, I would now be in a state of comparative comfort and at the summit of my wishes.

But my greatest misfortune is that I never knew how to turn a penny. How often have I wished a small share of my former Colleague's talent. He always could make of a twelve cents piece a dollar, and he would now be in an enviable situation if he had contented himself with occasional & not too striking deviations from the path of rectitude. . . . .[3]

When I took the pen, my intention was only to acknowledge the receipt of your letter, of the benign influence it has had upon my mind, and to pray you to indulge me with another so that I might regulate my steps with a view to our intended meeting, but the pleasure of conversing with you, has made me, however painful and laborious to me is writing, fill up an entire epistle. Fatigue forces me to put an end it.

Remember me to all inquiring friends & particularly to every member of your family tell Mrs. Gallatin that I hereby solemnly bind myself not to encroach upon your time of rest,

[2] By an act of March 5, 1816, bounties in land were granted to certain Canadian volunteers of the War of 1812, to be located in the unappropriated public lands in Indiana Territory.

[3] A reference to Nathaniel Ewing.

when we are together, & to be satisfied with the entire possession of your person from sunrise to eight o'clock at night.

Four succeeding years, the relief laws, by forcing my attendance in this office for the fall months, have left me exposed to the autumnal influence of this climate, which as often I had intended to shun, whether I shall be spared this fall is known only to that being who made us.

Fare you well my ever dear & beloved Friend For ever Yours &c

JOHN BADOLLET

[Addressed:] Albert Gallatin Esq'r New Geneva Fayette Co. Pen'a

[Endorsed:] Vincennes Sept'r 1825 [1824] J. Badollet

[Postmarked with stamp:] Vincennes Sep 7

[Badollet to Gallatin]

[May, 1825]

MY DEAR FRIEND,

I take the pen to acknowledge the receipt of your last,[1] and to inform you that I am making preparations for my intended journey, the precise time of which I am not able to fix, but hope to effect between June and July.

I am yet uncertain in what manner I will travel. I would prefer going on horseback, but doubt of my ability to bear the fatigue of such a long ride; a steam boat conveyance is both comfortable and speedy, but those boilers convey to my mind ideas not a little terrific, which utterly poison the pleasure which I would otherwise enjoy.

Last week an accident happened, which might have been a cause of general mourning throughout the United States had not Providence interposed: the Mechanic steam boat conveying Gen'l Lafayette and company to Louisville suddenly sank

---

[1] Not found.

between Evansville and the Falls, but thank God not a single life was lost.[2]

It will undoubtedly give you pleasure to hear, that one of the causes of my wretchedness has disappeared, the fees accruing under the act of the 18th of May 1824 having been sufficient to release me from my pecuniary embarrassments so that my present feelings are those of a mariner, who having struck on a rock and seeing destruction before his eyes, is unexpectedly saved by a friendly wave which wafts him unhurt to the beach.

I cannot write any more— I particularly charge you to convey to Mrs. Gallatin the assurance of my grateful and respectful remembrance. My kind compliments to Mr. Griffin Nicholson & families.

I need not tell you that my good Peggy & I join in sincere wishes for your health and content. Your affectionate Friend

JOHN BADOLLET

[Addressed:] Albert Gallatin Esq'r New Geneva Fayette Co. Penn'a

[Postmarked with stamp:] Vincennes May 17

[Endorsed:] Vincennes May 1825 J Badollet

[Badollet to Gallatin]

VINCENNES January 25, 1826

MY DEAR FRIEND

Mr. William Burtch, the Gentleman who will hand you this letter, is a merchant of this place enjoying and deserving the general esteem. Having married my niece (or rather third daughter) Margaret Hannah & my son Albert his sister;[1] the gratification I derive from that interesting connexion is so much the greater that he proves the most affectionate

---

[2] See Charles N. Thompson, "General Lafayette in Indiana," in *Indiana Magazine of History*, XXIV (1928), 67-68.

[1] William Burtch married Margaret Hannah, October 4, 1819, and Albert Badollet married Relief Burtch December 16, 1823. Knox County Marriage Records, I, 176; II, 43. Albert's first wife had died. See above, p. 260n. After his wife Relief died (see below), he married Rachael Barnet, September 29, 1832. *Ibid.,* II, 88.

husband & Albert has every reason to bless the day that united
him to a woman whose only ambition is to make him happy.
Any attention you will be pleased to shew him will be gratefully & feelingly acknowledged by me.

Mr. Burtch who intended to set off on his journey only
at the end of next month, having suddenly resolved to start
immediately, I write these few words in haste, and some time
hence I will undertake (what to me is now no little undertaking) another letter wherein I will range in my awkward
& desultory manner over sundry subjects which have occupied
my thoughts.

I waited, after your departure,[2] in the vain expectation of
a rise of the waters untill the 9th of November on which day
I took the stage at Wheeling and on the17th I reached home in
perfect health & with renovated spirts.[3] You would hardly
have known me to be the same man who, in your house &
every where else in my last journey, exhibited himself as a dull
& taciturn Ourang-outang and certainly a most unpleasant
inmate. But more anon on that subject.

Being forced by adverse circumstances to leave Sally Mc-
Clelland behind,[4] I had no occasion for the money you lent
me & I enclose it herein; I would have done it sooner, had a
safer conveyance than the mail offered itself.

If you can procure Malte Brun's Geography[5] & the price

[2] Gallatin had probably set out for Baltimore where he and his family
took up residence in the fall of 1825. Walters, *Albert Gallatin,* p. 528.

[3] On his way home from visiting Gallatin, Badollet wrote from Wheeling
to his son Albert in Vincennes: "The waters never were so low, & the
dry weather continuing [dry? MS torn] with no appearance of a change,
I have abandoned the idea of coming down stream & to morrow I take the
stage to Cincinnati, whence I will proceed by steam boat to Louisville.
Once there I shall find little difficulty in reaching you." Letter dated
November 4, 1825, in Badollet Papers, Indiana Historical Society Library.

[4] In the letter cited in the preceding note Badollet wrote, "I am grieved
that such untoward circumstances compel me to return without Wise's
sister, but having waited as long as I could, the lateness of the season forces
me on & I cannot support the idea of a longer absence."

[5] This would probably be Conrad Malte-Brun (1775-1826), *Universal
Geography, or a Description of All Parts of the World, on a New Plan,*

be not too high for my exchequer, send it to me in the packages of Mr. Burtch, with a map, if you can procure it, which I saw in your house, of the country through which the national road passes, & the various canals in contemplation, are to run.

If Mal. B. cannot be had now, I would be glad in the meantime to obtain the last edition, which must be at least the seventh, of Morse's Geography in 2 vol. large 8vo with the Atlass accompanying it.[6] The amount of either of those purchases shall be transmitted by the first safe opportunity.

My wife, and family reciprocate with thankfulness yours & Mrs. Gallatin's rembrance of them & we all join in earnest wishes that the happiness you now enjoy may never experience a drawback. You may now say with Gilblass Inveni postum &c

With my kind compliments to every individual of your family, accept the assurance that time has added to rather than substracted from the warmth of my feelings toward my old and indulgent Friend. Adieu Yours forever

John Badollet

P. S. At the termination of my letter I poured the inkstand instead of the sand box over my writing & I have neither time, power, nor indeed willingness to copy it.

I think that if Registers, whose burthens more than double those of the Receiver were allowed their percentage upon the amount transferred [it wou]ld be equitable & just, the amounts being considered as *new payments* similar to those formerly effected in stock.

[Addressed:] Albert Gallatin Esq'r Baltimore Md. Fav'd by Mr. Will'm Burtch

[Endorsed:] Vincennes 25 Jan'y 1826 J. Badollet

---

*according to the Great Natural Divisions of the Globe* . . . (6 volumes and atlas. Philadelphia, 1827-29). This is a translation of Malte-Brun's *Précis de la geographie universelle* (Paris, 1810-29). The atlas of the American edition was published in 1828.

[6] Jedidiah Morse, *The American Universal Geography: or A View of the Present State of all the Empires, Kingdoms, States and Republics in the Known World, and of the United States in Particular.* . . . A two-volume edition of this with atlas was published in Boston, 1819.

[Gallatin to Badollet]

NEW YORK 22d June 1826

MY DEAR FRIEND

Finding towards the end of the Session of Congress that the bill for the relief of the Registers was in great danger of being lost, for want of time and on account of a disagreement between the two houses as to the best mode of affording relief, I wrote to our Fayette C'y member of Congress, Andrew Stewart to use every exertion to push it forward. He is very kind & obliging and did his best, and I went to Washington the three last days of the session for the express purpose of assisting as far as I could. The bill very fortunately went through, being the last but one that was signed, and more than fifty being lost merely for want of two days more to go through the forms.[1]

As Mr. Graham[2] informs me that the law gives you about 1900 dollars besides y'r charge for extra clerk hire, I hope that it will relieve you; and the question now occurs whether you still intend to resign provided your son Albert can be appointed.[3] Cazenova[4] has already spoken to Mr. Graham, who will support the application; but it is thought best that it should be made during the recess of Congress, as there might be other applications made by some of your Senators or Members of Congress in favour of some friend or relation.

If therefore such is your intention, I advise the following course.

1 : Write a letter resigning the office on account of your age & infirmities, which you may address to the Commissioner of the land office or Sec'y of the Treasury, and in which, of course, you will say nothing of Albert.

[1] The act is in U. S. *Statutes at Large,* IV, 193. It allowed additional compensation to registers and receivers for extra services rendered by them under the relief act of 1821. See above.

[2] George Graham, commissioner of the General Land Office.

[3] Badollet did not resign at this time. See below, p. 326.

[4] Charles Anthony Cazenove, a fellow Genevan who had come to the United States. See Introduction, p. 12, above.

2dly Obtain the most respectable recommendation you can in favour of Albert, stating his moral character, integrity, and knowledge of the duties of the office.

3dly Enclose both the letters of resignation & recommendation to Cazenova, whose address is "Anthony Charles Cazenove Esqr Alexandria District of Columbia," requesting him to consult with Mr. Graham and not to deliver the letter of resignation and recommendation unless he can ascertain that there is a strong probability that Albert will be appointed in your place.

I am going to write to Cazenova to let him know all this, & will enclose him a recommendation signed by myself in favour of Albert and a private letter to the President, both to be delivered at the same time with your's.

The newspapers have informed you of my new mission to England. It has a specific object in view.[5] I take with me my wife and daughter and leave my two sons in Baltimore, where Albert has been admitted at the bar and expects to commence practice in September; but James has not yet succeeded in entering into business, which is at this time very precarious. We are all well, the baby included, and all join in affectionate compliments to you. I hope, God permitting, to be back in a twelve month and I leave sufficient pledges behind to secure my return as soon as practicable. I will not fail whilst in England to write to Dumont[6] as requested, and I hope in a manner that will be perfectly satisfactory to you and

[5] In May Gallatin had been appointed minister to Great Britain succeeding Rufus King. His chief duty was to open negotiations over the Oregon country. He sailed for England July 1, 1826, and returned arriving in New York, November 29, 1827. Walters, *Albert Gallatin,* pp. 330-42.

[6] Etienne Dumont, a fellow Genevan. In the Badollet Papers in the Indiana Historical Society Library there are some twenty letters from Dumont to Badollet written mostly from Geneva between 1780 and 1784, when Badollet was at Clairac. Dumont, born in 1759, in Geneva, was just a year older than Badollet. He left Geneva in 1784, living in St. Petersburg, London, and Paris. He served as secretary to Jeremy Bentham and translated his works into French. He returned to Geneva in 1814 and served in the representative council. Pierre Larousse, *Nouveau Larousse* . . . (7 volumes. 1898-1904), III, 878.

ought to remove that gloomy feeling you entertain respecting Geneva. It was highly gratifying to me to hear lately a very respectable member of the Baltimore bar, Mr. Pennington, speaking in the highest terms of you, calling you the faithful one amidst a scene of corruption &c. You stand equally high at Washington with the officers connected with you: and it will be a most pleasing office of friendship on my part to take care that you should also enjoy in your native country that reputation and fair name to which you are so justly entitled.

I received your letter with the forty dollars enclosed; but your friend did not call on me, and I could not find him out. Malte Brun's translation was not complete. I have left orders with my son James to get it whenever finished. Please to write to him directed Baltimore & to let him know how to forward it. If no Vincennes merchant comes, will it do to send it to James Nicholson or in any other way. If you had heard that he, Mr. Nicholson had got into some pecuniary difficulties, you will be happy to learn that he has been relieved by a sale of some portion of his Grandfather's estate.

Remember me most affectionately to your excellent wife, to whom mine sends also her best compliments. Give mine to your children. God bless you and them. I still hope to see you once more. Your visit did me much good and I think had the same effect on you.

So long as I breathe Ever Your's

ALBERT GALLATIN

[Addressed:] John Badollet Esqre Register of the land office Vincennes State of Indiana

[Badollet to Gallatin]

VINCENNES Feb'y 17, 1828

Welcome, thrice welcome, my Dear friend, to your country again in health and safety. I enjoy with the greater satisfaction the certainty of your being now surrounded by every member of your worthy family, that an uneasiness resulting from your exposure, with those so deservedly dear to you, to a treacherous element, could not be successfully combated.

But you are returned in evil times, the country is convulsed, the public mind is frenzied, the elements of discord are multiplying and in a state of fearful fermentation, and the press that blessing & curse of free states is scattering firebrands far & wide over the land. The language of vituperation so grosly & shamelessly indulged in by too many editors, & so keenly relished, is as disparaging to our national taste, as it is disgraceful to our morals, & must sink us in the estimation of the world. It is an afflicting reflexion, & deeply so, that our mad conduct must go a great way towards justifying the sinister anticipations of the enemies of liberal institutions, and extinguishing the hopes so fondly entertained by the friends of the liberty of both hemispheres. This deplorable state of things has so affected my mind, that when I anxiously cast my eyes into the vista of time, I can discover but a lurid light precursor of tempests. May God in his mercy disappoint such gloomy forebodings.

My mind is in a morbid state and requires some remedial assistance to restore its tone. You who have preserved the freshness & vigour of all your faculties condescend to come to my help, if you have any consolatory views to present on the present state of things in the United States, in charity communicate them at a moment of leisure.

Blessed be the heart which dictated and the hand which traced the last lines I received from you. Your voluntary attempt to lessen the obloquy, to which my thoughtless follies have exposed me in the place of my birth, has spread a ray of comfort upon my existence & shall be remembered with deeply felt gratitude to my last breath.

I have some time dreamed that in your next visit to Fayette with your indulgent wife & my kind lively & lovely Frances, you will take the stage to Wheeling, whence a steam boat will in less than four days land you in Evansville 50 miles from me from which place a four horse stage will bring you to Vincennes. There I can & will make you comfortable. It is only a dream to be sure, but too delightful not to be repeatedly indulged in.

Mr. William Burtch, the same Gentleman whom I introduced to your attention after my return home, will call upon you, soon after this letter shall have reached you, lose no time in getting ready Malte Brun for him, give him the bill that I may transmit you the amount I pray you, do not fail.

Give me some account of your correspondence with Geneva.

I am litterally unable to trace another line, my arm becomes so painful, so that I am forced to conclude, not however without tendering you the assurance of my affectionate remembrance of every member of your interesting family. My wife joins me in wishing you health & content.

Adieu Dear Friend Ever Yours

JOHN BADOLLET

I have transmitted $300 to my sister

[Addressed:] Albert Gallatin Esqr Baltimore[1] New-York

[Postmarked:] Vincennes Feb 18 Baltimore Mar 3

[Endorsed:] Vincennes Feb. 17, 1828 John Badollet

[Badollet to Gallatin]

VINCENNES Jan'y 10, 1829

It would have been, my Dear Friend, a highly valued gratification to me, to have received a few lines from you since your return, but I must confess I have not much right to complain being myself guilty of great neglect in that respect. But when you consider that to a flow of ideas beyond measure sluggish is superadded an encreasing physical difficulty in writing which makes a letter the work of the best part of a day, you cannot be surprised that I undertake that task with the wry faces of a child compelled to gulp down a dose of castor oil, & you will not withold your forgiveness.

The act of Congress passed for the relief of the land officers has been indeed a relief to me & has relieved my mind

---

[1] A line has been drawn through "Baltimore" and "New-York" added as a forwarding address.

of a part of its burthen.  In the application of that relief I was met by conflicting claims; to do complete justice to each was impracticable.  I was obliged to compromise: I transmitted to my sister $300.  I bought of Mr. Tabb (son in law of the late Charles Carrol of Bellevue now living at Washington & whom I wish you to see) his house & lot in a retired & pleasant situation on the bank of the Wabash & within the precincts of Vincennes.[1]  I was induced to make that purchase by considerations of some weight: My farm, since all my sons had left me, had become a burthen & a bill of expense to me, the necessity of leaving my wife almost every day in solitude at home & of my going to town three miles in all weathers at my age, was bearing harder upon me every day.  My wife whom undiminished affection & cheerful resignation was the solace of my often hopeless hours, required something at my hands in return.  By that purchase I provided for her comforts, she is surrounded by her sister her son Albert, her nieces, and by that dear Peggy Hannah (now the wife of Mr. Burtch) whom she raised & by whom she is loved, & when I am called away, her widowhood will not be cheerless.

The next application I made of the money I received, is for the reimbursement of Amat.[2]  I have $500 laid aside for that purpose; it is the sum which I received exclusive of interest, which, if I had to pay it now, would nearly reduce me to real poverty.  I hope this manifestation of a desire to atone for the error of thoughtless & romantic youth, will shew that, notwithstanding my long & almost inexcusable silence, I have preserved a lively sense of my old class mate's goodness of heart, & will be accepted in extenuation of my past wrongs.  How

[1] Moses Tabbs was a native of Maryland who married a daughter of Charles Carroll, a signer of the Declaration of Independence.  He was admitted to the bar at Vincennes in 1818, practiced successfully for several years, then returned to his native state. *History of Knox and Daviess Counties Indiana* (Chicago, 1886), pp. 194-95; Henry S. Cauthorn, *A History of the Town of Vincennes . . .* (Terre Haute, 1902), p. 188.

[2] Charles Jean Amat, a fellow Genevan.  Apparently Badollet and Gallatin had discussed this debt, which the former had incurred before he left Geneva, during Badollet's visit to Gallatin.

to forward that sum to you, I know not, except you should meet with a chance of drawing upon me at sight, in which case your draught shall be duly honoured. If you know any other mode, please to point it out.

I have taken the liberty of giving to Miss Frances Wright a few lines of introduction. That remarkable woman is a deep & fearless thinker, whose writings and lectures will go a great way towards unveiling the audacious schemes of the clergy & opposing a check to the flood of intolerant bigotry which threatens to overwhelm this land. Her rich fancy, reach of thought and in a style chastened by the most correct taste, rivet the attention of her hearers, and the saints are reduced to their customary shifts of abusing where they cannot refute. She may possibly go too far on certain points, & I am one who believes that she does, but we are not bound to adopt her ideas, if after a fair investigation they do not prove satisfactory to our minds, & there is this difference between her & our sanctimonious teachers, that she does not, like them, hurl us into damnation, if we chance to dissent from her.[3]

She informed me that one of your sons was at St. Louis; I have since thought that it must have been a mistake, arising from some similarity of name, otherwise Solomon or Nichol-

[3] Badollet had probably met Frances Wright at New Harmony located on the Wabash below Vincennes, where she was a member of the Owenite community. Miss Wright has been classified as a reformer and freethinker. She was born in Scotland. After her first visit to America she published *Views of Society and Manners in America.* She returned in 1824 and toured the western states as a member of the Marquis de la Fayette's party. She also called upon Thomas Jefferson and James Madison and interested them in her plans for the emancipation and colonization of Negro slaves. She carried out her plans with some success at the community which she founded at Nashoba in western Tennessee. In 1828 she came to New Harmony and in 1829 went to New York where she began publishing the *Free Enquirer.* As a public lecturer she brought the strongest criticism on herself since such performance was regarded as extremely "unfeminine" in that day. On the platform she attacked religion, the influence of the church on politics, and education based on authority. She defended equal rights for women and marriage based on moral obligation only rather than legal. *Dictionary of American Biography,* XX, 549-50. See Gallatin's comments on her conduct, below, p. 286, and Badollet's rejoinder, pp. 292-93.

son would have informed of the fact.

I have written to you once since your return, but being then ignorant of your removal to New York, I directed my letter to Baltimore & it may have not reached you, I am affraid, for after so many proofs of your kind affection toward me, it cannot be admitted that you would refuse me the few lines which I so eagerly solicited.

Mr. Cole who saw your family at New York informs me that your daughter lost some of that pleasing animation which a flow of health imparts. I hope that by this time she is entirely restored, & exhibits now the same amiable play-fulness & innocent gayety which pleased me so much when last with you. Tender her, I pray you, my affectionate re-membrance, as well as to Mrs. Gallatin to whose friendly attentions & kind indulgence I cheerfully pay the debt of a sincere & lasting gratitude. Remember me also to your son Albert who I presume is with you, & to James & his wife whom you will see on your return home. To yourself it is needless to repeat that I ever am Your affectionate friend

JOHN BADOLLET

P. S. I wish you could see Mr. Tabbs, he and his wife, an amiable & intelligent woman, have been friendly to me. Re-me[mbe]r me to them.

Perhaps Mr. Jennings or Blake[4] would pay you the money & take a draught upon me therefor. For obvious reasons it is my particular desire that the transmission of the said money should be effected through your own hands, you will not, I trust, decline the friendly task.

As I was going to mail this letter for Washington I re-ceived one from Solomon informing of your returning to New York— I have obtained at last Malte Brun, but no maps. Has he or has he not published any to accompany the work?

[Addressed:] Albert Gallatin Esqr New York

[Endorsed:] Vincennes Jan. 10, 1829 John Badollet

[4] Jonathan Jennings and Thomas H. Blake, members of Congress from Indiana.

[Gallatin to Badollet]

NEW YORK 26th March 1829

I duly received, my dear friend, your letter of 10th Jan'y last, and it would have been immediately answered, had not an accident deprived me of the use of my right hand. Rest has now partly restored it; but I am compelled to employ generally an amanuensis, and to write myself only on special occasions.

I have found no opportunity of negotiating a draft of 500 dollars on you, the current of commercial transactions running in the contrary direction. The money, if you can remit it to me will be immediately forwarded to the order of Amat though with a loss of 4 to 5 pr/c on the exchange. But is it certain that he is still alive? I think the best way for me will be to remit the money to Hentsch who, notwithstanding his colossal fortune (near ten millions of francs) has re-established in his own name his banking house at Paris, leaving that of Geneva to his children. He will pay it to Amat if alive and if not to his heirs. You should send me with the money a letter for him (Amat) explaining your motive for considering as a friendly loan what was by him intended as a gift. On your scruples on that point I can say nothing, though I do not share them and think that you have from over sensibility made yourself unhappy in that respect without sufficient cause.

I hope that, with your moderate wants, you find yourself now comparatively at ease. After much anxiety I find that our children must be left to cut their own way & to provide for themselves; and I have no other uneasiness respecting them than so far as concerns their health; that of Albert & Frances being extremely delicate, so much so indeed as may perhaps compel me to change once more my place of residence for one more southerly and favorable to their lungs. With great indolence and ever anxious wish to be rooted somewhere I was destined to be always on the wing. It was an ill contrived plan to think that the banks of the Monongahela, where

I was perfectly satisfied to live & die in retirement, could be
borne by the female part of my family or by children brought
up at Washington and Paris and unfortunately for them in
an artificial situation which has produced expectations that
can never be realised. Albert was the only one who was happy
and I was obliged to break up a comfortable establishment
and to attempt a new one in one of our sea-ports with means
inadequate to our support. Particular circumstances have
made Baltimore, which was my choice, objectionable in some
respects; and, on my return from England, in conformity
with the natural wishes of my wife, whose respectable mother
aged 85 is still alive, I settled here. What I may now do is
quite uncertain. To Washington I must proceed in a few
days on the business of the North East boundary which is
committed to my care & will be detained there till the 1st
of July. I must add that my public engagements in relation
to that important question will cease with the end of this year.

I am not pleased with the present aspect of public affairs,
still less with that of the public mind. Perhaps old age makes
me querulous: I care little what party and who is in power;
but it seems to me that now and for the last eight years, people
and leaders have been much less anxious about the public
service & the manner in which it should be performed than by
whom the Country should be governed. This feeling appears
to me to be growing and at this moment, every movement
seems already to be directed towards the next Presidential
election, and that not on account of any preferance of a
system of public measures over another, but solely in relation
to persons or at best to sectional feelings. Amongst other
symptoms displeasing to me I may count the attempt of the
West and particularly of your State to claim the sovereignty
& exclusive right to the public lands.[1] I wish they did of right

[1] In his message to the General Assembly on December 4, 1827, Governor
James B. Ray of Indiana, had contended that "it would not only be *just*, but
*wise*, to yield up the public domain to the States . . .," and continued at
length in support of his contention. The House committee agreed, reporting

belong to the several states and not to the United States. But the claim is contrary to positive compact and to common justice, any departure from which either in our domestic or external policy is the most fatal injury that can be inflicted on our political institutions, on the reputation of the Country, and indeed on the preservation of the Union. But we are going off the scene; I think that we have discharged our duties honestly and the next generation must provide for itself.

The country in which there is the greatest legal toleration is not the most tolerant in practice. There are also certain opinions which a woman of sound mind cannot support. She ought not at all events to exhibit herself in a theatrical manner. And I regret that one of as much talent and as I believe of pure mind as Miss Wright should have adopted a course so prejudicial to herself.

My wrist informs me that I must stop. My wife and children, Frances particularly with whom you are a great favorite, send their best compliments to you. Remember me most affectionately to your excellent wife and believe me ever Your friend

ALBERT GALLATIN

I have never seen Malte Brun's maps.

[Addressed:] John Badollet Esq're Register of the Land Office Vincennes Indiana

---

that "the State of Indiana has a right to the soil and eminent domain of all the unappropriated lands within her prescribed limits."

The following legislature (1828-29) passed a resolution instructing Indiana's senators and requesting her congressmen "to use every exertion in their power . . . to induce the United States, to acknowledge the vested right of the state; and place her upon an equal footing with the original states in every respect whatsoever, as well in fact as in name"; and Indiana's Senator William Hendricks proposed that the Federal government inquire into the expedience of ceding and relinquishing the public lands within the new states to the several states in which they lay. Dorothy Riker and Gayle Thornbrough (eds.), *Messages and Papers relating to the Administration of James Brown Ray . . . 1825-1831* (*Indiana Historical Collections,* XXXIV, Indianapolis, 1954), pp. 285-87n.

[Badollet to Gallatin]

VINCENNES July 8, 1829

DEAR FRIEND

I transmit you by the bearer Mr. William Burtch the same Gent'n whom I formerly introduced to your acquaintance as the husband of my ward & niece Margaret Hannah, the five hundred dollars destined for Geneva: But as circumstances might unexpectedly arise, which would render the retaining that sum convenient to him, I should wish you in that (improbable) case, to make a tender of it to him, & I shall find means to retransmit it.

A long lingering sickness & heavy business in the office under the last relinquishment laws have hitherto delayed my reply to your last letter, but I shall ere long undertake it however severe may, to me, be the task of writing.

You would do me a great favour by sending me a *fair* copy of your classification of Indian nations, the one I took with me is such a scrawl that I cannot read it.[1]

Make my respects acceptable to Mrs. Gallatin without forgetting the rest of your interesting family.

Dear friend Ever Yours &c

JOHN BADOLLET

[Addressed:]  Albert Gallatin Sen'r  Esq'r  New York Favoured by Mr. Will'm Burtch

[Endorsed:]  Vincennes 8 July 1829  John Badollet

[Badollet to Gallatin]

VINCENNES August 14, 1829

DEAR FRIEND

I have by Mr. Burtch transmitted you the $500 for our

---

[1] Gallatin had been interested in the various American Indian tribes and their languages since his first contacts with them in the District of Maine just after his arrival in America. In 1823, in Paris, at the suggestion of Alexander von Humboldt he had prepared a short essay classifying the tribes of North America. Adriano Balbi drew heavily upon Gallatin's classification for his *Introduction à l'atlas ethnographique du globe,* published in 1826. Walters, *Albert Gallatin,* p. 329. For publication of Gallatin's works on the Indians see below, p. 324n. Apparently what Badollet wanted was still in manuscript.

friend Amat, in hope that you may find an opportunity of having it remitted to its destination without the loss resulting from the unfavourable state of exchange between this country and Europe. I have not as yet written to him, the singular situation, wherein I find myself, rendering that step on my part both awkward and painful. To attempt to apologize for apparent forgetfulness and an unjustifiable silence of so many years, is an under[tak]ing, which would require an history of my life, the excentricities of & peculiarities of my character & long protracted childhood, to which I find myself unequal & from which I recoil with disgust. The retrospect of an ill spent life is infinitely galling to my feelings, without the additional pang which a detail of my errors and a picture of my thoughtlessness must of necessity inflict.

Another difficulty presents itself in writing to Amat. Shall I say nothing of Dumont, that first & warm friend, from whom not inconstancy but uncontrollable circumstances separated me. I once wrote to him when in England, but he answered not. Silly as my letter might have been, and perhaps it was, yet it came from one in taking leave of whom at St. Julian,[1] he shed a flood of sincere tears. That neglect on his part implied indifference, perhaps contempt. The first was well calculated to afflict me, but the last—Oh my friend estimate the dose of bitterness which that word conveys. I am conscious of having often been a legitimate object of friendly reproof, but never of contempt.

The difficulty attended to, is much increased by the silence you observe in relation to the result of the efforts you kindly volunteered to make at Geneva in my behalf. I infer therefrom that your benevolent endeavours have been unavailing & that the obloquy to which I subjected myself cannot be removed. If I could be assured of a friendly remembrance on the part of those early friends & class mates, that conviction would go a great way toward restoring a degree of health to my mind. But, unfortunately, I cannot expect at their hands

[1] A village in Savoy near Geneva.

the indulgence I experienced from yourself, who well knows that amongst my manyfold imperfections, there yet exists in me qualities of heart & mind, on which a degree of esteem can rightfully rest.

I have long partaken of your feelings, in relation to the present state of things & of the public mind & I have been made unhappy thereby. A moral & political degeneracy seems to me manifest. Our elections exhibit the influence of the vilest motives, instead of the proceedings of men who truly estimate the value of their political institutions, & know their *duties,* as well as their rights. Men, more than principles agitate the whole nation, & more & more assimilate us to the unreflecting multitude of the old world, in spite of our sneers, self congratulations, and fourth of July orations. The canvass of the two last Presidential elections has displayed a scene, which must have made the Aristocrats & Legitimates chuckle, has covered us with dishonour, and allarmed the true patriot. A majority of our editors are firebrands, retailers of ribaldry, & disseminators of lies, who fan the flame of party rancour, corrupt the public taste, & by sinking the national character, lessen the beneficial influence which our political institutions might have on other parts of the world.

Jefferson, as McKean had done before him, made a liberal use of his prerogatives in removing public officers. There existed then, perhaps, a necessity of diminishing the power and influence of a party, whose principles were little in accordance with those which had produced the revolution and who admitted in their ranks their well known opponents. But since that time, the exercise, with an unsparing hand, of that power of removal & reappointments bears a frightful aspect. It puts in violent agitation an immense mass of private interests, which more than the merits of the Candidates engross the public mind, & cause a political storm, the violence of which, the short interval of four years is insufficient to allay: before its waves have subsided, the periodical returns of the election cannot fail to accelerate their velocity and increase their violence & must ultimately prove fatal to the hopes so fondly entertained of the duration of our political happiness.

The remedy to such evils is to be found in the reduction of the enormous and still growing patronage of the President, & in extending his term to six or rather eight years with ineligibility for ever afterwards.

A trust in Jackson's integrity and the energy of his mind, have been the motive of my preference, but I must confess that his first steps—since his accession, in relation to removal & appointments, created in my mind disappointment & allarm. My fears however begin to yield to the hope that his acts in that respect proceed from more enlarged views than his adversaries are willing to ascribe to him, that he will respect the independence of all generous opponents & that those only have to fear, who misbehaved in office, or carried their opposition to an outrageous excess. In support of that impression, I can mention that in this State one Receiver only has been removed;[1] that for being a defaulter, that other land Officers, although ranged on the side of the opposition, remain undisturbed, as the deserving Postmaster of this place, & that a Receiver in Illinois, who had anticipated a removal by resignation has been reappointed notwithstanding his warm opposition. Is it unreasonable to suppose that in other states the same system of proper discrimination & forbearance has been pursued?

I have been agreably surprised by the indulgent recollection which your amiable daughter, as you inform me, has preserved of my poor individual. From my awkward manners, deafness, ineptitude to conversation, which imposes upon me an habitual silence in company, the reverse was to have been looked for.

[1] Perhaps Noah Noble, receiver at the Indianapolis Land Office, who was removed by Jackson. Noble, however, had not defaulted; the removal was political. Biographical account of Noble in *Messages and Papers* . . . *of Noah Noble, Governor of Indiana, 1831-1837,* edited by Dorothy Riker and Gayle Thornbrough (*Indiana Historical Collections,* XXXVIII, Indianapolis, 1958), pp. 10-11.

Being so pleasingly disappointed, I feel a proportionate degree of gratitude for her goodness.

Better founded are the favorable impressions she has left in my mind. I could not witness her unaffected manner, her constant cheerfulness, the offspring of purity & innocence, but above all her tender affection for her parents, without a lively interest which time and distance have not impaired. Be, to her, I pray you, the interpreter of these my sentiments.[2]

I trust that the uneasiness you betray on the score of Albert's health, are to be attributed more to parental solicitude, than to any fact calculated to justify it. Should your fears however have unfortunately some foundation, I have a proposal to make with which I seriously wish you would comply. Send him to me on *horseback* to spend a few weeks with your old friend. The exercise added to a temporary suspension of his sedentary occupations, the balmy air of the country, the new varied & interesting objects which will offer themselves to his observations, & this to him novel scenery of this region, will do more toward restoring the tone of his organs, than all the drugs of materia medica. I shall avoid mentioning as a motive to acquiescence the pleasure I should derive from a visit of your representative, since I can hardly hope of seeing you once more either here or even in Fayette.

Since we are on the subject, have you not drawn to liberally on the affection of that son & his readiness to gratify you, by inducing him to embrace the profession of the law, to which I presume he had no great inclination, & to which an ingenious mind must justly entertain strong objections. It seems to me that a mode of life that would keep mind and body in exercise, would be more congenial to his taste, certainly more conducive to his health. Are not forensic fame & possessions beyond competence mere bubles, when compared to happiness, which they do not necessarily confer. The last,

[2] Frances Gallatin, whom Badollet admired so much, at twenty-seven married Byam Kerby Stevens, a successful New York merchant, on April 6, 1830. Walters, *Albert Gallatin,* pp. 346-47.

by however simple means obtained, is after all the only legitimate object of a rational father's wishes in relation to his children.[3]

The doctrine lately broached by the designing Governor of Illinois (who no doubt had private views in starting the question) in relation to public lands, does not find as many admirers in the West, as one might be induced to infer from the proceedings of our Legislature.[4] On the contrary, I have reason to believe that it is generally disapproved by the thinking part of the community. It is a fact that the Legislature of Illinois took very little notice of it.

I trust that by this time you are more satisfied with the views of Miss Francis Wright, all directed, as it appears to the dispelling of antiquated prejudices & amelioration of the condition of man, & that you become reconciled to the extraordinary part she is acting by the consideration of the philanthropic motives by which she is actuated & the superior intellect she displays.[5] It is perhaps not improper to inquire whether the dissatisfaction we experience at the bold course she pursues, is not the result of prejudice, & whether such highly gifted female cannot without offending the modesty of her sex, openly utter her opinions in the manner she now does.

Those opinions whatever they may be, correct or erroneous, she offers without dogmatism to the scrutiny of reflecting minds; of the former we feel the force, the latter we may reject as we list, without incurring the damnation so liberally

[3] In the interest of his sons' future, between 1830 and 1832 Gallatin disposed of practically all his lands in western Pennsylvania and Ohio and settled with his family in New York City. He became president of the New National Bank of New York backed by John Jacob Astor. His sons, also with Astor backing, formed a trading firm, Gallatin Brothers, on Wall Street near the bank. Walters, *Albert Gallatin,* pp. 346-47. See his letter of February 7, 1833, below.

[4] Ninian Edwards was governor of Illinois at this time. His 1828 message to the General Assembly was a defense of the right of the states to the public lands. Theodore C. Pease, *The Frontier State, 1818-1848* (Illinois Centennial Commission, 1918), p. 122.

[5] See above, p. 282n.

awarded by our ghostly teachers to those who cannot chime with them.

I do not admit, for instance, her ideas on matrimonial union, or to speak more properly, I do not understand her, for the purity of her mind is not to be questioned, and that being admitted, it is difficult to conjecture what remedy she has to propose against the evils she so feelingly describes, which is not liable to more serious objections.

But waving the discussion of that topic, it may be asked, whether she is well founded in her premises; are those evils existing to such an extent, as she seems to admit? I think not: Unhappy marriages appear in bold relief & attract observation, whereas the numberless cases, if not of perfect bliss, certainly of domestic peace and content pass unheeded.

That exaggerated love of novels, is in this country & the present state of society a thing of rare occurrence, & marriages are contracted in most cases, in consequence of moderate not feverish attachments and are generally productive of concord and as much happiness as we can rationally wish for provided intemperance in the husband does not supervene, in which case the wife is an unfortunate & truly pitiable wretch.

Nature has wisely ordained, that in the approximation of the two sexes with a view to matrimonial connexions, the female shall not take the first steps, as inconsistent with that reserve & modesty which constitute their greatest charm. That law, severe as it seems to be to the sex, by compelling them to *accept* without the priviledge of *choosing* the future arbiters of their destinies, has been softened by the same being who enacted it & who in compensation has endowed them with a plastic disposition, by means of which they mould their affections, & with sincerity bestow them on the individual to whom circumstances have united them & who is to be the father of their children, their protector and friend. Once a very sensible girl expressed to me the same sentiments, and is now a living instance of their correctness. That marriages, as now regulated, are generally attended with happy results, that the contrary forms the exception and not the rule, and that the acceptance by a female of a man who would not have been her first choice, may yet be productive of happiness, my observations warrant me in believing, & I doubt not that your own will sustain me in that opinion.

The New York Free Enquirer, I rank amongst the best publications of the United States. We are certainly greatly indebted to its editors, for the importance of the subjects they introduce, the spirit of inquiry they excite & the boldness with which they breast the flood of superstition which threaten to inundate this land & expose the attempts made now by the Clergy to grasp political power & impose upon us the heaviest of curses, a clerical yoke. If that presumptuous, daring & tyranical body of men, dayly encreasing in number, wealth, and influence, is not unmasked & checked by that & other similar publications, I cannot see what can prevent us from becoming the most besotted priest-ridden nation of modern times.

In my children if I have much to approve, I have also much to deplore. James of whom I had formed sanguine expectations, has derived little or no benefit from his residence at West Point, not even a taste for reading, but he has on the other hand betaken himself to habits of industry and become a real Cincinnatus. But unfortunately having married,[6] much to my sorrow, in a family, the males of which were addicted to intemperance, he has received a degree of the infection, & the good qualities of his wife can constitute but an insufficient compensation for the evils of which she is the innocent cause & the first victim. My first step for his reformation has been to remove him from the vicinage of his brother in law's by placing him on my farm, which I shall give to him. To wean him by gentle means from that degrading propensity and elevate the tone of feeling, & give energy to the sense of

[6] James P. Badollet married Malinda McClure on January 18, 1820. Knox County Marriage Records, I, 182, in Genealogy Division, Indiana State Library.

self respect, is now my task, & I have reason to believe that I shall succeed.

Sidney is sober, honest and industrious. Albert is remarkable for his sober habits, application & a sterling integrity which has procured him the respect & confidence of the citizens of this and the adjoining counties. But all have evinced a singular reluctance to the acquisition of information & a notable deficiency I will not say of filial affection, but of those outward demonstrations of its existence so sweet to the heart of a parent. Albert in those unaccountable dispositions has taken the lead, & is perhaps their primary cause. Such is the seeming frigidity of his heart, that one would think he has no blood relations, he meets with brothers & sisters without apparent pleasure, parts with them without regret. As to myself he seldom manifests any token of filial attachment, and is equally sparing of those of common courtesy, in our intercourse he is unsociable & usually silent.

The above picture may possibly be overcharged, but my long wounded feelings have produced in me a morbid sensibility.

The foregoing observations by no means apply to my daughters in whose hearts nature has preserved her entire sway. But Sally lives one hundred miles off, & it is seldom I can see her, & Fanny whose good sense and endearing affections are the solace of my existence, is married to a man, who to a sobriety honesty & sound sense, which have rendered him very popular, joins such indolence & inattention to his interests, that she is & will ever be poor. She bears her hard fate with dignity & such habitual cheerfulness, that those who know little of her real situation, could not suspect the straightness of her circumstances & the extent of her privations. A brother of her husband, Mr. William Gilham merchant of Alexandria, took an early charge of, & raised the much lamented Lieutenant Samuel M. Brackenridge, son of a sister living in Kentucky, who perished by the explosion of the Fulton. It is very natural to wish that he could also be induced to take under his protection his nephew Fanny's eldest boy, a lovely, well disposed and promising child, but how to obtain the accomplishment of such a wish, I know not.

So prolific have my sons & daughters proved, that my grand children amount to the moderate number of nineteen.

Thus far my kind friend, have I indulged my desire of a free converse with you. That enjoyment was much obstructed at my last visit, by the reflexions growing out of the circumstances referred to in the first & last part of this letter, giving an air of discontent and a tinge of melancholy to my behavior, not a little augmented by your awful fits of musing, & a silence too much indulged in on your part, for which the length of this is a just retaliation.

The present communication, deficient as it may be in matter & manner, will, I am sure, be read with interest, as coming from an old, tried & warm friend; but the mechanical labour it required, has been long & severe: For this last at least, I hope you will give me credit, & make me glad, by a few lines in answer.

Make my respects acceptable to Mrs. Gallatin & tender my kind remembrance to the other members of your family. My wife joins me in good wishes for you all, & regrets that she cannot hope to see you once more.

Ever Yours &c

JOHN BADOLLET

P. S. Since writing the present letter, I have but too much reason to retract what I have said on the policy pursued by the present administration. The havoc has begun in this state, the best & most tried officers are unmercifully removed, & their stations filled by partisans, not even the post master of the most obscure country village can escape— I hope you have taken no step, as requested, in favour of Mr. Hill.

[Addressed:]  Albert Gallatin Esqr  New York

[Endorsed:]    14 Aug. 1829  Vincennes  John Badollet

[Gallatin to Badollet]

NEW YORK 11th Jan'y 1830

DEAR FRIEND,

I found here, on my return from Washington, where I had spent two months, a letter from Hentsch announcing others, all of which were received last Saturday by the Hâvre packet, and now enclosed.[1]

I had written to Hentsch, who being Banker at Paris was the most proper person to receive & pay the money, & to whom as my oldest friend, (since we were six years old) and also one of the few survivors amongst yours, I could address with most freedom, on what was nearer your heart. I stated that you felt hurt at not having received an answer from Dumont, and that your susceptibility made you apprehensive of having been entirely forgotten at Geneva. As you had not written to Amat, I supplied the defect by mentioning what you felt on the occasion & for him personally; and as I could not account for the delay otherwise than by truly stating the cause, I gave a short account of your life & explained how late it was that you could make the remittance which accompanied my letter. In doing this, I rendered that justice which was due to your private and public character, but without any suggestion and adhering strictly to truth. This I mention because you may think that there is a little colouring in the Article concerning you in the Geneva Journal what little there is, is due neither to me nor to your friends, but only to the Editor, who has given to you, the whole instead of the greater part of the credit for preventing the introduction of slavery in Indiana.[2] That is however no more than all

---

[1] At least two of the letters to Badollet which were in the packet are in the Badollet Papers in the Indiana Historical Society Library; one is from Hentsch dated November 24, 1829, and one from Etienne Morin Amat, son of Charles Jean Amat, November 25, 1829.

[2] A translation by Abraham Gimbel of the article in the *Journal de Genève* is in the Badollet Papers in the Indiana Historical Society Library. It reads:

"Thursday, Nov. 19, 1829.

"We are indebted to an obliging Communication from one of our

Journalists do, and you must let it pass and make allowance for a little national pride.

The satisfaction those letters will give you will be lessened by the account of the death of both Amat and Dumont. I have a few more numbers of the Geneva Journal containing his obituary notice, which I will try to send if I can find an opportunity.[3] Remember me most affectionately to your good wife & believe me ever Your's

ALBERT GALLATIN

J. BADOLLET ESQR VINCENNES

subscribers, for some important narrative, of a Mr. Badolet, our fellow country man, which will doubtless be interesting to our readers.

"Mr. Badolet emigrated to the U. S. of North America, about 52 years ago, & lived there a long time with out any determined occupation; his good conduct & acknowledged loyalty having attracted the attention, & gained the confidence of the American Government, obtained for him the appointment of Superintendent for the Sale of public lands in one of the Western Districts. That important function which he has filled for a period of over 25 years, with as much integrity as delicacy, has acquired enough consideration, to enable him, to render very important service to the State; also to prevent, by his influence, the establishment of Slavery, in that part of the country, where he lived. That worthy act has made him altogether recommendable & is the only distinguished official who retained his position, during the different commotions which agitated that beautiful country.

"His resources, which at first were scarcely sufficient to raise a numerous family, having increased since the last 3 years; his first use of that new wealth was, to refund to one of his friends at Geneva, an advance of money which he had received from that friend, before his departure; but now, since he is old & infirm, his principal thought, which troubles his mind, is, to be forgotten by his country & his friends.

"May our paper reach this respectable old man! It will be the interpreter of our fellow citizens who knew him, & who are yet alive, it will assure him, that he is not forgotten by them, & that they still love him, & that his fatherland takes a deep interest in his welfare, applauding him for the noble action, which has won for himself the esteem of his fellow Country men. To abolish Slavery in a part of the new world, was an act worthy of a Swiss; it shows the brilliancy of a virtue, which he, no doubt, gained from the rudiments of his first education."

[3] No copy of this has been found in the Badollet or Gallatin papers.

[Badollet to Gallatin]

VINCENNES Feb'y 27, 1830

MY DEAR FRIEND

The large packet from Europe, enclosing your friendly letter of the 11th ult'o, has been received. That interesting pacquet contained, beside authenticated receipts of the heirs of Amat two letters of our friend Hentsch, one from De Lasauzois, one from my youngest brother, one from each of my sisters, one from a cousin, one from John Cazenove, and one from Duby, all, especially my two first named class mates, expressing such kind feelings toward me, has affected me even to tears.

Of all the proofs of delicate & warm friendship which I have received at your hands, and they are not few, there is not one on which I set equal value, & which has made such profound and durable impression on me, as the step you have taken to write for me in transmitting Amat's money. That spontaneous and benevolent act of yours, has relieved me of a task from which I recoiled as often as undertaken & rendered unnecessary the awkward attempt—at reconciling self accusation with self apology. To your kind interference then, do I attribute the share I still possess in the affection and esteem of so many acquaintances & relatives and friends, and I cannot better acknowledge it, than by answering their kind remembrance, as soon and as rapidly as the state of my arm will permit.

But the gratification I have received by so many proofs of forgiveness & renewed friendship, is not unmixed with a strong dose of bitterness. Your letter having reached Europe subsequently to the death of our friends Dumont and Amat, to whose good opinion I was so anxious to be restored, I am left to deplore that they have departed under impressions of my unworthiness.

The little biographical account of my individual contained in the no. of the Geneva journal enclosed in the packet, might please the vanity of some under similar circumstances, but is not to my taste, as containing an assertion that is resting on no foundation. I have had no other share in keeping slavery out of this state, than that of other well intentioned men in efforts to resist the great influence of the Governor & his Prime Minister Parke over the population of this part of the Territory. It is true that I availed myself of the weight which at that time my office, more than my personal merit gave me, to encourage the despondent, and embolden the timid: that I wrote, was active and persevering in opposition, & wherever & whenever the opportunity offered, I seized it to refute his Excellency's sophistries; but it is not true that the Convention (for it is to my supposed agency in that body that the editor of the journal must allude) was prevented by any exertion of mine from admitting slavery. The simple fact is this, that at that time the public opinion was so strongly pronounced against it, that the hopelessness of any measure having that tendency was tacitly acknowledged by its most ardent friends, & not a whisper on the subject was heard in the Convention. I am sorry that that ornament has been added by the Editor, because my name cannot be properly connected with any thing that is not true, and because if the article was ever known in the U. S. I should be covered with ridicule, as the supposed author of that ornamental fiction.

Being unable to trace another line, on account of the increasing pain of my arm, though ever so desirous of continuing the confabulation with you, I feel that I must stop, not however without repeating that the service you have rendered me shall [be] recollected with the most heartfelt gratitude.

You have not told me whether I ever shall be favored with a visit of your son Albert.

My wife is frail & infirm, and joins me in tendering our respectful compliments to Mrs. Gallatin, your amiable daughter & interesting son. Rember [*sic*] me also to James & wife in your first letter  Dear Friend Yours forever

JOHN BADOLL[ET]

[Addressed:]  Albert Gallatin Sen'r Esq  New York

[Badollet to Gallatin]

VINCENNES April 1, 1830

Not knowing, my Dear Friend, how to direct properly the enclosed, I find myself under the necessity of trusting them to your friendly care, & I hope that you will neglect no means to insure their reaching their destination, either through Hentsch or John Cazenove. The various letters contained in the packet you sent me breathed such kind feelings towards me, feelings which I had not dared even to hope for, that it became my sacred duty to answer them with as much promptitude as my infirmity would permit. The task, under other circumstances, would have been delightful, but in the present state of my arm, required all my courage to undertake it, and needed no small share of perseverance to accomplish it. I hasten to transmit you what I have been able to effect, the rest (5 or 6 letters more) shall follow at no remote day. The trouble I give you shall not be required again, for I shall be in possession of my kind correspondents' respective addresses.

At the receipt and first reading of the letters referred to, I was thrown into a great agitation, which must account for, & excuse any incongruity which my last letter to you may contain, Now that I am calm, I duly appreciate the invaluable service you rendered me by writing to our friend Hentsch, & fully convinced of the sincerity & truth with which you portrayed your poor friend, I feel, deeply feel this kindest of all your kind acts towards me. To it I am indebted for my restoration to the kind feelings & good opinion of old friends and connexions. Would to God that Dumont & Amat had been permitted to be yet of the number, but they are gone, & with them all my hopes of once recovering a share of their esteem. This reflexion bitterly mars my present satisfaction.

I presume that the son of Hentsch has been, with the best intentions no doubt, the proximate cause of that colouring which the Editor of the Journal has given to the article that relates to me & I really wish that article had been spared;— I know myself too well to be much gratified by it. But what is really pleasing is the evidence it furnishes of the existence of the interest felt yet in Geneva for a countryman, who had but too many reasons to suppose himself forgotten. That part of it which attributes to me much more than I deserve in relation to slavery is what I am really sorry for. I had a notion to get a disavowal inserted, and would do it yet, if approved by you; but it is perhaps better to say nothing more about it, in as much as it is unlikely that that journal will ever be read in the United States & very probable that the recalling the public attention to that transitory notice of me by the insertion of any observation of mine might be viewed as savouring more of vanity than of modesty.

My wife's health has been very infirm of late, she is emaciated feeble & suffering, her ailments do not so totally however make an egotist of her as to let her forget your former kindness to her & be insensible to your affectionate & frequent recollections of her. She desires to be remembered to you & Mrs. Gallatin.

Upon experiment I find that french is a language to which I every day become more and more a stranger, its grammar, its words, its orthography itself retain no hold in my memory & that circumstance highly encreases the difficulty I experience in having so many french letters to write.

Another scurvy trick which Time has played me is this. It has so affected my poor brains, that for these few years, I forget in writing syllables, words, & often sentences in spite of me, & which causes those frequent erasures & interlineations you may notice in my writing. Otherwise, that great creator & destroyer has been kind to me, and, except for holding a pen, has left me the free use of all my limbs. I can actually walk twelve or more miles with ease.

Tender my respectful remembrance to Mrs. Gallatin, not forgetting your amiable daughter & son.

Adieu tried & Dear friend remember still Yours &c

JOHN BADOLLET

[Addressed:]  Albert Gallatin
[Endorsed:]  Vincennes April 1, 1830, John Badollet

[Badollet to Gallatin]

VINCENNES Nov'r 20, 1830

I have read, my Dear friend, with pleasure and thankfulness, your note appended to Hentsch's letter & I hasten to give you the information necessary for the safe transmission of that precious box to me.  Forward it to Philadelphia thus directed—

To Burtsch & Heberd  Vincennes
Care of Robert Toland.  Philadelphia

I have received with gratification the assurance of the present well being of yourself & family, much enhanced by the information of the happy mariage of your amiable daughter, convey to her my hearty congratulations, & my warm wishes for her happiness.

As to myself I feel the infirmities of age growing fast upon me & that the destruction of my poor frame has fairly begun. I am at this hour the prey of an epidemick intermittent which though often stopped, pertinaciously recurrs; my mind is in no better situation than my body. I have my full share of sorrows: My wife has been long sick, is surprisingly emaciated & enfeebled, but appears since September to grow better, she joins me in sincere wishes for your health & happiness.

Adieu my Dear Friend rember me to Mrs. Gallatin & drop me, if you can, some few lines of remembrance.

Ever Yours

JOHN BADOLLET

[Addressed:]  Albert Gallatin Sen'r Esq'r  New-York
[Endorsed:]  Vincennes, Nov. 20, 1830  John Badollet

[Badollet to Gallatin]

[January 20, 1833?]

At last, my dear friend, I find myself able with much

difficulty, & pain, & with a trembling hand to trace a few lines.

The letter which I wrote to you in answer to your last requesting me to point out to you a person at Philadelphia or Baltimore to whom the box sent me by Hentsch could be directed, was the last I could trace to the present time. Soon after its receipt I was seized with a dangerous and obstinate bilious fever, which encreasing daily in malignity, left not a shadow of hope that I could be saved. I was thought & was in fact dying & movement had begun to obtain my [MS illeg.] family was that at the very moment when all hope, in relation to myself had fled, and my last breath was every moment expected, the second wife of my son Albert actually died in a room below mine.

After many months however of suffering & progressive decay, my fever, as through a miracle, was suddenly stopped, but left behind a paralitic affection on my arms & legs which deprived me for a long time of the use of the latter & deadened the nerves of sensation in my hands, without however entirely destroying those of motion. I have been for a long time unable to stand & any way to help myself, & during that period of helplessness, I required all the services of a suckling child, services which were performed by my wife, even the most repulsive, with a patience & kindness truly angelick. Vain have frictions & warm baths been toward the restoration of the feelings in my hands, all I can now do, is to write with the greatest difficulty with a pencil, & with a pen to subscribe my name to official documents.

Extremely uneasy at a silence imposed upon me by circumstances so deplorable, the cause of which could not be known to my friends, as soon as I could walk with tolerable safety, I ventured in the stage to Harmony to get Mr. Ge[?] a friendly and estimable countryman of ours, to write for me the letters you must have received & one to Solomon, which he did with kindness. My trip proved rather favourable than injurious to me. But unfortunately from that time the health of my poor wife has rapidly declined, her life has been for a long period in jeopardy, she is better now, but emaciated to a frightful degree.

That box so kindly sent by Hentsch, has, by its interesting contents recalled many pleasing recollections; but at the same time that it has, with the packet of letters from Geneva received before, excited in my breast the most thrilling emotions of pleasure it has revealed a truth which at once humbles me and embitters my life. The neglect of corresponding with, & the apparent forgetfulness of the associates of my youth, whose good will has survived such long lapse of years, as evinced by their kind letters, can receive no other name than that of ingratitude. This observation applies with greater severity in relation to Dumont & Amat to whose friendship I owed so much, & the thought of having by their death lost the opportunity of testifying to them my repentance and the hope of revising their former sentiments toward me, has inflicted on my mind a wound which time cannot heal, & which will fester till I am no more.

In what precedes is to be found the secret cause, in part, of that dissatisfaction I betrayed [MS illeg.] Notice taken of me through kind motives perhaps not unmixed, as you seemed to think, with a little spice of national vanity, by the editor of the Geneva Journal. I hated to be held up as an object of approbation, which I was but too conscious of not deserving it sounded in my ears as a severe irony. The fact is that my mind was thrown into a sort of tumult at the receipt of that packet of letters—between the grateful sense of your kindness in writing to Geneva for me, kindness for which I never shall ceased to bless your name, & the conflicting feelings I have endeavoured to describe.

Your long silence has added not a little to my pains. A kind word from you, the assurance that the burthen of years lay light upon you, & that yourself & those dear to you enjoyed a competent share of health and content would have been a great relief to me. But excepting what I could glean in the newspapers assuring me that you were still alive, I have remained this long time in utter ignorance of your real situation, for both Solomon & Nicholson from whom I occasionally received intelligence concerning you and yours, have both ceased to write to me, & I know not to this day whether either is dead or alive.

If the latter yet lives there is, in his abrupt breaking off all correspondence with me, and the circumstances attending it, something which has sorely wounded my feelings  A lad who had lived with me, whose parents resided in Greene County in a state of poverty, had enlisted here & had died during the war. I had taken some steps to obtain for them the bounty land rightfully due to their son, but which from some cause, not necessary to mention, had not been allotted to him. It became necessary, therefore to establish legally their kinship. With this view I requested his assistance, & enclosed him a printed blank from the War office with directions how to proceed. By this appeal to the known kindness of his disposition, I felt convinced that I had enlisted his sympathies in behalf of the distressed individuals referred to, & that he would cheerfully embrace the opportunity of performing an act of benevolence; but to my astonishment he has not acknowledged the receipt of my letter, & has kept silence ever since.

It is possible that somme free & candid observations of mine elicited by the advice (friendly meant I sincerely believe) he gave me in a previous letter to prepare myself for the next world, may have allarmed his orthodoxy, but surely a supposed error in matters of faith, or the want of it, ought not to paralise friendly feelings of such long standing, still less to stop the flow of benevolence towards those who with the best claims to charitable assistance, were equally strangers to my person and to my opinions.

Solomon must believe me dead, or is strangely altered. I made out to send him a few lines, which, I hope will obtain me an answer.[1]

---

[1] In a long letter of January 15, 1833, Solomon apologizes for his long silence and says that he had been quite ill. He asks if Badollet feels well

I read with the greatest indignation the outrageous sally against you made by Mr. Clay on the floor of the Senate, if I mistake not, you have given greater proof of sincere american feelings & devotion to the interests of the country, than he ever did or will ever do. You must somehow, have offended his pride, when in your intercourse with him, when Secretary of State & thereby excited that degree of resentment & violence of ire which he manifested in such an unjustifiable manner: It is consoling however to know that the savage attack has met with a general reprobation.[2]

Ignorant of your present situation, but still believing you at New York I have been not a little allarmed by the apprehension that the scourge which has desolated that city, might have attacked you or some member of your family, I fondly hope you are all now safe, but would be happy to be assured of it.

Amongst the interesting objects sent me by Hentsch are a printed likeness of yourself & one of Dumont. When looking at the former, I behold my preserver, in his kind eyes I read the expression of the trusted friends[h]ip & of a generous indulgence for my many fold foibles & imperfections. The other seems to betray the feelings of an heart wounded by my guilty indifference, & to cast on me a look of asperity, which will be an incessant lesson of humility to me & no less incessant source of self reproach.

The black clouds gathering over our political horizon wear a portentous aspect, the fair fabric of our union seems to totter on its base & to threaten approaching demolition. The bare thought of the possibility of an event so calamitous and

enough to go to New Harmony, why doesn't he visit Washington. His letter is in the Badollet Papers in the Indiana Historical Society Library. See also Gallatin's letter immediately below.

[2] Probably a reference to Clay's speech on February 2, 1832, in which he attacked Gallatin for his stand against high tariff, which Clay regarded as a direct challenge to his own "American System." U. S. Congress *Register of Debates,* 22 Congress, 1 session, p. 267; Walters, *Albert Gallatin,* pp. 361-62.

pregnant with the destruction of the best hopes for the happiness of mankind which our inst[itu]tions inspired, that thought alone distracts the mind and harrows up the soul. I am not without hopes however faint indeed, but to which I cling notwithstanding the threatening aspect of the skies. May God stay the tempest and permit us to reach the harbour of safety.

I have run my race I have reached the goal,—and every moment the paralitic affection of which I have spoken, may reach the vital parts [MS illeg.] Before that event takes place I have long been anxiously wishing to write to you, but dreading the difficulty of the task, I have for month after month delayed the attempt. Summoning however all my courage, & all the patience I could command, I have at last performed it. The labour has been great, quitted and resumed at successive intervals, it has required many days & I trust that you will see in this communication an evidence of the gratification I enjoy in communing, perhaps for the last time with my old & tried friend.

I conjure you by the ties which have so long united us, to return or cause to be returned, (if unable to do it yourself) a few lines to me assuring me of your & family's well being, & affording the only pleasing sensation of which I now can be acceptable (having tasted in this place the cup of bitterness) the solace to be derived from the voice of friendship.

Present, I pray you, my best respects to Mrs. Gallatin, tell her that I recollect with gratitude her indulgence to my uncouthness & my singularities. Tender my kind rembrance to your son and daughter & accept my sincere wish that the evening of your days may be as serene & happy as your life has been honourable and useful.

To the last hour your devoted friend

JOHN BADOLLET

P. S. This rendered famous by the steam mill rag shop with her bank & many other minor villainies, has lately produced an instance of depravity in a public officer of which I may be able to give you an account hereafter.

[Gallatin to Badollet]

NEW YORK 7th February 1833

I am deeply and most sadly affected by your letter of 20th ult'o. It has indeed, my dearest friend, been a source of constant regret and the embittering circumstances of my life, that not only we should have been separated during the greater part of our existence, but that your lot should have been cast in the comparatively unhealthy climate, to which your repeated bilious attacks and their sad consequences must be ascribed. But what else could be done? The necessity of bringing up a family and of an independent existence is imposed upon us. And although I should have been contented to live and die amongst the Monongahela hills, it must be acknowledged that, beyond the invaluable advantage of health, they afforded either to you or me but few intellectual or physical resources. Indeed I must say that I do not know in the United States any spot which afforded less means to earn a bare subsistence for those who could not live by manual labor, than the sequestered corner in which accident had first placed us. We can but resign ourselves to what was inevitable. And yet, I have often thought that we boasted too much of the immense extent of our territory, which, if it makes us more powerful as a nation and offers so large a field for enterprize, carries within itself the seeds of dissolution, by expanding weakens the bonds of union and the devotedness of genuine patriotism, and in the mean while destroys the chords of local attachment, separates friends and disperses to most distant quarters the members of the same family. In your remote situation, thrown at the age of 45 amongst entire strangers, and amidst the afflictions of which you have been visited, two great comforts have still been left to you; the excellent wife with which you have been blessed, that bosom friend from whom there are no secrets, that faithful partner of all your joys & sorrows, that being who had your and gave you her undivided affection, with tender feelings without the least affectation, gentle and prudent, such indeed as meant to have been a special gift Heaven intended for you. Add to this the consciousness not only of a life of integrity but of a pure life, of one which either as private or public should satisfy you and has gained you general consideration and the respect of all that have simply known you. And as to those who have been more intimately acquainted with you, who has been more generally beloved and could always count more sincere friends than yourself?

My dear friend, you judge yourself with too much severity. For want of greater offences you seek for specks, and your extreme susceptibility magnifies them into unpardonable errors. I tell you the truth, Badollet, when I assure you that, in the course of a life which has brought me in contact with men of all ranks and of many nations, I have not known a more virtuous & pure man than yourself. Your education, that of a student, and your simplicity, and your unsuspecting integrity unfitted you for that active life of enterprize which is the characteristick of this Nation, and made you unable to cope with the shrewdness of those by whom you were surrounded. Still you have to the last resisted every temptation and struggled for existence by honorable means. Yet it is true that both you and I, during the years of youthful hopes and those which succeeded of arduous labor, identified with our new country and surrounded by new and dearest objects of domestic affection, it is true that we both neglected to correspond with the friends of our youth and to preserve ties which could not be replaced. The penalty for that offence we have paid & have been the greatest sufferers. I have been far more to blame in that respect: and yet please to God that I had nothing more to reproach myself with.

It may be that J. Nicholson took some offence at your daring to avow your want of orthodoxy, for he is extremely weak on that point. But his neglect in the business you allude to must be principally ascribed to his extreme indolence of which I have experienced the effect of late in a remarkable degree. A better apology may be found in the affliction which he has for several months suffered by the gradual decay & final death of his eldest son James who was the best hope of his family. As to Solomon's silence I can easily account for it. His wife, after twenty years of nervous indolence during which she hardly left her bed, all at once put herself in a stage and fell like a *bombe* on her husband and his Batchelor's comfortable establishment. Casenove says that she behaves decently and that he bears this total derangement of plans & habits with composure: but I have not, from that time, about nine months, had a single word from him. He has been living comfortably but prudently, saving enough out of his salary of 1000 dollars to allow her 250 a year and to have paid his most urgent old debts in Geneva. When I was last in Washington, his plan was, if living long enough, to save enough—say 4000 dollars—that the interest should afford his wife the same allowance during her life and the principal to be applied after her death to the payment of his remaining creditors, of whom D'Ivernois[1] is I believe the principal.

My family continues in good health. James has no other child than the one you saw who is a very amiable boy & of tolerable talents. Albert remains unmarried & with a delicate health. Although admitted at the bar in Pennsylvania & at Baltimore and capable, he has from timidity and want of energy declined practicing. I gave them all my property at New Geneva & remaining western lands. The sale of these engaged their time for three years. They have realized twenty thousand dollars with which they have entered in copartnership and commenced business as Bankers & Stock & Exchange brokers; the two professions being here united. We continue to live together, with the exception of my daughter who is

[1] François D'Ivernois, a fellow student of Badollet's and Gallatin's in Geneva. He became a political writer and diplomat of some note. Walters, *Albert Gallatin*, p. 6.

married to Mr. Stevens, a very amiable man and a merchant in this City. They have already a son & a daughter. We all went to Greenfield Connecticut during the Cholera & escaped that calamity; but during our absence we lost Mrs. Nicholson who died in August of old age (88).[2] It was principally on her account that Mrs. Gallatin wished, on our return from England to settle here. I found after a while that my income was not sufficient for this conspicuous & expensive city: and this induced me to accept the place of President of a new Bank (the National Bank of N. York) which I have now filled for near two years with a salary of 2000 dollars. I might now give it up so far as concerns myself, as the additional income derived from my wife's property is sufficient for us; but whilst my health permits I may remain in it, as it gives me opportunities of introducing my sons in business. Although I neither suffer pain or can complain of serious illness, I grow gradually weaker, thinner, & more and more liable to severe colds & derangement of the bowels. My faculties, memory of recent events or reading excepted, are wonderfully preserved; and my two last essays on currency, and on the tariff have received the approbation of the best judges here and in Europe. I had another favourite object in view in which I have failed. My wish was to devote what may remain of life to the establishment, in this immence & fast growing city, of a general system of rational & practical education fitted for all & gratuitously opened to all. For it appeared to me impossible to procure our democratic institutions & the right of universal suffrage, unless we could raise the standard of general education & the mind of the labouring classes nearer to a level with those born under more favorable circumstances. I became accordingly the President of the Council of a new University originally established on the most liberal principles. But finding that the object was no longer the same, that a certain portion of the clergy had obtained the controul, and that their object though laudable was special & quite distinct from mine,

[2] Mrs. Gallatin's mother.

I resigned at the end of one year rather than to struggle probably in vain for what was nearly unobtainable.[3]

The present aspect of our national politics is extremely discouraging. Yet, having heretofore always seen the good sense of this nation ultimately prevailing against the excesses of party spirit and the still more dangerous efforts of disappointed ambition, I do not despair. But although I hope the dangers which threaten us may for the present be averted, the dissensions & the acts which have already taken place have revealed the secret of our vulnerable points, dissolved the charm which made our Constitution and our Union a sacred object, and will render the preservation of both much more difficult than heretofore. I have always thought that the dangerous questions, arising from the complicity & in our complex, half consolidated, half federalistic form of government, doubtful rights of individual States & United States, should, if possible be avoided; that the bond of Union if made too tight would snap; and that great moderation, in the exercise even of its most legitimate powers, was, in our extensive country with all its diversified & often opposite interests, absolutely necessary on the part of the General Government. This is a general observation and more applicable to futurity than to the present. The acts of S. Carolina are outrageous and unjustifiable. The difficult part for our Government is how to nullify nullification and yet to avoid a civil war. A difficult task, but in my humble opinion not impossible to perform.

Do not write to me long letters which tire you; but now and then drop me three or four lines. All my family unite in affectionate rememberance & sympathy. Give my love to your wife and tell her that whilst I live, she has a friend to whom she may apply under any circumstances. Farewell my dear friend. May God throw comfort on your last years.

[3] This was New York University. See Walters, *Albert Gallatin*, pp. 350-51.

Ever your own faithful friend

ALBERT GALLATIN

JOHN BADOLLET  Vincennes

[Badollet to Gallatin]

VINCENNES September 22, 1833

MY DEAR FRIEND

I have the pleasure of introducing to your particular notice the bearer Mr. Phiquepal[1] formerly of Harmony, a gentleman the qualities of whose head & heart entitle him to the attentions which he will undoubtedly receive at your hands. A keen & judicious observer of men & things, he can give you much interesting information on the present state of the present state [sic] of Europe, of the public opinion there, & of the mighty events which are slowly but certainly maturing in the womb of time. Permit me to add that he is an intimate friend of my brother & is kindly disposed towards me.

Surrounded as I am at present by distressing objects, my poor & good wife in a bed of allarming sickness with four children at the same time contending with violent fevers render my house a scene of gloom & prevent me from detailing at present to you the reasons of my silence how an injury in the testis & repeated attacks of bilious fever have confined me for months to my bed et left me but few days of comparative well-being.

Drop me a few lines, I beseech you, upon you and your family & let me have the consolation to know that the evening of your days continues mild & serene, clear of the clouds which of late have darkened my existence.

Remember me affectionately to your children & tender my respectful salutations to Mrs. Gallatin. Adieu my Dear Friend

[1] William S. Phiquepal (Guillaume Sylvan Casimir Phiquepal d'Arusmont). A teacher of the Pestalozzian system, he came to New Harmony in 1826. In 1831 he married Frances Wright. Their marriage ended in divorce. Arthur E. Bestor (ed.), *Education and Reform at New Harmony* . . . (Indiana Historical Society *Publications*, XV, No. 3, Indianapolis, 1948), index.

Ever Yours

JOHN BADOLLET

[Addressed:]  Albert Gallatin Esq  New York  Favoured by Mr. Phiquepal

[Endorsed:]  Vincennes Sept. 22, 1833.  John Badollet

[Badollet to Gallatin]

VINCENNES Jan'y 10 1834

Your last letter, my dear friend, has been a balm to my wounded spirits, & would have been answered ere this, if a series of severe visitations had not engrossed my thoughts and embittered my existence.  About twelve months ago, I received an injury in the *testis* which produced a prodigious enlargement & induration of the organ & presented the threatening alternative of a fatal [MS illeg.] or its extirpation.  Three months have I been in bed, during which every effort made by medical skill to soften the induration & reduce the enlargement has proved vain.  The pain at last disappearing & my health rather improving, I ventured to get up, & using a suspender I found that I could walk without much inconvenience.

My ill luck did no terminate there, attacks of bilious fever have off & on poisoned my existence, so that I have not, for the last twelve months, enjoyed for five or six successive days a state of well being.  Add to all this, that last autumn five of my daughters children were, at the same time, attacked by most allarming fevers & with difficulty saved, & you can see how little enviable my situation has been.  I have also felt & do yet feel mental distress flowing from another source, of which I shall omit the afflicting detail.

But a more severe stroke was in reserve for me; my dear wife, the patient & affectionate sharer of my joys & sorrows, after many months of gradual decay, has at last, after much suffering, sunk into her eternal rest on the six of this month, leaving me forlorn  a prey to never ceasing & bitter regrets.  May you my beloved friend never witness such scene as it has been my lamentable lot to behold.

If any circumstance can in any degree mitigate the bitterness of my present feeling, it is this, that I have justified the confidence reposed in me by the commission with which I have been honoured, witness my successive reappointments, although I never took a solitary step to Obtain them, witness also the openly declared approbation of the correct state of my office by the late examiner.

I am unable to trace another line, and as unable to think, I must therefore terminate here this melancholy scrawl with a request to be kindly remembered to every member of your family.

Adieu my kind and tried friend, drop me a few lines, they will be a great relief to me in my disconsolate situation. Dear friend farewell. Ever yours, &c

JOHN BADOLLET

[Addressed:] Albert Gallatin Sen'r Esq'r New York
[Endorsed:] Vincennes Jan. 10, 1834 John Badollet

[Badollet to Gallatin]

VINCENNES Dec'r 26, 1834

It is now a little less than a year, my dear friend, that I communicated to you the heavy loss I had suffered in the decease of my poor wife, & from that moment I have daily & anxiously looked for a kind notice of my letter & a word of sympathy from you. What can have been the cause of that long silence I am at a loss to conjecture, except that, like myself, you can not write without insufferable labour, or not at all. I[f] such was your unfortunate situation, I entreat you to obtain from one of your sons, or Mrs. Gallatin a few words, assuring me of your present welfare, & that of all the members of your family.

Since fate has placed us at such a distance from one another, that an approximation is not to be thought of, would it be too much for me to hope that you may induce your son Albert to pay me a short visit. The means of travelling are now so rapid that his absence could not be long. This last mark of your friendship, would be highly appreciated by me, & be a solace in my approach to the grave.

Fare well my ever dear friend, remember me respectfully to Mrs. Gallatin & believe me for ever Yours &c

JOHN BADOLLET

P. S. January 18, 1835. In the request I made you of a visit from your son Albert, I am serious & no less sanguine, & I cannot but renew my earnest solicitation, that you may consent to grant me this last favour. To the eye of an inquisitive & reflecting mind, the view of the beautiful Mississipi valey, & its growing states, will be prented [*sic*] objets both phisical & moral, which must command the most earnest attention, & excite the warmest interest. And who knows whether he would not hereafter locate himself in this western world. By his modesty and aimable diffidence, he is exposed in the crowded atlantic cities to being jostled out of the road to distinction & preferment by the multitude of ardent & bold aspirants by which it is choaked : inconvenience which exists in a less degree in these infant states. He might call first at Nicholson's to whom such a visit would be highly gratifying, & embarking at Wheeling reach Evansville in this state fifty-five miles from Vincennes to which a stage runs in one day twice a week. He might return in stages through the state of Ohio, take the Erie canal & descending the Hudson in a steamboat, reach home after a comparatively short absence. I cannot form the idea of a more interesting tour.

Have the goodness to forward the enclosed; & should our friend Hents[ch] be unfortunately no more, send it to his son.

Return me two lines. Adieu Dear Friend,

J. B.

Met une enveloppe à la lettre pour Hentsch.

[Addressed:]  Albert Gallatin Sen'r  Esq'r  New York
[Endorsed:]  Dec. 28, 1834  J. Badollet

[Gallatin to Badollet]

NEW YORK, 3d Feb'y 1834 [1835]

MY DEAR FRIEND

I have received your's of 15th January and will transmit that to Hentsch by next packet.

I sympathised most truly and deeply with you in the irreparable loss with which you have been afflicted. I had no consolation to offer you, and felt so painfully that very wrongfully and shamefully I postponed and postponed writing to you. Even now, what can I say but what must renew and embitter your grief? For no one knew more thoroughly, appreciated more highly than I did the worth of your beloved partner. She was the solace of your checkered and in many respects troubled life, a singular blessing bestowed on you and long preserved. With heartfelt thanks to Him who gave it, resignation to his will is a duty, but this does not lessen the loss or the pain. Maybe it was best that of the two, you should have been the survivor. Do you now live with any of your children and with which of them? I hardly dare ask how your health stands.

I have no other infirmities but a derangement of the functions of the stomach which I manage without medicine and an unusually enervating debility which none could cure. It is only within the last year that I have discovered a sensible diminution in the facility of thinking and committing thoughts to writing. But this and other symptoms advise me that my active career is at an end and that I cannot continue to vegetate very long. My two sons, James's wife and their only child now ten years old continue to live under my roof. Both are engaged in business under the firm of Gallatin brothers, and although they do not together make one thousand dollars a year, it is better than idleness. I thank you for your invitation to Albert the motive for which I feel. Whether he may, engaged as he now is, find time for that journey, I cannot yet tell. He is destitute of ambition and indeed of energy, with considerable talents and the highest & purest moral feelings. His very delicate health and nervous susceptibility unfit him for any considerable exertion. My daughter has already three children who engross the attention of my wife. Mine has for some time been turned & will be still more devoted to the education of James's son, who has tolerable talents with a most engaging disposition. He is the only young male of my name, and I have hesitated whether, with a view to his happiness I had not better take him to live and die quietly at Geneva, rather than to leave him to struggle in the most energetic country, where the strong in mind & character serves every body else, and where consideration & respectability are not at all [MS illeg.] in proportion to virtue & modest merit. Yet I am so identified with the country which I served so long that I cannot detach myself from it : I find no one who suffers in mind as I do at the corruption and degeneracy of our Government. But I do not despair and cannot believe that we have lived under a perpetual delusion and that the People will not themselves ultimately cure the evils under which we labour. There is something more wanted than imposed forms of government. There is something wrong in the social state. Moral, still more than intellectual education & habit are wanted. Had I another life before me my faculties would be turned towards that object much rather than to political pursuits. But all this is for our posterity. Farewell my dear friend.

Ever most affectionately Yours

ALBERT GALLATIN

My wife & children unite in affectionate remembrance. [Addressed:] John Badollet Esq're Vincennes Indiana [Postmarked:] New-York Feb. 4

[Badollet to Gallatin]

VINCENNES June 10, 1835

I have read your kind letter, my dear friend, with feelings of sincere gratitude, the tone of indulgent kindness which had uniformly characterized your communications with me, is so affectingly preserved in it, that it has greatly contributed to compose my mind, & to lessen the bitterness of many unwelcome retrospections.

Henry Gilham husband of my daughter Frances, is a man of sound sense, great sobriety, correct moral & political principles, & remarkable for his affectionate treatment of his wife:

But unfortunately he thought fit to abandon a gainful trade in which he was eminently skilful. He wasted thus in indolence several years, reckless of the future & of the fate of an encreasing family, relying for subsistance on a commission of Justice of the peace in Illinois nine miles from Vincennes, & on hunting, of which he was immoderately fond. My poor daughter condemned to an humble cabin bore her privations with resignation & dignity.

You may easily conceive my distress at the unhappy fate of a dear & deserving child. To relieve her from such a situation, to bring her to the assistance of her mother who was less & less able to keep house & to whom she was tenderly attached; & to put her husband in a way to provide for his family, I called him to my house, made him some advances to enable him to resume his trade. He accepted my offer which combined the advantages of all, applied to business successfully & I had the prospect of contented days when the death of my wife cast again a gloom over my existence. Still I possessed my affectionate daughter, who I knew would & did by endearing attentions fill the place of her departed mother & I had the prospect of enjoying the evening of my days with some degree of comfort & of terminating my existence in the arms of a dearly beloved child.

But fate reserved me an harder fate & it is now my melancholy task to inform you of the severest trial which your poor friend could be condemned to undergo. Fanny, that child of my affection, who by her good sense & warm attachment was the solace of my declining days & who I fondly hoped would close my eyes, is no more, she fell a victim to a short but malignant complaint. Her death by no means anticipated, was to me a thunder stroke— You understand, & I am sure you partake my distressed feelings on the occasion.

As a relief from the painful feelings which the foregoing details must undoubtedly cause you, I have the consolation to inform you, that the arrangements rendered necessary by my new situation, have happily contributed to restore my mind to a state of composure & blunt the asperity of my regrets. Albert, whose wife I have long known, who possesses an angelic temper, & is perhaps the only being who can fill the void left by the exit of my Fanny & supply her place, has moved to my house & I am in state of comparative comfort.

I have put Gilham in possession of another house of mine wherein Albert previously lived, & is now doing well.

Under my present circumstances, a visit from your son Albert would be doubly welcome, but keeping my gratification out of view I cannot avoid submitting to your consideration the probability, nay the certainty of such a journey being advantageous to his health.

A few lines from & about you will, you know, be welcome, they will cheer up my mind & be antidote to the sadness which I am not always successful in repelling.

I pray you to tender my kind remembrance to the members of your family & to accept my warm wishes for their health & welfare.

Adieu Dear Friend, Yours &c

JOHN BADOLLET

[Addressed:]   Albert Gallatin Sen'r Esq'r New York
[Endorsed:]   Vincennes June 10 1835 John Badollet

[Badollet to Gallatin]

VINCENNES July 15, 1836

MY DEAR FRIEND

The bearer of this is William Gilham son of my deceased daughter, going to the military academy at West Point.[1] He is a youth of the best dispositions, [MS illeg.] possessing the capability of the exertions necessary for the acquirement

[1] William Gilham enrolled in the Academy July 1, 1836, and graduated 5th in his class July 1, 1840. He became commandant and professor of chemistry and geology at the Virginia Military Institute. During the Civil War he fought with the South. Afterward he became president of the Southern Fertilizing Company of Richmond, Virginia. Letter of his son W. H. Gilham, of Richmond, to Vigo Badollet, Vincennes, April 14, 1878, Badollet Papers, Indiana Historical Society Library; Heitman (comp.), *Historical Register of the United States Army*, I, 456.

of knowledge. Any advice you will be pleased to give him for his government will, I am sure, be treasured up by him. Your interest for him & kind superintenance during his noviciate is warmly solicited, & in anticipation gratefully appreciated by me.

I have been long without intelligence from you. I ascribe it to difficulty of writing, which unfortunately I experience myself. If that be the case, one of your sons might drop me a few lines.

Present to them my kind remembrance & make my respects acceptable to Mrs. Gallatin.

Yours &c

JOHN BADOLLET

[Addressed:]   Albert Gallatin Sen'r Esq'r New York Fav'd by Mr. William Gilham

[Endorsed:]   Vincennes July 15, 1836  J. Badollet

[Gallatin to Badollet]

NEW YORK  3d Sep'r 1836

MY DEAR FRIEND

Your grandson Gilham arrived here safely, and with great propriety remained but two days & proceeded at once to West Point. I gave him an introductory letter for Major De Russie the Superintendent, and told him to write to me in case of any incident or difficulty. I was not without apprehension, that some might arise, on his examination for admission, from the want of preparatory study in any of the branches taught in that school. As that examination takes place in August, and he has not written to me, I conclude that every thing has gone right. He is modest and prepossessing: but it will require great efforts on his part and some native mathematical talent to keep pace with his fellow students and to go through the severe scientific course adopted in that institution. About one half of those admitted are dismissed within two years after, for want of sufficient proficiency. I had intended to go myself to West Point; but chronical infirmities, always aggravated by travelling, have kept me the whole summer in the City.

It is not that I have any right to complain, being only troubled with obstinate costiveness and feeling sensibly the gradual &, lately, rapid decay of strength both of body & mind. The last affects me most; memory is greatly impaired, and that great facility of labour with which I was blessed has disappeared. It takes me a day to write a letter of any length: and unfortunately the excessive increase of expenses in this City and a heavy loss by last winter's fire (in fire insurance stock) compel me, for the sake of the salary, to continue the irksome & mechanical labours of President of a Bank.[1] I cannot think of withdrawing to the country, on account of my dearly & justly beloved daughter, married to an excellent man (Mr. Stevens) a merchant in moderate circumstances by whom she has four children. James has but his only son now 12 years old, a good & rather promising boy. His family and Albert still single & with a delicate health continue to make part of my family. Though industrious and in business these four years, they do not yet earn enough to sustain a separate establishment. Neither I, nor they have the talent of making money any more than yourself, though the Genevase are rather celebrated for it. Mrs. Gallatin enjoys excellent health and so does the family generally. Your grandson gave me a more favourable account of your's than I had hoped to hear: and I was also much gratified by the appointment of your son as your successor in the Land Office.

My last work, written in 1835 at the request of the Antiquarian Society of Massach's, is a synopsis of the Indian tribes of the U. States east of the Rocky Mountains and of those of British and Russian America north of the States. It will contain, besides an explanatory Map, about 200 pages of text and 300 of comparative vocabularies & grammatical

---

[1] Gallatin continued to serve as bank president until June 7, 1839, when he resigned. He was succeeded by his son James who "played a leading role in the New York banking community for the next twenty-five years." Walters, *Albert Gallatin,* p. 347.

notices.[2] I had expected to have sent you a copy before now; but the printing has been unaccountably delayed by the publisher employed by the Society. I have material for "Supplementary considerations on Banking & currency."[3] But I have not the courage to reduce them to order, and though they might perhaps be of some use, the Bank paper mania has extended itself so widely, that I despair of its being corrected otherwise than by a catastrophe. The energy of this nation is not to be controlled: it is at present exclusively applied to the acquisition of wealth and to improvements of stupendous magnitude. Whatever has that tendency and of course an immoderate expansion of credit receives favour. The apparent prosperity and the progress of cultivation population commerce and improvement are beyond expectation. But it seems to me as if general demoralization was the consequence; I doubt whether general happiness is increased, and I would have proposed a gradual, slow, & more secure progress. I am however an old man; and the young generation has a right to govern itself.

.    .    .    .    .    .    .

I had expected to write only a few lines and have fallen into digressions of little personal interest to you. The fact is that as I grow less capable of thinking, I have become quite garrulous. I only wish I could enjoy once more the pleasure of practicing in that respect with my old friend, as talking is not at all, and writing is quite a labour to me. Fare you well, and whether silent or writing believe me, ever whilst I still breathe, Your old & faithful friend

ALBERT GALLATIN

.    .    .    .    .    .    .

[2] The title reads: "A Synopsis of the Indian Tribes Within the United States east of the Rocky Mountains, and in the British and Russian Possessions in North America," in American Antiquarian Society *Transactions and Collections,* II, 1-422 (Cambridge, Mass., 1836). For his other writings on Indians see Walters, *Albert Gallatin,* pp. 353-55.

[3] In February, 1831, Gallatin had published a pamphlet *Considerations on the Banking and Currency System of the United States.*

I was rather astonished to hear that Harrison had a majority in Indiana.[4] In the Presidential election I will take no part.

Mrs. Gallatin, my son & my daughter pray to be affectionately remembered to you.

[Addressed:]  John Badollet Esq're  Vincennes  Indiana

[Badollet to Gallatin]

VINCENNES October 7 1836

A thousand thanks, my dear & good friend, for your kind letter, it has removed the uneasiness your long silence occasioned, & I am happy to learn that yourself & every member of your family are in the enjoyment of health & content. I knew that the awful conflagration of last winter could not immediately affect you, your residence being distant from the scene of destruction, & of course felt no alarm on your account and I now learn with regret that the [MS illeg.] has reached you & curtailed your ressources.

Hitherto the candidates for the Presidency were men conspicuous for talents, moral worth, & sound political principles, it was reserved for our degenerate times to see a man sadly deficient in those important qualifications presuming to aspire to the distinguished station, & what is to be lamented supported in his ambitious views by numbers. But be not deceived, he will not receive the electoral vote of Indiana, he is too well known here: his supporters are the friends of slavery which when Governor he strained every nerve to have admitted in the territory, & many will vote for him out of gratitude for the services of his father rather than his personal worth.

In rumaging amongst my old papers, I found the following which was written by me at the request of many who were indignant to see exhibited as diamond what in reality was

---

[4] In the presidential election, on November 7, 1836, Indiana cast 41,000 votes for Harrison and 33,000 for Van Buren. *Indiana Election Returns, 1816-1851,* compiled by Dorothy Riker and Gayle Thornbrough (*Indiana Historical Collections,* XL, Indianapolis, 1960), pp. 21-28.

nothing but paste.[1] For reasons unnecessary to mention, it was not sent, but it will serve to shew in what estimation he was then held. If I could write without pain, or once more pay you a visit, I could mention many facts & circumstances which would let you into the true chara[c]ter of that man. But alas, I can do neither.

I have to thank you for the kindness you have shewn to my grand son.[2] I have no doubt but he will prove himself not undeserving of it. From my knowledge of his capacity & disposition, I am convinced that he will not be deficient in the exertions necessary to go with credit through the severe ordeal of the institution. The boy deserves praise that he is not spoiled, for his father, who is indolence personified, took him away from me when progressing hopefully in study, & made him waste years in doing little more than nothing. If he knows anything, he owes it to his personal efforts unaided by parental care or advice. I hope you will continue his friend & inspire him with courage & perseverance.

Albert was appointed without any agency on my part except the signing of my resignation. His appointment has been approved throughout the district, & I do not believe there is a solitary individual of a contrary opinion.[3]

After my resignation I received the following letter

TREASURY DEPARTMENT
January 11th  1836

SIR

Your letter of resignation addressed to the President has been referred to this department and its acceptance. I take

[1] Not found.

[2] William Gilham. See above, pp. 321-22.

[3] Albert Badollet was appointed by President Jackson register of the Vincennes Land Office January 8, 1836, to succeed his father. He was confirmed by the Senate on January 13. His commission, dated January 14, is in the Badollet Papers in the Indiana Historical Society Library. He was reappointed by President Van Buren on December 28, 1839, and confirmed by the Senate on January 3, 1840. This commission, dated January 4, 1840, is also in the Badollet Papers. U. S. Senate *Executive Journal,* IV, 504; V, 237, 239. He resigned in 1841. *Ibid.,* V, 383.

occasion to say that while a regret is felt for the loss of services so long & faithfully rendered to the Government, a sincere hope is entertained that in the retirement to which you go, the evening of your days may be unclouded & happy.

I am &c

LEVI WOODBURY
SECRETARY OF THE TREASURY.[4]

I learn with sorrow for the first time the death of our friend Solomon, I regret him sincerely, he was a man of sterling worth. . . .

I repeat it I feel greatly pleased that yourself & concerns enjoy health, the incommodity you mention may be relieved by a tablespoonful of *sacred tincture* taken in the evening, you will find its composition in the pharmacopeia.

With regret I must now take leave of you, I am unable to write more—My health is very precarious, my bodily strength is daily wasting & I have been sick the best portion of summer.

Now my dear friend tender my kind remembrance to all the members of your family, jointly & severally—I am gratified to hear that your amiable [daughter] is happy, I have preserved an interesting recollection of her— I cannot but regret that you could not consent to Albert's visiting your old friend. I still think that the journey would invigorate his constitution.

Adieu, may health & content attend you, try to drop me a few lines.

Yours, for ever

JOHN BADOLLET

[Addressed:]  Albert Gallatin Sen'r Esq'r  New York
[Endorsed:]  Vincennes  Oct. 7, 1836  J. Badollet

[Badollet to Gallatin]

VINCENNES October 26 1836

I avail myself, Dear & old friend, of the short period of

---

[4] This letter is in the Badollet Papers.

existence yet allowed me, to commune once more with you before nature's fiat is pronounced, & the chain that has linked, happily for myself, our fates together, is ultimately & for ever severed.

I have in my memory a budget of facts relative to the *hero* of Tippicanoe which would throw much light upon his character & show how far he is entitled to public confidence. I will select a few. Under the presidency of the elder Adams, in the hey days of federalism & aristocratic aspirations, if memory does not deceive me, he discharged a philipic against militia, for which & his zeal for the federal party he was rewarded with the governorship of Indiana territory;[1] & some years afterward having left it unprovided for defense & obtained by intrigue in Kentucky an illegal commission of Major General to supersede Gen'l Winchester, he made a stump speech to the army wherein he contrasted the free & high-minded militia of Kentucky with the regulars as *slaves*.[2] And here one cannot but being astonished at the weakness of Pres't Madison who instead of removing him for his shameful abandonment of the Territory in time of need & danger

---

[1] Harrison's appointment as governor of Indiana Territory generally has been attributed to his championship of the bill dividing the Northwest Territory. Freeman Cleaves, *Old Tippecanoe. William Henry Harrison and His Time* (Charles Scribner's Sons, 1939), pp. 30-32; Dorothy Burne Goebel, *William Henry Harrison, a Political Biography* (*Indiana Historical Collections,* XIV, Indianapolis, 1926), pp. 48-52.

[2] In a letter to Governor Isaac Shelby of Kentucky on September 18, 1812, Harrison had written, "Yes, my dear sir, I anticipated in this campaign a glorious triumph to our arms, and an equally glorious triumph to republicanism, since it will prove the falsity of the theory which proclaims the necessity of standing armies, or, in other words, that a man must become a slave before he can be made a warrior." However, only a few months later he was writing to the Secretary of War, "It is impossible that the impolicy of relying upon Militia, for the prosecution of the war, can be more strongly impressed upon the mind of any person than it is upon mine. . . . Militia can only be employed with effect, to accomplish a single distinct object which will require little time and not much delay, on the way." Esarey (ed.), *Messages and Letters,* II, 138, 405. For objective comment on this and Harrison's appointment to command the Northwest Army see Goebel, *William Henry Harrison,* pp. 137 ff., 151.

conferred on him the commission for which he panted & which he disgraced: for on a dispassionate view of his military operations, one cannot resist the conviction that in a military point of view he is a mere driveller.—But return.

One day at Mr. Vigo's, in company with Ewing, he violently declaimed against the admission of foreigners in the U. S. expecially Irishmen, echoing the sentiments of Rufus King. I became exasperated, & told him that I was a better American than himself, for he was born & grew the dutiful subject of his Britannic Majesty, that events in the bringing about which he had no share had ranked him amongst republicans, & that if his lot had been cast within the limits of the Turkish empire, he now would be the Sultan's most humble slave. Not so with me, I had come to the U. S. through choice & predilection for their political institutions. In the excess of my anger I told him that I had a mind to write a pamphlet wherein I would contrast the numerous foreigners who had lavished their blood in the defence of their adopted country, & honoured it by their talents & virtues, with the natives who disgraced it by their vices or their crimes. The same consistant man at a public dinner in Vincennes went into an elaborate encomium of the Irish; amongst the guests was an Irish family of some influence lately come, who were devoted to him.

There had been at my arrival at Vincennes a paper war carried on against the Governor by one Darneille a lawyer at St. Louis formerly of Vincennes.[3] For aught I know his charges against him might be true. Be that as it may, one day Parke who was the tool of Harrison approached me as a cat does a mouse, & slily & insidiously suggested the propriety of my taking up the quill in defense of his Excellency. To a man lately arrived, stranger to the character of the parties & to the matter at issue between them, the proposal was sufficiently absurd to ensure its prompt rejection; but it was intended to try my metal, & had I been silly enough to fall into the snare, I would have been judged, & set down for a fellow destitute

[3] See above, pp. 61-62n.

of brains, & fit only to be a tool, which it was no doubt the object of the governor to ascertain.

I have read in the biography of Black Hawk (said to be dictated by himself) that unfair means had been used to obtain his land. That brought back to my recollection, that Col. Vigo, who attended at the treaty by which Harrison purchased for the U. S. a large tract of both side of the Mississipy, informed me upon his return, that the Indians when called upon to sign the treaty declared that they were not proper chiefs, & had no right to alienate the lands of their tribe, but sign they must & sign they did. Such perhaps was the first seed of Black Hawk's desolating war.

Is it not surprising that from insignificant stock as my humble self should have sprung so numerous sprouts? I have no fewer than 28 grand children. Albert has but two children, he is now united to his third wife, the first was a devil incarnate, the second a blind bigot, the present one, formerly a widow, is a sensible excellent woman, of an angelic disposition, & as kind & attentive to me as a real daughter.[4] I live with them & am as comfortable as my bereavements permit me to be.—James is quite reformed, farms, & is very industrious; he has a progeny of 9 children—Sidney[5] is at the head of a cabinet making shop 8 1/2 miles from Vincennes in Illinois, has a family of 6 children—Sarah Caldwell my remaining daughter has since the death of her husband removed to Lawrenceville close by Sidney & has 9 children—Fanny has left 5 children of whom William is the eldest.

I would willingly prattle longer with you, but the strength is wanting, if I live, I may perhaps add a few more anecdotes in the biography of the great Harrison, but I am compelled to stop here. One more reflection. Former candidates for the Presidential chair preserved a dignified & left the decision of the question to their fellow-citizens; Is it not lamentable to

[4] For Albert Badollet's marriages, see above, pp. 260n, 273n.

[5] Algernon Sidney Badollet. He married Julia Armstrong on January 2, 1822. Knox County Marriage Records, II, 24, in Genealogy Room, Indiana State Library.

witness the unprecedented & degrading steps taken by that
man to reach a station so honourable, to see him travelling
from place to place begging votes? The mind sickens at the
thought of such a meannes [*sic*], the whole country shares
the humiliation.

Remember me affectionately to Mrs. Gallatin & the rest of
your family.

Adieu, my dear & good friend, yours for ever

JOHN BADOLLET

[Addressed:]   Albert Gallatin Sen'r Esq'r  New York
[Endorsed:]   Vincennes  Oct. 26, 1836  J. Badollet

# APPENDIX

## ENCLOSURES IN BADOLLET'S LETTER OF NOVEMBER 13, 1809

### A

### [Petition to the General Assembly]

To the Council and House of Representatives of the Territory of Indiana in General Assembly met—The Petition of sundry inhabitants of this said Territory most respectfully sheweth[1]

That Congress guided by an enlightened, humane and consistent policy embracing not only the present but future interests of this portion of the Union, have in the Ordinance providing for the organization of the Territory North West of Ohio, enacted, that Slavery or involuntary servitude never should be admitted into the said Territory.

That in evasion if not in manifest violation of said Ordinance a law has been passed introducing here a qualified Species of Slavery and such a law has received the sanction of the Executive the appointed guardian of that same Ordinance.

That repeated Petitions have been transmitted to the national Legislature expressing the wishes of the minority of the inhabitants of Indiana for a modification of the Ordinance so far as to admit Slavery into this Territory.

Your Petitioners have not been inattentive to these proceedings and though hitherto silent have not remained indifferent to their banefull tendency.

The poverty of the arguments adduced in support of the measure, was not calculated to create very serious allarms, but a continuance in a State of inaction on the part of your Petitioners would induce a belief abroad, that the sentiments avowed in the Petitions before mentioned are universally approved and would eventually deprive this fertile country of the active and interesting population of the middle and eastern States, and of that numerous descriptions of persons from the Southern States, who wish to fly

---

[1] See above, pp. 104-5, and note. The petition was introduced and referred on October 8, 1808. Thornbrough and Riker (eds.), *Journals of the General Assembly of Indiana Territory*, p. 225.

from a system, which a melancholy experience of its innumerable evils, has taught them to detest. Your Petitioners deem it now encumbent upon him to undeceive the public and correct a general error.

Your Petitioners therefore prompted by a sense of sacred duty, beg leave to express in the most unequivocal manner, their disapprobation of and their determination to resist henceforward by every lawfull means, every attempt to introduce into this infant country a system attended with the most calamitous consequences— A system outraging at once the laws of natural justice, the principles of our institutions, the maxims of sound policy, and the holy religion which we profess. A system which has the most deleterious influence on the manners and morals of Society, which it intends to corrupt and brutalise, which debasing every kind of usefull industry drives the husbandman and mechanic to more congenial climes, and throws into the hands of the negroe-holder the wage of daily labour, only means of subsistence left to the poor— A system which keeps every country afflicted with it in a permanent State of debility and fear; which makes our fields resound, not with voices animated by liberty and hope, but with the groans of the oppressed wretchedness, which converts power into right [?], familiarizes the mind with the idea of usurpation, which resting upon injustice begets daily new acts of injustice to uphold its hideous fabric, gives birth to the most iniquitous laws and sets principles and practice in constant opposition— A system the consequences of which are deprecated by every benevolent mind, which is reprobated by every Statesman of the age & which all the enlightened patriots of the southern States never cease to deplore— A system in fine which is advocated by none, but those who are either incapable, or whom contracted views of imaginary and present interest, render unwilling, to take a comprehensive and correct view of the subject.

Such being the sentiments of your Petitioners and their sollicitude to avert that momentous evil, they respectfully approach your honourable body, with an earnest prayer, that the law before mentioned may be repealed, that no further step may be taken, to obtain from Congress the admission of the iniquitous system alluded to; and that no person may be delegated to the federal Legislature, but such as shall have given the most unequivocal assurances of his determination to oppose it.

Your Petitioners do not address you as supplicants, to call your attention to objects of a local, circumscribed, or subordinate nature; to the fleeting interests of a moment, theirs is of a far greater importance; the permanent prosperity, the happiness of this rising country. They feel a conscious pride, that their motives are contaminated by no alloy, their judgment perverted by no sordid views. They are aware of your constitutional powers, that to your honourable body appertains the right of decision, but they are also sensible, that on a question involving interests of such magnitude, your wisdom will not permit you to decide without duly weighing their reasons, their views and their motives.

And your Petitioners as in duty bound will ever pray, &c.

## C.

### [Badollet's letters, signed A Farmer, to the editor of the *Western Sun*]²

MR. EDITOR,

When in the discussion of political subjects an author descends to scurrility and personal abuse, we may fairly conclude, that his cause is a bad one, that he fears the investigation of its merit, and that the perpetuation of error, is his object. For no man in his right senses will, if placed on strong and defensible ground, substitute insults for arguments, and use threats, when he can convince. Such stratagems have often succeeded here; by a violent attack on a writer, you draw him off his guard, force him to a personal defence, and make him loose sight of the real object he had in view, the public attention is diverted to another point, and the main question is forgotten in the disgusting tumult of personal squable.

I was led into these reflections by the perusal of some publications over the signature of Slim Simon, to which a piece called the Citizen of Vincennes, seems to have given rise. To me, equally unacquainted with both, it is a matter of perfect indifference whether the last is a bad man, or, his antagonist immaculate: the only thing wherein I feel myself concerned, is, whether their principles and opinions are correct, every thing else is perfectly irrelevant.

My object in these numbers is to try the solidity of whatever has the semblance of argument in Slim Simon's productions. In my endeavours to perform that task, I shall address the under-

² The clippings from the *Western* Sun of these four letters, which are in the Gallatin Papers, bear the ironic label "Documents which prove the disaffection and enmity of John Badollet to his Country." They appeared in the issues of March 4, 18, and April 15, 1809, and probably April 7. There is no known surviving complete issue of April 7; copies of the other three papers are in the Indiana State Library.

standing, and not the passions of my readers, and shall at least claim the merit, rare in this place, of having treated them with becoming respect.

But before I enter into this investigation it becomes unavoidable to say a few words on the piece which has created so much irritation.

The obvious object of the Citizen of Vincennes, was to obtain from the candidates for the general assembly, a public declaration of their opinion respecting slavery, a subject which with hundreds of others, he justly considers as of vast importance. The voters have an unquestionable right to know the political sentiments of the candidates for the legislature, that they may make a rational choice, and give their votes to such as will represent them in reality, and not in name only. That is no electioneering trick with a view of carrying a particular person, it is the open and avowed purpose of electing only such, as will oppose every measure tending to the introduction of slavery. A request to that effect is certainly proper, and cannot offend the honest candidates, be their opinions what they may, and no man of honour will decline avowing the principles under the guidance of which he proposes himself to act.

That the Citizen has used expressions of severity, and some others wherein malignity will see personal allusions, will be readily admitted; but those defects will find their excuse in the warmth of an honest heart, indignant at the vices which infest society, and are but too apparent here. With the same readiness I'll confess that he has materially erred in the following instance,— he divides the people of this county into two descriptions of persons, federalists and republicans; the first, friends of, and the second opposed to slavery. There never were two such parties discoverable here, the country so long debased by a territorial government, exhibits the same uniformity of complexion, it is not union of sentiment, it is torpor. The Citizen's distinction is therefore incorrect, and calculated to mislead. Had he said that the friends of slavery were aristocrats, his position would perhaps have been more tenable, for a friend to slavery must not only be an aristocrat in his heart, but one of the worst kind. Common aristocrats have not, notwithstanding their inventive faculties, arrived at the ultimatum of oppression, many means of afflicting the human race, have by them been left unattempted. The negro aristocrat may with justice be said to outstrip them all, he preys upon man himself, makes his person, his endless labours, his offspring his own, and in the fulness of his own impotence often starves the friendless who feeds him. Upon the whole, the piece signed a Citizen of Vincennes, notwithstanding the blemishes above mentioned appears to me, to be the work of a well designing man, actuated by motives of public good. This judgment which I have formed on mature reflection, and which I doubt not many of my readers will acquiesce in, is further confirmed by his subsequent numbers, wherein, in an attitude of tranquil dignity, he further developes his motives and his views, opposes arguments to declamations, and silence to personal insults.

I will now proceed to Slim Simon, and first discard that enormous mass of extraneous matter, which overloads his pages. His arguments will then appear to be in substance as follows:

*"The existance of slavery in the Southern States, threatening those states with danger, it is consistent with good policy to open a new outlet for slaves in this territory, and by scattering them to render them less dangerous."*

We may feed our fancies with delusive dreams, but the unchangeable laws of nature never will cease to operate, moral and natural causes never will cease to produce their wonted effects, and except you exterpate the means of propagation, the negroes like every other species of men, when, by what causes soever their condition is rendered more happy, or less deplorable, will proportionably multiply. By no other principle can the rapid population of these states be rationally explained, and it is absurd to suppose that the population of negroes would remain stationary, either in the territory receiving, or the state furnishing the supply, when their condition, would, by the proposed plan, have been in some degree meliorated. Besides, it is a well known fact among commercial men, that the productiveness of a commodity will always meet the demand, and since, to our shame, the negro is an article of traffic, it will follow that opening a new market for blacks to the southern states, will have the infallible effect of keeping up their numbers there.

This reasoning a priori will, I trust satisfy every reasonable mind, that the argument so much relied on, and so ostentatiously repeated, is destitute of all kind of solidity. But I am not content to suffer the question to rest upon analogical deductions, and I will proceed to prove *by fact* the fallacy of Slim Simon's reasonings, and that the exportation of negroes from one of the southern states, has not diminished their numbers there.

By calculations made by mr. Jefferson, in his notes on Virginia, the correctness of which has never been questioned, it appears that in the year 1782, the number of negroes amounted in Virginia, to nearly 270762, and by the census taken in the year 1800, to 345796 (Kentucky at the former period being as it were lately discovered, and in a weak and incipient state, cannot affect the correctness of our conclusions). Thus we see, that during a space of 18 years, nothwithstanding the vast exportations of negroes to Kentucky, Tennessee, and other parts, their number has not only suffered no diminution, but has actually considerably increased; and it is but fair to presume that the reception of slaves in the Mississippi territory, New Orleans and Louisiana, has not sensibly lessened their numbers in the other slave states.

I will now ask the candid reader whether I am not justifiable in inferring from the facts above stated, that the admission of slavery in Indiana could not much vary the result, and, as it is not likely that the middle and eastern states could be made converts to that strange doctrine, that the only fruit we should reap from that improvident measure, would be, to see ourselves placed by our own choice exactly in the same perilous situation, whereinto the southern states have been forced, and which excited so much sympathy for them amongst us.

A FARMER

Mr. Editor,

There is nothing more tempting, when we have a favourite object to accomplish, than to deceive others, and nothing more common than to deceive ourselves as to the real motives by which we are actuated. This observation is fully exemplified in the following argument of Slim Simon and his associates in favour of the admission of slavery.

*Humanity militates in favor of the measure, because negroes imported here would be better fed and better cloathed and placed in a state of comparative happiness.*

How humanity can be enlisted on the side of slavery, is not easy to conceive, except it is that kind of humanity which impells the British merchants to keep Africa in a constant state of dissolation and war, to obtain supplies of that unfortunate race, to pack up and fasten those victims of avarice, on shelves in the hold of their ships, where cruelty, unwholesome food, and diseases, where the more destructive mental anguish and black despair terminate the existence of numbers, who are daily thrown over board in the passage, and to vomit the wretched remnants on the shores of the West Indies where another portion perishes in the seasoning, and the rest reduced with their posterity to the condition of beasts, remain living monuments of the cool blooded barbarity of the whites. (Such a plea has really been urged on the floor on the Parliament of Great Britain to justify the slave trade.) Where is the friend of slavery who, laying his hand upon his heart can assert, where is the man in possession of his understanding who can for an instant believe that humanity has any thing to do in the business? Pride and avarice are at the bottom of all this. Who is accustomed to the servile obedience of humble negroes, cannot bear the erect attitude of men proud of their independence, and who can command a multitude of blacks, for no other consideration, than the obligation which his interest imposes, of keeping them alive, will not readily pay the price which a free man sets upon the exertions of his industry.

Where the clamorous friends of that measure well supplied with slaves to feed their cupidity, or minister to their vanity with submission and without reward, it is not likely that the dangers threatening the southern states or the sufferings of the Virginia or Carolina negroes would much disturb their night slumbers.

That the negroes would for a time, be better fed and better clothed, may by way of accommodation be granted, we will concede that a generous supply of rags or coarse garments would be allow'd them, that for a few years we would not behold numbers of them in a state of perfect nudity, that the allowance of a peck of corn a week, or of cotton seed for their support, would not be immediately resorted to. But how long would that state of *bliss* last? Just as long as the causes which produce it, as long as the native fertility of the soil would remain unimpaired and make their maintainance easy, as long as the smallness of their number would render them more precious, as long as the cultivation of some valuable commodity for exportation would not force the planter to contract the ground allowed for their support. Any change in those circumstances, would more and more assimilate their fate to that of the same class of men in the southern states.

Besides, food and raimant are not the only ingredients of happiness, and the negroe, however well provided for as to those objects, may still suffer misery under an hideous variety of shapes. The immigrating master will bring with him his passions and his habits, and the negroe will as certainly feel here the effects of his inhumanity as on the banks of the Roanoke. He will be sold like a beast, his family will be bartered away, and his back lacerated with as much composure on the Wabash, as in Georgia. Kentucky has been emphatically called the Paradise of negroes (just God

what Paradise?) and every traveller may bear ample testimony to
the inhuman punishments daily inflicted at the nod of every
little despot. The writer of these numbers has himself witnessed
there such horrid acts of deliberate cruelty, that did no other
objection exist, he would ever oppose the introduction of a
system which can convert civilized man into a barbarian.

It will not be preposterous here to add, that, our ideas of
happiness or misery are most commonly relative. Before the
negroes are numerous enough to be disposed of in quarters, they
will be more mixed and live in greater connection with the
whites, a ray of knowledge will penetrate their minds, they will
be enabled to take a view of their situation, they will learn that
those rights, which we deservedly hold so dear, are, as far as it
relates to them, laughed at, and outrageously violated; those
reflections will add poignancy to their other sufferings, and the
sum of their afflictions will be proportionable encreased.

Of those whining (one is almost tempted to say hypocritical)
arguments, every one is able to estimate the solidity, it would be
supurfluous to spend more time in their further refutation.

But Slim Simon takes a bolder flight, and setting his own
opinion in opposition to that of the most eminent statesmen, he
pronounces that *slavery is no political evil.*

When the population of a country is composed of two classes
of men, one oppressing, the other oppressed, is that state of
things no political evil? Is that opposition of interests, that state
of continual alarm on one side, that deep rooted sense of mighty
and aggravated wrongs on the other, that unextinguishable hatred
in both, no political evil? Is that action and re-action between
the slaves forming, and their tyrants counteracting plans of vengeance no political evil? And are the scenes of dissolation and
horror, which, sooner or later will take place, no political evil?
The political happiness of a state results from the perfect harmony
of all its parts, from an unity of efforts towards the general
good, but when such jarring elements, as are to be seen in the
slave states compose the body politic, elements which have no
affinity together, but constantly effervesce and threaten explosion, we are warranted in asserting, that such a state of things
is political evil of the first magnitude.

In considering slavery in this point of view, another consideration claims our most serious attention. We acknowledge certain
primary and immutable principles, on which all our political
institutions rest, and the permanence of these, depends in a great
measure on the former being held as sacred and in no instance

violated. The existence of slavery must inspire doubts on their excellence and solidity, it goes to establish the doctrine, that there may exist cases wherein those principles find no application and may be entirely disregarded. The liberties of a nation cannot indeed be thot secure on such tottering base, and it is not probable that the dangerous projects of criminal ambition can be checked by the influence of principles to which such a great portion of our fellow creatures have appealed in vain. In a few years we may perhaps become a state, our first objects in forming our constitution, will certainly be to recognize the sacredness and immutability of those same principles, and, if slavery were admitted, we would present to the world the scandalous spectacle of a people asserting in one page, what they deny in the next, declaring in almost the same breath, that *all* men are born free, and yet that a number of men are born *slaves*.

A FARMER

MR. EDITOR,

The permanence of political institutions, and the internal peace of a people depend less upon the coercive power of the laws, than upon happiness being so generally, and we may say, so evenly diffused, that every member of the state feels the strongest attachment for the present order of things, and dreads nothing more than changes, by which he can be made to lose, but never to gain. If such a sense of present happiness is not generally felt, if discontent circulates through any part of the body politic, revolutions are at hand.

If those premises are true, and I trust no body will contest their correctness, what shall we think of the political situation of a country, the population of which is partly composed of a description of persons, whose condition can by no possible events be made worse. What has not such a country to fear from foreign attack, which contains an enemy within its own bosom. In him an inveterate or crafty foe will find a faithful ally. Power may for a long time stifle their murmurs and palsy their arms, but a change of circumstances, commotions within, or storms from without, may, in one instant transform the abject slaves into the intrepid avengers of the wrongs of their own race, and the patient negroes into ferocious beasts, panting for vengeance, slaughter and destruction. The heart is in distress, the mind is convulsed with agony, at the reflection, that such is the awful situation of more than one half of the United States. Let those of my readers whose hearts are honest, whose minds are open to conviction, ponder upon the probable consequences, of the British landing, at such moment as this, by the assistance of their new friends the Spaniards (for whom our deep politicians of the day express such sympathy) an army in Florida; and after having with their gold divided the north, arming the negroes in the south; let them ponder on the complication of horrors which, if we had slaves in Indiana, the united cruelty of the Indians and negroes would in case of war inevitably produce, & let them, if they can, refrain a burst of indignation at those, who, to gratify selfish views, and for reasons destitute of solidity, would deliberately introduce in Indiana a policy so criminal, and attended with so disastrous consequences. I will ask again whether slavery is, or is not a political evil?

But, says Slim Simon, *Slavery is not a moral evil,* and the southern states are by no means inferior in point of morality to their northern brethren.

That the white inhabitants of the southern states observe, with regard to one another, moral rules cannot be denied; their own preservation, if no other reason existed, would compel them to it: But strange ideas indeed, must men entertain of moral obligations, who can, when in the way of their interest, cancel them all. Is there no danger of those moral ties being considered as mere matter of convenience, which, as soon as opportunity offers may be broken asunder? What evidence have we that the laws of justice and humanity, which are utterly disregarded in relation to the negro, will be better submitted to in relation to the whites, when interest or passions point out the benefit to be derived from their violation? The man who can calmly tear, for a few dollars the child from its mother's arms, will not feel great qualms of conscience at taking his neighbour's horse, is the right of one more sacred than the other? It is in vain to attribute to the perversity of human nature the vices which disgrace society, the folly and even perversity of some of our institutions, are their prolific source. Of that number is slavery. We may renew the laws of Draco, and as our deep legislature have done, write them with blood, but except you cleanse and purify the fountain, the streams issuing from it will remain impure and corrupt. This truth I would wish to inculcate. I would wish to shew its great import-ance, but I must confine myself at present to my subject.

Is a practice which sears the heart and renders it callous to other's woes, no moral evil? Is the spirit of wild dissipation produced in youth by a state of inactivity and idleness incident to, and inseparable from the existence of slavery, no moral evil? Is common decency not outraged, is female modesty not insulted or destroyed by the frequent exposure of men and women in a state of complete nakedness to public view? And is that no moral evil? The existence of so many thousand mulattoes evinces a general dissoluteness of manners where slavery obtains, and the practice of selling and dooming to eternal slavery those unfortunate fruits of unbridled and savage lust followed by their parents themselves, has no parallel, except amongst the most savage nations of the earth. Will any of our wiseacres dare to assert that such enormities are no moral evil?

*But slavery is not inconsistent with republicanism, inasmuch as the southern states are all republican.*

Shall we not mistrust our own senses at hearing that slavery and republicanism can walk hand in hand together! But from this fact I would form a very different conclusion. I would infer, that since the southern states are so attached to republican principles and institutions, in a manner which does them honor, the thinking and influential part of those states, the real states-men must abhor (which is really the case) a system productive of, and threatening the most calamitous evils. As to those who love slavery for slavery's sake, who like our wise politicians of Indiana, carry their views no further than the present moment, are unused to reflect and to calculate effects from given causes, their opinions cannot contribute to stamp a character on those states, their being republican because the best informed part is so, cannot affect the present question, made to be led they would be federalists in Connecticut.

But those states found slavery existing among them at the breaking out of the revolution, they would not decline joining their brethren and forego its advantages, they joined in the grand contest, proclaimed the same fundamental principles of freedom, abolished the slave trade, which under the king they had never been able to effect, and trusted to the slow but sure progress of reason, for the total eradication of an evil of which they then lamented, and to this day lament the existence. The hitherto insuperable obstacles which have since prevented the attainment of that desirable event, hold out to Indiana an awful lesson not wilfully and rashly to plunge into a labyrinth of difficulties and dangers, which may be foreseen, but it will be too late to avoid. Were the southern states unincumbered with slaves, it is almost a sacrilege to assert, that among the patriots of those states a single one could be found to advocate their introduction in the country;

and it belongs exclusively to a few sapient men of Indiana, to hail in the nineteenth century the adoption of a system which owes its existence to the most baneful passions of the human heart, sloth, cruelty, pride and sordid avarice, and is a source of eternal regrets to every sincere lover of his country.

Religion is not opposed to slavery inasmuch as we find the Patriarchs had slaves.

It is unfortunately not the first time, that religion, that gift of Heaven, that bond which (as its name imports) was destined to unite by its ties of gratitude man to his Creator, and to excite him in imitation of that Heavenly father to deeds of justice and benevolence, it is not the first time that its sacred name has been used for the perpetration of the blackest crimes; and the propagation of the most dangerous doctrines; and the imprudence of Slim Simon, cannot but excite an indignant surprise at the renewal of such profanation. If that is the way to lull asleep the conscience of the religous, the undertaking is worthy of a demon.

But who can read without amazement that the period when the science of government is reduced to simple and certain principles, that the United States, profiting by the errors of preceding ages, have adopted a policy best calculated to ensure general happiness, the territory of Indiana is seriously advised to recurr to the infancy of society for institutions proper for her to adopt; As well they might offer to our imitation the indiscriminate massacres of age and sex committed on the Cananites by the children of Israel, whom God, in the inscrutable ways of his providence had chosen to execute his judgments upon those devoted nations. Besides, we are Christian and not Jews, and the new dispensation has abolished the laws and prophets. The divine and benevolent founder of the Christian system has incessantly endeavoured to inculcate a spirit of charity and brotherly love. Love all men, and even your enemies, was his constant theme, he taught men to consider themselves as brothers, and as children of the same Heavenly parents. From the tenor of his life, and the general bearing of his precepts, an active philanthropy appears to have filled his breast, and no where can we infer from the writing of his apostles, that he did countenance or permit the reducing of our fellow creatures to the condition of beasts, that we may wear down a poor black, goad and starve him, without offending that God who gave his life and liberty to all, without provoking his often tardy, but always sure and unavoidable vengeance.                    A FARMER

Mr. Editor,

Slim Simon in his inconsiderate zeal for slavery, hesitates not to bring forward revered names, insidiously to induce a belief, that because Jefferson, Giles and other eminent patriots of Virginia, *hold* negroes, they therefore approve the system of slavery. That attempt to mislead those who not consulting their understandings, rely upon the conveniency of precedents to stifle the murmurs of their consciences, cannot be too severly reprobated. It tends to the destruction of the native independence of man's mind, and to introduce an unreflecting spirit of servile imitation, more likely to propagate the errors of eminent men, than to inspire the virtues by which they are counterbalanced.

But it is not true that to *hold* slaves is to be a friend of slavery; in a country where no other labouring hands are to be found, imperious necessity compels the best of men to use negroes on their farms, or to abandon cultivation. They cannot, they ought not, indiscriminately to be set free, to the nation alone, and not individuals, belongs the difficult and almost desperate task of totally extirpating the evil.

With a view to make amends to the readers for the imperfections of these sketches, I will now offer to their reflexions the sentiments of one of those worthies of Virginia on this subject. Speaking of the manners of that state mr. Jefferson expresses himself thus.

"There must doubtless be an unhappy influence on the manners of our people, produced by the existance of slavery amongst us. The whole commerce between master and slave, is a perpetual exercise of the most boisterous passions, the most unremitting despotism on the one part, and degrading submission on the other. Our children see this and learn to imitate it, for man is an imitative animal. This quality is the germ of all education in him. From his cradle to his grave, he is learning to do what he sees others do. If a parent could find no motive either in his philanthropy or his self love, for restraining the intemperance of passion towards his slave, it should always be a sufficient one that his child is present. But generally it is not sufficient. The parent storms, the child looks on, catches the lineaments of wrath, puts on the same airs in the circle of smaller slaves, gives a loos to his words of passion, and thus nursed, educated, and daily exercised in tyranny cannot but be stamped by it with odious peculiarities. The man must be a prodigy who can retain his manners and morals undepraved by such circumstances. And with what execration should the statesman be loaded, who permitting one half the citizens thus to trample on the rights of others, transforms those into despots, and these into enemies, destroys the morals of the one part, and the amor patriae of the other. For if a slave can have a country in this world, it must be any other in preference to that in which he is born to live and labour for another; in which he must lockup the faculties of his nature, contribute as far as it depends on his individual endeavours to the evanishment of the human race, or entail his own miserable condition on the endless generations proceeding from him. With the morals of the people, their industry also is destroyed. For in a warm climate, no man will labour for himself who can make another labour for him. This is so true, that of the proprietors of slaves a very small proportion indeed is ever seen to labour. And can the liberties of a nation be thought secure when we have removed their only firm basis, a conviction in the minds of the people that these liberties are the gift of God? That they are not to be violated but with his wrath? Indeed I tremble for my country when I reflect that God is Just: that his justice cannot sleep for ever: that considering numbers, nature and natural means only, a revolution of the wheel of fortune, an exchange of situation is among possible events: that it may become probable by supernatural interference! The Almighty has no attribute which can take side with us in such a contest— But it is impossible to be temperate and to pursue this subject through the various considerations of policy, of morals, of history natural and civil. We must be contented to hope they will force their way into every ones mind. I think a change already perceptible, since the origin of the present revolution. The spirit of the master is abating, that of the slave rising from the dust, his condition mollifying, the way I hope preparing, under the auspicis of heaven, for a total emancipation, and that this is disposed in the order of events, to be with the consent of the masters, rather than by their extirpation."

From the perusal of Slim Simon's productions we feel ourselves compelled to lament that talents which might have been devoted to the destruction of error, and the dissemination of correct principles, should have been unfortunately misapplied to the thickening of the veil which selfish passions throw upon the most sacred truths and the accomplishment of the most nefarious purpose. I say *nefarious* because however grating that expression may be to some, it is correct and true.

After what has been written by the first statesman of our country and has been read above, it would be presumption to add any thing more on this momentous question, I therefore will terminate here the task which I had imposed upon myself, in the performance of which, I have not, I trust, violated any rule of decorum. I have as far as it lay in my power, endeavoured to recal the taste for chaste and temperate discussion, to which we have been so long strangers. My abilities were not, I feel, equal to the importance of the undertaking, and much remains to be said upon so prolific a subject, but if I have contributed to induce those to reflect, who seemed to have hitherto delegated to a few eminent men their privilege of thinking, if I have wakened them to a sense of their independence, if I have succeeded in persuading that in matters of opinion, but especially on questions which involve the happiness of ourselves and posterity, no other authority ought to be submitted to, than that of eternal reason and truth, then my feeble efforts shall not have been exerted in vain. *Truth* having been my *guide and the public weal my aim,* I feel a conscious pride that I have contributed my mite towards the public good, and now resign the pen to those who actuated by the same honest motives, are more able to use it.

A FARMER

---

H

[Badollet and Ewing to the editors of the Vincennes *Western Sun*][3]

GENTLEMEN

It is the right and certainly the duty of every virtuous citizen to watch the conduct of public servants and to detect and expose when there is real cause of complaint every prevarication in office and it is undoubtedly no less true that such a sacred duty must be discharged in a manner which will evince the purity of the motive the indignation of offended virtue and not the rankling of a malignant heart.

But to come forward in an anonymous shape under the mask of friendship as Doctor Samuel McKee has done in a late publication to give currency to accusations conceived in the dark bosom of some abandoned wretch and brought forth in the revels of

[3] Printed in Vincennes *Western Sun,* August 22, 1807. It was signed by John Badollet and Nathaniel Ewing. The copy which Badollet sent to Gallatin is in long hand.

intemperance, to say in substance to the superintendants of the public sales, you may have been hitherto men of integrity but the country now rings of your turpitude: Stand forth and prove your innocence, is a proceeding as novel in practice as it is outrageous to Justice decency and common sense; that act not so much of a friend as of an insidious enemy. Sad indeed must the state of that society be, where men of approved morals may unexpectedly be dragged before the public in such a wanton manner by loose and general charges, and reduced to the intolerable alternative of either sanctioning their condemnation by their silence or proving a negative and resorting to unavailing asservations of innocence. And are thus the fruits of a life of rectitude to be ravished from us in a country boasting of justice and humanity. But we will dismiss those querulous declamations and come to the point at once. The Dr. having authorised you to inform the public that his criminations were not intended to apply to Gov'r Harrison. The business is drawing to a point and we may then fairly conclude that we are particularly aimed at. We therefore through the medium of your paper Solemnly entreat, nay we challenge Doctor Samuel McKee, if he value his own reputation to come forward with specific charges with the mention of every fact that would in any measure justify his insinuations or even cast a shade however slight upon our integrity or to produce the name of every person who is in the possession of any. We will do more we will request every good man of this Territory whose heart recoils at the idea of corruption to join his efforts for the detection of those mal practices which have been so broadly alledged to have taken place. Let our conduct as superintendants of the Sales be strictly investigated let every step of ours during their continuance, be traced up, let a mass of light be thrown upon our proceedings, and let your columns proclaim to the world the criminals and the crimes. Nay more let the same reach the seat of government that the high tribunal to which we are accountable for our official conduct, may institute the proper inquiries and award us the punishment which our very iniquities shall be found to deserve.

But if Dr. McKee decline this solemn invitation if he avoid naming his principals or prompters or substantiating the rumours of which he has so obligingly become the publisher, the consequence is obvious he must resign himself to that disgrace which such conduct is calculated to produce. Gentlemen though indignant at the wanton and unprovoked attack made upon us we have not sullied your pages nor disgraced our selves by any expression of scurrility or abuse, our object is not to wreek our vengeance on a man of whom we had a good opinion and who must now feel himself sufficiently humbled and a real object of pity. We are sensible that intemperance of language appears more like the writhing of a guilty conscience than the accents of injured innocence. So low we shall certainly not stoop, we wish and invite investigation, if our solemn call is not attended to we are but too well avenged.

[John Badollet

[Nat'l Ewing]

I

[Deposition of John Johnson and John Rice Jones][4]

WE JOHN JOHNSON AND JOHN RICE JONES OF THE COUNTY OF KNOX IN THE INDIANA TERRITORY Attornies at law Do hereby certify That immediately on Dr. Samuel McKee being served with a writ out of the General Court of the Territory at the suit of John Badollet for publishing a piece in the western Sun under the signature of "a friend to the Commissioners" charging the Commissioners of the Land Office of the District of Vincennes with improper conduct in the sale of the Public Lands he employed us as his attornies to defend the said suit at the same time and at several others informing us that he never meant to implicate Mr. Badollet in his piece that he was perfectly convinced Mr. Badollet was in no wise concerned in the speculation made upon the United States at those sales by giving or receiving what was denominated "Hush" money. That in consequence of this information we determined to make our defence on the ground that Mr. Badollet was not meant to be implicated in that piece and to prove that the superintendent of the Sales meaning the Governor was concerned with others (not in office) in giving and receiving Hush money at the sales which in effect depreciated the price of the Public Lands.— And we further certify that Dr. McKee several times informed us that he never authorised the Printer of the Western Sun to assert the author of "the Friend to the Commissioners" had directed him to declare that the Governor was not meant to be implicated in that charge.— That he Dr. McKee had asked the printer how he could have made such an insertion in one of his Papers who made answer to the following effect "That he the printer was poor, depended a good deal on the Governor's support and partonage and also that he expected

4 This is a copy in Badollet's hand.

the legislature would give him the printing of the Laws through the influence of the Governor which was promised to him and conclude by begging Dr. McKee not to injure him by contradicting his the Printers paragraph exculpating Gov'r Harrison."

And we further certify that Dr. McKee from the first time he spoke to us on the subject of this improper conduct of some of the commissioners at the time of the sales of the Public Lands to a little before his death frequently informing us that he meant and intended in his Piece signed "a friend to the Commissioners" to implicate and criminate the Governor who he was convinced was highly culpable in his conduct as Superintendent of the sales of Public Lands.— And he further informed us that the premeditated attack made upon him by the Governor at the Secretary's office in the presence of several Gentlemen called for the purpose he the Dr. was taken by surprise at the moment but he had a little after fully written his sentiments to the Governor about the conduct of some of the Commissioners at the Sales but that the Governor had never written him an answer. The Dr. never shewed us a copy of his letter to the Governor.

Signed JNO. JOHNSON<br>
JNO. RICE JONES

VINCENNES  23d Nov'r 1809

# ENCLOSURE IN BADOLLET'S LETTER OF DECEMBER 10, 1809

[November 13, 1808]

To the Freeholders of the County of Randolph
Fellow Citizens,

In pursuance of a promise made to several of my constituents, it now becomes my duty to give you a short account of the principal transactions in our Legislature during the last session of the second General Assembly of this Territory, in which I had the honor of representing you. This promise would have been complied with sooner, had I not been obliged to leave the seat of Territorial government the day after the dissolution of the Legislature, which placed me under the necessity of writing this Circular in Kaskaskia and sending it for publication to the St. Louis Press.

The session commenced with prospects peculiarly auspicious to your interests, and every thing was done by your representatives which they conceived would have any tendency to lighten the burdens of the people, or promote the prosperity of the country. The Legislative Council, however, in which during the whole session only three members attended, two of whom were from the western counties, uniformly and with mysterious pertinacity, but no doubt from the best, the very best of motives, opposed every measure of importance which originated in the house of representatives; almost every bill sent up to the Council was either mutilated by way of amendment, passed over without notice, or rejected without ceremony—but let it not be thought that I mean to question the reputed wisdom of that body—we all know and have sometimes felt that it is placed too high above the people to be controuled by their opinions; and is it not intended by the ordinance, that excellent epitome of the British constitution, to operate as a milestone about the necks of your representatives, should they dare to think too freely or act too boldly in the performance of their Legislative functions.

The contested election, after much unnecessary delay, was decided in favour of the sitting members; for as it appeared to the House that the election had been fairly conducted on the part of the successful candidate; that not one of the votes taken

(351)

in the township of Springfield was proved to be bad; that the magistrate who had omitted to take the oath prescribed by an act of the previous session, swore that he conceived himself acting under the sanction of his oath of office; and as it also appeared that he was ignorant of the existence of the law, the revised code not having reached the county till some days after the election, it was considered that the intention of the Legislature, which was merely to secure a fair election, had been fulfilled in every essential respect; and it is a rule of construction well established in our laws, that when the intention of the Legislature can be clearly ascertained, it is incumbent on every tribunal to pursue that intention, even though it may seem to militate against the express letter of the law. To diminish the weight of taxes; to send a man to Congress who would favour or at least not oppose a division of the Territory, and to obtain, if possible, such alterations, in the ordinance as would abridge in some degree the extraordinary powers of the executive, were the three great objects which the representative branch kept constantly in view from the beginning of the session—and I may affirm with confidence that more was done towards effecting these objects than we had any reason to expect considering the mass of influence that opposed us. An act originated in the House of Representatives, and was finally passed, repealing so much of the law regulating county levies as laid a tax on neat cattle and young men, and in lieu of it laying a tax on located lands, at the rate of ten cents in every hundred dollars valuation, to be exclusively appropriated to county buildings—by the original bill the tax was taken off work horses also, but the council amended it by striking out that part of the bill so that horses of every description remain taxable as heretofore. An effort was made to take from the Judges of the Common Pleas their salary of two dollars and a half per day, which at present exhausts nearly all the county taxes, and to substitute in the place of it the fees upon law proceedings payable, as the law now stands, into the county treasury;—but as a majority of the Legislative council consists of judges, they would only agree to take off fifty cents per day from their immoderate salary, and to save appearances, chose, by an amendment to the law, to make the tax upon poor suitors double what it had formerly been—a strong evidence of the impropriety of mixing the legislative and judicial functions, which according to the soundest maxims of policy should ever be kept separate and distinct; it is dangerous to suffer legislators to be the judges and expounders of their own laws—it is preposterous to permit public officers to give salaries to themselves in the capacity of law makers, nor would it be tolerated in any well regulated community jealous of its freedom. A bill was introduced to remedy this intolerable defect in our laws and also to amend the election law so as to prevent in future the frauds of Sheriffs, but was treated with such contempt by the council that they would not even honour it with a rejection, but let it lie unnoticed on their table to the end of the session.

The Governor observed in his speech to both houses at the opening of the session, that he had barely allowed time for the deliberate choice of a delegate and for his arrival at the seat of Government by the time fixed for the meeting of congress—the House of Representatives accordingly made early offers to go into the election, but the council, with many marks of disrespect for that House and with a conduct unprecedented in Legislative proceedings, delayed it on various pretences till they thought they had secured a majority in favour of their own candidate; they actually put the Territory to considerable expence, and made a sergeant at arms of the Governor by directing him to dispatch couriers in quest of such absent members as they supposed would forward their views; and even endeavoured to persuade Samuel Gwathmey, esq. to resume his seat in the council, tho' he had sent his resignation to the Governor and then held, and still holds, an office incompatible with a seat in either House.[1] A behaviour so impolitic, so derogatory to the honor, so contrary to the interest of the Territory, must evince to every impartial observer who reads the Journals of the late session, to our constituents and to the world that all this caballing and confusion arose from improper conduct in one or both branches of the Legislature, but it is consolatory to reflect that the representatives of the people are able to vindicate themselves in the fullest manner from the charge of having been the cause of that confusion and to shew that in all their proceedings they paid the strictest attention to the right and privileges of their fellow-citizens, and to their own dignity as the immediate organs of the people. At length a few days before the close of the session the council sent down word that they were ready to go into the election—the manner in which it terminated must be known to you all, but to such of my fellow-citizens as will favour me with a conversation on the

[1] Gwathmey had been appointed register of the land office at Jeffersonville on December 8, 1807. He declined to resume his seat. Ewbank and Riker (eds.), *Laws of Indiana, 1809-16*, pp. 830n-31n.

subject, I shall be happy to give a circumstantial account of the singular scene—a recital of the intrigues and cabals that preceded the choice of a delegate would astonish a veteran of the courts of St. Cloud, and would convince every reflecting man of the danger of having a governor with the powers of a king, whose influence must for the most part be quite irresistible when exerted upon a Legislature, which when full consists of twelve members, nearly one half of whom form a little aristocratical assembly totally independent of the people, and the remainder are selected from a thin population scattered over an immense country, of different local interests, and without the means of communicating with each other on political subjects. Kings, indeed, in many monarchical governments have enjoyed much less power and influence than the executive of this Territory—he has the unlimited disposal of offices, may convene, prorogue and dissolve the Legislature at pleasure as it suits his private convenience, interest or caprice, and may put his absolute negative on any law without being obliged even to give a reason for his dissent. Resolutions of the House of Representatives were therefore forwarded to the General Government urging such alterations in the Ordinance as would in some degree abridge these great prerogatives of the Governor; for as it is the nature of ambition to be unsatiable, so it is the nature of man to be ambitious and liable to be corrupted by power—when he possesses a little he will grasp at more if he thinks it within his reach; and who will say that our present governor is in this respect infallible? among several acts which he negatived at the late session was one establishing circuit courts and a court of appeals; he rejected it merely because it contained a reasonable proviso requiring him to remove clerks on the request of a majority of the judges;—but innumerable instances might be adduced to prove that he is perpetually on the watch to increase and enlarge his prerogatives, when occasion offers—it is of course the primary duty of the representatives of the people to be equally vigilant in preserving and extending the rights and privileges of their constituents. Resolutions were also passed praying that the Delegate to Congress and the members of the legislative council may in future be elected by the people—should we succeed in obtaining these important changes in our system of government, it will at least render our condition much more tolerable, and in case we fail in procuring a division of the Territory, enable us to sustain for a few years longer our present unnatural connection with the Eastern side of the Wabash. On the question of the division a Resolution passed the House of Representatives instructing the Delegate to use all the means in his power in order to obtain it.—the council on the last day of the session attempted to pass a counter resolution—but their President insisting that the rules of the House could not be dispensed with unless by unanimous consent, thus prevented them from counteracting the interest and wishes, at least of this part of the Territory. An act passed both houses and received the sanction of the governor forming a new county out of the counties of Knox and Clark; but the Representatives from this country, conceiving that Randolph was justly entitled to another member, refused to vote for the bill till they had obtained a promise from the governor that he would give an additional member to this county; he made a proviso, however, that Dr. Fisher and myself should procure certificates on oath from one or more magistrates or other respectable authority in different parts of the county, stating it as their belief that it contains at least 300 free male inhabitants; a condition which I have no doubt can be easily complied with—as at the last census the county contained nearly seven hundred exclusive of about one hundred and forty which were improperly given to the county of Knox instead of this county; and there must surely have been an increase of several hundred since that time.

The session was not very productive of new laws; but among others there is one in addition to the criminal code making horse-stealing punishable with death for the first offence, and another increasing the jurisdiction of Justices of the Peace to forty dollars, to take effect from the first day of January next.

Instructions were forwarded to the Delegate to endeavour to obtain the passage of a law authorising the actual settlers of the district of Kaskaskia who have no titles to the land by them respectively improved, to cover their improvements with Donation rights confirmed by the commissioners of the Land-office for the land district; to obtain a sum of money sufficient to open a road from the Ohio by the Saline below the mouth of the Wabash to Kaskaskia or any other place in the district; and to obtain authority for surveying into quarter sections and for the sale of the lands in the said district over which the indian title has been extinguished.

I shall conclude by referring you for a confirmation of what I have stated, to the two representatives of the county of St. Clair, and to the Journals of both houses that are shortly to be published in the Vincennes weekly paper and with the warmest wishes for your individual happiness and political prosperity, subscribe my-self,

Your Fellow-Citizen

RICE JONES

KASKASKIA, Nov. 13th, 1808.

# INDEX

Adams, John, President, 204, 283.

Adams, John Quincy, President, 26n; presidential candidate, 266.

Agun, Jane M., *see* Badollet, Jane M. Agun (Mrs. Albert).

Allegre, Sophia, *see* Gallatin, Sophia Allegre (Mrs. Albert).

Amat, Charles Jean, 281, 284, 288, 297, 298, 305.

Amat, Etienne Morin, 297n.

Armstrong, Julia, *see* Badollet, Julia Armstrong (Mrs. Algernon Sidney).

Astor, John Jacob, 292n.

Backus, Elijah, 75.

Badollet, Albert, 11, 44, 103, 115-16, 204, 295, 330; sickness, 37, 60; serves as deputy register, 260; succeeds father as register, 21, 276, 277, 326; volunteers for militia service (April, 1809), 129; on Tippecanoe expedition, 197-98n, 204, 206, 209; marriages, 260n, 273.

Badollet, Algernon Sidney, 11, 21, 116, 245, 261, 295; marriage, 330.

Badollet, Frances (Fanny), *see* Gilham, Frances Badollet (Mrs. Henry).

Badollet, Jacques, of Savoy, 9.

Badollet, James P., 11, 21, 116, 240, 261, 330; West Point cadet, 245-46n; marriage, 294.

Badollet, Jane M. Agun (Mrs. Albert), 260n.

Badollet, John, birth and education, 9; comes to America, 10; marriage, 11; joins Albert Gallatin & Co., 11-12; activities in Pennsylvania, 12-13; commissions to lay out roads in Northwest Territory, 13; correspondence with Gallatin, 14-15, 15-16, 16-17; on St. Clair's defeat, 15; on French constitution, 15; member Constitutional Convention, 1816, pp. 16, 21, 261; drafts article on education, 262-63; character and disposition, 17-18; ardent Jeffersonian, 18; disillusionment with American democracy, 18; anticlerical beliefs, 18-19, 282, 294; defends Frances Wright, 19, 282-83, 292; interest in education, 19, 262-63; president Vincennes Historical and Antiquarian Society, 21; member Vincennes Library Company, 21; place in Vincennes society, 21; trustee Vincennes University, 21, 64n, 180; disagreement with Harrison in regard to University, 107, 177; recommendations in regard to University, 179-80; description of, 21; personal finances, 33-34, 58, 59, 65-66, 67-68, 94-95, 97-98, 102-3, 263, 270-71, 273, 280-81; indebtedness to Gallatin, 33, 66, 78-79, 95, 99, 100; settlement of debt, 256, 257; advised by Gallatin, 30, 33, 42-43, 106-7; health and illnesses, 37, 50, 60, 166, 258-59, 263, 272, 280, 300, 301, 302, 303, 304, 308, 315, 327; returns to Pennsylvania, 41; writes of family, 44, 115-16, 204-5, 245-46, 260-61, 294-96, 330; recommends Benjamin Parke to adjust land claims, 46; on act incorporating company to construct Ohio Falls Canal, 48; appointed judge of Court of Chancery, 50n; description of Vin-

granted, 124n; 1809, pp. 109-10, 119-29; (1811), pp. 191-92. *See also* Jennings, Jonathan; Parke, Benjamin; Thomas, Jesse B.

"Detector Detected," letters by, 125.

Detroit, 56.

Detroit Land Office, 25.

Devin, Rev. Alexander, 189n.

Dill, James, 132n, 211, 213.

D'Ivernois, François, 311n.

Downs, Thomas, 181, 208.

Duane, William, 52, 129n, 136n.

Dubois, Toussaint, 60n, 137, 153, 154, 155, 162, 165, 170; sent as emissary to the Prophet, 155n, 169; trustee Vincennes University, 180; influence with Indians, 234n; on committee to prepare address vindicating militia, 244n; denies participating in militia meeting, 244, 247, 251-52n.

Duels, 20; Rice Jones challenged by Bond, 117-18n; McNamee challenged by Randolph, 119-20.

Dumont, Etienne, 265, 277, 288, 297, 298, 301, 305.

Dunlap, Dr. James, shoots Rice Jones, 118-19n.

Dunlap, Joseph, 150.

Dunmore, Lord, 48, 51.

Education, Badollet's interest in, 19, 262-63; Gallatin's interest in, 311-12; article on, 1816 Constitution, 262. *See also* Vincennes University.

Edwards, Ninian, 186, 292n.

Eel River Indians, annuity, 132; treaties with, 51n, 183n.

Eppes, John W., 128.

Eustis, William, secretary of war, 175n; vetoes establishment of outpost, 171n.

Evans, Robert Morgan, 175, 178.

Ewing, Nathaniel, 37, 39, 40, 41, 42, 44, 61, 63, 64, 65, 98, 154, 155, 237, 238, 329; sketch of, 27n; description of the Prophet, 20, 163; re-

turns to Pennsylvania, 41; goes to Washington, 43, 45; recommends Benjamin Parke to adjust land claims, 46; trustee Vincennes University, 64, 180; land speculation, 83-85, 160-61; suit against Hurst, 82-83n, 139-40n, 161; wounded by Hurst, 82; opposition to slavery, 104-5; relays report on John Randolph, 113; aspiration to be Governor reported, 145; on difficulty of doing public business in Vincennes, 147; at meeting to consider Indian situation, 162, 165; accused of opposing memorial for extension of credit on public lands, 191; joins in thanks to Col. Boyd, 219-20; accused of opposing relief for militia, 241; of opposing extension of credit to purchasers of public lands, 241; of interfering with military appointments, 241; president Vincennes Bank, 260n, 263n; ability to make money, 271;

*and Governor Harrison*: incurs Harrison's hostility for opposition to slavery, 102, 121, 156-57, 161; Harrison's estimate of, 111; alleged to be seeking Harrison's removal, 111; disloyalty of, hinted by Harrison, 132; seeks Gallatin's protection against, 159; on Harrison's speculation in lands, 159-61; Harrison's hostility toward, 170, 188, 247; accused by Harrison of corresponding with Indians, 170, 197, 203, 241; attempt of Harrison to get indictment against, 170-71;

*receiver of Vincennes Land Office*: appointment, 27, 30, 32-33; absent from office, 68, 69, 77; attack on, 73; report as commissioner of land claims, 73; incurs hostility in settling claims, 80-81; charges against as super-

162; account of meeting, 165; territorial treasurer, 176; joins in thanking Col. Boyd, 219.

Johnson, John, 150, 165, 182, 236, 237; trustee Vincennes University, 64n, 179-80; candidate, delegate to Congress, 110n, 129; attorney for Badollet, 141n; calls Vincennes meeting to consider Indian situation, 156n-57n; joins in thanks to Col. Boyd, 219, 220n; recommended for judge of General Court, 225, 226n; member Constitutional Convention, 262; deposition in regard to McKee's charges, 349-50.

Johnston, Capt. ——, 164.

Johnston, General Washington, 135, 143n, 156n, 190, 191; trustee Vincennes University, 64n; answers charges of fraud against superintendents of land sales, 81n; attorney for Ewing, 83n; defends election of Davis Floyd as clerk of House, 91n; representative, 105n; in 1810 session, 180-81; introduces bill to create new board of trustees of Vincennes University, 178; representative, on petition for Harrison's appointment, 212n; on advancement to statehood, 213n; opposed as judge of General Court, 226n.

Jones, John Rice, 112, 182; clerk to land commissioners, 44, 73n; representative, 48; trustee Vincennes University, 64n; witness for Ewing, 83n; political enemy of Harrison, 117; attorney for Badollet, 141n; deposition in regard to charges of McKee against land commissioners, 349-50.

Jones, Michael, 147.

Jones, Peter, 82n, 135, 175; trustee Vincennes University, 64n, 180; accompanies Harrison to Fort Wayne, 132n; auditor of territory,

176; representative, 180-81, 213n; secretary of militia meeting, 249-50.

Jones, Rice, representative, 118n; challenged by Shadrach Bond, Jr., 117-18n; political enemy of Harrison, 118; assassinated, 118-19n, 147; address to constituents, 147, 351-56 (text).

Jones, Thomas, 85, 160, 161, 236; deposition in regard to charges against Ewing, 87-88.

Jones, William, 178.

Jordan, Ephraim, 189n.

Kaskaskia, road from Vincennes, 74n.

Kaskaskia Land Office, 25, 65; receiver, 236.

Kentucky, sends troops on Tippecanoe expedition, 197, 198-99.

Kickapoo Indians, 232, 235.

King, Rufus, 277n, 329.

Knox County, militia, resolutions in regard to Battle of Tippecanoe, 214-16; effect of Indian unrest on settlement of, 201.

Kuykendall, Jacob, trustee Vincennes University, 64n, 180.

Lafayette, Marquis de, 272.

Land claims, see Vincennes Land Office, settlement of claims.

Land grants, in Vincennes district, 28-29n; speculation in, 80-81. See also College township; Illinois Land Company; Vincennes Land Office, settlement of claims; Wabash Land Company.

Land sales, see Vincennes Land Office.

Lands, public, speculation in, 20, 81-82n, 83-86, 123n, 159, 160-61, 349-50; memorial for relief of purchasers of, 191; reduction of price, 259; extension of time allowed for payment, 241, 252, 269; sale of forfeited, 222, 230, 246,